INTERFACING TEST CIRCUITS WITH SINGLE-BOARD COMPUTERS

BY ROBERT H. LUETZOW

TAB TAB BOOKS Inc.
BLUE RIDGE SUMMIT, PA. 17214

NOTICES

The TRS-80 is a trademark of the Tandy Corporation.
The SYM-1 is a product of Synertek, a Subsidiary of Honeywell.
The AIM-65 is a product of Rockwell International
The VIC-20 and VICMON are trademarks of Commodore Business Machines, Inc. The KIM-1 was also manufactured by Commodore.
The Blue Line power supply is a product of Standard Power a Subsidiary of Acme Electric Corporation.
AIRPAX is a trademark of the Airpax Corporation.
The BASIC programs in Chapter 15 were written by Greer Computer Consultants.

A special thanks is given to:
Larry J. Torok
Leonard F. Martin
N. S. (Scotty) Maxwell
Gary Greer
Benard J. Miller
Lawrence Denbo

FIRST EDITION

FIRST PRINTING

Printed in the United States of America

Library of Congress Cataloging in Publication Data

Luetzow, Robert H., 1944-
Interfacing test circuits with single-board computers.

Includes index.
1. Automatic checkout equipment. 2. Computer interfaces. I. Title.
TK7895.A8L83 1983 681'.2 83-4852
ISBN 0-8306-0183-X
ISBN 0-8306-0583-5 (pbk.)

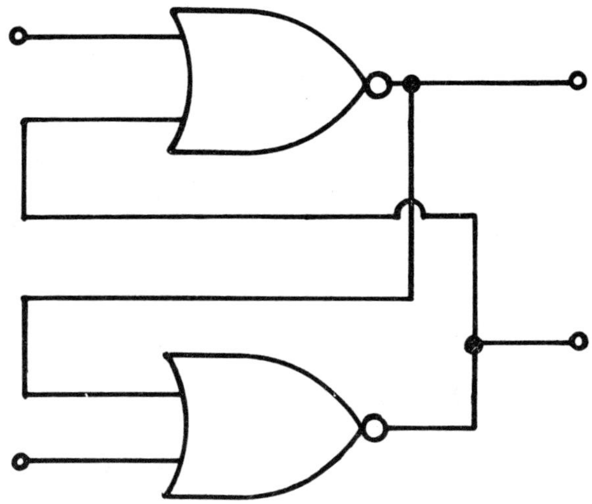

Contents

Introduction

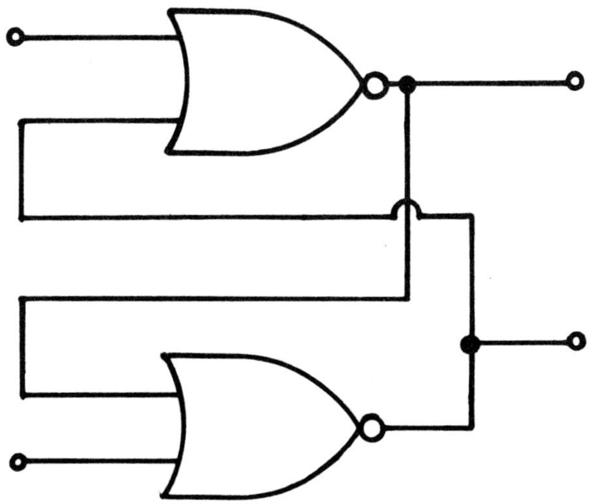

When I purchased my first single-board computer, which was a 6502-based KIM-1, I jumped into an area that was quite new to me and a lot of other people too. While I was going to school (1968-1971), a single-board computer like the KIM-1 or an all-in-one combination such as the TRS-80 Model I were not even yet dreamed about. I did have a two-hour college course about the larger computer systems of that time, but back then, the only time I ever saw a computer was in the data processing section of large companies.

Now, when I look back over the last four or five years, I think how much easier it would have been for me if there would have been a book published about interfacing basic electronic circuits to a single-board computer (SBC) system and a few computer programs that would have made these circuits work. The learning curve of using the single-board computer would have been much shorter. Today, when I meet other engineers and technicians who have not had a chance to use the newer and even lower cost SBC systems, I usually end up spending a while, and sometimes quite a while, answering a few questions and explaining how easy it really is to use the SBC systems. One day I talked to an individual who told me how much he would like a book about the ways and methods I use with the SBC systems. When I investigated the current books on the market, I discovered that an area did exist between the "how to operate SBC systems" and more complex systems and computer methods. None of the publications I reviewed actually presented test circuit interface methods and compatible programs to make them work. I made up my mind then to write a book that could be used as a stepping-stone between the books that tell you how to operate a SBC system and the more advanced computer books written by PhDs.

This book is about building and controlling the electronic test circuits that are common to most industrial electronic and electrical manufacturing. The main point presented is how to use a single-board computer to control a test circuit and then determine if the secured test data is good or bad. You will not be instructed on how to build a high-level electronic wonder or be flooded with a lot of reedited technical data sheets. You will simply learn how to interface some of the common electronic circuits that will test resistance, capacitance, and inductance with a SBC system. You can then let the SBC system do the boring repetitive tasks of performing the same basic electronic tests over and over and obtain the excellent accuracy and repeatability that a SBC system can deliver.

It is hoped that a practicing engineer who has not been able to keep up with the fast pace of the computer world and the technical-school student who is currently studying computers can use this book to easily learn how to use the SBC systems that are currently on the market.

This book is dedicated to my family:
Peggy
Laura and Jennifer

Test System Design and Measurements

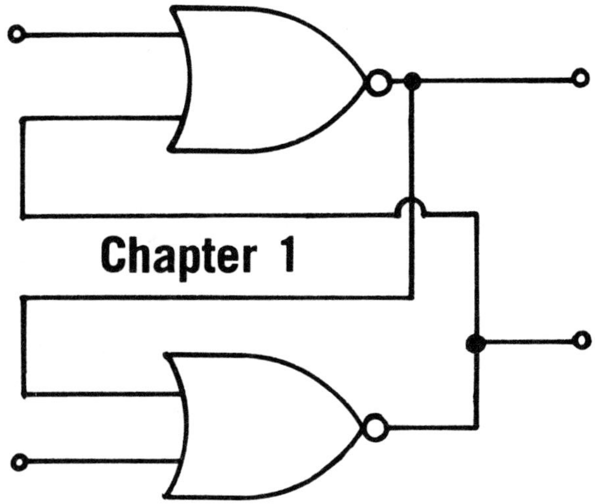

Chapter 1

The design and construction of an electronic test system in today's high technology world is generally an industrial application of performance-proven integrated circuits and microprocessors. A well thought-out design approach using a little creativity and ingenuity with the currently available integrated circuits and single-board computers will give one a highly sophisticated and reliable test system at a relatively low price. Basically, time and experience are the true instructors of ingenuity and creativity, so I will show you some expedient test circuit designs and single-board computer programs and then let time and experience do their thing.

TEST MEASUREMENT SYSTEMS

Electrical and electronic test measurements made in a factory production environment, school laboratory, or home hobby shop will usually fall into one of the following fundamental categories:

- ☐ Resistance measurements
- ☐ Inductance measurements
- ☐ Capacitance measurements
- ☐ Ac and dc voltage measurements
- ☐ Ac and dc current measurements

Test equipment construction has been greatly simplified with the various integrated circuits that have been marketed over the past ten years. The test circuits, which would have taken a great number of transistors ten years ago, can be constructed with only a few integrated circuits. You can now build a complete test system that is very reliable and stable with only a few integrated circuits and a single-board microcomputer for control purposes.

The new single-board computers that have been marketed over the past few years have added a new dimension to test system design because the control system can also do high-level math functions and decision making while performing the standard function of controlling the test system.

RESISTANCE MEASUREMENTS

In the electrical and electronic world, the word resistance in general will have something to do with the opposition to the flow of electrons which a specified material exhibits. The resistance of a material gives it the ability to limit the flow of electricity. The unit of resistance is the *ohm*. Another term which should be discussed at this time is the unit of conductance which is the siemens. The siemens is the reciprocal of resistance and is used to describe the ability of a material to conduct the flow of electricity. The relationship of the units of conductance and resistance to voltage and electric current is called Ohm's law. Ohm's law is a linear function which means that the resistance or conductance of a material does not change as different ac or dc currents flow through it.

In an industrial production environment, resistance measurement usually falls in one of four areas.

- ☐ Continuity checks
- ☐ Low resistances of less than one ohm
- ☐ Resistance between 1 ohm and 22 megohms
- ☐ Very high resistance of 22 megohms and over

Continuity checks will often be used to verify that a path for the flow of electrons exists between two points. Low resistance measurements are often needed to measure solder-joint resistance, relay-contact resistance, and circuit-board pad resistance. The vast majority of all resistance measurements will fall in the area of 1 ohm to 22 megohms. A quick study of all resistance measurements that my test systems made in 1979 showed that the mean average resistance measurement was 1,089.6 ohms. The very high resistance measurements which are in the area of 22 megohms and higher are most often used to verify the integrity of an insulation material or process.

There are many methods available to check the resistance properties of an electrical component. A Kelvin bridge circuit can be used to measure resistances that are below one ohm and the Wheatstone bridge circuit is used to measure resistances in the more average range of one ohm to 22 megohms or so. Very high resistance measurements are generally done with high voltage and a dielectric strength test circuit. Other circuits such as a window-comparator circuit can be used to do high speed production testing. The window comparator and the bridge circuits will be discussed in a later chapter along with the interface circuits required to connect them to a single-board computer.

INDUCTANCE MEASUREMENTS

Inductance measurements are one of the most measured electrical parameters in an industrial environment. Just about all industrial electrical machines have some type of inductive device like a motor, solenoid, relay, or transformer that is used to control the machine.

The unit of inductance is the *henry* (H). The general range of inductance measurements will be between a few microhenrys (μH) and about 25 henrys. Of course there are times when inductance measurements outside of this area are needed, but they are generally for special purpose devices and not within the scope of this book. The most commonly measured characteristics of an inductor are:

- ☐ Inductance
- ☐ Hysteresis
- ☐ Eddy currents
- ☐ Inductor Q
- ☐ Inductor copper losses

Inductors that are encountered in industrial applications are usually in one of the following areas:

- ☐ Air core rf inductors
- ☐ Iron core inductors
  - A. Relays
  - B. Chokes
  - C. Solenoids
  - D. Transformers
    1. Power Transformers
    2. Audio Transformers
- ☐ Various forms of electric motors

The inductance characteristic which most test circuits measure is mainly inductance in henrys. A later chapter covers a turns comparison test circuit that can be used to test inductors. This is usually a little easier and faster than making actual inductance measurements with some form of ac bridge circuit. The inductor comparison test circuit will not be able to test all forms of inductors, but when you are producing a large number of inductors of the same type, the inductor comparison method can be quite useful and expedient.

CAPACITANCE MEASUREMENTS

Capacitor measurements in the majority of the industrial applications will be for a quality audit or general troubleshooting repair measurements unless you are actually in the business of making capacitors.

The basic unit of capacitance is the *farad*. The farad is an extremely large value, so most capacitor values that one will encounter will be in the area of .001 μF (microfarad) to about 20,000 μF. Capacitance below .001 μF is usually referred to as picofarads (pF) where 1000 pF=.001 μF. Capacitance values above 10,000 μF are generally used in filter circuits of highly accurate power supplies and are not found too often in general electronic use.

The capacitor characteristics which are usually measured using some form of test system are given below.

- ☐ Capacitance value
- ☐ Dissipation factor (dielectric losses)
- ☐ Leakage current
- ☐ Leakage resistance
- ☐ Resistance losses (ESR or effective series resistance)

- ☐ Breakdown voltage

The type of capacitors that one will encounter in an industrial environment come in many styles and sizes, but all of them will generally be one of the following types:

- ☐ Oil filled capacitor
- ☐ Plastic film capacitor
- ☐ Mica capacitor
- ☐ Ceramic capacitor
- ☐ Electrolytic capacitor

There are other types of capacitors but they are not as common as the ones listed above.

Capacitor testing can easily become quite complex and the capacitor parameters and test system can easily be a little above the scope of this book. The main capacitor testing objective that will be presented in this book will be the comparison testing methods which may be used for high-volume and high-speed capacitor inspection.

VOLTAGE AND CURRENT MEASUREMENTS

The voltage and current measurements are probably the most used measurement characteristics in the area of electricity and electronics. Even though the test system engineer may be measuring resistance, capacitance, or inductance, the test circuit that is performing the test is converting the measurement characteristic into a voltage or current level which is a characteristic representation of the parameter which was measured. The characteristic voltage or current level can be directly presented as the measured parameter via a calibrated ac or dc metering device.

The voltage and current measuring circuits presented in this book will be of the go no-go type which will give the test engineer an indication of "more than" or "less than" a given quantity or an indication that the measured voltage or current is between two given points. We will also discuss using the BCD outputs of a digital meter with a small single-board microcomputer to give you a hard copy printout of the digital meter reading.

ACCURACY, ERROR, PRECISION, RESOLUTION, AND STABILITY

It is impossible for any measurement to secure the true value of an unknown quantity. The difference between the measured quantity and the actual quantity is generally called *error*. The accuracy, error, precision, resolution, and stability of test measurements have been the subject of much study and debate. People have spent their entire lives studying in this area of tests and measurements in order to help improve accuracy and reduce error. Since this book is about connecting single-board computers to test circuits of various forms, we are not going to become involved in a big, long, and drawn out essay on the subject of accuracy and error. We will, however, touch upon the subject.

You will usually run into about three types of errors when using test systems. Error number one will be the "tough luck error" or whatever you want to call it. This type of error, which is usually a mistake, is caused by some form of carelessness. Whether the carelessness is because someone did not study the full details of the test situation or they did not have a good handle on what you were doing, an error was caused and that error will have to be corrected. This is the easiest type of error to cure by just researching the job completely before attempting to do it.

The second type of error that is encountered will be system or equipment errors. This type of error will usually be due to incorrect operation or application of the test equipment. Some of the test systems that are in operation today are quite complex and it is very easy to let an error sneak in the back door if you do not study and know the system completely. These errors are very hard to stop and sometimes experience is really the best and only tool you can have to fight this type of error problem.

The third type of error problem you will probably encounter will be an environmentally related error. These errors will result from some type of external problem due to temperature, noise, magnetic fields or electric fields such as radio signals from a local radio station. The changing of the seasons, such as, summer to fall or winter to spring are times when the test system engineer must keep an eye on his test systems, especially the ones that are in a factory production area. Again, sometimes experience is the best weapon to use against environmentally related errors, but they are also very easy to foresee and avoid by placing the test system in areas which will be least affected by environmental happenings.

Accuracy, precision, resolution, and stability are really design functions of the equipment you are using. A frequency counter is generally a high precision instrument with good resolution that is generally capable of reading one hertz in 50 million hertz, but if the reference clock oscillator in the counter is not calibrated accurately, the high precision and resolution mean nothing. Next, if the clock oscillator drifts very much due to warm-up or vibrations, the stability of the instrument will cause problems. The specifications of a test instrument will explain all of the above data for that instrument. These specifications should be studied very carefully before using a test instrument in a test system.

TEST SYSTEM SPECIFICATIONS

Keep it simple and fundamental is the best suggestion that I can give a new test engineer. I have known engineers who have built test systems that were more elaborate than was really needed for the situation so they could impress someone. All one really secures from a test system that is over-engineered is a big price tag and test system that sooner or later will have unnecessary downtime. A test system that has a lot of downtime will not allow very many products to be shipped, and shipping a product to a customer on time and at a reasonable profit is basically what industrial production is all about.

One of the first things a test system engineer will need to establish is a set of specifications which characterize the test system that he is going to build. These specifications are not easy to establish all the time because the Design Engineering Department will usually want a technically sophisticated test system and the Manufacturing Department, who usually pays the bill, will want an inexpensive test system. Also, if you are employed by a large enough company, the Quality Control Department will want a separate test system of their own. The test system engineer can also find himself in a situation where the Design Engineering Department will not agree with the QC Department about how a given product should be tested.

Well, in order for the test system engineer to protect himself from building a system that won't work, it is well worth the effort to have some type of test system specification form to fill out which will characterize the test system to be built.

CONTROLLING FACTORS OF TEST SYSTEM CONSTRUCTION

When the test system engineer is designing a test system, there are many different factors which dictate how he will construct the test system. Some of the more important factors that must be considered are:

☐ How much capital is allocated for the test system construction?

☐ How long do you have to build the test system?

☐ How complex will the test system be?

☐ How many years must the test system last?

☐ How many parts must the test system test?

☐ How can the test system be built with readily available parts?

The amount of capital (money) that is available to spend on the test system is generally determined in one of two ways. The first way would be for the company that is producing the product to finance the test system. If this is the case, the company will naturally want to invest the lowest amount of corporate capital that will give them a functional tester because a low cost test system will give them a better bottom-line profit figure. The second way of financing the tester is to have the company that is requesting the product pay for the test system as part of the tooling cost. This is how most of the larger corporations such as the automotive companies buy their vendor parts. In order for the purchasing company to secure their part at the lowest possible price, they will request product quotation prices from competing industrial companies. The cost of the test system must be figured as part of the "tooling cost" and added to the "part price" quote to generate a "complete product price." So, the test-system engineer will again be under pressure to design a low cost test system so his company will be able to submit the lowest product price quote and secure the production contract.

In today's economics, the amount of time that it will take to tool up and produce a product can be just as big a factor as the product price in winning the production contract. So, this makes the time factor very important in building a test system because it will dictate the length of time the test engineer will have to design the test system, order parts, and construct the test system. Sometimes the best testing methods for building the test system can not be used because the required technical items can not be secured in the allocated time limit. In this situation, an inventive test-system engineer who can design and construct a functional test system with the parts that are quickly available will have a very big advantage over the competition.

The complexity, life expectancy, and operating speed of the test system are also important items, but they do not play as big a role in management's eyes as the "how much does it cost" and the "how long does it take" factors. The test-equipment engineer must understand that he is dealing with management people in the ivory tower who have business degrees or have come up via the "road of hard work" and do not care to understand the "ohms" part of a production test system. The company management generally will not say too much about a production test system until its cost is too much or its delivery is late.

THE QUALITY CONTROL DEPARTMENT

The Quality Control Department (QC) is one department that is growing in importance in today's industrial and technical society. The quality of a company's product is becoming a very significant factor when a customer is deciding to purchase their product. [1]

The QC Department directs their efforts toward acquiring a positive customer reaction toward the company's products, development of an appropriate level of reliability in the company's products, securing a firm control of the company's production processes, and the establishment of a good relationship between the customer and company. [2]

Well it is very obvious that a relationship between the QC Department and the Production Test Department must exist in some form or another. The general relationship that will result is that of interdepartment cooperation built toward test equipment and product standards calibration. Really, the job of both departments is to see that a quality product is shipped out of the back door.

WHY USE A SINGLE-BOARD COMPUTER?

The field of electronics which is involved with the use of microprocessor-controlled equipment is one of the most active areas of electronics today. The microprocessor has found a permanent home in small dedicated control systems. The main reason for its acceptance lies in its small size, low cost, and unlimited uses. The applications of the microprocessor is only limited by the designer's abilities. A few of the areas in which the microprocessor is doing a great job are listed below.

- ☐ Automobiles and trucks
- ☐ Calculators
- ☐ Communications terminals
- ☐ Games and toys
- ☐ Kitchen cooking systems
- ☐ Medical equipment
- ☐ Manufacturing and production equipment
- ☐ Word processing systems

One can not watch the television very long without seeing an advertisement about one of the above items which has a microprocessor control system as one of the main attracting features.

The microprocessor is a complete processing system inside a single integrated circuit device which generally has about 40 pins configured in a dual-in-line package (DIP). The internal parts of a microprocessor are an accumulator, arithmetic logic unit, program counter, storage registers, and a logic bus structure (address, data, and control busses). The microprocessor will generally have a 1 MHz or higher crystal-controlled clock circuit. The ability to operate at one million clock cycles per second is why the microprocessor can function so fast and accurately. We will discuss the operation of the microprocessor in later chapters.

The microprocessor does not function by itself but it must be designed into a system with some support integrated circuits. When the microprocessor is put into an operating system, it then becomes a microcomputer or minicomputer in accordance to the size of the system. The small systems that will be discussed in this book are called single-board computer systems because the microprocessor and all the support chips will be located on one circuit board. The small single-board computer gives the test equipment design engineer an almost unlimited variation of control functions and math capabilities. This wide range of programmable functions makes the small computer a very handy control system because it gives the designer the ability to make engineering changes without making hardware changes. Often, when the test engineer has trouble with a new design, all he needs to do is to change the program a little which costs nothing but programming time.

The single-board computer handles all of its functions without relays or contacts and thus, the life expectancy of the computer will be very long. The cost savings of using a single-board computer to control production test equipment can be quite significant because the computer system can be purchased tested and ready to go from the computer store. Thus, the test equipment engineer will not have to design and build a complete control system.

We mentioned the on-board crystal-controlled clock which controls the speed of operation of the computer. This accurate clock will give the test engineer the ability to produce very precise waveform pulses to an accuracy of almost one microsecond. The clock also gives the test equipment engineer the ability to measure pulses and event times with similar accuracy.

When one considers the ability of the single-board computer, it is very hard to justify the cost and time involved in building a TTL control circuit from scratch to compete with the single-board computer.

THE ELECTRONIC TEST ENGINEER AND TECHNICIAN

Industrial applications of automatic electronic test-

1. Total Quality Control, A. V. Feigenbaum, Page vii, McGraw-Hill Book Company, Inc., 1961.
2. Ibid 1.

ing are becoming very important because of the high level of economic competition. The small industrial companies are finding it very hard to produce and market some of their electronic devices because of the electronic testing requirements and the capital expenditures that are involved in electronic testing. The problems that small companies face fall into two areas. One area is the expensive cost of commercially constructed test systems, and the other problem is in finding qualified technicians to keep the test systems functional.

Larger companies do not have similar problems in the area of test equipment because they have the funds to support a large test equipment engineering department that is staffed with highly skilled and specialized technicians. This type of test department will solve their test equipment problems by simply investing enough money into the product to purchase an expensive test system for even the simplest testing function.

Whether you work for a large or small company, if you have a broad enough understanding of electronics to design and build production test systems that function in an expedient and reliable manner your future will be very secure. The ideas presented in this book will help the new engineer, the technician, and even the experienced engineer to quickly learn the methods of interfacing test circuits to today's modern single-board computers.

Choosing a Control System for Test Circuitry

Chapter 2

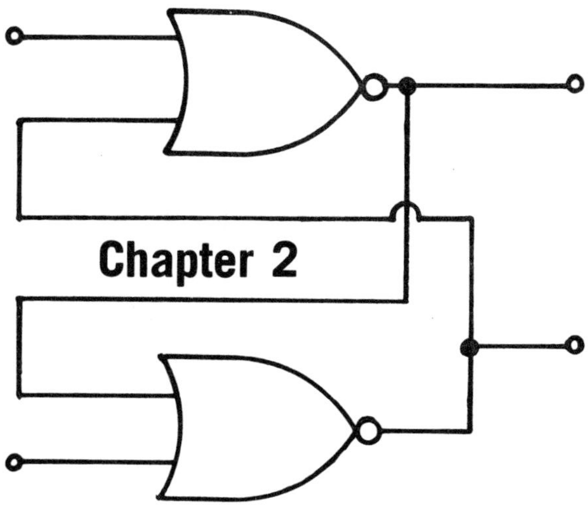

Solid-state test system control is a technique of electronically controlling a test system by means of integrated circuits and other devices which can control the test system signals without mechanical movement. Some of the reasons for using solid-state devices for automatic test system control are better reliability, faster test system speeds, reduced maintenance costs, increased productivity, and a more flexible and accurate control system. With all the good things that can be said about solid-state control, you must remember that electromechanical devices have done a good job at controlling machines and test systems for many years and they will not disappear overnight.

A SIMPLE TTL SEQUENCE CONTROLLER

Not all test systems are complex enough to require a single-board computer to run the system. Sometimes it is faster and cheaper to build a small TTL controller to run the test system. One must compare the cost of the TTL controller to the cost of a complete single-board computer which can be purchased tested and ready to go. After one has learned how to program a single-board computer, it will always be simpler to buy and not build. But for now, we will consider our test system to be very simple and describe a very easy-to-build TTL control system which has an elementary logic summing circuit to generate a part-good or part-bad signal.

The control system will be based on TTL integrated circuits which are easily obtained at the local hobby store. Now don't laugh at hobby store parts because, if one is very careful when they are obtaining these parts, the parts will function just as well as parts purchased from commercial supply houses. Also, hobby store parts are available when you need them but they are somewhat more expensive than parts purchased through commercial outlets. The total cost of this control system is about $40.00 at 1982 prices.

TTL CONTROL SYSTEM CIRCUIT DESCRIPTION

The TTL control circuit is designed around several common integrated circuit devices. These devices are the 555 timer circuit, the 7402 quad 2-input NOR gate, the 7404 hex inverter, the 2N2222 transistor, and the 1N914 silicon switching diode. The other items such as the relays, LEDs, indicator lamps, and terminal strips are easily found items. This control system circuit has been built several times with the indicated parts and has worked for quite long periods with no downtime.

The control system is designed and built around four 555 IC timer circuits which are the same as the basic timer circuit that is shown in Fig. 2-1. This timer circuit is a standard configuration for the 555 timer with a few modifications for this particular application. Resistors R2, R3, and R4 along with capacitor C1 form the time

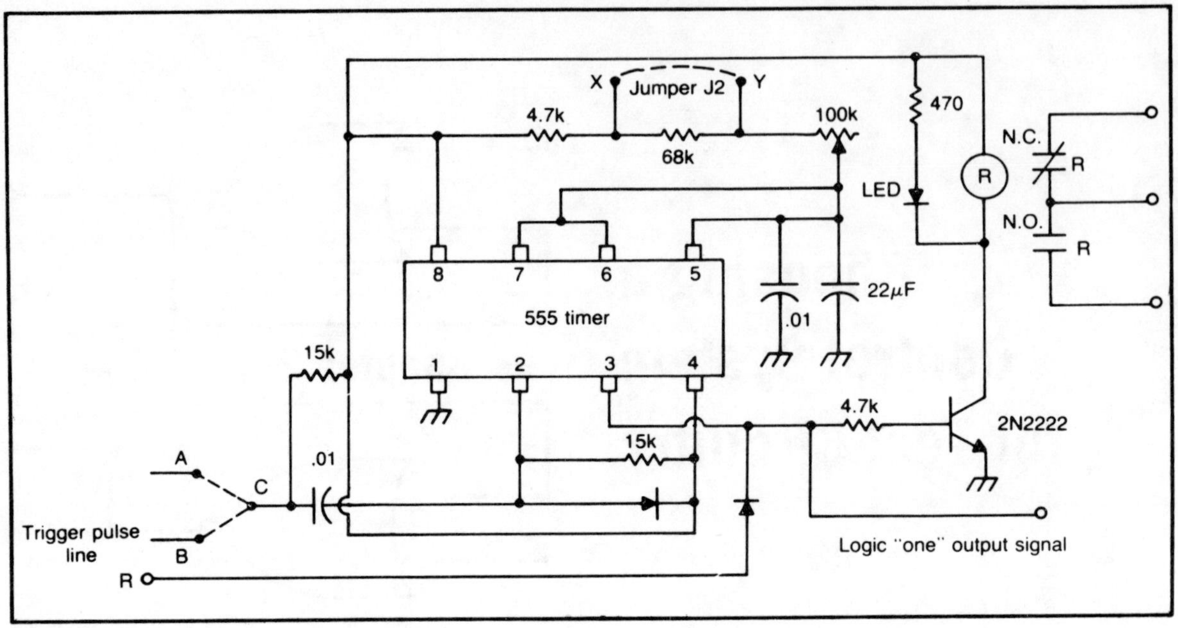

Fig. 2-1. The basic 555 timer control circuit.

constant network. When the jumper (J2) is connected between points X and Y, the circuit will have a time delay between 0.3 and 4 seconds. With the jumper disconnected, the time delay will be 3 to 7 seconds. The time delay will depend upon the setting of R4, the 100 k trim pot. I have observed that the specified time constant parts will give one a time constant change of ± 0.2 seconds over a period of three years.

The timing sequence of the 555 timer circuit is triggered by holding pin 2 at the positive level of pin 8 and then dropping the pin 2 voltage level to that of pin 1 which is ground potential or zero volts. The timing sequence will start on the negative voltage transition of the pin 2 voltage level. The negative voltage transition which is applied to pin 2 is generated by a differentiator circuit consisting of resistors R1 and R5, capacitor C1, and diode D1. Resistor R5 is the pull-up resistor which keeps the pin 2 voltage at the +V level (See Fig. 2-2). Capacitor C3 is held at +V level by the two resistors R1 and R5. When point C is shorted to ground-voltage level by a push-to-start switch or the preceding timer stage, capacitor C3 is discharged and a negative voltage transition pulse is generated. When the trigger pulse is applied to pin 2, pin 3 which is at the ground voltage level will go high to the +V voltage level for duration of the time delay when it then will go back to the ground-voltage potential. The jumper wire J1 is used to choose the trigger mode of operation for the timer circuit. When J1 is connected between points A and C, the timer circuit will be triggered by the time out of the preceding timer stage. When J1 is connected between points B and C, the timer circuit can be triggered by an external push-to-start button.

When the 555 timer period starts and pin 3 goes high, a positive voltage will be applied to the base of transistor Q1. With a positive voltage applied to the base of the transistor, a dc current, which is limited by the resistance of resistor R6, will flow to the transistor base and turn on the transistor. When Q1 is turned on, the relay "RA" closes and the LED will turn on. The relay will stay closed and the LED will stay on until the 555 timer period has timed out. Diode D2 is used to couple and dc-isolate the timer circuits. If the reader has not worked with a 555 timer circuit before, it would be well worth the effort to construct this circuit on a modular IC breadboard set-up such as a Radio Shack 276-174 breadboard.

The complete control circuit, shown in Fig. 2-3, will use four timer units. We will assume that one timer will be used to control the test fixturing or whatever holds the part being tested. This will leave three timer circuits left to control the testing circuits. The relays used in this circuit have a contact load rating of one ampere. If you wish to control higher power circuits or use a transistor interface circuit instead of the relays shown, you can use the interface circuits that are shown in Chapter 4 with this controller.

The heart of the logic summing circuit is a NOR latching circuit, shown in Fig. 2-4, which uses two of the four NOR circuits in a 74LS02. When a logic one signal (+5 volts) is applied to the input of NOR "A", the output will go low (zero volts). A zero logic signal from the output of NOR "A" will force the output of NOR "B" to become a logic one. The logic one at the output of NOR "B" will keep the NOR "A" output at a logic zero until a logic one (reset pulse) is applied to the input of NOR "B".

The complete test logic summing circuit is shown in Fig. 2-5. This circuit contains five of the NOR latching circuits. The NOR latching circuits A,B, and C are used to store the data from the test circuits. The logic states of these three circuits are designed so the test circuits must supply a logic 1 if the part being tested is good. If no logic 1 is received by any one of the NOR latching circuits a part-bad signal will be generated when the end of test pulse is received. A logic level change (zero to one or one to zero) should always be used in test detection circuits in order to check the testing circuits. If you would design a test detection circuit to generate a logic one output only when the part being tested was bad, there would be no part-bad signal generated if the testing circuits malfunctioned. *Beware* of this type of circuit design situation.

When the +V voltage is applied to the logic summing circuit, all five of the NOR latching circuits will turn on in some random logic order. We must dictate the logic outputs of each of the NOR latching circuits when the circuits are initially turned on and at the beginning of each test sequence. A reset pulse is generated by the circuit of Fig. 2-6 when the +V voltage is turned on (power on reset) and at the beginning of each test (test sequence reset).

The reset pulse will set the outputs of all of the NOR latching circuits to a logic zero state. The power on reset pulse is caused by time delay action (differentiator) of capacitor C1 and resistor R1. During normal operation, the output of U4D will be a logic one which will turn on transistor Q5 and cause a voltage drop across resistor R28 setting up a logic zero in the collector circuit of transistor Q5. When the power is turned on, the differentiator action of R1-C1 will cause a short positive pulse to appear at the input of U4D. This will cause the output of U4D to go to a logic zero which will cause transistor Q5 to turn off. When Q5 is off, there will be no voltage drop across R28 and a logic 1 will be placed on the reset line as the power no reset pulse. The test sequence reset pulse is generated in a similar manner with the input to U4C being connected to timer trigger pulse line. A test sequence reset pulse will be generated when the negative voltage transition occurs on the timer trigger pulse line. The reset pulse duration will be about .3 seconds long.

An end-of-test pulse which is generated by the circuit of Fig. 2-7 will be required to trigger the decision making circuitry at the end of the testing cycle. The input to IC U4E will be connected to the last timer circuit to time out. When the output of the timer drops to zero volts, a 0.3 second positive pulse will be generated at the output of U4F. When the end-of-test pulse is generated, the outputs of U2C and U2D will depend upon the state of

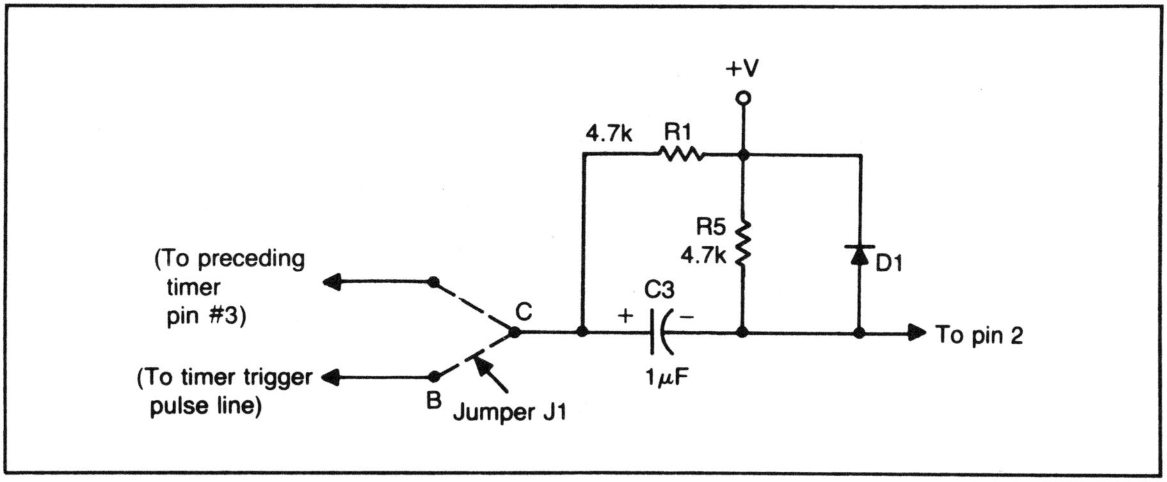

Fig. 2-2. The 555 timer trigger circuit.

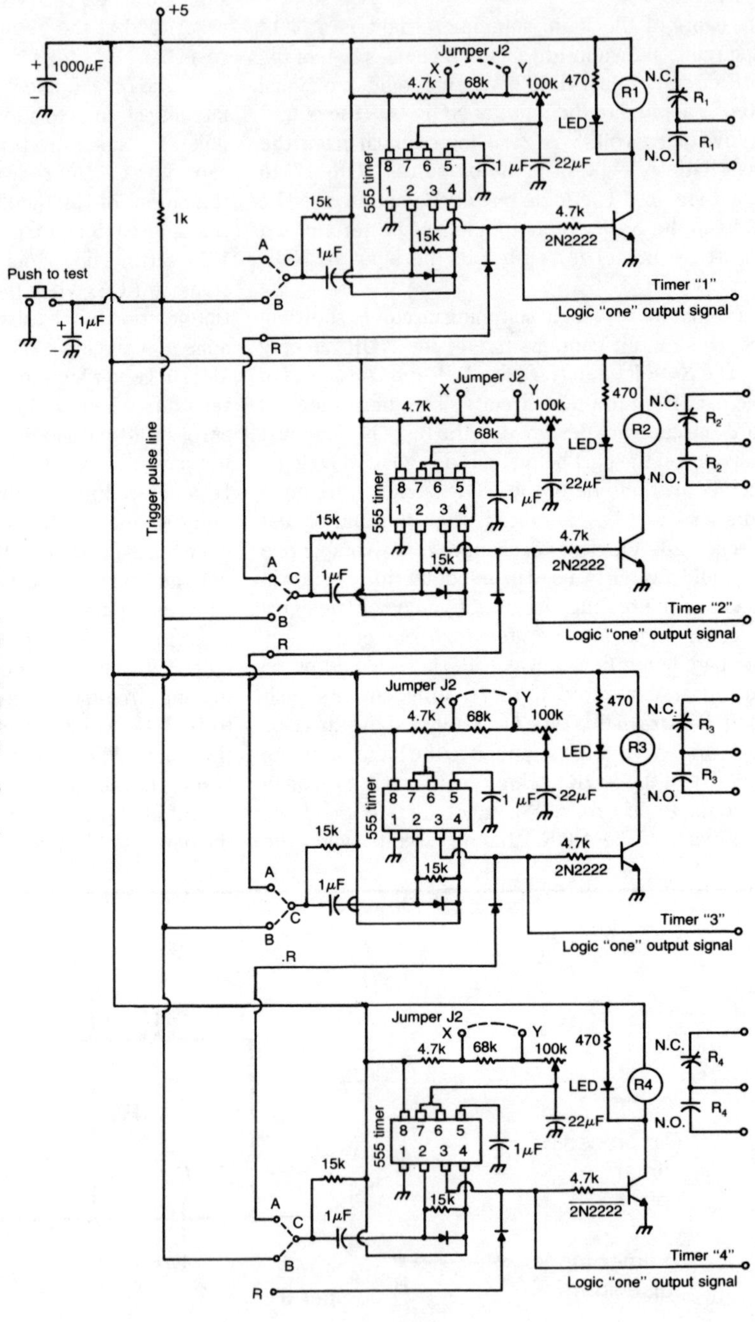

Note A: When the J1 jumper is in the "B—C" position, the timer circuit will start when the push button is pushed.

Note B: When the J1 jumper is in the "A—C" position, the timer circuit will start when the preceding timer circuit times out and its output voltage drops to zero volts.

Note C: The X/Y jumper is used to control the time delay period.

Note D: Relays R1, R2, R3, and R4 should be Radio Shack 275-216.

Fig. 2-3. The complete 555 timer-sequence control circuit.

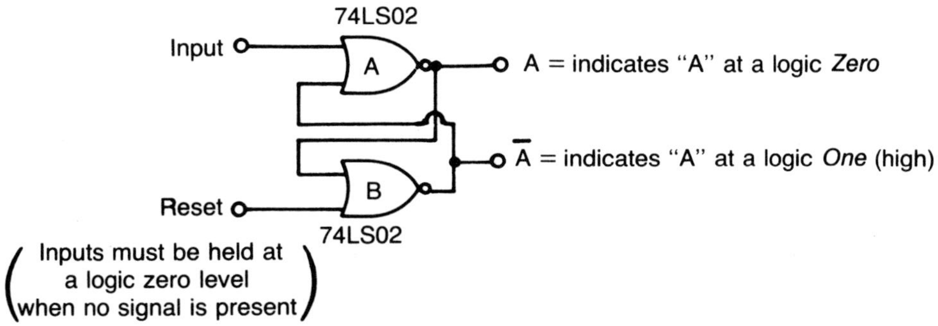

Fig. 2-4. The basic NOR latch circuit.

logic line "A". If one or more of the test inputs A, B, or C indicated a bad part, logic line "A" will stay at a logic one level and the output of U2C will go high when the end-of-test pulse occurs. When U2C goes high, the "part-bad light" will be turned on. If logic line "A" is set to a logic zero, which indicates a part-good condition, the output of U2D will go high when the end-of-test pulse occurs and the "part-good light" will be turned on.

The audio circuit which is shown in Fig. 2-8 will give the test system the capability to generate an audio indication of whether the test sequence was good or bad. The circuit will have to be supplied with 12 volts to be heard in a production area which is noisy. With the audio indication circuit, the operator who is running the test system will not have to look at the test indicator lights to know if the part tested was good or bad.

USING A SINGLE-BOARD COMPUTER AS A TEST SYSTEM CONTROLLER

A single-board computer (SBC) is a microprocessor with all of its support electronics located on one printed circuit board. There are quite a few single-board computers on the market. The selection of the proper SBC for the test system can be quite difficult for an inexperienced test system engineer or production engineer. Most of the SBC systems, which range from very simple to quite complex, start out at about $200 and go up in price as the system's sophistication increases. You must investigate the test system design parameters very closely to see what advanced computer features must be incorporated in the test-system computer to insure reliable operation.

While pondering the question of what SBC system to use, the test system engineer must ask himself the following questions to determine what features are required in the SBC.

- ☐ Do I need a video terminal?
- ☐ Do I need a system printer?
- ☐ Do I need more than 4K of RAM memory?
- ☐ Do I need a programming language such as BASIC?

For most of the small test systems that a test engineer will build, the answer to all of the above questions will be "no". If the answer is no, then you will not have to buy a big expensive computer. Now, let's examine some of the characteristics that are required for a test system SBC.

The four of the most important characteristics that are required for a test system SBC are listed below.

- ☐ Microprocessor operation speed
- ☐ Number of input and output ports
- ☐ Monitor control program
- ☐ Reliability

The microprocessor speed (machine cycle time) becomes very important when you are trying to record very short pulse times or generating high-speed pulse waveforms. It is also nice if the microprocessor clock frequency is a nice even number like 1 MHz, 2 MHz, or 10 MHz. Using an even number will make pulse measurement and pulse generation parameters much easier to calculate. Also, a fast clock frequency does not give you a high-speed computer if the computer requires a lot of machine cycles to execute a given microprocessor instruction.

The number of input and output ports (I/O ports) is a very important SBC characteristic because the number of

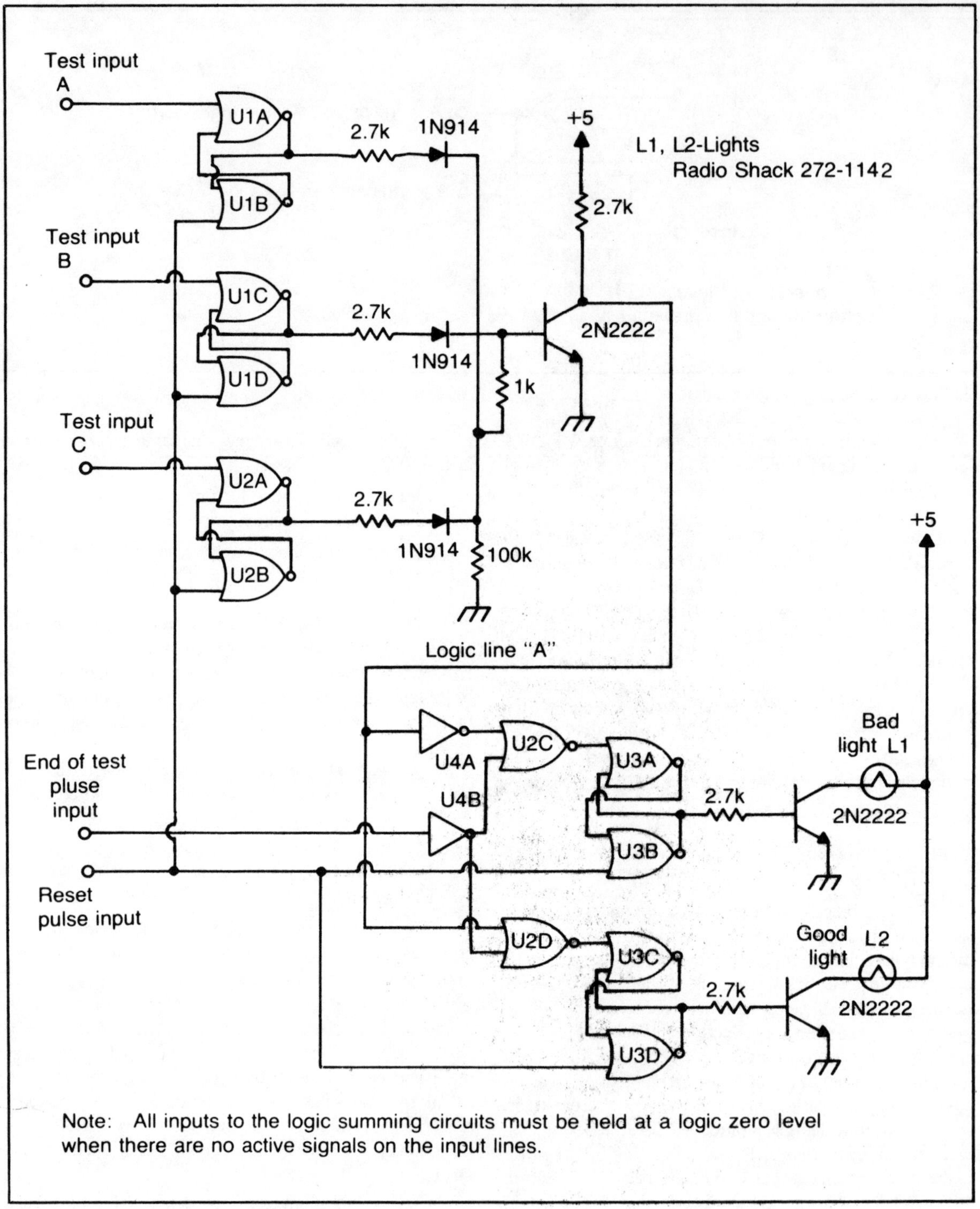

Fig. 2-5. The logic summing circuit.

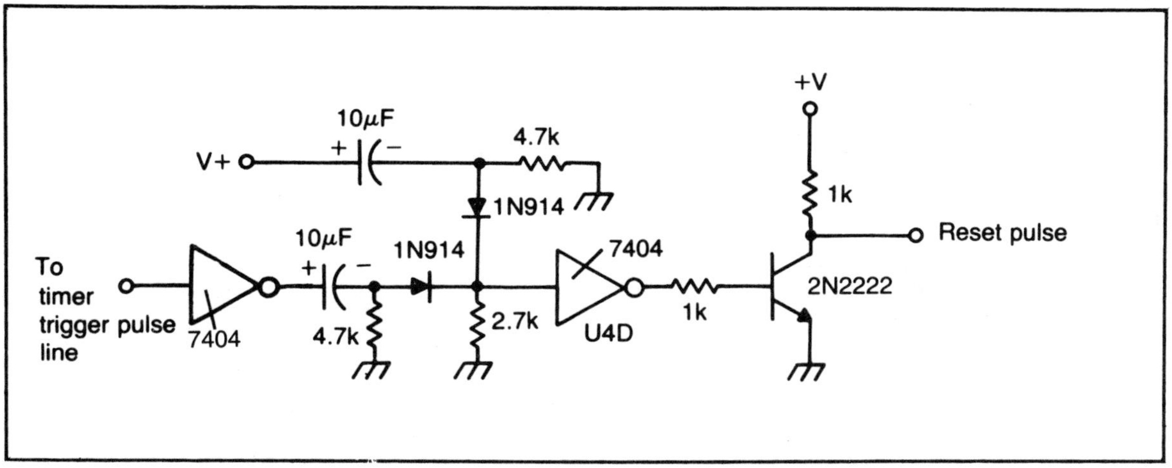

Fig. 2-6. The power-on and reset pulse circuit.

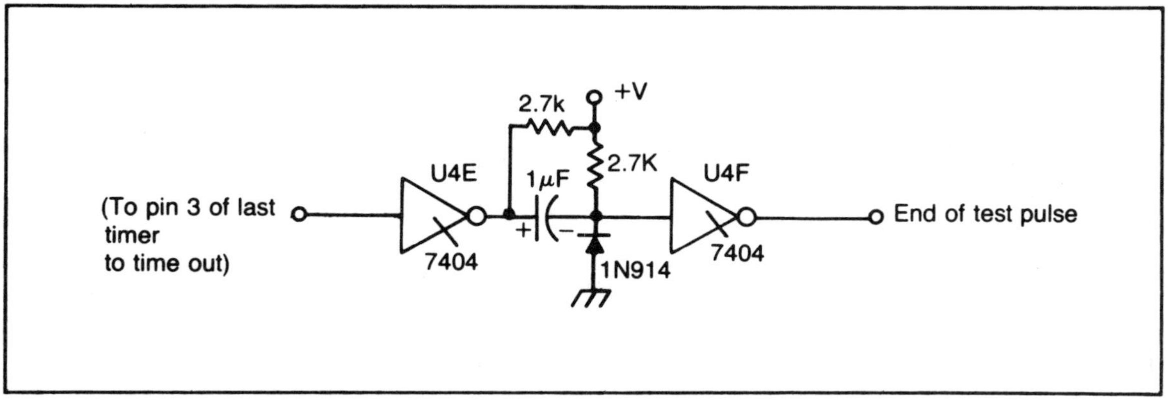

Fig. 2-7. The end of test pulse circuit.

ports will limit the size of test system that the computer will control. One can always hard wire an I/O port chip to the computer, but that can be a very difficult and unrewarding experience for a person who is new to computers. So, when looking over the characteristics of an interesting SBC, always check to see how many I/O ports it has and if you can expand the number of I/O ports by simply inserting an I/O port integrated circuit (IC) chip into an on-board expansion socket.

The monitor program of a single-board computer is the software that controls the way the computer operates and dictates the methods the programmer can use to enter and run the testing program. A monitor program for the test system controller must be able to handle the machine language coding of the SBC's microprocessor. The machine language is the functional coding that tells the computer what to do and how to do it. Of the four listed parameters, the monitor program is the most important characteristic to consider. If the monitor program is not powerful and creative, the work involved in programming the computer will be difficult and time consuming.

The test engineer should take a very close look at the computer reliability aspects. If the computer has a lot of fancy attachments, such as a printer or fancy monitor display, it is bound to be less reliable than another computer which has only a LED readout display. Keep the computer as simple and basic as possible because it is not fun working on a computer if you do not have the right test instruments and background experience for the task. A computer which is fancy looking might impress a lot of people, but when it is not working, it will not impress the right people. I would like to point out that a high priced and fancy looking computer is not always the best com-

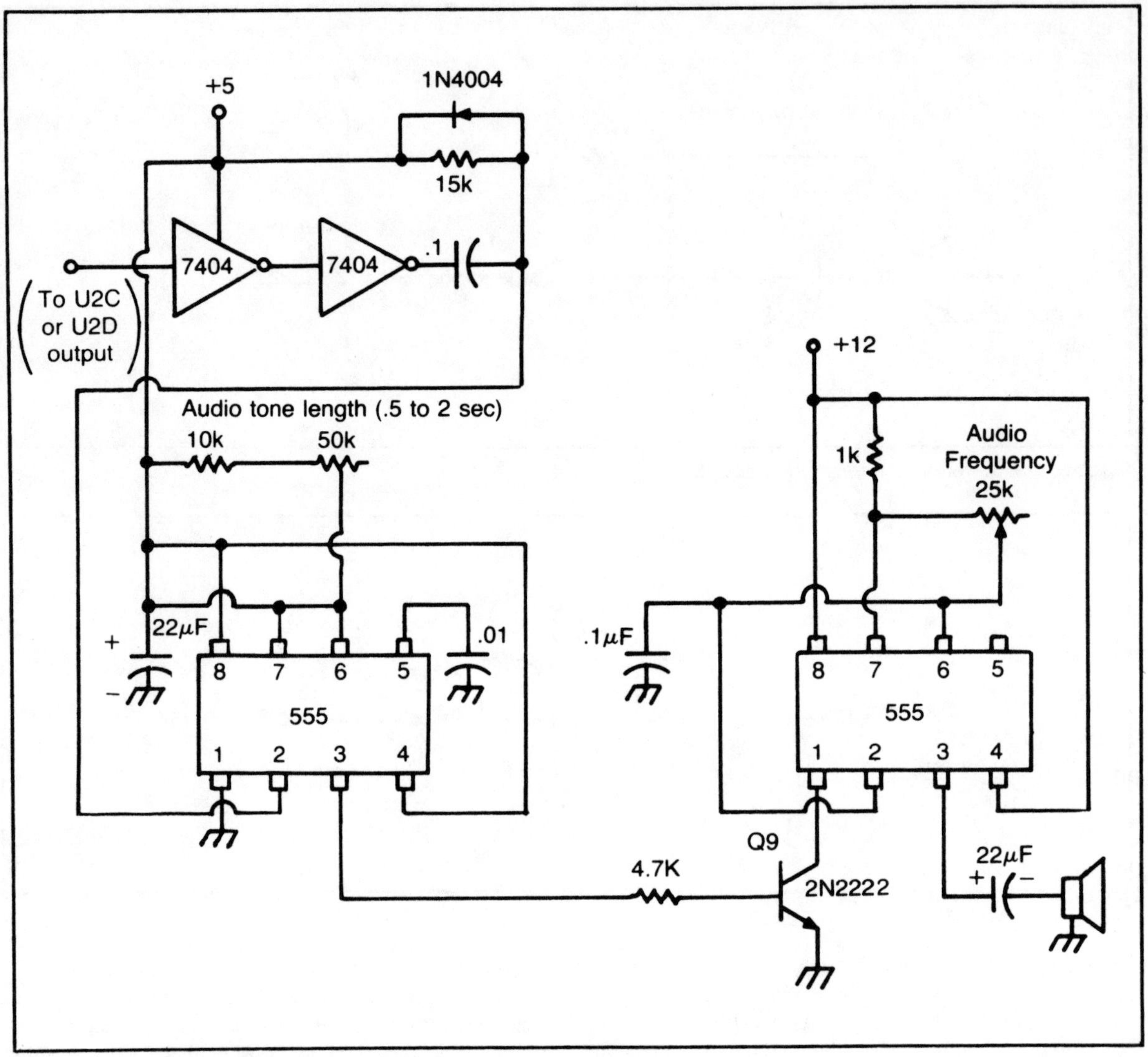

Fig. 2-8. The logic-triggered audio oscillator.

puter to use for a test system. A correctly selected computer can cut the time of building a test system by as much as fifty percent.

USING THE 6502 BASED SINGLE-BOARD COMPUTER AS A TEST CONTROLLER

There are basically three popular 6502 single-board computers which are the SYM-1, the KIM-1, and the AIM-65. All three computers are very good machines with each one being designed a little differently from the other. But, all three can control a test system very easily. Each of the three single-board computers has its own personality which is set up by the system-monitor program that is designed into the computer. In this book, we will talk more about the SYM-1 single-board computer than the other two because the SYM-1 is designed to handle machine language programs a little more expediently and will also fit into the test department's budget a little easier.

A BRIEF DESCRIPTION OF THE KIM-1

The KIM-1 was designed and marketed by MOS

Technology to demonstrate the ability of their 6502 microprocessor. It was the first highly successful single-board computer. The KIM-1 is not being manufactured anymore, but you can still find a lot of the single-board computers for sale and many of them are used in school computer labs. The low cost of the KIM-1 gave many test-system engineers their first chance to use a true one-chip microprocessor-controlled single-board computer to run an automatic test system. The KIM-1 turned out to be a very useful learning tool for schools and educators. I learned on a KIM-1 and would recommend it because there are several published books on the KIM-1 which will enable the operator to use the computer for entertainment while learning at the same time.

The KIM-1 is a complete microcomputer which includes the following items on-board.

- ☐ 6502 CPU
- ☐ 1-MHz crystal clock
- ☐ Two 6530 ROM-RAM-I/O-timer
- ☐ Hexadecimal keyboard
- ☐ Six LED data readout
- ☐ Tape recorder interface
- ☐ Teletype interface
- ☐ Application and expansion connector pinouts

DESCRIPTION OF THE ROCKWELL AIM-65 MICROCOMPUTER

The AIM-65 is marketed by the Rockwell International Corporation. Rockwell terms the AIM-65 as the professional's microcomputer and indeed it is a step above the rest of the single-board computers. One can expand the AIM-65 into a really elaborate system by using Rockwell's RM-65 plug-in card cage system. The AIM-65 contains the following on-board items.

- ☐ 6502 CPU
- ☐ 1-MHz clock pulse system
- ☐ One 6522 VIA with two 8-bit output ports
- ☐ 1K of RAM expandable to 4K
- ☐ Tape and teletype interface
- ☐ Hard-copy printer
- ☐ 20-character alphanumeric display
- ☐ 54-key alphanumeric terminal style keyboard
- ☐ Advanced interactive monitor program

If one needs a hard copy printout of the test system data, an AIM-65 with a "BASIC" Program PROM is the way to go. If one is going to be building a really big test system, a RM-65 Card Cage system with the AIM-65 can be expanded to fit most any test system that a small test system department could build.

The AIM-65 can be considered a miniature computer when you take into consideration that it has a printer, an LED 20-character alphanumeric display, and if a video monitor system is needed, a RM-65 CRT card can be used to complete a full computer system that is almost on a single board. The monitor program in the AIM-65 is what the Rockwell International Corporation calls an *Advanced Interactive Monitor*. While handling machine language on the AIM-65 is not as easy as using machine language on a SYM-1, you must remember that there are many higher level features on the AIM-65 than there are on the SYM-1, so other considerations besides machine-language routines must be taken into consideration when you appraise the AIM-65. Two of the Advanced Interactive Monitor software features which the AIM-65 has are the *mnemonic assembler program* and the *machine language disassembler program* which will make the programming task much simpler for a beginner who does not have the 6502 machine language codes memorized.

Figure 2-9 presents the AIM-65 application port pinout and Fig. 2-10 shows an AIM-65 with a RM-65 Card Cage System that is checking four dc parameters and eight waveform parameters of an ignition sensor device for an automotive application.

A BRIEF DESCRIPTION OF THE SYM-1

Most single-board computers (SBC) that can be seriously considered for a test system controller cost in the area of $175 to around $700. The SYM-1[1] SBC costs about $239 at 1982 prices. It is in the low end of the SBC price range, but it has more abilities and functions for that price than any of the other SBC units. The SYM-1 is a nice unit because it has plenty of I/O ports, up to six timers if needed, and a good monitor program that will control them easily with machine language. The SYM-1 is shown in Fig. 2-11.

Based on the 6502 microprocessor (central processing unit or CPU), the SYM-1 is designed to permit a wide variety of solutions in the area of test system design as well as other applications too. A system software monitor called Supermon is stored in 4K bytes of read only memory which gives the test engineer a very powerful machine-language-oriented monitor to use. After the test engineer has the test system up and running, he can store his test program on an EPROM (erasable programmable read only memory) and insert it into one of the on-board prom sockets. By changing on-board jumpers, the SYM-1

1. Some of this information is from the SYM-1 Reference Manual and reproduced by permission of Synertek Inc.

PIN	SIGNAL	PIN	SIGNAL
22	(−12V)*	Z	(+24V)*
21	CA2	Y	SERIAL INPUT
20	CA1	X	
19	CB2	W	TAPE 1A
18	CB1	V	TAPE 2A
17	PB6	U	TTY PTR
16	PB5	T	TTY KYBD
15	PB7	S	TTY PTR RTN (+)
14	PA0	R	TTY KYBD RTN (+)
13	PB4	P	AUDIO OUT HI
12	PB3	N	+12V
11	PB2	M	AUDIO OUT LO
10	PB1	L	AUDIO IN
9	PB0	K	
8	PA7	J	TAPE 2B
7	PA6	H	TAPE 2B RTN
6	PA5	F	TAPE 1B
5	PA4	E	TAPE 1B RTN
4	PA1	D	R/$\overline{W}$
3	PA2	C	$\phi 2$
2	PA3	B	
1	GND	A	+5V

*These signals are jumper options on PA00-D100-005 and subsequent AIM-65 boards.

Connector J1 Pin Assignments (Back View)

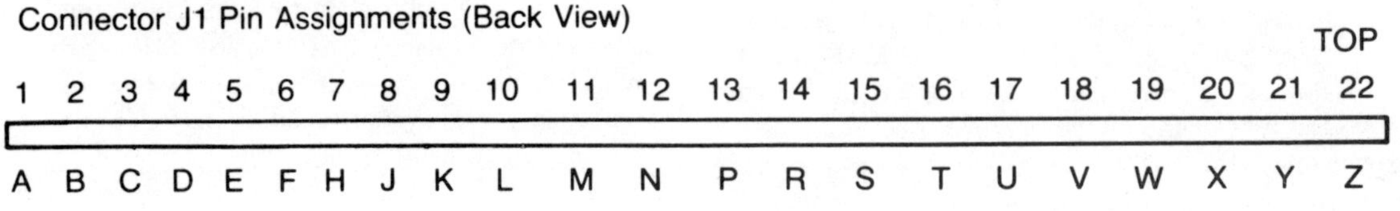

Connector J1 (Application) Signals

Fig. 2-9. The AIM-65 applications port pinout (courtesy of Rockwell International).

can be set up to respond to test system software as soon as the power is turned on.

The SYM-1 comes equipped with 1K of random access memory for programming use, and sockets are available on-board for plug-in expansion up to 4K. Those of you who have larger computer system are probably saying "only 4K!" Believe me, 4K of machine language can handle a pretty big test system. There are 47 easily usable input-output ports on the SYM-1 and that can be increased to 71 if needed. The ability to expand this single-board computer without having to worry about interfacing hardware components, address decoding, and mother boards is one of the most important points about the SYM-1 when it comes to a low-cost and flexible single-board computer.

The SYM-1 is really an advanced version of the KIM-1. One will not be able to do any more with a SYM-1 than they can do with a KIM-1, but it is easier to expand than a KIM-1. A photo of a SYM-1 that is being used as a central controller of a test system is shown in Fig. 2-12. In this test system, the SYM-1 is being used to control a test sequence that is testing coil resistance, dielectric strength, and coil turns count. As well as controlling the test data, it is also controlling a stepper motor, all of the

Fig. 2-10. This test system is operated by an AIM-65 which controls the spinner rpm speed, all test sequence operations, and all testing logic functions and decisions.

air solenoids, and keeping track of how many good parts and bad parts that have went through the test system. All of this with less than 2K of memory loaded with machine language.

The SYM-1 computer contains the following on-board items.

- ☐ 6502 CPU
- ☐ 1-MHz Crystal Clock
- ☐ Two 6522 VIA, expandable to three
- ☐ 1K of RAM, expandable to 4K
- ☐ Hexadecimal keyboard
- ☐ Six LED data readout
- ☐ Tape recorder interface
- ☐ Teletype interface
- ☐ Terminal control interface
- ☐ An oscilloscope display circuit
- ☐ Two applications and one expansion connector pinouts

The application port pinout for the SYM-1 is shown in Fig. 2-13. If you compare the application port pinouts of

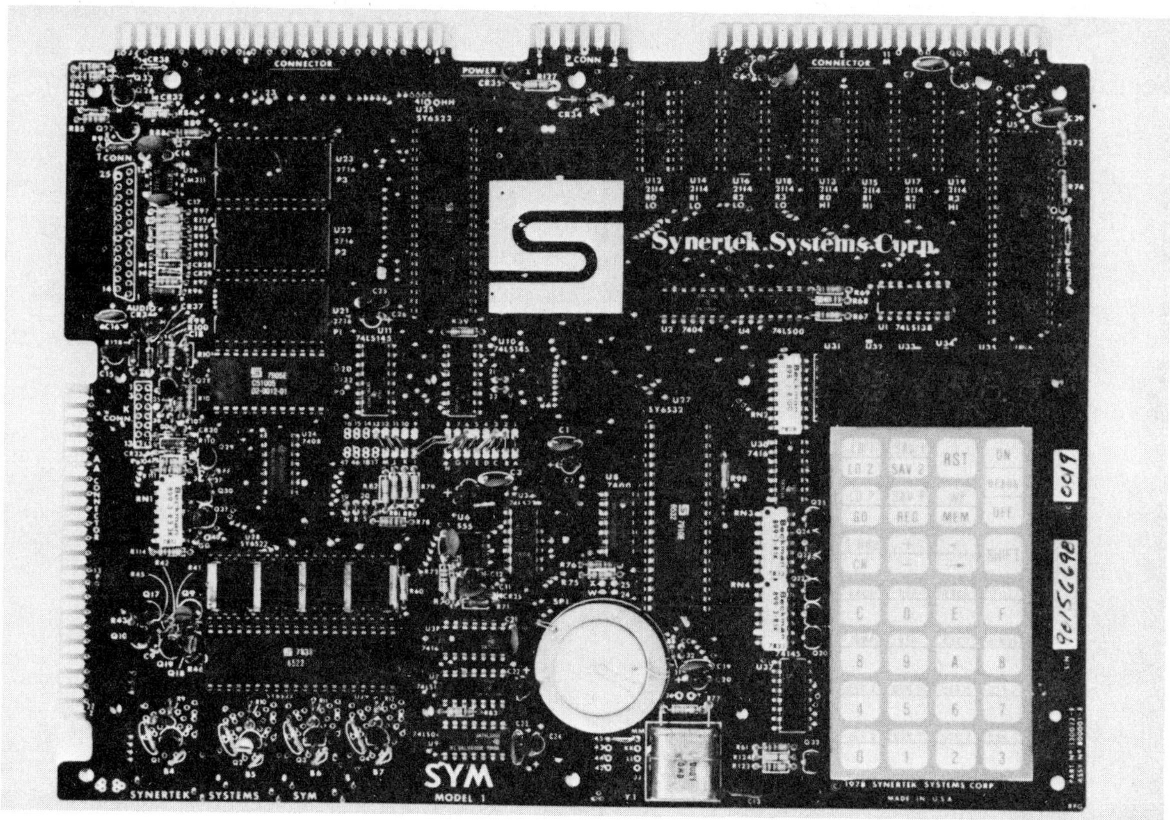

Fig. 2-11. A SYM-1 single-board computer (courtesy of Synertek Inc.).

Fig. 2-12. The SYM-1 SBC in this test system is controlling six major test system functions plus all the other minor functions. The ability to perform a math function (which can create a problem for a hardware style TTL logic controllers) is the one big reason for using a single-board computer.

1	GND	A	+5V
2	APA3	B	$\overline{00}$
3	APA2	C	$\overline{04}$
4	APA1	D	$\overline{08}$
5	APA4	E	$\overline{0C}$
6	APA5	F	$\overline{10}$
7	APA6	H	$\overline{14}$
8	APA7	J	$\overline{1C}$
9	APB0	K	$\overline{18}$
10	APB1	L	Audio In
11	APB2	M	Audio Out (LO)
12	APB3	N	RCN-1 (1)
13	APB4	P	Audio Out (H1)
14	APA0	R	TTY KB RTN (+)
15	APB7	S	TTY PTR (+)
16	APB5	T	TTY KB RTN (-)
17	KB ROW O	U	TTY PTR (-)
18	KB COL F	V	KB ROW 3
19	KB COL B	W	KB COL G
20	KB COL E	X	KB ROW 2
21	KB COL A	Y	KB COL C
22	KB COL D	Z	KB ROW 1

Fig. 2-13. The SYM-1 application port pinout (courtesy of Synertek Inc.).

the SYM-1 and the KIM-1, you will find that the I/O pinouts of PA0 to PA7 and PB0 to PB7 are the same on both SBC units.

CONCLUSION

In this chapter you have been introduced to a TTL controller system and three single-board computers. Any four of the described units will control a test system very expediently. Chapter 3 describes a set-up for controlling a test system with the Radio-Shack TRS-80 Model III computer. We are giving the Model III a separate chapter because it is a Z80 computer. Chapter 4 presents some I/O interface circuits which will connect any of the control systems to the outside world. Chapter 5 gives you some elementary computer programs for each of the interface circuits described in Chapter 4 which can then be used on the SBC units described in Chapters 2 and 3.

Using the TRS-80 (Model III) as a Test Controller

Chapter 3

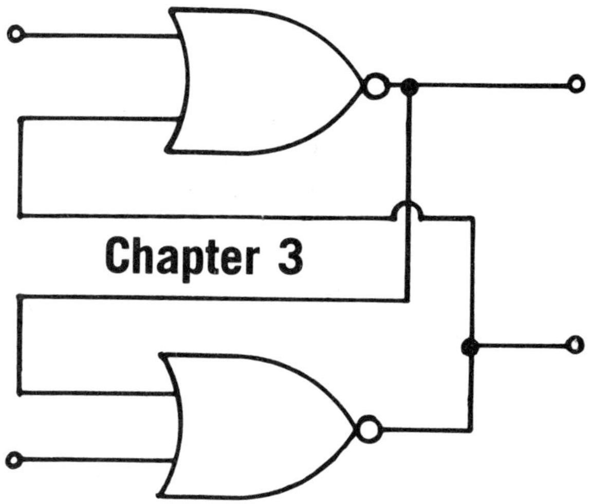

Thus far we have been concerned only with the 6502-based single-board computers mainly because they were the first and the lowest cost single-board computer systems that were available to the test system engineer. Obviously, no book showing how to interface test circuits to a small computer system would be complete if one of the largest selling small computer systems was left out. Using the interface circuitry described in this chapter, you will be able to control the test circuits which are shown later in this book with the TRS-80 Model III Level II Computer system.

The TRS-80 Model III Computer System as purchased from the Radio Shack Computer Center is not designed to control electronic test circuits. The computer system is mainly sold as a hobby, business, and educational machine and does not come equipped with a PIA I/O port like the 6502-based single-board computers have that were described in Chapter 2. The TRS-80 does have a completely buffered I/O port that can be used to control a test system if its operation is understood and the proper interface circuitry is utilized. The system operation of the TRS-80 is quite different from the KIM-1, the SYM-1, and the AIM-65 because the TRS-80 uses a Z-80 microprocessor and the other three use the 6502 microprocessor.

This chapter deals mainly with four TRS-80 related topics: the explanation of the TRS-80 I/O port operation, the construction of an I/O Port Parallel Interface Board (I/O-PIB), an experimenter's interface board for the I/O PIB (the I/O-PIB Experimenter 80), and the software that is needed to test the two hardware boards. If you complete the hardware interface boards in this chapter, you will be able to control the test circuits presented in this book and also generate a video and hard-copy printout of the test data that is secured.

USING THE I/O BUS PORT

The Model III has a nice output port set-up which is quite easy to use if you are willing to put forth the effort to learn a little about machine language programming. The Model III resets its I/O port system after each BASIC instruction is completed, and this port system reset prevents the programmer from directly operating the I/O bus port with a BASIC language program.

It is quite easy to use the BASIC language USR (X) instruction along with a Z-80 machine language routine (assembly language to some people) to completely take charge of the I/O port system. When you have accomplished this task (and we will try and make it easy), you will be able to use your machine to its full potential. One can really build an impressive test system with a TRS-80 by using the I/O port system, the video display, and a Line VIII Printer. The ability to use the Z-80 machine language to run the functional test circuits and the BASIC program to do all the decision making, math calculation, and printout will make a complicated test system almost simple.

If you are going to use the Model III I/O bus system, you will have to buy a TRS-80 Model III Service Manual (Radio Shack part number 26-1061/1062/1063) and a DEBUG Software program (Radio Shack part number 26-2000) so you can insert the Z-80 machine language into the TRS-80. The DEBUG software is really a small but well thought-out machine language monitor program which is similar to the monitor program that is used on the KIM-1. I would also suggest the purchase of a TRS-80 Model III Series I Editor and Assembler software package (Radio Shack part number 26-2011/26-2013) because it has a very good explanation of the Z-80 machine language and if you are going to write any programs of over thirty instructions it will save you time too. The programs in this book have already been assembled, so you can get by with only the DEBUG program.

When you have placed the Model III in machine language operation by using the DEBUG program, you will have to start all I/O routines with a DI Instruction (Disable Interrupts) and then set bit "4" in memory location 00EC H (hexadecimal) to a logic in order to use the I/O port. We will explain more on this later because you will receive step-by-step programming instructions and all you will have to do is follow them and then watch the machine language work for you.

The I/O port technical data is not too involved and can be outlined as follows:

1. The I/O port requires a 50-pin edge connector (T&B/Ansley P/N). All odd numbered pins are data pins and the even numbered pins are all ground pins.

2. All machine language programs that are going to use the I/O port must begin with a "DI" machine-language instruction.

3. The I/O port must be enabled by placing a logic one into bit "4" of address location 00ECH.

4. The I/O signals that will be used in this book are the data bus signals XDB0 through XDB7, the address bus signals XA0 through XA7, and the control lines XIN, XOUT, IOBUSINT, and EXTIOSEL. (See page 39 of the Model III Service Manual.)

5. The control lines are enabled at a logic one data level (+5 volts) by address 00ECH and are considered active when a logic zero is on the line. Example, when an OUT signal is placed on the XOUT control line by the Z80 microprocessor, a logic zero will be available at the XOUT pin for three full clock cycles.

6. The data bus and address bus lines are enabled at a low logic level state and are considered active when a logic one is on the bus lines.

7. The EXTIOSEL signal is required to reverse the I/O port buffers so an input signal can be received. The EXTIOSEL signal is not generated in the Model III, so you must generate the EXTIOSEL signal in your own logic hardware on the I/O interface circuit board.

8. The I/O port must be controlled by a Z80 machine-language program because a BASIC language program will not work. You will, however, use the machine language IN and OUT instructions just like you would use the BASIC IN and OUT instructions.

9. All I/O bus lines are TTL and CMOS compatible.

After you have studied pages 19, 20, 21, 22, and 39 in the Model III Service Manual, you should have no problems understanding the information in the technical outline above. If you are still a little fuzzy on what we are talking about, you may not be technically far enough along to attempt using the I/O bus port. Although the I/O lines are fully buffered, you still can wipe out a bus buffer integrated circuit if you make a mistake in the I/O bus pin connections.

In outline item number 7, the fact was pointed out that a special signal (EXTIOSEL) was needed to set-up the I/O bus buffers in the Model III so an input signal can be received. There is no requirement like this when using the I/O port for an output port because all of the I/O buffers are always set-up for output operation unless changed over by an EXTIOSEL input signal.

THE 80 I/O-PIB (INPUT/OUTPUT-PARALLEL INTERFACE BOARD)

The 80 I/O-PIB (shown in Fig. 3-1) is a simple and small eight-bit parallel-interface board that is designed for the TRS-80 Model III I/O bus port. It requires only five integrated circuits and all but two parts, a 7430 IC and a 50-pin I/O port edge connector, can be purchased from a Radio Shack store. When you are finished with the I/O board construction part of this chapter, you will be given functional step-by-step instructions on how to bring the 80 I/O-PIB to life. Once the interface board is up and running, you will have the ability to use the eight output lines and the eight input lines for any test function described in this book.

The functional block diagram of the 80 I/O-PIB is shown in Fig. 3-2 with the schematic shown in Fig. 3-3. There are three functional connection points to the board which are the 40-pin ribbon connector, the 44-pin edge-card connector, and the 6-pin edge-card connector. The

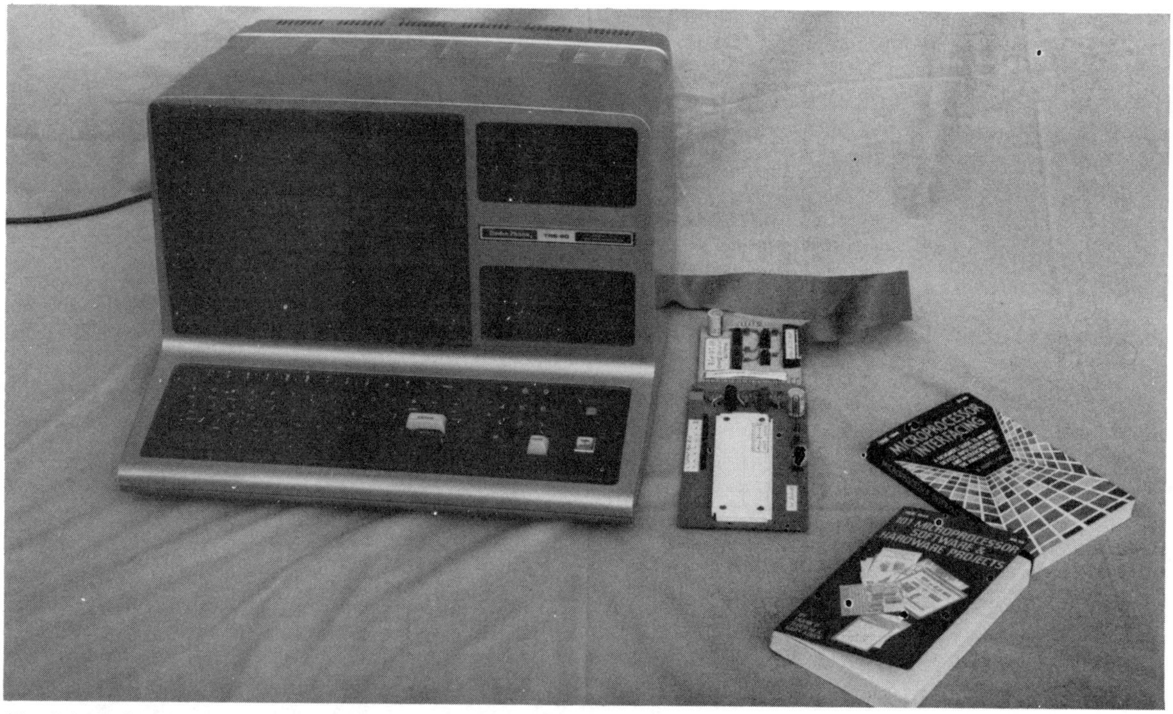

Fig. 3-1. A pictorial view of the 80 I/O-PIB connected to the Model III.

40-pin ribbon connector assembly is for all the data signals that are sent between the I/O board and the TRS-80. The 44-pin edge-card connection points are for the I/O applications connector and the 6-pin edge-card connector is for dc power supply connection.

The main parts of the functional block diagram (Fig. 3-2) are the 7430 address decoder circuit, the TTL logic control circuits, the 74LS244 bus driver circuit, and the 74LS373 data latch circuit. All four block functions are only using the most elementary forms of digital logic operation for these circuits so the total circuit complexity and number of parts could be kept to a minimum. Since one of the basic objectives of this I/O board is to keep it simple and fundamental, provisions for only one I/O port address (6FH or 111 decimal) is used in the design.

Figure 3-4 shows the address decoder circuit. The address decoder circuit uses one 7430 (8-input NAND gate) and two 7404 (HEX INVERTER) integrated circuits. The basic operation of U3 and 7430 NAND gate dictates that the output will go low only when all eight inputs are high. When a hexadecimal 6F (01101111) is placed on the address bus by the Z80 microprocessor, the two inverter circuits U2B and U2C will invert bits 7 and 4 from logic zeros to logic ones which puts logic ones on all eight inputs of U3 and forces the output of the 7430 to a logic zero. The only time that the output of U3 can go to logic zero is when a 6FH (H stands for hexadecimal) is placed on the address line. The output of the address decoder circuit goes to the control logic circuit.

The control circuit shown in Fig. 3-5 is very simple, but it does the job that is required of it very well. The control circuit's main functions are to control the two integrated circuits (U5 and U6) plus generate the EXTIOSEL logic pulse that is used by the Model III when it is reading the input data at the I/O port. In order for you to understand the I/O operation a little easier, an elementary diagram of the I/O timing relationships between the IN and OUT commands and the data bus and address bus signals is presented in Figs. 3-6 and 3-7.

The OUT instruction data signals are shown in Fig. 3-6. This diagram shows that, while the data bus and address bus signals are stable at a logic one level, the XOUT logic signal (logic zero) is generated and is available at pine 35 on the fifty-pin I/O edge connector. This XOUT logic signal is used (along with the decoded address logic signal) to control U5 the 74LS373 IC by making it latch onto and hold the active data that is presented on the data bus lines during the OUT instruc-

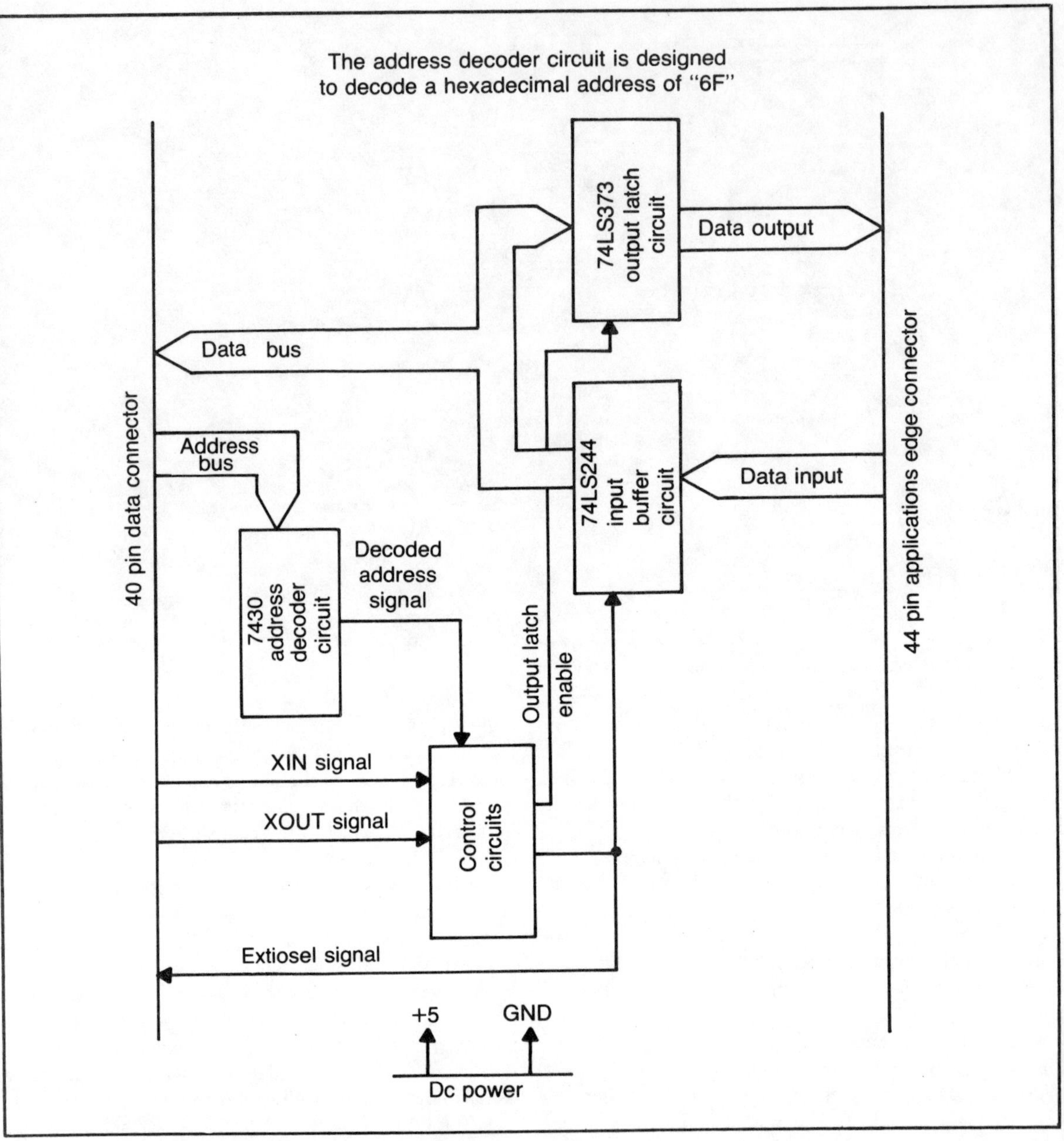

Fig. 3-2. The functional block diagram of the 80 I/O-PIB.

tion. The output data is held in the eight latch circuits until another OUT instruction is used to place new data in the output latch circuits of U5.

The IN instruction data signals are shown in Fig. 3-7. This diagram shows that when the address bus data is stable, the XIN signal is then generated in the Model III circuitry. The EXTIOSEL signal is generated by the I/O board hardware when the decoded address bus logic signal and the XIN logic signal are gated through the NOR gate of U1B and inverted in the logic inverter of U2A. The EXTIOSEL signal, which is needed by the Model III to reverse the data direction of the data bus buffers in the

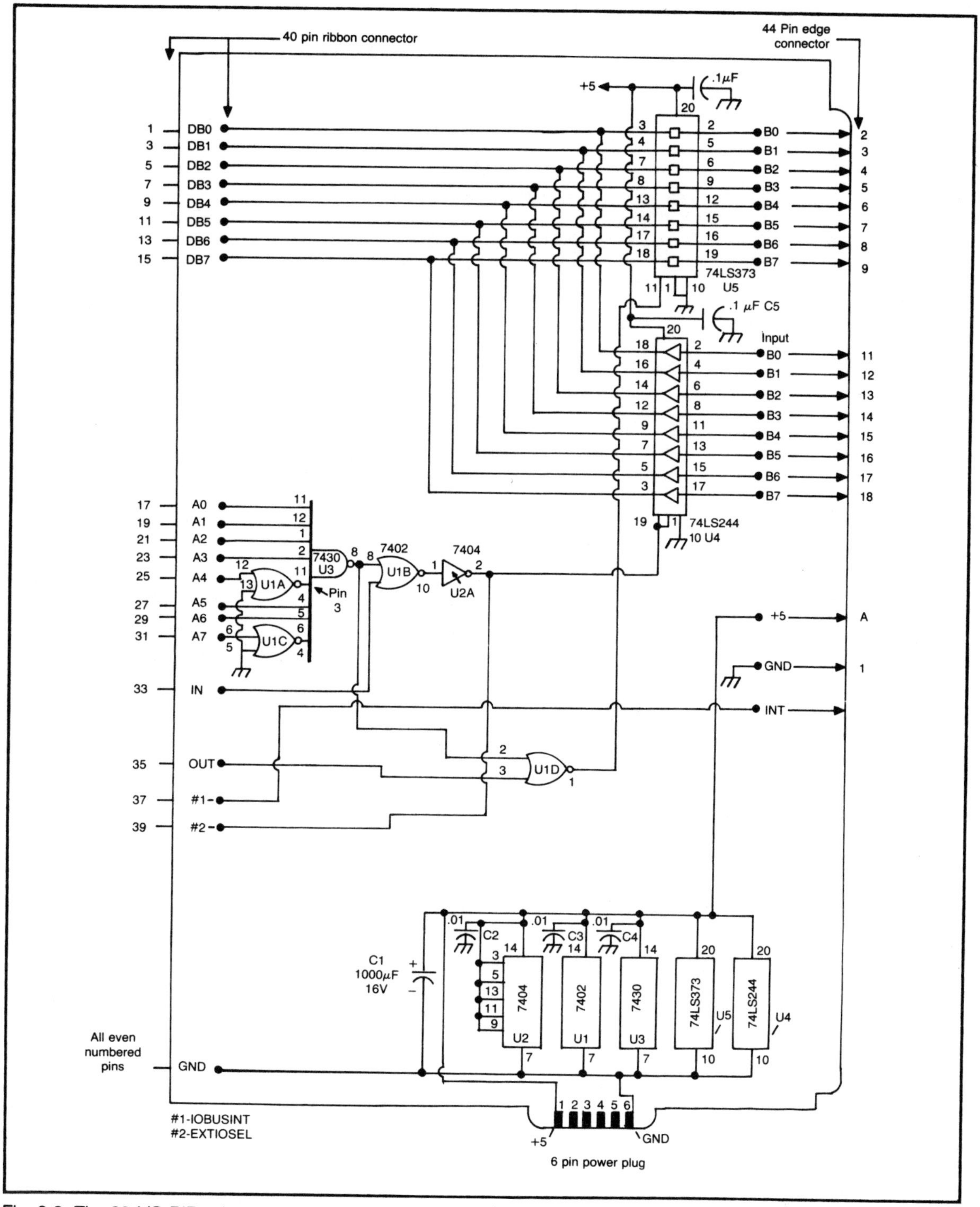

Fig. 3-3. The 80 I/O-PIB schematic diagram.

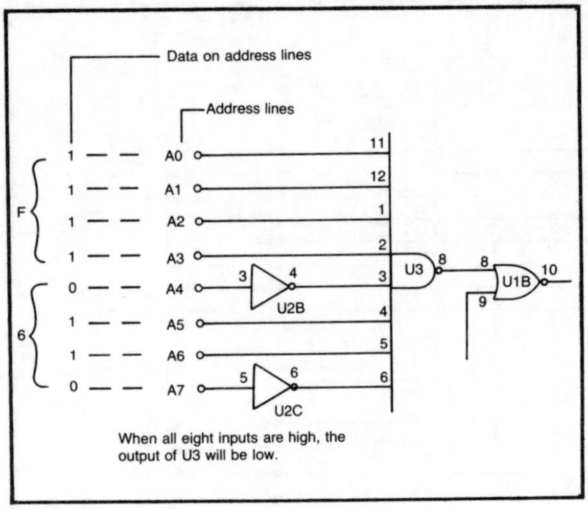

Fig. 3-4. The address decoder circuit.

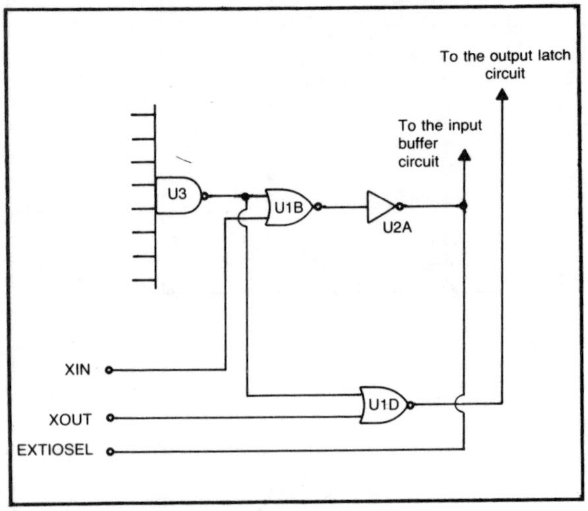

Fig. 3-5. The logic control circuits.

I/O port, is the same signal that must be used to turn on U4 the 74LS244 and place the input data on the I/O bus data lines.

We will repeat again that you should note a bar on top of the XIN and XOUT means that they are a logic one when the I/O port is enabled and that an active signal is on the control lines when they are in a logic zero state. You should also note that the address bus lines and data bus lines are a logic zero when enabled and they are active when logic one data is present on the bus lines. It is very important to understand the I/O port data and control signals and their timing relationships to each other because if any problems come up when you try to use I/O port, you will have to have some knowledge of their timing relationships to do any troubleshooting.

In Fig. 3-6 you were presented with the timing relationships between the different output port logic signals. You can easily see that the output data is available on the data bus lines for only an instantaneous portion of time. You must have an output circuit that can capture and hold the information that is on the data bus lines long enough so it can be used to perform a given function. A circuit which can do this capture and hold function is called a latch circuit. The output latch circuit that is used in the 80 I/O-PIB is shown in Fig. 3-8. This circuit uses a 74LS373 IC as U5, and connected so it will latch onto the information that is on the data bus lines when pin 11 is taken from a logic zero to a logic one and then back to a logic zero. The actual data latching occurs on the negative transition from a logic one state to a logic zero state. The data that is latched into this circuit will be held until pin 11 is again raised to a logic one level by an OUT machine-language instruction.

Figure 3-7 shows that when reading input data you are again dealing with very small amounts of time. When an IN machine language instruction is given, the Model III I/O port can be set-up to receive input data when the XIN logic signal is a zero. In order to input data into the Model III, you must have some way of placing input data onto the data bus lines when the XIN logic pulse occurs. But, if you are also going to use the same data bus lines as output lines, there must be some method used to decouple the data bus lines from the input data circuitry so they will not load down the data bus lines. An integrated circuit which can do this function is a National DM74LS244 Octal tri-state buffer IC. Tri-state means that the output buffer lines can be programmed into a high input impedance state by software control so they will not load down the data bus lines. Figure 3-9 shows the input data circuit in the 80 I/O-PIB which uses a DM74LS244 as U4 for the input buffers. The circuit is connected so the buffer outputs are always in the high impedance state. When a XIN logic zero pulse is received with a decoded address signal, pins 1 and 19 are taken to a logic zero state and the DM74LS244 is taken out of the high impedance mode of operation and the input data that is present at the buffer inputs is allowed to pass to the buffer outputs and the input data is then placed on to the I/O data bus lines. When the XIN instruction is over, the input buffers will again be placed in the high impedance mode of operation.

Now that we have discussed the I/O port timing signals and how the input and output circuits operate, you

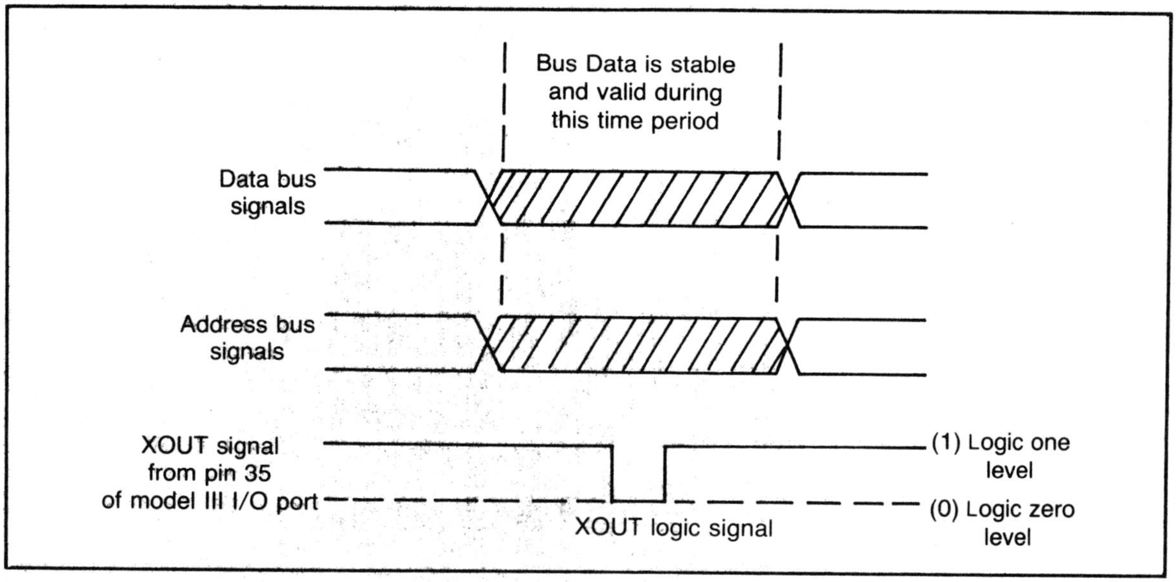

Fig. 3-6. The OUT command timing signals.

should be able to tie the complete 80 I/PIB system operation together. Remember, the control circuit serves two functions which are the generation of the EXTIOSEL signal and the controlling of the input and output IC circuits U4 and U5.

The EXTIOSEL signal that is required by the Model III to set-up the data bus transceiver for an input instruction cycle is generated when the decoded address signal (A logic zero from U3) and the XIN signal (a logic zero from pin 33 of the 50-pin I/O port connector) are logically NORed in the NOR gate of U1B. When the two logic zeros are on the inputs to the U1B NOR gate, the output will go high. The high output from NOR gate U1B is then inverted by the inverter circuit of U2A. The inverted

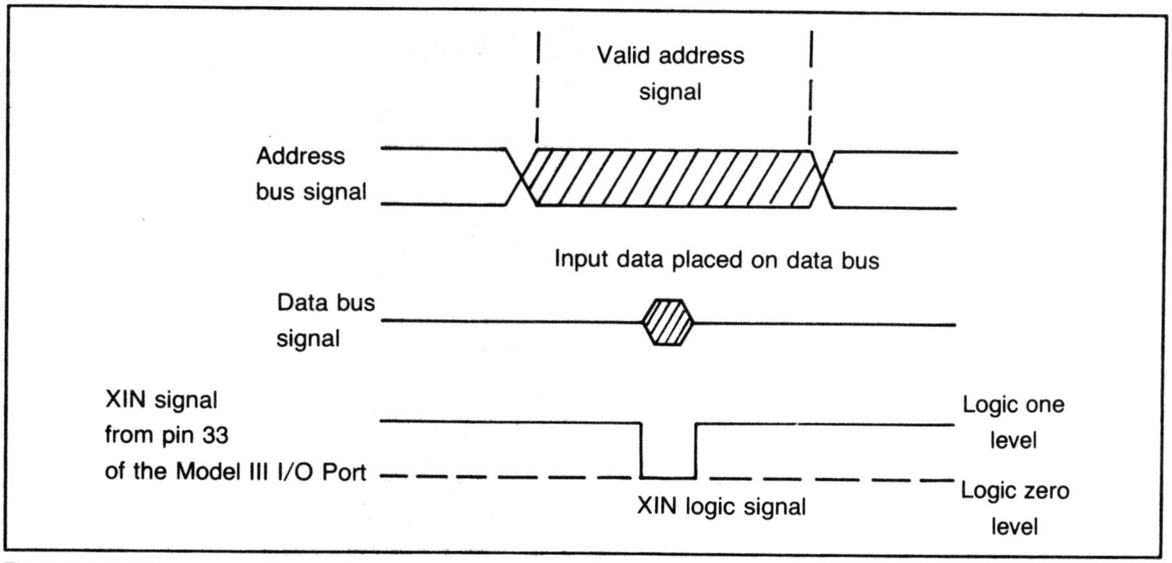

Fig. 3-7. The IN command timing signals.

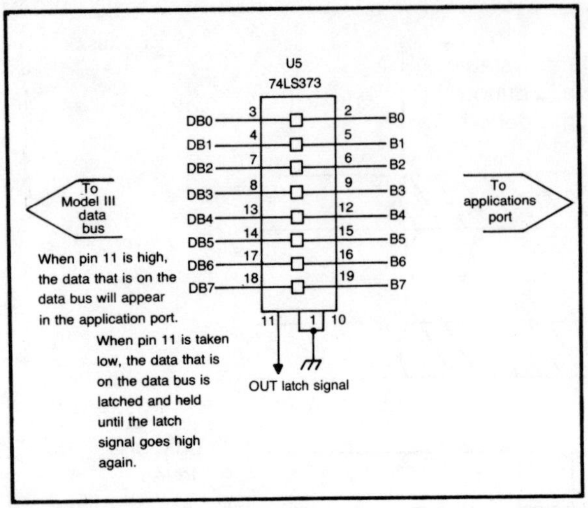

Fig. 3-8. The output latch circuit.

logic signal is the hardware generated EXTIOSEL signal. The EXTIOSEL signal is used by the 80 I/O-PIB to switch the input buffers of IC U4 out of their high impedance state so they can place the input data, which is present at the buffer inputs at this time, onto the data bus lines.

The output I/O transceiver of the Model III is in the output mode of operation normally, so there is no special signal required for an OUT instruction cycle. There must, however, be a logic signal generated so the 80 I/O-PIB knows when to latch an output signal on the data bus into its output latches. This logic signal is generated by NORing the decoded address signal from U3 (a logic zero) and the XOUT signal (a logic zero from pin 35 of the 50-pin I/O port connector). When these two signals are NORed, a logic one pulse will be generated. This logic one pulse is sent to IC U5 where it is used to open and set the latches when the output data is valid on the I/O bus lines.

Constructing the 80 I/O-PIB

The construction of the 80 I/O-PIB is not critical at all and no problems should be encountered while building it. The unit that is pictured in Fig. 3-1 took about three evenings to build and troubleshoot. If you follow the instruction details presented here, you should be able to duplicate the unit and have it up and running in a far shorter time.

The 80 I/O-PIB layout shown in Fig. 3-10 is built on a Radio Shack Experimenter's board. An optional dc power supply edge connector was epoxied to the experimenter's board so a separate 6-pin dc power supply connector could be used. This extra connector keeps any wires that must go to the power supply off of the port applications connector which means that the application edge connector only needs to connect to the I/O device you are using. This way, if you must disconnect the I/O device to work on it, you do not have to cut any dc power supply wires or drag the 80 I/O-PIB power supply over to the work bench.

Probably the oddest arrangement of the whole I/O set-up is the ribbon cable that is used to connect the Model III to the 80 I/O-PIB. The Model III requires a 50-pin connector to connect to its I/O port edge connector, and at the writing of this book, Radio Shack did not sell a 50-pin edge connector. I did discover that most of the local electronic hobby stores did sell 40-pin ribbon cables and connectors and that one of the local computer stores had the 50-pin connector that was needed for the I/O edge connector. Since all of the I/O port signals are not used by the 80 I/O-PIB, it was decided that a 50-pin edge connector and a 40-pin ribbon cable could be used. This cable arrangement is shown in Fig. 3-11. You should note that only odd numbered pins of the Model III I/O port carry data signals and that all even numbered pins are used as ground pins. (See page 39 of the Model III service Manual.)

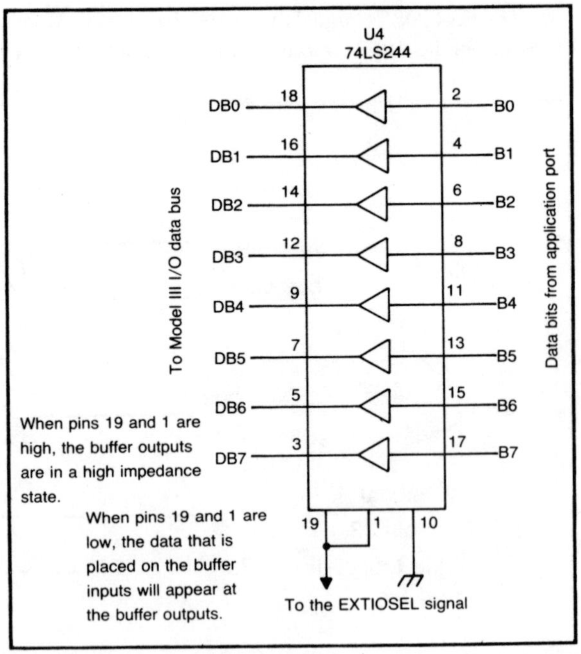

Fig. 3-9. The input data circuit.

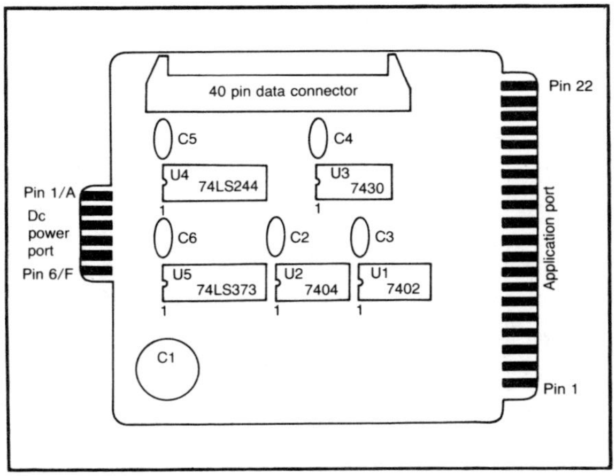

Fig. 3-10. The 80 I/O-PIB board layout.

Pictures of the top and bottom of the 80 I/O-PIB are shown in Figs. 3-12 and 3-13. When using this type of construction, you must be careful when you solder all the connecting wires so there are no solder bridges. Also remember to clean off the copper side of the experimenter's board with fine sand paper or steel wool so the soldering will be easier. When you are soldering the wires to the under side of the board, very carefully keep track of the IC socket numbers. The order of construction I used was to connect all of the data bus connections first, all of the address bus connections second, all of the application port connections third, and the control circuit connections were last.

Testing the 80 I/O-PIB

After you have constructed the 80 I/O-PIB, the in-

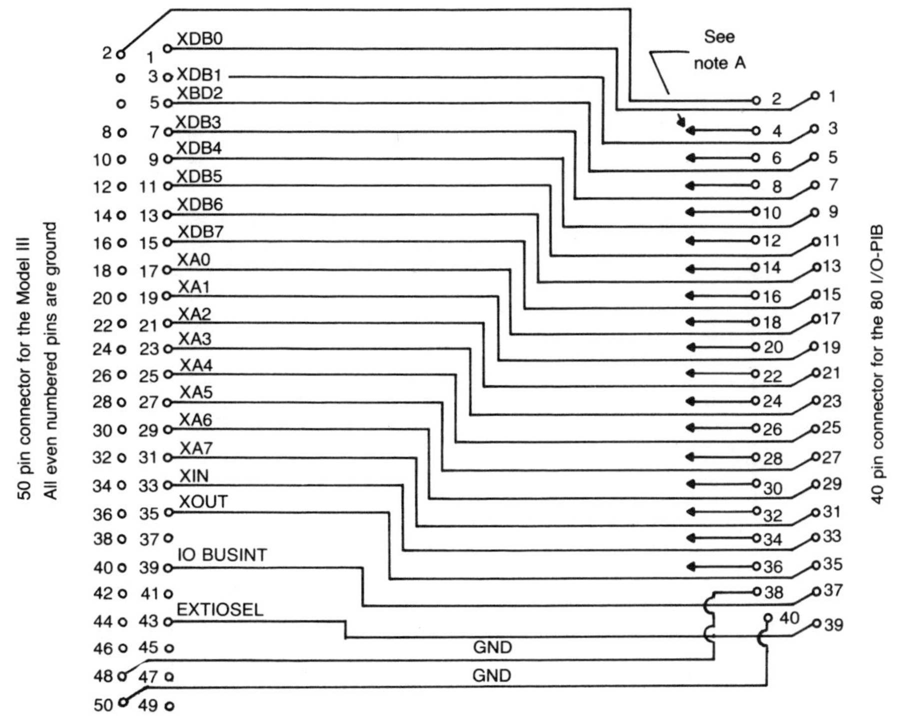

Note A:

All even numbered wires of the forty wire ribbon cable are ground wires. Only wires 2, 48, and 50 are connected to the Model III ground system. The other even numbered wires are not connected to the 50 pin connector but are cut off at the 50-pin connector and are connected to the 80 I/O-PIB ground system bus at the 40 pin connector.

Fig. 3-11. The ribbon-cable connection diagram.

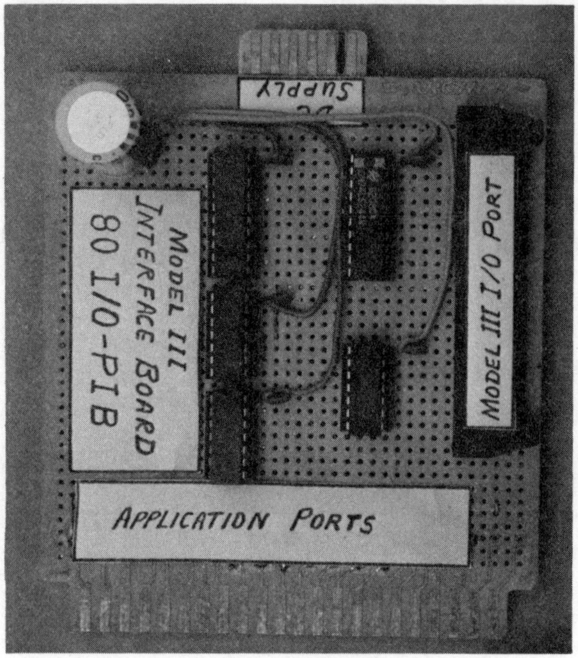

Fig. 3-12. A view of the 80 I/O-PIB top.

terconnecting ribbon cable assembly, and the dc power supply cable, you are ready to test the whole system. The first thing to do is to test the ribbon cable assembly with the ohmmeter or some other type of continuity checker and make sure all wires go to the right pins and that there are no shorts between pins or wires. The next job is to check the power supply and power supply cable. You need to make sure that the power supply voltage is +5 volts and that the right voltage polarity is applied to the power supply edge connector pins. Next, check the 80 I/O-PIB board dc power connections pins (Pin #1 positive and Pin #6 Negative) for shorts on the board. This can be done by connecting the ohmmeter to the pins 1 and 6 of the power supply connector which should give you a low reading at first and then the reading should increase as the ohmmeter charges up the 1,000 μF capacitor C1. When C1 is charged by placing the ohmmeter's positive lead (red) to pin 1 and the negative lead (black) to pin 6, the resistance reading should be no less than 1,400 ohms when using a Simpson 260 Multimeter on the 1,000 ohms scale. Now, recheck all wiring to make sure that all data bus wires, all address bus wires, all application port wires, and all control logic wires go to where they should go. If you connect all of these wires to the right place on the first try, you are better than me!

If you have checked all of the above suggestions and have found no problems, you are now ready to connect the completed 80 I/O-PIB to the Model III I/O port. Remember to carefully watch how you plug the 50-pin connector into the I/O port because there are no orientation slots in the I/O bus edge connector. Note: all even numbered pins on the I/O edge connector are grounded (see Fig. 3-14).

Bringing the 80 I/O-PIB to Life

In order for one to use the 80 I/O-PIB with the Model III, you now must tackle the biggest, the most feared, the hardest, and the most time-consuming task to be attempted or tried by the avid TRS-80 BASIC programmer. The task is that of using the Z80 machine language! Machine language programming is really simple, easy and fun to use, but you must realize that you are using simple and individual machine instructions and a lot of machine-language instructions are required to perform one BASIC language instruction. To go any further now, you must have the DEBUG software program which is sold at all Radio Shack stores. We will also assume that you have a Radio Shack Series 1 Editor/Assembler Instruction Manual or some other Z80 assembly-language programming book which you can refer to for clarification.

The DEBUG program is a short program to load into the Model III. Once the program is loaded, you can look into any memory location in your machine and see what data is in that location. From here on, we will be dealing with both hexadecimal and decimal numbers, so be on your toes and keep them straight. We will also assume

Fig. 3-13. A view of the bottom-side of the 80 I/O-PIB.

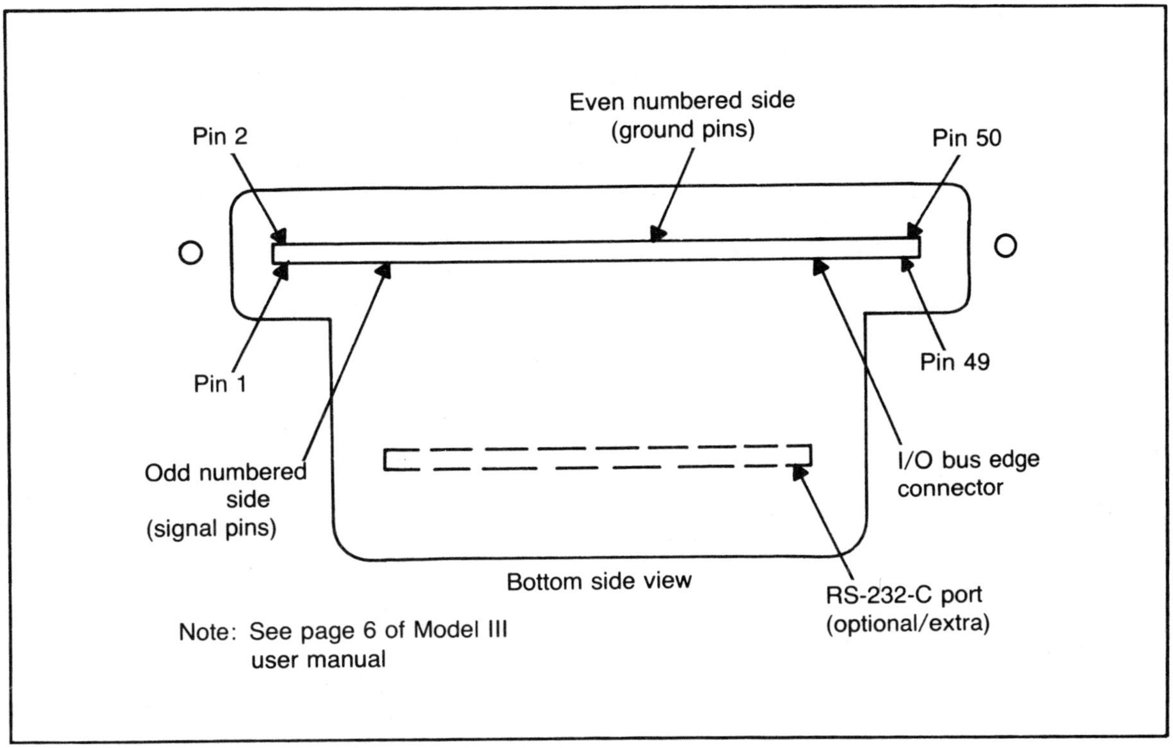

Fig. 3-14. The Model III I/O port edge-connector data.

that you are familiar with the first eleven pages of the DEBUG program instruction manual and have run through all of the listed program examples.

We will be using only a few of the Z80 machine-language instructions to start with but we will add a few more here and there so you can increase your machine-language knowledge. I must now point out that this is not a book on using the Z80 machine language and we'll only be using the instructions that must be used for controlling test circuits. The instructions that are listed below are the ones that we will need to test our 80 I/O-PIB. All of the object codes, address locations, and operands will be given in the hexadecimal (hex) numbering system.

Instruction Mnemonic—Object Code

1. LD A,n 3E LOAD Command

This instruction loads into register A the hex number that is represented by the operand n.

2. OUT (n),A D3 OUTPUT Command

This instruction is used to place the contents of register A into the output port specified by the hex number contained in the operand (n). The "OUT (6F),A" instruction command will be used to place the contents of register A into the output latch circuit of the 80 I/O-PIB. (6F is the output port address location of the 80 I/O-PIB)

3. DI F3 DISABLE INTERRUPTS

This instruction disables maskable interrupt.

4. IN A,(n) DB INPUT Command

This instruction will read and place the contents of the output port specified by operand (n) into register A. The "IN A,(6f)" instruction will place into register A the input data that is present at the input of U4 on the 80 I/O-PIB when the IN instruction command is executed.

5. JP nn C3 JUMP Command

This instruction will cause the program to jump to a new location which is specified by the hex address contained by operand nn.

The instruction commands that were just described will be used to write the programs that are needed to test our 80 I/O-PIB.

The first circuit that will be tested will be the address decoder circuit. An oscillator will be used to monitor the output of U3 which will show you the decoded address logic pulse which will be generated when the hex

6F data is placed on the address bus by the Z80 microprocessor. The first step in testing the address decoder circuit is to write a machine-language program that will enable the Model III I/O port and then write some output data to the 80 I/O-PIB at port address 6FH. A machine-language program which can do these functions is given in Table 3-1. This program should be loaded into the Model III using the DEBUG program and the M command as shown in Table 3-2. When the program is loaded, it can be executed by using the J command of the DEBUG program.

After the program is loaded and running, place the oscilloscope probe on pin 3 of IC U1D. Each time that you run the program, a logic one pulse should be seen on the oscilloscope screen, as shown in Fig. 3-15. This pulse tells you that the I/O port is being enabled. Now connect the scope probe to pin 8 of U3. When the test program is ran, you should see a zero logic pulse as pictured in Fig. 3-16. If you are receiving an I/O port enable pulse but are not generating the address decode pulse, check your wiring and make sure that everything is set-up for an I/O port address of 6FH.

After the address decoder circuit is working, we will verify that the circuitry which controls the OUT instruction signals is functioning normally. Connect the scope probe to pin 3 of U1D again and check for a logic zero pulse like the one shown in Fig. 3-17 which is the OUT instruction pulse. If you are receiving the OUT instruction from the Model III, connect the scope probe to pin 1 of U1D and verify that a pulse like that of Fig. 3-18 is present. If the address decoder circuit is working and you are receiving the OUT instruction pulse, there should be no problems in getting the OUT instruction control circuit to function properly.

Now that the OUT instruction control circuitry is functioning, you must check the IN instruction control circuitry. To do this, you must enter a new machine-language program into the Model III which uses the IN machine language instruction. A program which will input a byte of information from the 80 I/O-PIB into the Model III is given in Table 3-3. You should load this program into the Model III using the DEBUG program, and when the program is up and running, you are ready to test out the IN control circuitry.

Connect the scope probe to pin 9 of U1B and check for a waveform like that of Fig. 3-19. This logic zero pulse is the IN instruction pulse that is needed to generate the EXTIOSEL signal and to gate on the input data buffer circuits. After you have verified that you have the IN instruction pulse, place the scope probe on pin 10 of U1B. You should be able to observe a waveform like the one in Fig. 3-20. When the waveform of Fig. 3-20 has been observed, connect the scope probe to pin 2 of U2A and check for the waveform that is displayed in Fig. 3-21 which is the EXTIOSEL signal. If you can observe the EXTIOSEL signal on the scope, you have the whole IN instruction circuitry working properly.

At this point in your attempt to bring life into the 80 I/O-PIB, you have all of the control circuitry functioning properly. The next circuits that need checking are the

Table 3-1. This Z-80 Machine-Language Program Can Be Used to Test the Output Latch Circuits of the 80 I/O-PIB.

```
THIS  ROUTINE IS USED  TO  TEST THE  OUTPUT  LATCH  CIRCUITS
USING THE DEBUG PROGRAM.
ADDRESSES, OP CODES, AND BYTES ARE IN HEXADECIMAL NUMBERS

ADDRESS---INSTRUCTION-OPERANDS-DESCRIPTION
LOCATION   OP CODE      B1  B1
5000       F3                   DISABLE INTERRUPTS
5001       3E           10      PLACE 10H IN REGISTER A
5003       DE           EC      PLACE 10H IN PORT ECH
5005       3E           AA      PLACE AAH IN REGISTER A
5007       D3           6F      PLACE AAH IN OUTPUT PORT 6F
5009       USE DEBUG J COMMAND TO RETURN PROGRAM BACK TO
           DEBUG SOFTWARE
NOTE:  10H  MEANS TEN IN HEXADECIMAL NUMBERS
       AAH  MEANS "AA" IN HEXADECIMAL NUMBERS
```

Table 3-2. A Method of Entering Maching Language into the Model III.

Loading The Test Routines Using The Debug Program.

A. LOAD and RUN the Debug Program in the Model III.
B. When the Program is Running, press "D" and address 5000H.
C. When the 5000H Block of memory is displayed, press M and address 5000, then press the space bar.
D. Type in the following coding for the output routine.

```
F3   Press space bar
3E   Press space bar
10   Press space bar
DE   Press space bar
EC   Press space bar
3E   Press space bar
AA   Press space bar
D3   Press space bar
6F   Press space bar
```

Now press "ENTER" to terminate the "M" command

The top line labelled 5000 should now read:
5000 F33E 10D3 EC3E AAD3 6FXX XXXX XXXX XXXX . . . .

The XXXX means "Does not matter what data is in these locations".

Insert the input routine in the same manner and when finished the 5000 line should read as shown:
5000 F33E 10D3 ECDB 6FD3 6FC3 0050 XXXX XXXX . . . .

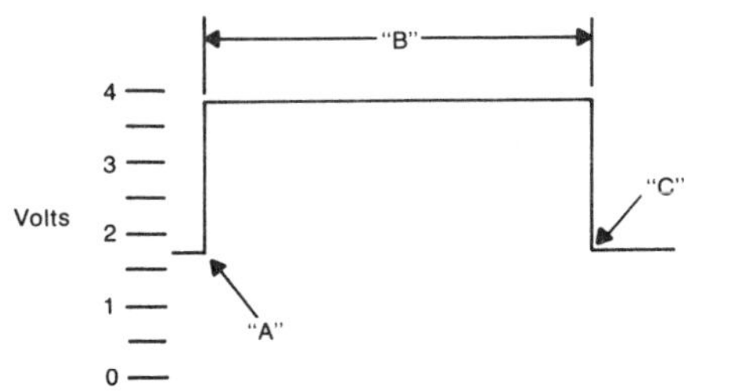

"A" The nonactive voltage level of XOUT or XIN signal lines when connected to the 80 I/O-PIB is about 1.7 volts.
"B" The I/O port active time is about 1200 microseconds when using the OUT instruction routine of Table 3.
"C" The logic ONE level of the active lines is about 3.9 volts.

Fig. 3-15. The I/O port "active" voltage levels.

data input and data output circuits. We can only check these circuits if we have something to connect to them that places the proper TTL loads on their input and output circuits. Before going any further in the check-out phase of the 80 I/O-PIB, an experimenter's board will be described which will plug into the applications edge-connector pins of the 80 I/O-PIB and enable you to easily connect input and output circuits to the I/O board.

THE EXP-80 EXPERIMENTER'S BOARD

The EXP-80, which is shown in Fig. 3-22, is designed to enable you to easily connect I/O circuits to the Model III via the 80 I/O-PIB. The EXP-80 is built on a piece of circuit board material with a 44-pin edge connector mounted on one end. This edge connector will connect to the application port of the 80 I/O-PIB. There are eight LEDs which will keep you informed of what logic data is currently on the eight output port lines. The LED which is marked LED 1 will light up when the +5 volts supply to the board is turned on. A +5, volts and a ground connection are available from the red and black binding posts on the EXP-80 for operating the I/O circuits. A standard experimenter's board from Radio Shack is used for the I/O circuits and the input and output line connections.

The schematic for the EXP-80 is shown in Fig. 3-23. There is no high level logic circuits used in this circuit and no problems should be encountered when building the unit and testing it. Connections to the experimenter's board is made by cutting a hole in the support board and then peeling the plastic backing tape off of the experimenter's board so you can solder the connecting wires directly to the terminal pads as shown in Fig. 3-24.

After you have the EXP-80 completed and checked for wiring errors, plug it into the 80 I/O-PIB. When the power supply is turned on, all nine LEDs on the board should light up. You are now ready to complete the task of bringing life into the 80 I/O-PIB.

CONCLUDING THE TESTING

At this point in your attempt to bring life into your 80 I/O-PIB, there is really not much left to do except run both of the IN and OUT program routines and see if you secure the proper results. If you do not observe the proper results, about the only problem that can be left is some type of wiring error in the output latch circuit or the input buffer circuit. This assumes that there are no wiring errors in the EXP-80.

Now, load the OUT instruction routine into the Model III and execute to routine using the J command.

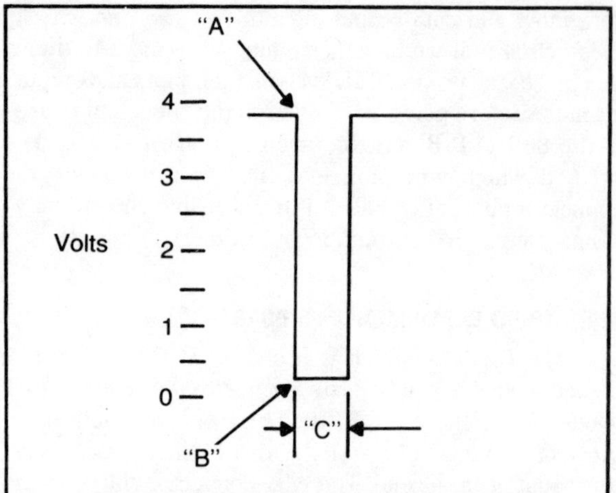

"A" The logic ONE voltage level is about 3.9 volts.
"B" The logic ZERO voltage level is about .2 volts.
"C" The pulse width is about 2 microseconds.

Fig. 3-16. The address decoder signal at pin 8 of IC U3.

After the program is executed, the output LEDs should show the HEX number of AA which is 10101010. If you did get AAH, change location 5006 to read 55H. Now when you execute to routine, you should observe the HEX number 55 on the LEDs display which is 01010101.

Now that you have the data output system functioning, you can load the IN instruction routine into the Model III and execute the routine. Set-up the J execute command in the following manner; J, ADDRESS= 5000,5009 (ENTER). This J command sequence will stop the program at memory location 5009 and return program control back to the DEBUG program. If you do not stop the routine at 5009, the routine will go into a closed loop caused by the JUMP command which jumps back to location 5000. Once you get into this closed loop, you will have to reset the Model III to get out of the loop and then reload the DEBUG system tape again.

When you execute the IN instruction program, all of the output LEDs should stay on. Connect a ground wire to the black binding post and insert it into the B0 (Bit 0) hole

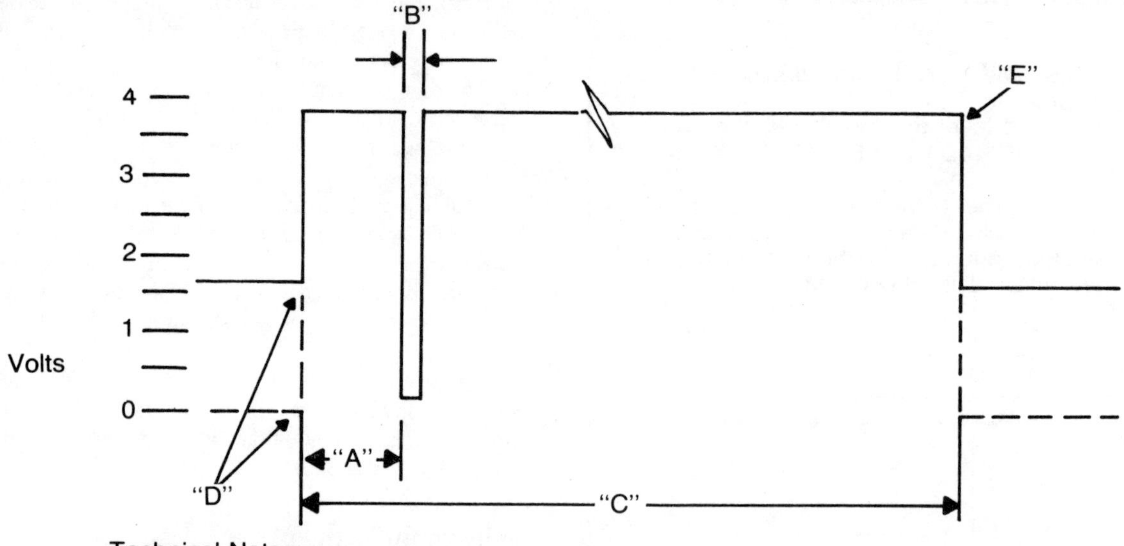

Technical Notes:
"A" The OUT Instruction pulse starts about 8 microseconds after the program is started.
"B" The OUT Instruction pulse is about 1 microsecond long.
"C" The I/O port is enabled about 1200 microseconds when the program is executed.
"D" The voltage will be about 1.7 volts at pin 3 of U1D, but will be zero volts if U1D is not installed.
"E" The logic ONE voltage level will be about 3.9 volts.

Fig. 3-17. The OUT instruction signal.

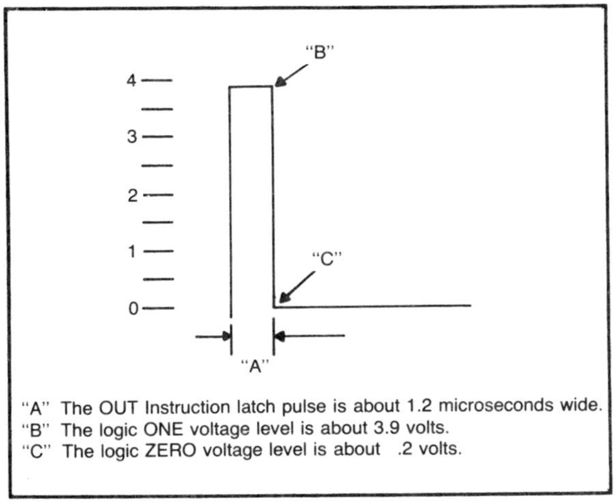

Fig. 3-18. The OUT instruction latch pulse.

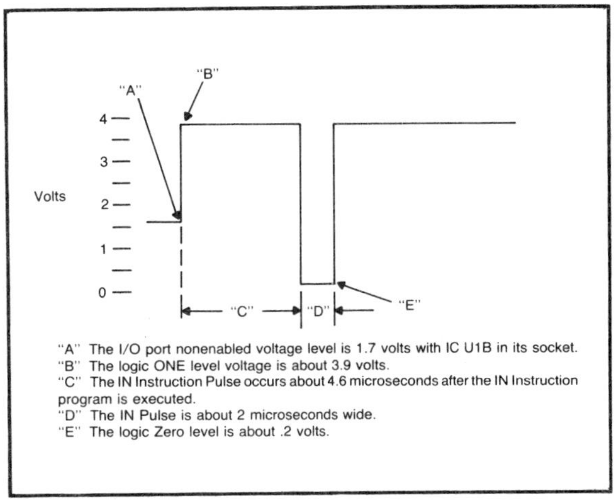

Fig. 3-19. The IN instruction phase.

on the breadboard and execute the program. Since B0 is now at a zero logic level, Model III will read a FE (Hex 1111 1110) at the input port and then it will place the FE data into the Z80's A register. The Z80 will write the FE data into the output which will turn off the B0 LED. After the routine is run, all of the LEDs should be on with the exception of LED B0. If this was the result that you observed, you can now run the IN instruction program routine in a closed loop fashion. When running in a closed loop, you should be able to plug the ground wire into any input port connection hole and watch the corresponding output LED go out indicating that the output port bit is a logic zero. Again, if you do not observe the correct results, check all of the wiring and make sure that the EXTIOSEL signal is getting to the Model III. If all of the control circuits are working, there are not too many reasons why the input and output circuits should not work also.

If you have followed the instructions presented in this chapter, you should now have an up and running I/O

Table 3-3. This Z-80 Machine-Language Program Can Be Used to Test the Input Buffer Circuits of the 80 I/O-PIB.

```
THIS  ROUTINE IS USED  TO  TEST THE  INPUT  BUFFER  CIRCUITS
USING THE DEBUG PROGRAM.
ADDRESSES, OP CODES, AND BYTES ARE IN HEXADECIMAL NUMBERS

ADDRESS---INSTRUCTION-OPERANDS-DESCRIPTION
LOCATION  OP CODE     B1  B1
5000      F3                   DISABLE INTERRUPTS
5001      3E          10       PLACE 10H IN REGISTER A
5003      D3          EC       PLACE 10H IN PORT ECH
5005      DB          6F       READ AND PLACE INPUT PORT
                               DATA INTO REGISTER A
5007      D3          6F       PLACE CONTENTS OR REGISTER
                               A INTO OUTPUT PORT 6FH
5009      C3          00  50   JUMP TO LOCATION 5000H
500C      USE DEBUG J COMMAND TO RETURN PROGRAM BACK TO
          DEBUG SOFTWARE
NOTE: "10H" MEANS TEN IN HEXADECIMAL NUMBERS
```

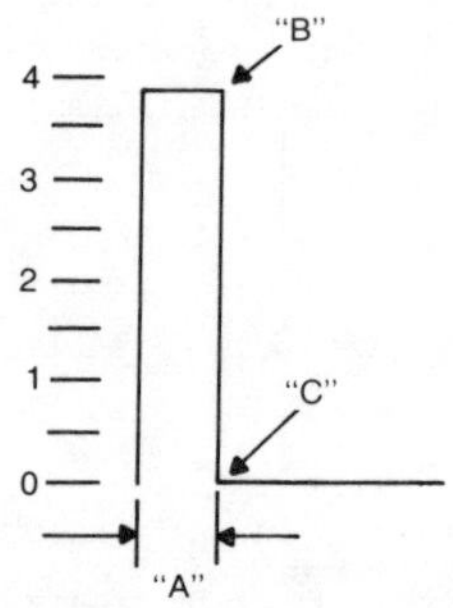

"A" The gated output pulse of IC U1B is about 1.2 microsecond wide.
"B" The logic ONE voltage level is about 3.9 volts.
"C" The logic Zero voltage level is about .2 volts.

Fig. 3-20. The gated output signal of U1D.

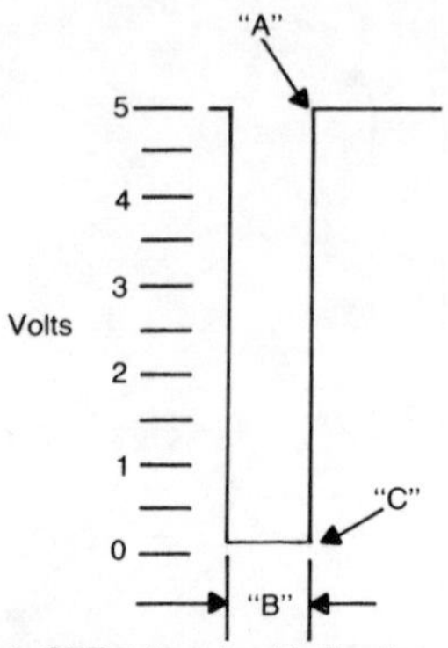

"A" The logic ONE voltage level is 5 volts.
"B" The EXTIOSEL logic pulse width is about 1.2 microseconds long.
"C" The logic ZERO voltage level is about .2 volts.

Fig. 3-21. The Extiosel pulse.

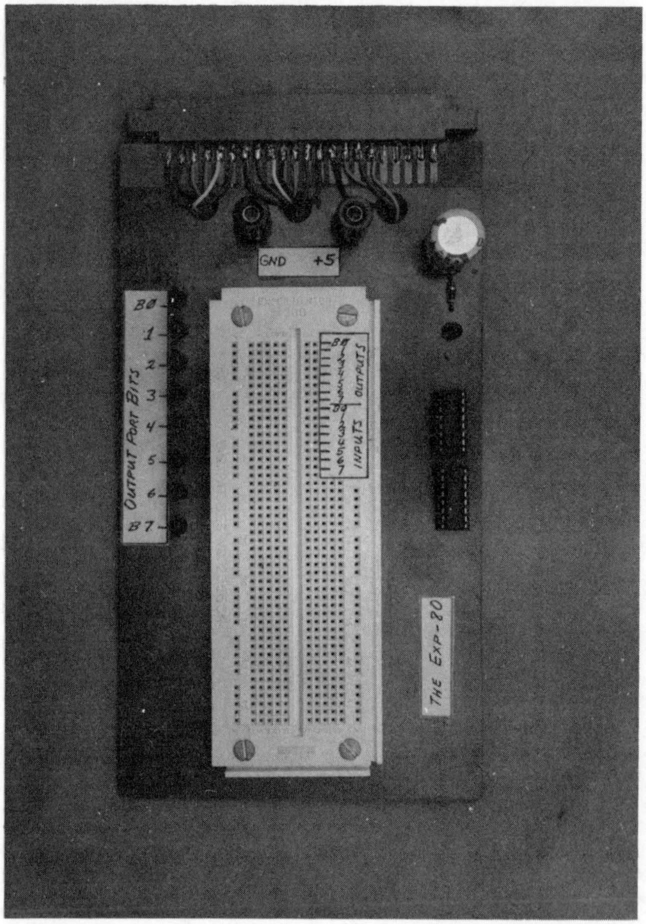

Fig. 3-22. A view of the EXP-80 top-side.

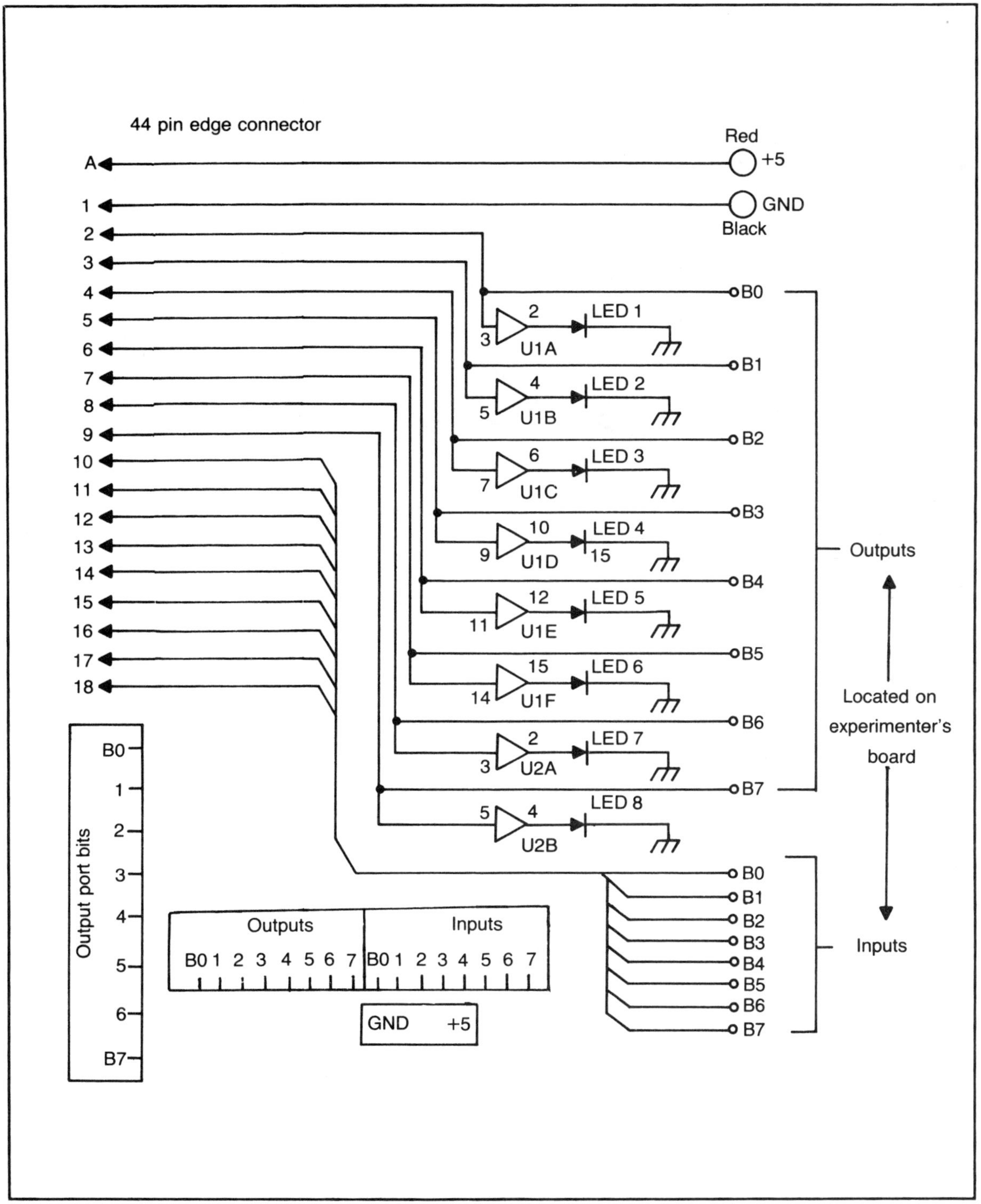

Fig. 3-23. The schematic diagram of the EXP-80.

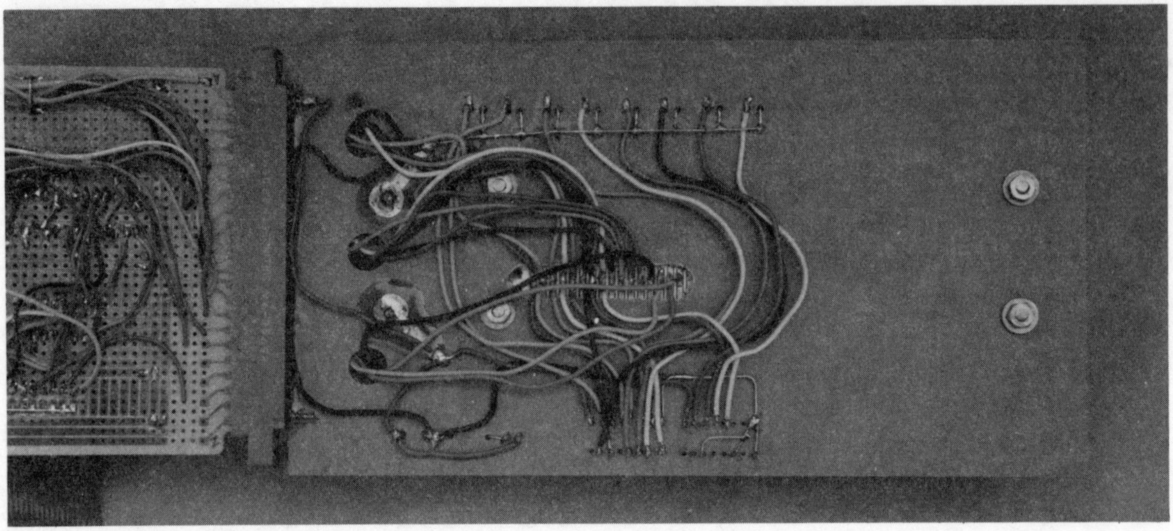

Fig. 3-24. A bottom view of the EXP-80.

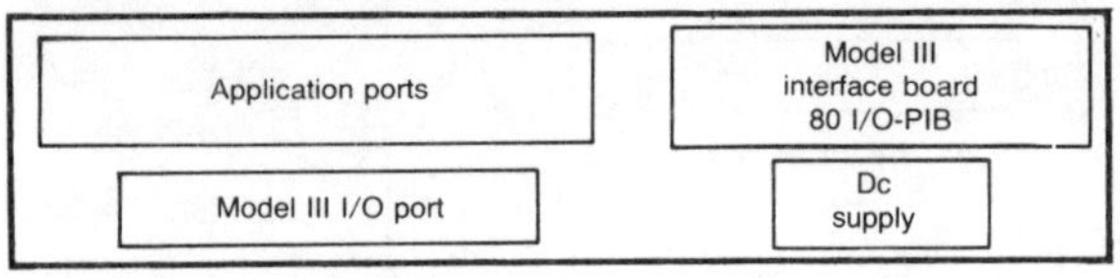

Fig. 3-25. The 80 I/O-PIB cut-out labels.

port which will allow you to interface and operate any test circuit which is described later in this book with a Model III. I would suggest that you read Chapter 4 before using the 80 I/O-PIB and the EXP-80 with any operational circuits. Figure 3-25 shows the 80 I/O-PIB labels that can be copied, cut-out, and glued to the board.

Interfacing Circuits for a Control System or Microcomputer

Chapter 4

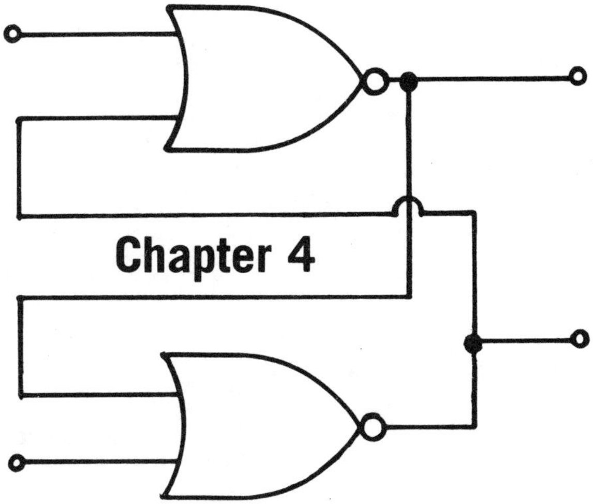

The terminology of "interfacing circuit" in this book will mean a circuit that is designed to connect a control system or microcomputer to the outside world for the purpose of performing a given technical function. The interfacing circuits discussed in this chapter are fundamental building blocks of the functional test circuits that will be described in later chapters, and are designed to work with the TTL Controller, the 80 I/O-PIB, or the three single-board computers that were described earlier in this book.

ALWAYS PROTECT THE COMPUTER

The interfacing circuits are the parts of the control system that give our computer muscle. Without the interface circuits, our single-board computers would be nothing more than play-things. When you interface the computer to an external circuit there is a right way, a wrong way, and a hazardous way of doing it. There are many right ways to connect the computer to external circuits and I will point out a few methods which I have used with good results.

One point you must remember whether you are young or old is to "always protect the computer" when you are connecting it to external circuits. A general rule that will sooner or later protect your computer (unless you do not make mistakes) is to always use a buffer circuit between the computer and the interface circuit. This way, when you "smoke" an interface circuit, you will only torch the buffer circuit and not the computer output port. It is cheaper to replace a fifty cent IC than it is to replace a twenty dollar I/O port chip.

The single-board computers that have been discussed in this book can interface easily with either TTL or CMOS circuit chips. It can sometimes be very advantageous to intermix both TTL and CMOS circuits in order to use the optimum operating parameters of both which are generally considered to be the high input impedance of the CMOS circuits and the current-sinking ability of TTL circuits. You will be able to observe this intermix in several of the chapters that follow.

Before we start describing the different basic interface circuits, it will be assumed that the reader has a basic background in electronics and can understand how a npn transistor can be turned off and on and knows a little about the logic families TTL and CMOS. There are a lot of good electronics books at the local library; so, if you are strong in programming and light in electronics, you should study some of these books. Learning how to interface I/O circuits to a computer is somewhat comparable to learning how to program a computer because a little hands on experience can be better than two thousand words and a whole bunch of pictures.

THE EXPERIMENTER 6522

The Experimeter 6522 is a breadboard set-up that

Fig. 4-1. The EXP-6522 connected to the SYM-1 single-board computer.

presents an expedient and safe method of experimenting with I/O circuits using the 6522 VIA (Versatile Interface Adapter) chip that is used on the SYM-1 and the AIM-65. Of course the breadboard set-up will work with other I/O port chips such as the 6530 RRIOT (Rom-Ram-I/O-Timer) that is used on the KIM-1. The Experimenter 6522 is shown in Fig. 4-1 with the nonmenclature label layout in Fig. 4-2. The labels can be copied, cut-out, and glued onto the circuit board. The breadboard set-up is designed to give the inquisitive programmer or engineer the ability to use all the single-board computer functions with the I/O interface circuits that will be described in this chapter.

The edge connector assembly which connects to the single-board computer will work with either the SYM-1, the KIM-1, or the AIM-65 because their application port bus pinouts are compatible. There are differences between the three computer application port pinouts but none that will interfere with the operation of the breadboard set-up. The Experimenter 6522's circuitry, shown in the schematic of Fig. 4-3, secures its dc power from the computer's power supply through the application port bus. One must be sure that no shorts occur on the breadboard which would overload the power supply and drop the voltage level because this will cause the loss of any program that is stored in the computer memory. It would also be wise to use an overload protected power supply or at least have a fuse in the power supply dc line that is a little over what the computer will consume.

The main features of this breadboard system is the bus buffering to protect the I/O port chip and the LEDs which show what logic level is on the I/O bus lines. The I/O port lines PA0 through PA5 are always used as output ports, but PA6 and PA7 can be used as input and output port lines by changing switches S1 and S2. Using PA6 and PA7 as inputs will give the user the ability to try out the 6501 BIT instructions to test for pulses, open or closed switches, and other possible uses. I/O lines PB0 and PB7 are also brought out to the breadboard circuit which will give one the opportunity to experiment with Port B on a small scale and use the ability of PB7 to generate square waves or other various programmable waveforms. When

PA6 and PA7 are set-up as input ports, a logic signal voltage between zero and twenty volts can be interfaced to the computer because the 4050 CMOS chip used in this circuit is designed for voltage conversion applications.

The logic data I/O connections to the experimenter's board are wired to pin row locations 1 to 10 using columns F,G,H,I, and J. The actual connections to the layout board are made by peeling off a portion of the plastic backing tape on the back of the board and soldering the lead wires directly to the pin rows. The +5 volts dc operating voltage for the user applications on the EXP-6522 is made available from the red and black binding post.

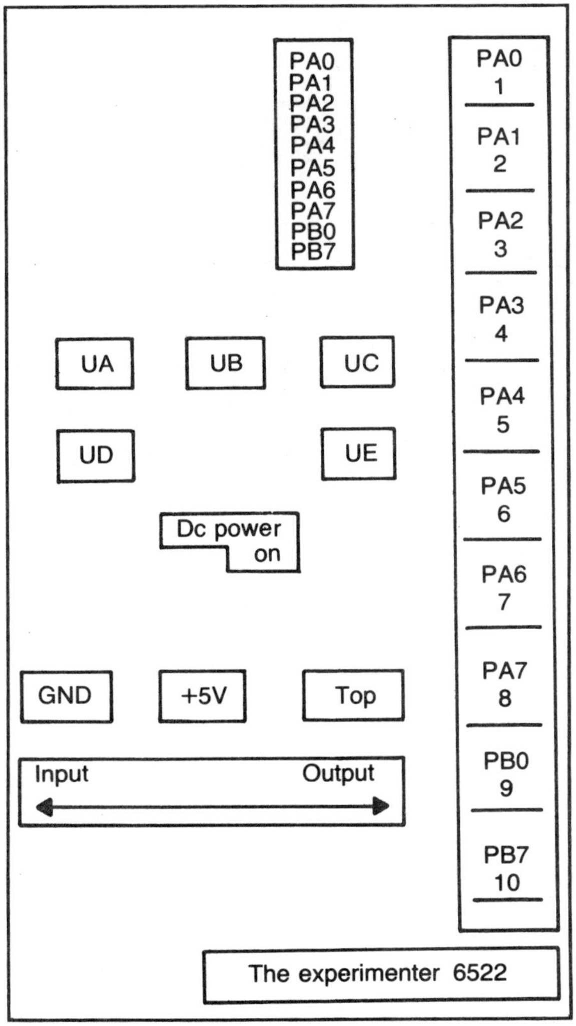

Fig. 4-2. The EXP-6522 board labels.

The complete Experimenter 6522 breadboard system is built on a piece of G-10 board using point-to-point wiring (Fig. 4-4). This type of construction was chosen because it would give the builder a larger selection of assembly options. The total cost of the breadboard system if Radio Shack parts are used should not be over $35 at 1982 prices. When this experimenter's system is connected to the single-board computer simulator that is described at the end of this chapter, you will have a complete breadboard system for developing computer interface circuits safely.

THE SINGLE-BOARD COMPUTER'S INPUT/OUTPUT PORT

The single-board computer will have some type of I/O port in order to communicate with the outside world. The integrated circuits that are used for the I/O port functions are usually referred to as PIA (Peripheral Interface Adapter) integrated circuits. Generally, you will be using a more elaborate chip call a 6522 VIA (Versatile Interface Adapter) which is used on both the SYM-1 and the AIM-65. A 6530 RROIT (Rom-Ram-I/O-Timer) is used on the KIM-1. The parallel I/O port lines of both I/O circuits chips will interface easily to the same electronic circuits because both chips have similar I/O capability. A short description of the 6522 VIA I/O port system will follow because the 6522 is used on most of the single-board computers which you will encounter that use the 6502 microprocessor.

Each 6522 VIA has two I/O ports which are called Port A and Port B. Each of the two I/O peripheral ports have eight bidirectional port I/O lines which can be set to either an input or output line by software control. Each I/O Port line is given a descriptive label and number. The port line label description will be either PA or PB according to whether it is Port A (PA) or Port B (PB), and the line number will be in accordance to the line bit significance starting at bit zero (0) for the least significant line to bit seven (7) for the most significant line. The sixteen I/O lines will be PA0, PA1, PA2, PA3, PA4, PA5, PA6, PA7, and PB0 to PB7. The I/O line data direction (input or output) assignments for each port line is determined by a register called the Data Direction Register (DDRA for port A and DDRB for port B). The process of using software instructions to assign a data direction to each port I/O line is called *port initialization*.

As an example, the 6522 VIA that is on the AIM-65 uses addresses A000,A001,A002, and A003 (Hex) for the I/O ports. Addresses A000 (Port B) and A001 (Port A) are the data ports and addresses A002 (DDRB) and A003 (DDRA) are the data direction registers. Placing a logic

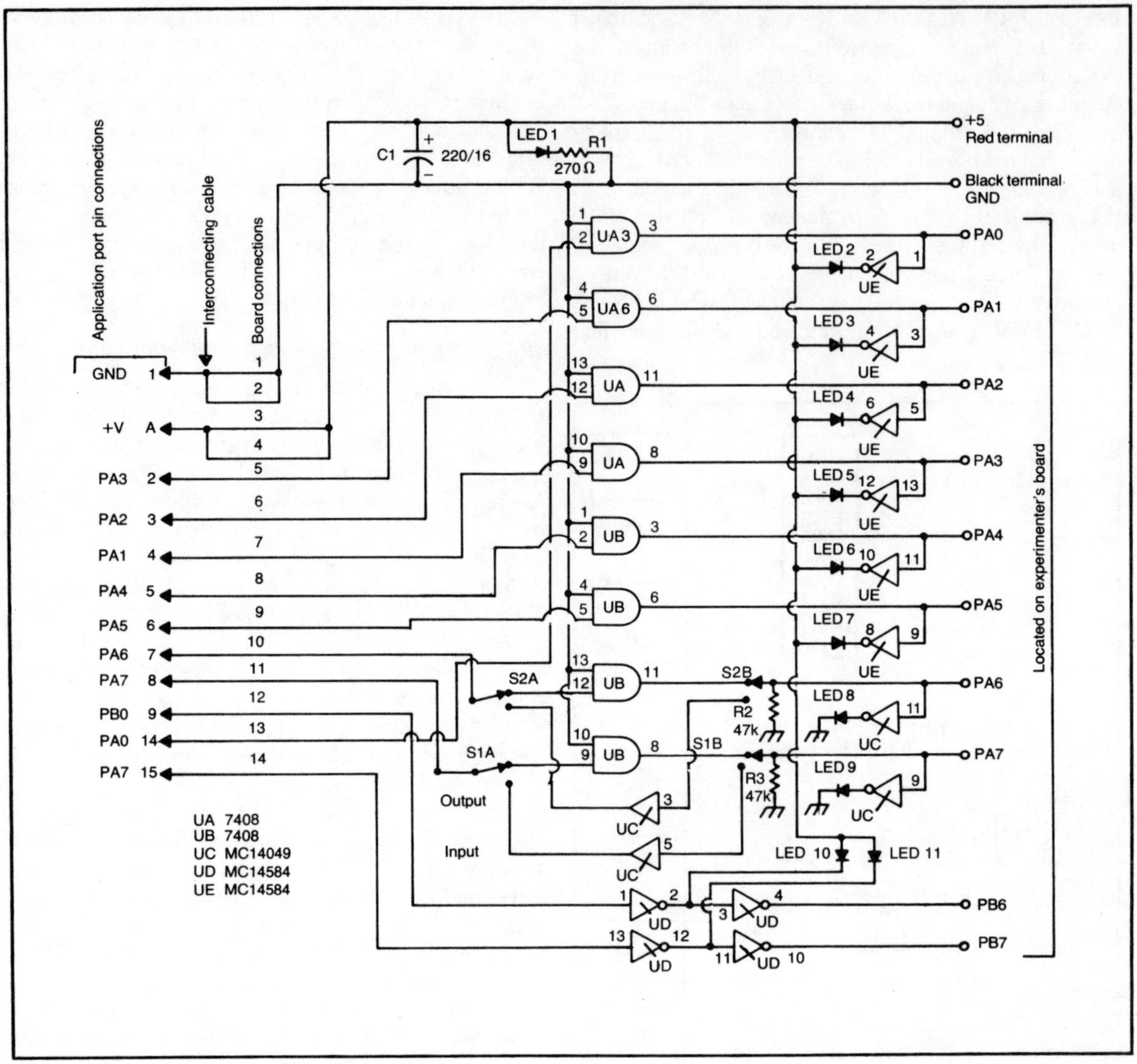

Fig. 4-3. The EXP-6522 schematic diagram.

one (1) in bit 0 of register DDRA will make port line PA0 of data port A an output port. Placing a logic zero (0) in bit 0 of register DDRA will make port line PA0 of data port A an input port. Software control will be discussed further in Chapter 5.

Port A and Port B are TTL and CMOS compatible with each port line having the ability to drive one TTL load in the output mode and represent one TTL load in the input mode. Port B also has the capability of sourcing 3.0 mA at 1.5 volts in the output mode (the Rockwell R6522), counting input pulses using port line PB6, and generating a square wave output signal on port line PB7. Most generally the logic one (1) output voltage on the PA port lines will be around four volts and the PB lines will be over 2.4 volts. The logic zero (0) output voltage on both port lines will be 0.4 volts or less.

The total capabilities of the 6522 VIA are many and can become quite complex if the total utility of the 6522 is needed. The main objective of Chapter 4 and Chapter 5 is to describe the basic methods of using the two I/O ports with different input and output interface circuits along with the special functions of PB6 and PB7 port lines.

DISCRETE TRANSISTOR INTERFACE CIRCUITS

The first of a number of different computer interface circuits that are described in this chapter will be the transistor output circuits. The transistor output circuits will enable the programmer to operate a wide variety of dc components with the speed, accuracy, and repeatability that is inherent in a computer. The transistor circuits will be divided into three categories: low power, medium power, and high power driver circuits. All of the circuits can be built and tested using the Experimenter 6522 so you can easily learn how to use them with a computer.

In all of the transistor circuits, the transistors will be specified as Q1 for lower power applications, Q2 for medium power applications, and Q3 for high power applications. The transistor specification for each of the three applications is described in Table 4-1 for low power applications, Table 4-2 for medium power applications, and Table 4-3 for high power applications along with the transistors that fulfill the specified requirements. These transistors were selected because one or more of them will usually be available at an electronic supply house close to your location.

The transistor buffer circuit which is shown in Fig. 4-5 is the basic npn transistor switch circuit. The operation of the circuit is very simple in that when a positive voltage is applied to the base circuit of transistor Q1

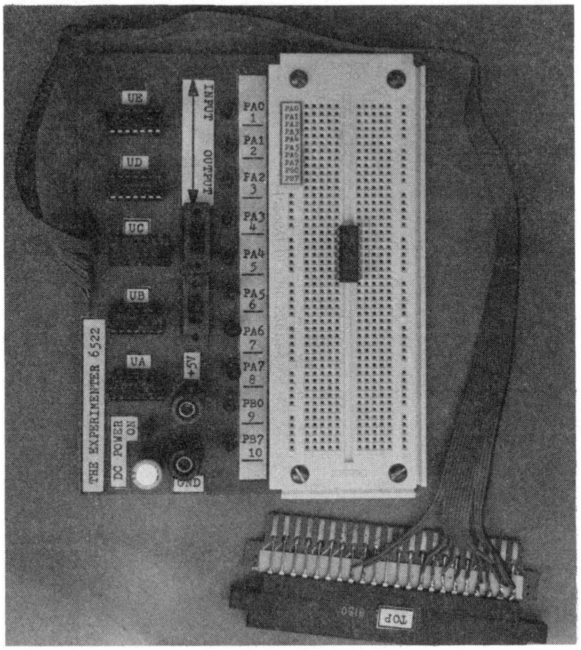

Fig. 4-4. A view of the top of the EXP-6522.

Table 4-1. Transistor Q1 Technical Specifications.

The low power transistor for circuit application as Q1 in the transistor output interface circuits.

Required Transistor Specifications	
Type	NPN
Material	Silicon
Power Dissipation	.5 Watts
Collector Current	.5 Amp
Maximum Usable Frequency	30 MHz
Base to Emitter Voltage	5 Volts
Collector to Emitter Voltage	40 Volts
Input Base Current	4 mA
Transistor Gain	150

Some transistors which meet or exceed the low power transistor specifications and are available at most retail electronics stores are given below.

Manufacturer	Part Number
Calectro (CG Electronics)	J4-1628
Radio Shack	276-2009
Sylvania	ECG-123
RCA	SK-3444
GE	GES6004
2N Type Number	2N2222A

(through resistors R1) which is high enough to supply the required base current, the transistor switches on. If there is no positive voltage applied to the base circuit of Q1, the transistor will remain in the off-state and no current can flow in the collector circuit. With no current flowing in the collector circuit, there will be no voltage drop across resistor R2 and the voltage level at the collector output of Q1 will be a +5 volts (A logic one level). If there is a positive voltage applied to the base circuit (+5 volts), a base current will flow and Q1 will switch on. When Q1 is switched on, a collector current will flow which is limited by the resistance of resistor R2. Transistor theory will tell us that a voltage drop across a silicon npn transistor will be about 0.7 volts when the transistor is turned on completely. This fact will cause a voltage drop across R2 of 4.3 volts and will cause a collector output voltage of 0.7 volts at the output of transistor Q1 (0.7 volts is considered a logic zero state). Now you can see how a logic

Table 4-2. Transistor Q2 Technical Specifications.

The medium power transistor for circuit application as Q2 in the transistor output interface circuits.

Required Transistor Specifications	
Type	NPN
Material	Silicon
Power Dissipation	5 Watts
Collector Current	1 Amp
Maximum Usable Frequency	3MHz
Base to Emitter Voltage	4 Volts
Collector to Emitter Voltage	40 Volts
Input Base Current	400 mA
Transistor Gain	15

Some transistors which meet or exceed the medium power transistor specifications and are available at most retail electronics stores are given below.

Manufacturer	Part Number
Calectro (C G Electronics)	J4-1649
Radio Shack	276-2018
Texas Instruments	TIP 29
Sylvania	ECG-188
RCA	SK-3893
GE	D44C4
2N Type Number	2N1701

Table. 4-3. Transistor Q3 Technical Specifications.

The high power transistor for circuit application as Q3 in the transistor output interface circuits.

Required Transistor Specifications	
Type	NPN
Material	Silicon
Power Dissipation	40 Watts
Collector Current	3 Amp
Maximum Usable Frequency	3 MHz
Base to Emitter Voltage	5 Volts
Collector to Emitter Voltage	40 Volts
Input Base Current	1 Amp
Transistor Gain	20

Some transistors which meet or exceed the high power transistor specifications and are available at most retail electronics stores are given below.

Manufacturer	Part Number
Calectro (C G Electronics)	J4-1654
Radio Shack	276-2017
Texas Instruments	TIP 31
Sylvania	ECG-152
RCA	SK-3054
GE	D44C5
2N Type Number	2N1486

one (+5 volts) is applied to a npn transistor-switch circuit to generate a logic zero (0.7 volts) in the output circuit. The npn transistor-switch circuit is also called a logic inverter circuit.

One of the main uses of the inverting buffer circuit is to add muscle to the computer I/O port since the I/O port can only drive one TTL load per output. The inverting buffer circuit (the transistor switch) will come in handy when there is a requirement to drive a group of TTL circuits or other similar higher driver requirement situations.

When a single-board computer is turned on, all of the I/O ports will be initiated and turned on as input ports and a logic one will appear on the I/O port bus line if there is no zero logic load connected to the line. This logic one will turn on any output interface circuit that is connected to a port bus line until the I/O port is set to an output port by software control. An inverting buffer circuit will keep any output circuit in the off state until the computer can be programmed and the I/O port set to the proper state (input or output) and set to the proper logic level (one or zero).

The circuit of Fig. 4-6 is a reed relay driver circuit. Most five volt reed relays will draw about 10 mA or so which is easily within the current rating of transistor Q1. The operation of the relay driver circuit is about the same as the inverting buffer circuit but the collector load is a reed relay and not a resistor. When transistor Q1 is turned on by a logic one signal, the reed relay will close. The reed relay circuit is very good for switching low power ac signals such as an audio oscillator output signal. The voltage drop across an average set of reed relay contacts is high enough that you should not attempt to switch ac signals which are less than ten millivolts peak

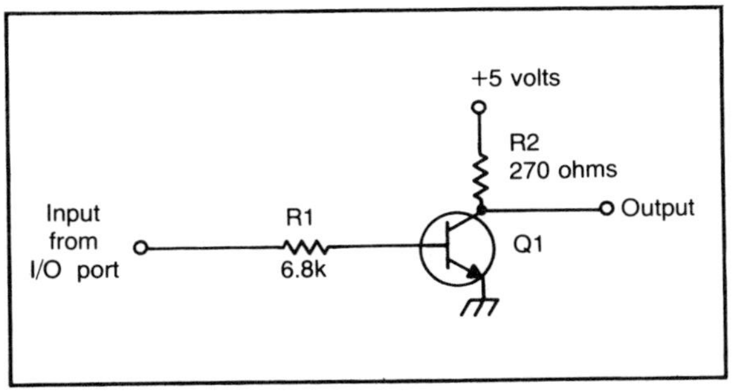

Fig. 4-5. A transistor inverting-buffer circuit for increasing the output port drive.

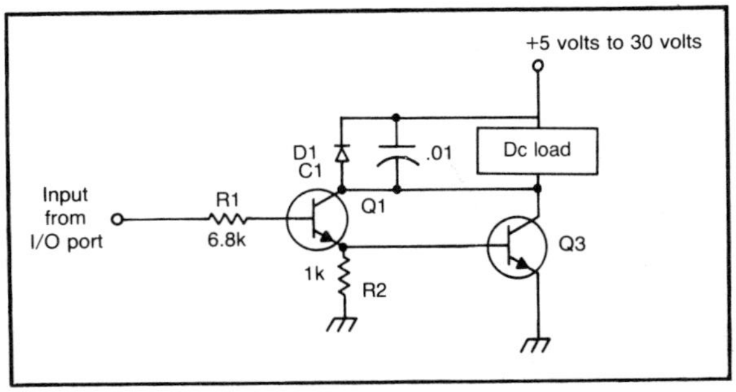

Fig. 4-7. A power driver circuit for loads of up to 3 amps resistive or inductive.

to peak. One can buy a reed relay which has special contact plating that will work at levels below ten millivolts.

The circuit in Fig. 4-7 is a power Darlington driver circuit which is used to control larger dc relays and solenoids. The gain of both transistors Q1 and Q3 are multiplied together to find the total gain of the Darlington circuit. Since the circuit has a high gain, the low output drive of the I/O port can control the high current requirements of the load. Diode D1 and capacitor C1 are used to suppress the inductive flyback voltage that is generated when an inductive load such as a relay is turned off. The dc lamp driver circuit of Fig. 4-8 is very similar to Fig. 4-7, but since the dc lamp is a resistive load, a capacitor and diode will not be needed.

Two LED driver circuits are shown in Fig. 4-9. These two circuits are more examples of how an inverting buffer circuit may be used for a given function. In circuit A, a logic one signal at the base input of transistor Q1 will turn on the transistor and a current will flow through the LED which will make it light up. The current is limited to a safe value by resistor R4. In circuit B, a logic one signal at the base input of transistor Q1 will turn on the transistor and limit the voltage across the LED to 0.7 volts so the LED will not light up. When a logic zero signal is at the base of Q1, the transistor will remain off and a current will flow through the LED which is limited by resistor R4. These two circuits show how to build circuits which will indicate a logic one or zero condition.

The circuit that will be described next is not a circuit that should be built on an experimenter's board. The circuit, shown in Fig. 4-10, is an ac control circuit which is an extended application to the reed relay driver circuit. The operation of the circuit is very simple. when a logic one signal is put into the base circuit of transistor Q1, the transistor turns on and energizes reed relay Ra. When the reed relay contacts close, triac TR-1 will turn on supplying power to the ac load. This circuit is designed for 120 volts ac operation. The ac line voltage and current that are used in this circuit can easily burn up an experimenter's board if a short circuit occurs in the ac load! So, Don't build this circuit on the Experimenter 6522 or any other breadboard system that is similar!

Table 4-4 contains general information about other parts that are used in the transistor interface circuits. The parts that are listed were chosen because they are generally available at most retail hobby electronics stores.

INTERFACE CIRCUITS FROM INTEGRATED CIRCUITS

TTL and CMOS integrated circuits are generally

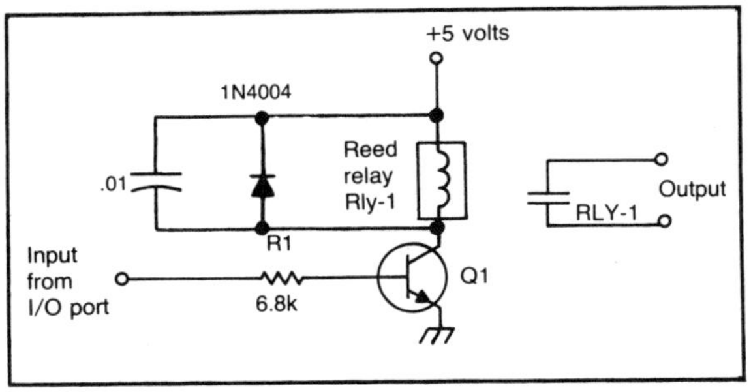

Fig. 4-6. A transistor reed relay driver circuit.

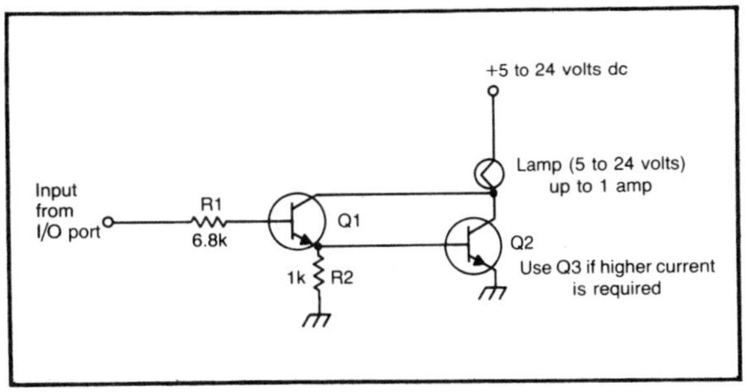

Fig. 4-8. A dc lamp driver circuit.

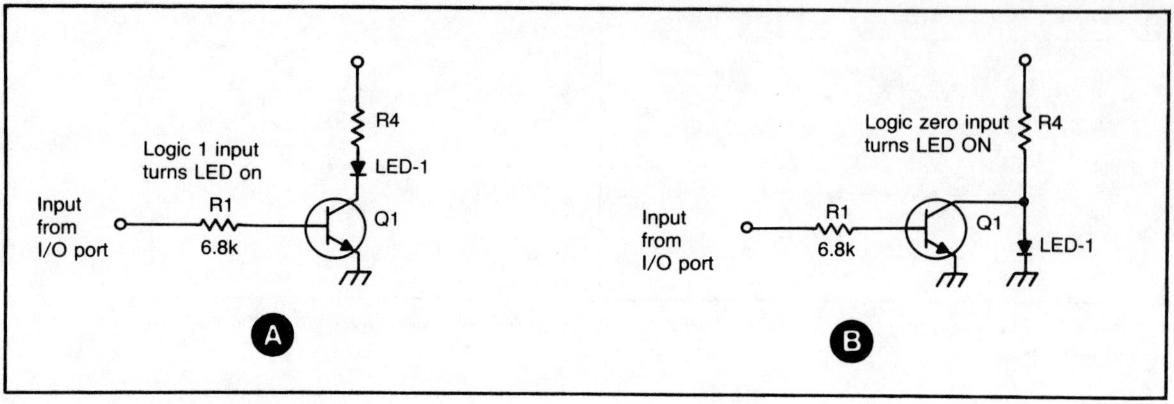

Fig. 4-9. Transistor LED driver circuits.

more useful for input interfacing than they are for output interfacing for computers. The majority of all computer interfacing can be done with just a few circuit chips. The TTL and CMOS chips that are used in this chapter can be purchased at most electronic hobby stores, so, those of you who will be building these circuits on the Experimenter 6522 will not have any problems. We are not going to present a complete guide of using logic circuits because there is an ample supply of this type of information already published. We will present some tried and true TTL and CMOS circuits plus the information that is needed to use them. In Chapter 5 the computer programming that is required for using these circuits will be presented.

The scope of this book assumes a little background in using logic circuit chips. Tables 4-5, 4-6, and 4-7 give some specific information that will help in successfully using these circuits.

Schmitt-Trigger Logic Circuits

A Schmitt-trigger logic circuit has the special ability to turn on at a specific positive-going voltage and turn off at a specific negative-going voltage. These voltage trip points are referred to as the positive- and negative-going threshold voltages. The threshold voltages are set so the positive threshold trip point is a little higher than the negative threshold trip point giving what is called an area of hysteresis. The hysteresis area between the positive threshold point and the negative threshold point is generally about 0.6 volt to 1.0 volt for logic circuits with 5 volt supply voltages. Since slow rise and fall time signals are a no-no for most logic circuits, one can use a Schmitt

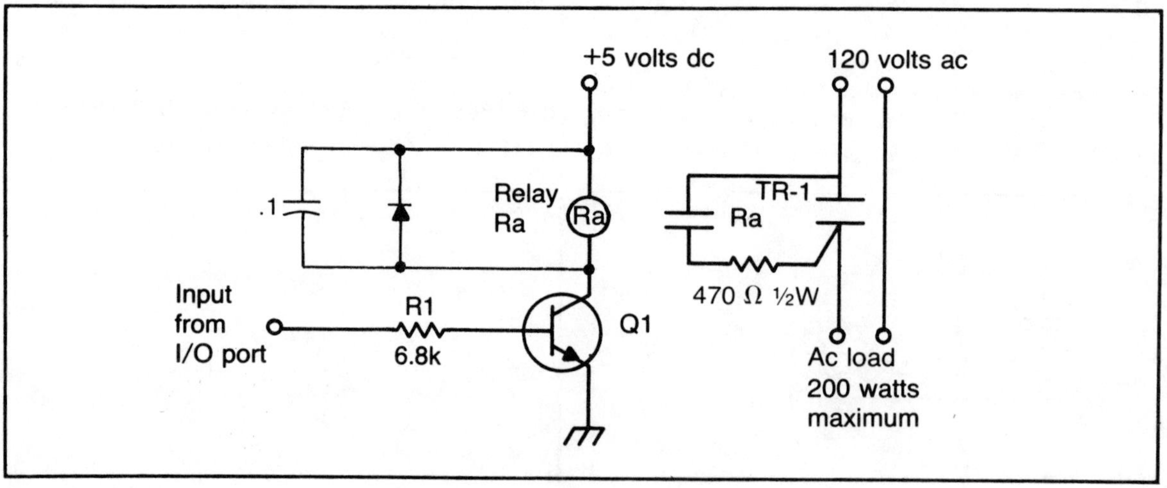

Fig. 4-10. An ac control circuit for small loads such as lights, fans, and radios.

Table 4-4. General Parts Description for the Interface Circuits.

Resistors

R1-----6.8k ¼ Watt
R2-----270 Ohms ¼ Watt
R3-----1.0k ¼ Watt
R4-----5 Volt Supply---470 Ohms ¼ Watt
9 Volt supply---680 Ohms ¼ Watt
12 Volt supply--1.0K Ohms ¼ Watt
R5-----470 Ohms ½ Watt

Relay, Ra, 5 Volt dc coil, Radio Shack 275-216
Reed Relay Rly-1, 5 volt dc coil,

LED-1, Radio Shack 276-035
Triac TR-1, Radio Shack 276-1001
Lamp--- 5 Volts Supply---#47
12 Volts Supply---#1891

Table 4-5 General TTL Characteristics.

A. Dc power connections: +5 volts and ground or common.
B. TTL circuits should be bypassed by a .1 μF capacitor at the +5 volts input pin.
C. Unused inputs should be tied to +5 volts.
D. Know what type of output circuit is in the TTL chip you are using; standard, open collector, or 3 state output (High-low-open circuit).
E. Input conditions: A "One" Logic level must be more than about 2.5 volts. A "Zero" logic level must be below about .8 volts.
F. The operating speed of the TTL gates are generally between 10 and 30 nanoseconds, which is far faster than any low priced single board computer can operate.
G. Output Drive (Fan-Out) The 7400 series will drive ten 7400 series inputs. The 74LS. . series will drive two 7400 series or ten 74LS series inputs.

Table 4-6. General CMOS Characteristics.

A. Dc operating current requirements are very small compared to TTL.
B. All inputs are high impedance inputs which require no driving power.
C. The design characteristics give CMOS chips good noise immunity.
D. The CMOS "B" series chips will function from 3 volts to over 15 volts with some operating up to 20 volts.
E. The output voltage will go from the positive voltage supply level to ground level. (complete + to − voltage swing.)
F. All inputs "must" be connected to an input line or to the + voltage line or ground line. CMOS is a high impedance input logic family and unconnected inputs can easily pick up noise.
G. The operating speed of CMOS is not as fast as TTL at the 5-volt supply level. The best supply voltage for CMOS circuits is between 9 and 12 volts.

Trigger circuit to convert a slow rise and fall time signal to a fast rise and fall time signal. Schmitt-trigger circuit technical data for the chips that are used in this book is given in Table 4-7.

Schmitt-trigger circuits are very useful for interfacing computers because they can be used with great success in preventing noise from getting into an I/O port. The word noise is used to describe any electrical type of interference such as switch or contact bounce static, inductive oriented electrical spikes, and other electrically generated disturbances.

Schmitt-trigger circuits will be used many different ways in the various circuits found in this book. A few of the functions which the circuits will be performing are switch or push-button conditioning (debouncing), noise elimination from slow rise and fall time signals, accurate threshold voltage detection in peak-detector circuits, and oscillator circuits.

CMOS Interface Circuits

A few CMOS interface circuits are shown in Figs. 4-11 and 4-12. These circuits are by far not the only ones

Table 4-7. Schmitt-Trigger Circuit Characteristics

CMOS Schmitt-trigger
Circuits: (4093 and 4584)

A. The hysteresis voltage will be about .9 volts at a supply voltage of 5 volts and 2.3 volts with a supply voltage of 10 volts.
B. A positive going waveform will cause the output to switch logic levels at about 58% of the power supply voltage and a negative going waveform will cause the output to switch logic levels at about 46% of power supply voltage.
C. The propagation delay time of the Schmitt-trigger circuits are longer than the standard CMOS chips being in the area of 190 nanoseconds typical to a maximum of 380 nano seconds for worse case values at a power supply voltage of 5 volts.

TTL Schmitt-trigger
Circuits: (7414 and 74LS14)

A. Has a low input impedance of about 6k.
B. The hysteresis voltage range is about .8 volts.
C. A positive going waveform will cause the output to switch logic levels at 1.7 volts and a negative going waveform will cause the output to change logic levels at .9 volts with the standard 5 volts supply.
D. The propagation delay is about 20 nanoseconds.

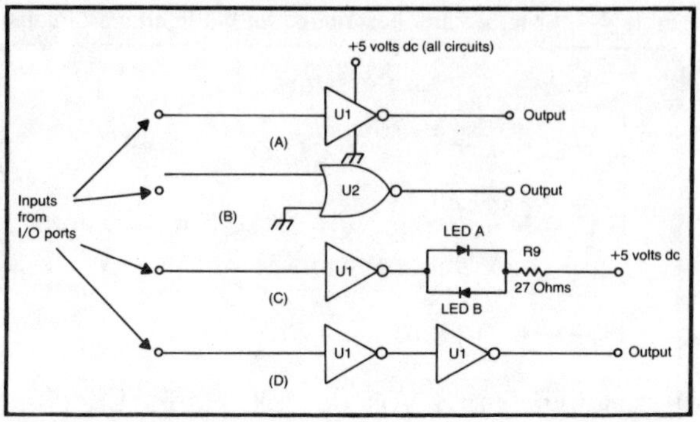

Fig. 4-11. CMOS output-buffer circuits for a single-board computer.

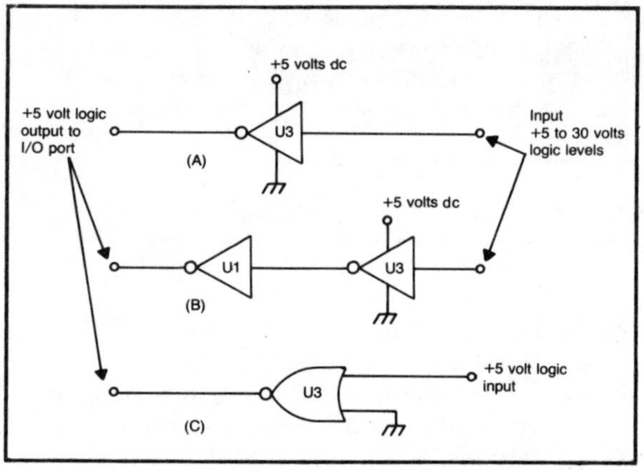

Fig. 4-12. CMOS input-buffer circuits for a single-board computer.

that are usable as interface circuits, but they do demonstrate the basic ideas of interfacing to a single-board computer. In general the CMOS circuits will be used more for input interfacing than for output interfacing.

Figure 4-11 shows several interface buffer circuits which can be used between the computer and a transistor interface output circuit. Figure 4-11A is a standard inverting buffer circuit. One of the main uses of this circuit is to invert the I/O port logic level because all I/O ports of the three named 6502 single-board computers are initiated as input ports when they are turned on, and a high logic level voltage appears on the port which has enough drive ability to turn on a transistor interface circuit. Inverting the I/O port logic level will keep the interface circuits from turning on until the I/O ports are configured as output ports and set to the proper logic levels. Figure 4-11B simply shows how a NOR circuit can be used to perform the same function as that of Fig. 4-11A. Figure 4-11C demonstrates how a noninverting buffer circuit and two LEDs can be connected to indicate the I/O port logic level. Figure 4-11D is basically the same as 4-11A with the exception that the logic circuit is the noninverting type. The main purpose of all of the output interface circuits is to place a buffer for protection purposes between the I/O port and whatever circuit is being driven.

Figure 4-12 shows three circuits which demonstrates some basic methods of interfacing input signals to a computer. Figure 4-12A shows an inverting buffer circuit using a 4049 hex inverter chip. The 4049 is very handy for interfacing to logic voltages which are higher than five volts. Figure 4-12B is similar to 4-12A but it is of the noninverting type with the same voltage level interfacing capability. Figure 4-12C is an example of how a Schmitt-trigger circuit can be used to interface the computer to a switch or relay without having any contact bounce problems. Again, one of the main purposes of using these interface circuits between the I/O port and the outside circuit is to prevent one from smoking up an I/O port chip in the event that some type of over-voltage condition occurs.

TTL Interface Circuits

The TTL circuits shown in Figs. 4-13 and 4-14 perform interface functions that are similar to the CMOS circuits just described. One of the advantages that the TTL logic family has over the CMOS family is the ability to develop a higher output drive signal.

The I/O port output circuits shown in Fig. 4-13 are used to interface circuits that need higher input drive requirements. The I/O ports can drive one TTL load, so, if there is a need to drive more than one TTL load, some form of interface driver circuit must be used. The resistor R_x is use as a pull-up resistor to give a full five volts logic signal swing. Some TTL circuits like the 7406 hex inverter chip have open collector circuits which can handle output voltages of up to thirty volts giving one the ability to generate a thirty-volt square wave.

Figure 4-14 shows some basic TTL input interface circuits. All three circuits will handle the standard five volts TTL logic levels. When it comes to input circuits, CMOS circuit chips such as the 4049 and 4050 have an advantage over the TTL chips because they can easily interface with other logic input voltage levels.

AUDIO OSCILLATORS

An audio oscillator is a very handy circuit to use in a control system. It can be used to indicate whether a test has been good or bad, or if some part of the production system is not functioning properly. It is not too hard to use a single-board computer to generate audio, but while the computer is generating audio, it can not do other needed tasks. Why use a $250 single-board computer to generate audio when a circuit that will cost about two dollars will do a better job?

The circuit that is shown in Fig. 4-15 is a simple 555 IC audio oscillator that is turned on by the transistor switch circuit of Q1 and Q2 when a logic one signal is received from the computer I/O port. The audio oscillator circuit shown in Fig. 4-16 is designed around the RCA CD4093B Schmitt-trigger CMOS IC. Only two oscillator circuits are shown in the schematic, but four circuits could easily be built since the CD4093B had four NAND gate in the IC package. This CMOS audio oscil-

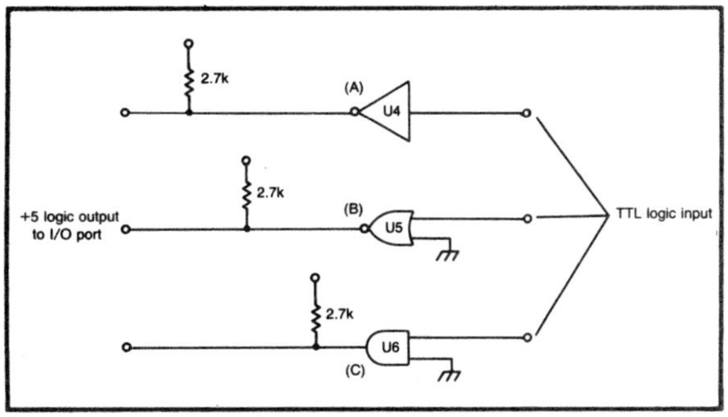

Fig. 4-14. TTL input-buffer circuits for a single-board computer.

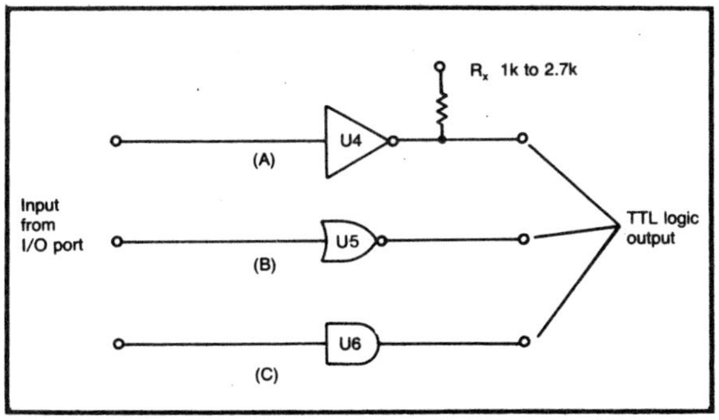

Fig. 4-13. TTL output buffer circuits for a single-board computer.

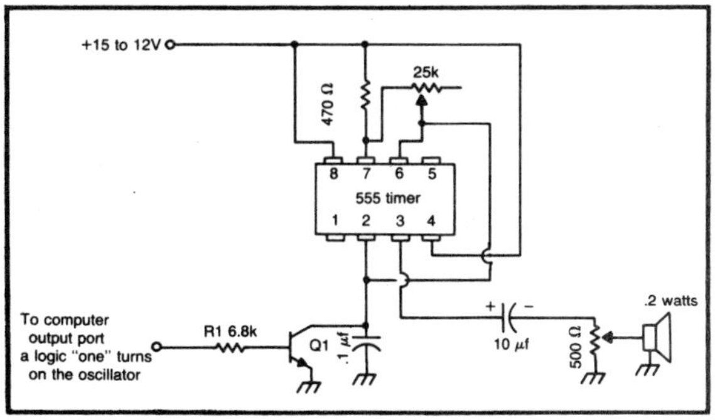

Fig. 4-15. A 555 audio oscillator circuit.

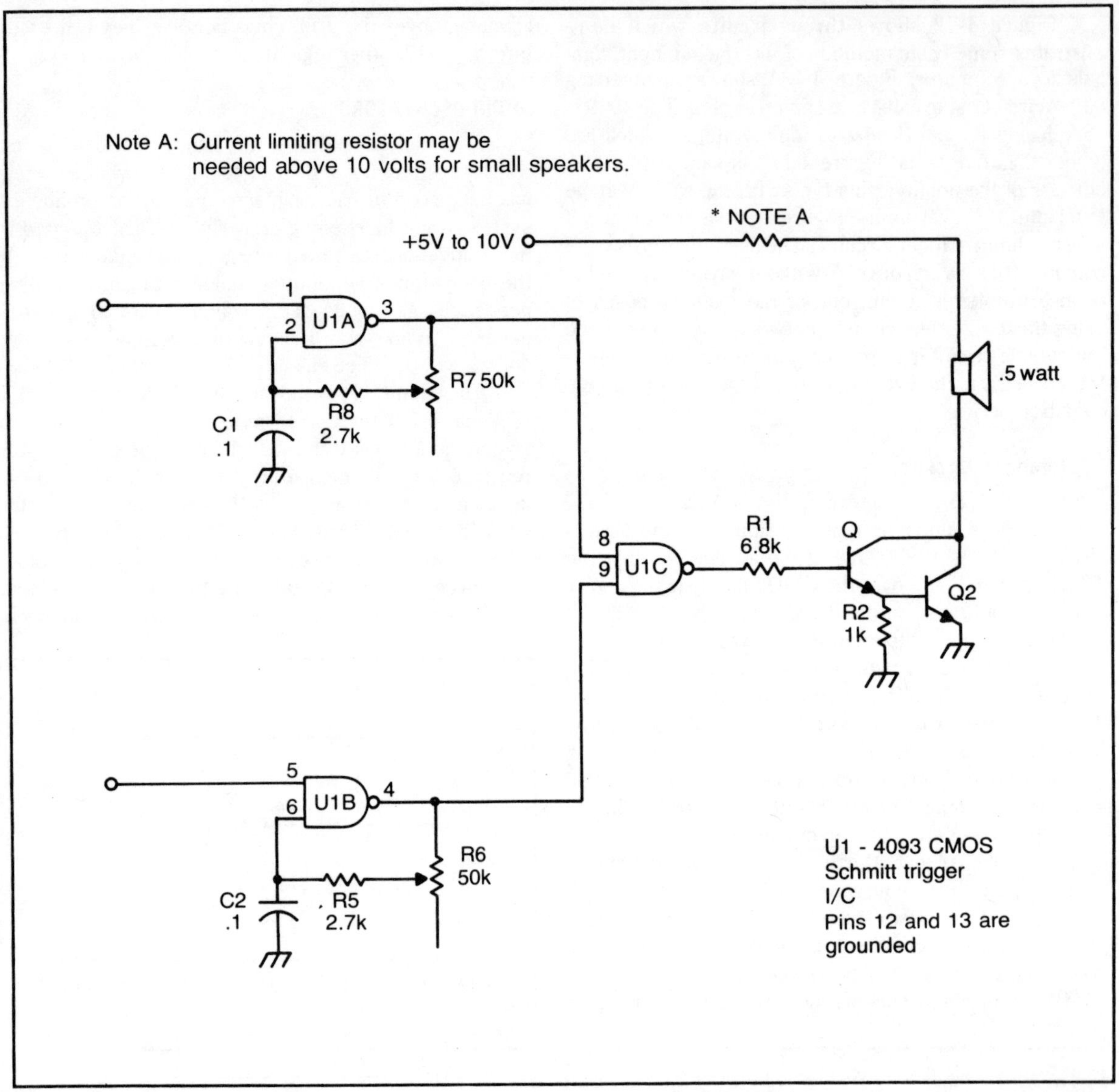

Fig. 4-16. A dual-tone audio oscillator.

lator can be easily turned on by placing a logic one voltage on the unused input gate of the NAND circuit. The audio oscillator generates a really loud audio sound for a small five-volt oscillator.

THE SINGLE-BOARD COMPUTER SIMULATOR

The SBC simulator is designed for use with the Experimenter 6522 so you can test your breadboard circuits before they are connected to the computer port. If you know that your interface circuit works properly, then you can spend all your time and mental ability on writing and debugging your computer program.

Figure 4-17 shows the circuit schematic of the SBC simulator which is designed to plug into the I/O port connector of the Experimenter 6522. The port logic signals can be made a logic one or zero by changing the switches labeled PA0 to PB7. The dc power for the simulator is supplied by four AA batteries. The 6.0 volts

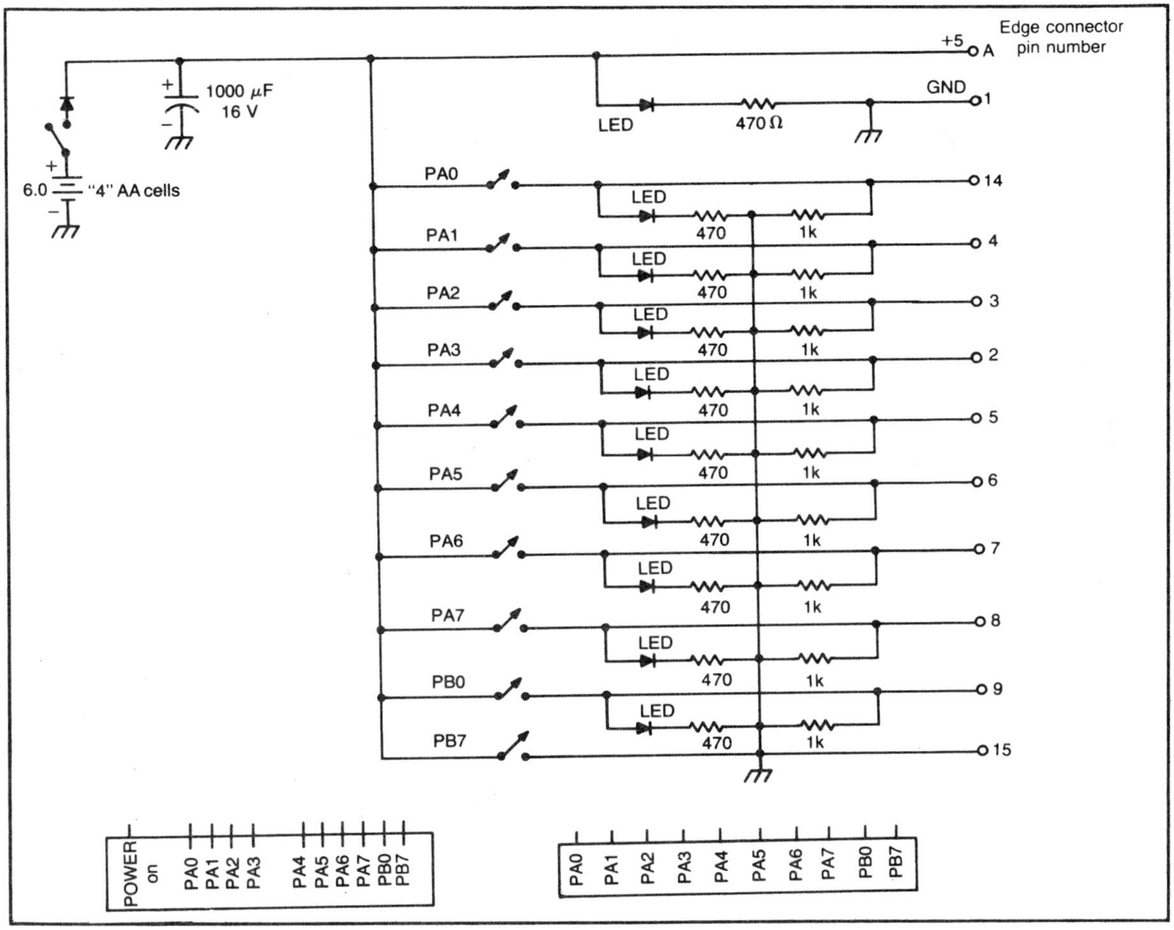

Fig. 4-17. The schematic of the SBC Simulator.

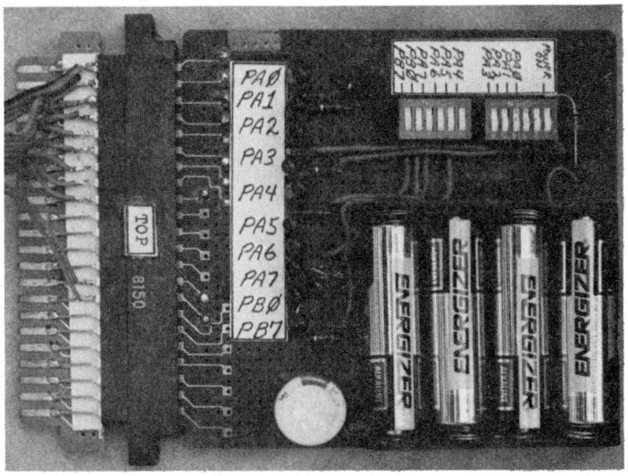

Fig. 4-18. A view of the SBC simulator connected to the EXP-6522.

from these four batteries is dropped to 5.3 or so by the 0.7 volt voltage drop of diode D1. The capacitor C1 does a good job of despiking the +5 volts line which is turned off and on by one of the bank switches. When one of the switches is turned on, a logic one (+5 Volts) is put on the I/O port line pin and the LED that corresponds to the switch label will light. The SBC simulator which is connected to a EXP-6522 is shown in Fig. 4-18.

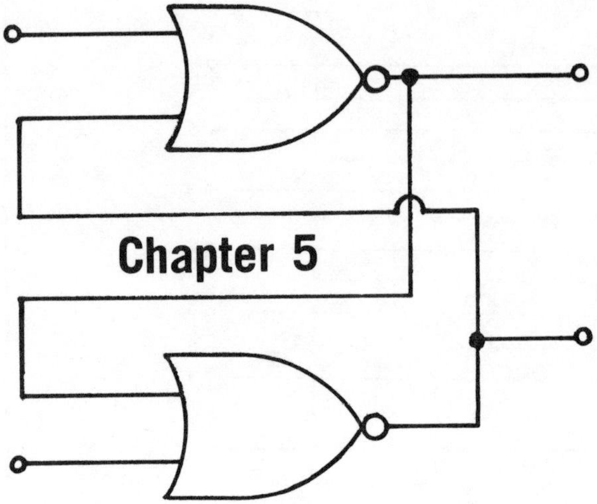

Chapter 5

Single-Board Computer Routines for I/O Functions

We are now ready to make our single-board computer system perform some useful functions for us. As we proceed through this chapter, you will start to see how versatile the single-board computer really can be if it is used to its full potential. After you have finished this chapter, you will not be a highly trained computer programmer, but you will have a better practical understanding of the programming that is required to operate some of the I/O circuits that are presented in this book.

The I/O functions of a single-board computer are a basic requirement if the computer is going to serve any useful purpose in a manufacturing environment or a school lab. A single-board computer that can not service the outside world can really be nothing more than a learning tool or a programmable calculator. Learning how to use the I/O ports can be very hard if you do not have the proper tools. This is one reason why we went to great lengths in the preceding chapters to build the experimenter's boards so you will have the tools to learn the ins and outs of I/O port functions.

We will now assume that you have a 6502 or Z80 machine. First we will discuss some computer program routines which will make the I/O circuits of Chapter 4 work. Then we will present other 6502 programs which can be used to control test systems. The ability to operate and run these programs in this chapter will be very important when you attempt to use the test circuits that are described in the rest of this book. If you have never operated with I/O circuits before, you will be very fascinated when you watch your computer really operate some active electronic circuits.

THE I/O REGISTERS

The first thing that we must do in order to use the I/O ports on our single-board computers is to properly set up the data direction registers in the I/O port chip. If you are using the Model III, you do not have to worry about the data direction because that was designed into the 80 I/O-PIB for you. If you are using a KIM-1 or a SYM-1 or a AIM-65, you must set up the I/O ports as an input port or an output port. (The three SBC units initiate all I/O ports as input ports when the computers are turned on.) After you set up the data direction register (DDRA for port A and DDRB for port B), you then can write data to the I/O port or read data at the I/O port. Also, all eight bits do not have to serve the same function. You can arrange then in any order you wish, three input and five outputs, all inputs, all outputs, or whatever is required.

When you arrange an I/O port, you must use a logic 1 (one) to make the port bit an *output* bit or use a logic 0 (zero) to make a port an *input* bit. Where do you find the data direction registers so you can insert the ones and zeros? You look up the SBC memory map and hunt up the

I/O port addresses. Grab your SBC instruction manual and look up page 4-19 if you have a SYM-1, page 39 if you have a KIM-1, or page 7-49 if you have an AIM-65. The data direction registers are located as shown in Table 5-1.

You may want to note that both the AIM-65 and the SYM-1 use the same I/O port DDRA and DDRB addresses which are A000 through A004. You can insert a "1" or a "0" into these register bit locations by using the computer's monitor program or you can do it under actual program software control.

After the data direction registers have been set up, you can then read the input bits or write to the output bits of the I/O data registers. Each data direction register in a 6522 I/O chip has a companion I/O data register which it controls. Since all of the I/O operations with the computer are done using the I/O data registers, the data direction registers are generally set up at the beginning of the computer program and not altered or used after that point. To sum up the register situation, you might say that after you have once set up the data direction registers, all other input and output functions are done using the I/O data registers. The I/O data registers and their addresses are given in Table 5-2.

USING THE PRESENTED PROGRAMS

The computer programs that are presented here have been used to control test systems and manufacturing equipment ever since the KIM-1 computer system was introduced many many moons ago. These programs are very simple. They do not use high-level addressing techniques or any other advanced programming methods. Only thirteen 6502 instruction codes were used to write all of the programs that are presented in this chapter and even fewer of the Z80 instruction codes were used. Even though only a few of the many machine instructions are used, you can do some very elaborate controlling with a single-board computer using the programs presented in this chapter. Only two programs are presented for the Model III. But, when you use the two input and output programs as USR functions of a BASIC program, you can do a lot of controlling with a Model III.

Table 5-1. The KIM-1, SYM-1, and AIM-65 Data Direction Register Memory Locations.

The Data Direction Register Addresses

Computer	Address	Register
KIM-1	1701H (Hex)	Data Direction Register "A"
	1703H	Data Direction Register "B"
SYM-1	A002	Data Direction Register "B"
	A003	Data Direction Register "B"
AIM-65	A002	Data Direction Register "B"
	A003	Data Direction Register "A"

Table 5-2. The KIM-1, SYM-1 and AIM-65 I/O Register Memory Locations.

The I/O Data Register Addresses

Computer	Address	Register
KIM-1	1700H	I/O Register A
	1702H	I/O Register B
SYM-1	A000H	I/O Register B
	A001H	I/O Register A
AIM-65	A000H	I/O Register B
	A001H	I/O Register A

The presented programs are really machine-language routines which can be coupled together to form a computer program. All program routines start at location 200 for the 6502 programs, but they can be located anywhere in the user RAM memory of the host machine. You can not start all routines at location 200 because there is only one location 200 in every machine. But, you can easily relocate the location 200 routines if you start inserting the routine at location 210, 250, 300, 400, 460, or any other address which is the next zero hexadecimal address following the last routine. All of the routines can be linked together by JUMP or JSR instructions. This type of programming may waste a little memory here and there, but most small test systems that use a single-board computer with 4K of memory will have memory to burn because 4K of RAM will do a lot of test system controlling.

Once you have mastered the use of these control routines, you will have no problems adding other machine-language instructions to the routines to increase the power and functional ability. Operating a control system using machine language is not too hard. But when you start doing math problems and playing games, the level of programming that is required increases at a very rapid

Table. 5-3. A KIM-1 Hex-Data Output Routine.

```
A. This routine is used to set up port A  at address 1700 as
an  output port and  then write  the  hex  data  "AA" to the
port.
B. This routine will work on a KIM-1
C. Use DDRA at address 1701 and I/O DRA at address 1700

Address--Instructions--Mnemonic--Description
Location B1--B2--B3
200        A9  FF          LDA      LOAD FF INTO THE ACCUMULATOR
202        8D  01   17     STA      STORE FF IN DDRA AT 1703
205        A9  AA          LDA      LOAD AA INTO THE ACCUMALATOR
207        8D  00   17     STA      STORE AA IN DRA AT 1700
20A        00              BRK      STOP PROGRAM

Note:  If you wish to enter different data  into the  output
ports, change the hex data in location 206.
```

rate. But wait!! You do not have to do math functions or play games in machine language if your machine has a BASIC language program with a USR function. The AIM-65, the SYM-1, and the Model III all have that ability, so you've got it made in the shade.

SIMPLE OUTPUT ROUTINES

One of the two basic functions which the control system computer must do is to generate output data signals for the I/O circuits. The output data signals will be logic-ones or zeros which will turn on and off the selected I/O circuits. The three output routines presented in Tables 5-3, 5-4, and 5-5 will control all of the output circuits that are described in Chapter 4.

Table 5-3 is used to output data signals from a KIM-1 and Table 5-4 is used to output data signals from the SYM-1 and the AIM-65. The program routines are very simple using only the Load, the Accumulator, and Store

Table 5-4. A SYM-1 and AIM-65 Hex-Data Output Routine.

```
A. This routine is  used to set up port A  as an output port
and then write the Hex data "AA" to the port.
B. This routine will work on a SYM-1 and an AIM-65.
C. Use DDRA at address A003 and I/O DRA at address A001

Address--Instructions--Mnemonic--Description
Location B1--B2--B3
200        A9  FF          LDA      LOAD FF INTO THE ACCUMULATOR
202        8D  03   A0     STA      STORE FF IN DDRA AT A003
205        A9  AA          LDA      LOAD AA INTO THE ACCUMULATOR
207        8D  01   A0     STA      STORE AA IN DRA AT A001
20A        00              BRK      STOP PROGRAM

Note:  If you wish  to enter different data  into the output
ports, change the hex data in location 206.
```

Table 5-5. A Model III Machine Language Hex-Data Output Routine.

```
A. This routine is used to output data to  your external I/O
   devices using the Model III and the 80 I/O-PIB.
B. Use this routine  to turn  on and  off  the I/O interface
   circuits described in Chapter four using output port  bit
   number one.

Address--Instructions--Mnemonic--Description
Location B1--B2--B3
5000       F3              DI     DISABLE INTERRUPTS
5001       3E  10          LD     LOAD 10H IN REGISTER A
5003       DE  EC          OUT    OUTPUT 10H TO PORT EC
5005       3E  01          LD     LOAD 01H IN REGISTER A
5007       D3  6F          OUT    OUTPUT 01H TO PORT 6FH
5009       76              HALT   STOP PROGRAM

NOTE:  When  using  the  DEBUG  program, the J command  will
stop the program at location 5009.
```

the Accumulator machine-language instructions. These two routines can be used to set the output port bits to logic-ones or logic-zeros which will turn on and off the I/O circuits that are connected to the respective output port pins. You should read the portion of your computer instruction manual that explains the operations of the I/O ports before using these output routined.

The Model III output routine is not much different from the routine you used to test the 80 I/O-PIB. So, we will assume that you will be familiar with its use.

SIMPLE INPUT ROUTINES

The other basic function that our control system computer must do is to input data from the external I/O circuits. The input routines that are presented in Tables 5-6, 5-7, and 5-8 will read the addressed input port pins and then place the received input data in a location which will store the data for later use.

Table 5-6 presents an input routine which can be used on a KIM-1 single-board computer. A similar routine is shown in Table 5-7 that will work on a SYM-1 and the AIM-65. Again the input routines are just as simple as the output routines because they only use the basic LDA and STA machine-language instructions. These input routines are fairly fast, giving you the ability to read an input port about once every fifteen microseconds if needed. You must be careful that noise is suppressed on the input port pins because it is very easy to mistake a noise spike for a logic one signal.

Table 5-8 presents an input routine for the Model III which will store the eight-bit logic data that is present on the input port pins of the 80 I/O-PIB in register A.

PROGRAM ROUTINES

The rest of the programs in this chapter are control function routines that can be used to assemble a control program for a complete test system. These program routines again use simple programming style and could be considerably shorter if advanced programming style was used. But, we will leave the advanced programming for some time in the future. Right now, you want to insert a machine-language routine into your single-board computer and watch it do something.

These program routines can be used to check for an open or closed switch, look for logic-ones and zeros, count logic pulses, generate pulses and square waves, measure pulse width, and do various other timing functions. You will be able to assemble about any control program that will be required to run your test system and still have plenty of computer left over to do other things like printing out the resulting test data after the test sequence is finished.

The first group of program routines that will be presented are the bit-test routines. These routines will

Table 5-6. A KIM-1 Data Input and Store Routine.

```
A. This  routine is used to set up port A at address 1700 as
an  input port and then  place the  data which is at the I/O
port in memory location 210H.
B. This routine can be used on the KIM-1
C. Use DDRA at address 1701 and I/O DRA at address 1700.

Address--Instructions--Mnemonic--Description
Location B1--B2--B3
200       A9  00        LDA     LOAD 00 INTO THE ACCUMULATOR
202       8D  01  17    STA     STORE 00 IN DDRA AT A003
205       AD  00  17    LDA     LOAD INPUT DATA AT I/O PORT
                                A001 INTO THE ACCUMULATOR
208       8D  10  02    STA     STORE THE I/O DATA IN MEMORY
                                LOCATION 210H
20B       00            BRK     STOP PROGRAM

Note A: When  this  routine is  used with the EXP-6522, only
port  bits  PA6  and PA7 of  address  A001 may  be  used  as
inputs. To  make a  port bit a zero,  connect a ground  wire
between  the  black  binding  post  and  the  PA6  and  PA7
connection point on the experimenter's board.
```

Table 5-7. A SYM-1 and AIM-65 Data Input and Store Routine.

```
A. This routine  is used  to set up port  A as  an input port
and then  place the data which is  at the I/O port in memory
location 210H.
B. This routine can be used on the SYM-1 and the AIM-65.
C. Use DDRA at address A003 and I/O DRA at address A001.

Address--Instructions--Mnemonic--Description
Location B1--B2--B3
200       A9  00        LDA     LOAD 00 INTO THE ACCUMULATOR
202       8D  03  A0    STA     STORE 00 IN DDRA AT A003
205       AD  01  A0    LDA     LOAD INPUT DATA AT I/O PORT
                                A001  INTO THE ACCUMULATOR
208       8D  10  02    STA     STORE THE I/O DATA IN MEMORY
                                LOCATION 210H
20B       00            BRK     STOP PROGRAM

Note A:  When this routine  is used with  the EXP-6522, only
port  bits  PA6  and PA7 of  address  A001 may  be  used  as
inputs. To  make a  port bit a zero,  connect a ground  wire
between  the  black  binding  post  and  the  PA6  and  PA7
connection points on the experimenter's board.
```

Table 5-8. A Model III Data Input and Store Routine.

```
A. This routine is  used to input data from  an external I/O
   devices using the Model III and the 80 I/O-PIB.
B. Use this routine to read data from  any  of the input I/O
  interface circuits described'in Chapter four.

Address--Instructions--Mnemonic--Description
Location B1--B2--B3
5000       F3               DI     DISABLE INTERRUPTS
5001       3E   10          LD     LOAD 10H IN REGISTER A
5003       DE   EC          OUT    OUTPUT 10H TO PORT EC
5005       DB   6F          IN     READ AND PLACE THE DATA
                                   FROM INPUT PORT 6F INTO
                                   REGISTER A.
5006       76               HALT   STOP PROGRAM

NOTE:  When  using the DEBUG  program,  the J  command  will
stop the program at location 5006.
```

check ports PA6 and PA7 for a logic one or zero condition. The bit-test instruction makes the job of checking for open or closed switches very easy. All you have to do is to wire a switch, as shown in Fig. 5-1, to the input port so that a logic-one or zero will be present under the correct situation. Once you place the computer in the bit-test routine loop, it will stay there until the one or zero condition that is required is fulfilled. When the correct logic condition is fulfilled, the program loop will be terminated and the program will continue on to the next routine. Now you should look up the bit-test instruction in the 6502 programming manual and after you understand what is happening, you can check out one of the bit-test routines that are presented in Tables 5-9 through 5-16. These programs are designed to run on the KIM-1, the SYM-1, or the AIM-65 single-board computers. You can plug the EXP-6522 into any of these computers and build your switch circuit on the experimenter's board in order to observe how one of the bit-test programs operate. The bit-test routines can be incorporated into a complete program by using JUMP instructions or JSR instructions to join it with other routines.

The next group of routines that are going to be presented are the pulse generation and counting routines. There are always operations that require you to generate or count a certain number of pulses. You may need to keep track of an index table position or you may need to index a test table a certain number of degrees which you can correspond to a given number of pulses received from a sensor element that is mounted on the index table. You can also use this program to count the number of parts that have been tested or you can stop a particular function after a given number of operations have been performed,

In the last sentence, you may have noticed that I referred to the routine as a program. If you check the programs that are presented in Tables 5-17 through 5-20, you will observe that you are doing some bit-testing, memory decrementing, branching, and jumping which really forms a small stand-alone program. Just as you used a switch on the EXP-6522 to observe the bit-test routine function, you can connect a pushbutton to the EXP-6522, as shown in Fig. 5-2, in order to observe the pulse counting and pulse generation programs in action.

The following two software programs will make your computer into a square-wave generator which generates programmable waveforms at frequencies between 1 Hz and 10,000 Hz. Someone might say that running a software program such as this is a wasteful use of the computer, but if you need a square wave for a specified function, you can generate it with just this program. Since your computer uses a crystal-controlled clock, the clock frequency will be as stable as a "rock", and your waveform frequency will not drift from its programmed characteristics.

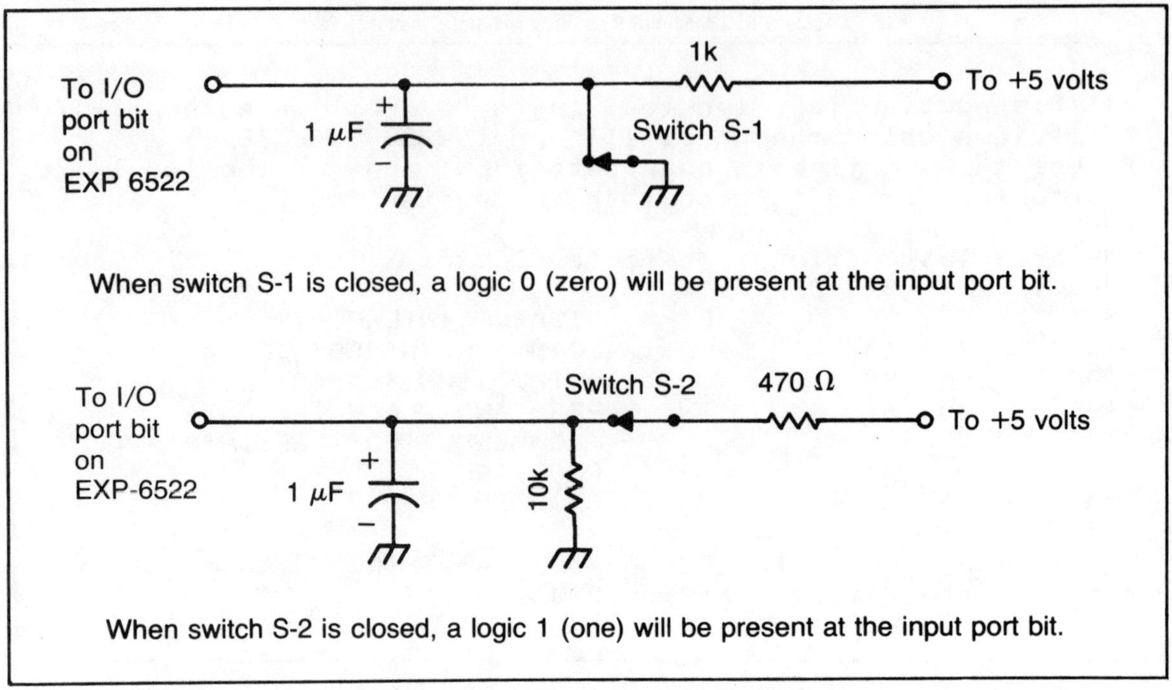

Fig. 5-1. The switch connection diagram for experimenting with the bit-test instruction.

Table 5-9. A KIM-1 PA6 Logic-Zero Bit-Test Routine.

```
A. This routine will  check for a logic "0"  (ZERO) on  port
bit PA6.
B. This routine can be run on a KIM-1.
C. Use DDRA at address 1701 and I/O DRA at address 1700.

Address--Instructions--Mnemonic--Description
Location B1---B2--B3
200       A9   00        LDA      LOAD 00 INTO THE ACCUMULATOR
202       8D   01   17   STA      STORE  00  INTO DDRA AND MAKE
                                  ALL PORT BITS INPUT BITS.
205       2C   00   17   BIT      BIT TEST PA6
208       50   FB        BVC      IF PA6 IS A ZERO, GO TO NEXT
                                  INSTRUCTION. IF PA6 IS A  "1"
                                  GO  BRANCH BACK  TO  LOCATION
                                  205 AND BIT TEST AGAIN.
20A       00             BRK      STOP PROGRAM

NOTE:  The bit test only takes a few microseconds to run and
branch  back  for  another  test, so care  must be  taken to
insure that there is  no noise  or voltage spikes allowed on
the PA6 input line from the outside circuits.
```

Table 5-10. A SYM-1 and AIM-65 PA6 Logic-Zero Bit-Test Routine.

```
A. This routine will check for a logic "0" (ZERO) on port
bit PA6.
B. This routine can be run on a SYM-1 or a AIM-65.
C. Use DDRA at address A003 and I/O DRA at address A001.

Address--Instructions--Mnemonic--Description
Location B1---B2--B3
200       A9    00         LDA     LOAD 00 INTO THE ACCUMULATOR
202       8D    03    A0   STA      STORE 00 INTO DDRA  AND MAKE
                                   ALL PORT BITS INPUT BITS.
205       2C    01    A0   BIT     BIT TEST PA6
208       50    FB         BVC     IF PA6 IS A ZERO, GO TO NEXT
                                   INSTRUCTION. IF  PA6 IS A "1"
                                   GO  BRANCH  BACK  TO LOCATION
                                   205 AND BIT TEST AGAIN.
20A       00               BRK     STOP PROGRAM

NOTE: The bit test only takes a few microseconds to run and
branch back for another test. Care must be taken to insure
that there is no noise or voltage spikes allowed on the PA7
input line from the outside circuits.
```

Table 5-11. A KIM-1 PA7 Logic-Zero Bit-Test Routine.

```
A. This routine will check for a logic "0" (ZERO) on port
bit PA7.
B. This routine can be run on a KIM-1.
C. Use DDRA at address 1701 and I/O DRA at address 1700.

Address--Instructions--Mnemonic--Description
Location B1---B2--B3
200       A9    7F         LDA     LOAD 7F INTO THE ACCUMULATOR
202       8D    01    17   STA     STORE  7F  INTO DDRA AND MAKE
                                   PORT BIT PA7 AN INPUT BIT.
205       2C    00    17   BIT     BIT TEST PA7
208       30    FB         BVC     IF PA7 IS A ZERO, GO TO NEXT
                                   INSTRUCTION. IF PA7 IS A  "1"
                                   GO  BRANCH BACK  TO  LOCATION
                                   205 AND BIT TEST AGAIN.
20A       00               BRK     STOP PROGRAM

NOTE:  The bit test only takes a few microseconds to run and
branch back for another test, so care must be taken to
insure that there is no noise or voltage spikes allowed on
the PA7 input line from the outside circuits.
```

Table 5-12. A SYM-1 or AIM-65 PA7 Logic-Zero Bit-Test Routine.

```
A. This  routine will check for a logic "0"  (ZERO)  on port
bit PA7.
B. This routine can be run on a SYM-1 or a AIM-65.
C. Use DDRA at address A003 and I/O DRA at address A001.

Address--Instructions--Mnemonic--Description
Location B1--B2--B3
200      A9  7F       LDA       LOAD 7F INTO THE ACCUMULATOR
202      8D  03   A0   STA       STORE 7F INTO  DDRA AND MAKE
                                BIT PA7 AN INPUT PORT BIT.
205      2C  01   A0  BIT       BIT TEST PA7
208      30   FB       BMI       IF PA7 IS A ZERO, GO TO NEXT
                                INSTRUCTION. IF PA7 IS A  "1"
                                GO  BRANCH  BACK  TO LOCATION
                                205 AND BIT TEST AGAIN.
20A      00               BRK       STOP PROGRAM

NOTE:  The bit test only takes a few microseconds to run and
branch back for  another test. Care must be  taken to insure
that there is  no noise or voltage spikes allowed on the PA7
input line from the outside circuits.
```

Table 5-13. A KIM-1 PA6 Logic-One Bit-Test Routine.

```
A. This  routine  will check for a logic "1"  (ONE)  on port
bit PA6.
B. This routine can be run on a KIM-1.
C. Use DDRA at address 1701 and I/O DRA at address 1700.

Address--Instructions--Mnemonic--Description
Location B1--B2--B3
200      A9  00           LDA       LOAD 00 INTO THE ACCUMULATOR
202      8D   01   17    STA       STORE 00 INTO  DDRA AND MAKE
                                   ALL PORT BITS INPUT BITS.
205      2C  00   17    BIT       BIT TEST PA6
208      50  FB           BVC       IF PA6 IS A ONE, GO TO NEXT
                                   INSTRUCTION.  IF PA6 IS A "0"
                                   GO BRANCH  BACK  TO  LOCATION
                                   205 AND BIT TEST AGAIN.
20A      00                BRK       STOP PROGRAM

NOTE: The bit  test only takes a few microseconds to run and
branch back  for another test. Care  must be taken to insure
that there is no noise or voltage spikes allowed on the  PA7
input line from the outside circuits.
```

Table 5-14. A SYM-1 or AIM-65 PA6 Logic-One Bit-Test Routine.

```
A. This  routine will check for a  logic  "1" (ONE)  on port
bit PA6.
B. This routine can be run on a SYM-1 or a AIM-65.
C. Use DDRA at address A003 and I/O DRA at address A001.

Address--Instructions--Mnemonic--Description
Location B1--B2--B3
200         A9  00         LDA      LOAD 00 INTO THE ACCUMULATOR
202         8D  03   A0    STA       STORE 00 INTO DDRA AND  MAKE
                                    ALL PORT BITS INPUT BITS.
205         2C  01   A0    BIT      BIT TEST PA6
208         50  FB         BVC      IF PA6 IS A ONE, GO TO NEXT
                                    INSTRUCTION. IF PA6 IS  A "0"
                                    GO  BRANCH BACK  TO  LOCATION
                                    205 AND BIT TEST AGAIN.
20A         00             BRK      STOP PROGRAM

NOTE: The bit test only takes a  few microseconds to run and
branch  back for another test. Care must be taken  to insure
that there is no noise or voltage spikes allowed  on the PA7
input line from the outside circuits.
```

Table 5-15. A KIM-1 PA7 Logic-One Bit-Test Routine.

```
A. This  routine will check for  a logic "1"  (ONE)  on port
bit PA7.
B. This routine can be run on a KIM-1.
C. Use DDRA at address 1701 and I/O DRA at address 1700.

Address--Instructions--Mnemonic--Description
Location B1--B2--B3
200         A9  7F         LDA      LOAD 7F INTO THE ACCUMULATOR
202         8D  01    17    STA      STORE 7F INTO  DDRA AND MAKE
                                    BIT PA7 AN INPUT PORT BIT.
205         2C  00   17    BIT      BIT TEST PA7
208         10  FB         BPL      IF PA7 IS A ONE, GO TO NEXT
                                    INSTRUCTION. IF  PA7 IS A "0"
                                    GO  BRANCH  BACK TO  LOCATION
                                    205 AND BIT TEST AGAIN.
20A         00             BRK      STOP PROGRAM

NOTE: The  bit test only takes a few microseconds to run and
branch back  for  another test. Care must be taken to insure
that there is no noise or voltage spikes  allowed on the PA7
input line from the outside circuits.
```

Table 5-16. A SYM-1 or AIM-65 PA7 Logic-One Bit-Test Routine.

```
A. This routine  will check for  a  logic "1"  (ONE) on port
bit PA7.
B. This routine can be run on a SYM-1 or a AIM-65.
C. Use DDRA at address A003 and I/O DRA at address A001.

Address--Instructions--Mnemonic--Description
Location B1--B2--B3
200        A9   7F          LDA       LOAD 7F INTO THE ACCUMULATOR
202        8D   03   A0     STA        STORE 7F  INTO DDRA AND MAKE
                                      BIT PA7 AN INPUT PORT BIT.
205        2C   01   A0     BIT       BIT TEST PA7
208        10   FB          BPL       IF PA7 IS A ONE, GO TO NEXT
                                      INSTRUCTION. IF PA7  IS A "0"
                                      GO BRANCH  BACK  TO  LOCATION
                                      205 AND BIT TEST AGAIN.
20A        00               BRK       STOP PROGRAM

NOTE: The  bit test only takes a few microseconds to run and
branch back for another  test. Care must be taken to  insure
that there is no noise or voltage spikes  allowed on the PA7
input line from the outside circuits.
```

Table 5-17. A Pulse-Generating Routine for the SYM-1 or AIM-65.

```
A. This routine can be used to generate up to 255 pulses on
any output Port A bit. The pulse width can be programmed to be
between 50  microseconds and 1/2  second wide, and  the time
between  pulses  can  be  programmed  also  to be between 50
microseconds and 1/2 second.
B. This program will run on a SYM-1 and a AIM-65.

Address--Instructions--Mnemonic--Description
Location B1--B2--B3
200        A9   20          LDA
202        85   00          STA    STORE 20 IN LOCATION 00
204        A9   20          LDA
206        85   01          STA    STORE 20 IN LOCATION 01
208        C6   01          DEC    DECREMENT LOCATION 01
20A        DO   FC          BNE    IF LOCATION 01 IS NOT ZERO,
                                   BRANCH BACK TO LOCATION 208.
20C        C6   00          DEC    DECREMENT LOCATION 00
20E        D0   F4          BNE    IF LOCATION 00 IS NOT ZERO,
                                   BRANCH BACK TO LOCATION 204.
210        60               RTS    RETURN TO PROGRAM
```

Table 5-17. A Pulse-Generating Routine for the SYM-1 or AIM-65 (continued from page 60.)

```
211      00                   THIS LOCATION NOT USED
212      A9  FF         LDA
214      8D  03 A0      STA   MAKE PORT A AN OUTPUT PORT
217      A9  00         LDA
219      8D  01 A0      STA   SET OUTPUT PORT TO ZERO
21C      4C  34 02      JMP   JUMP TO LOCATION 0234
21F      00                   NOT USED
220      A9   20         LDA   THIS TIME LOOP IS  THE SAME AS
                              ONE AT LOCATION 200
222      85  00         STA
224      A9  20         LDA
226      85  00         STA
228      C6  01         DEC
22A      D0  FC         BNE
22C      C6  00         DEC
22E      D0  F4         BNE
230      60             RTS
231      00  EA EA            THESE LOCATIONS ARE NOT USED
234      A9  01         LDA
236      8D  01 A0      STA   SET PA0 TO A LOGIC-ONE STATE.
239      20  00 02      JSR   JUMP TO SUBROUTINE AT 200
23C      A9  00         LDA
23E      8D  01 A0      STA   SET PA0 TO A LOGIC-ZERO STATE
241      20  20 02      JSR   JUMP TO SUBROUTINE AT 220
244      4C  54 02      JMP   JUMP TO 0254
247      EA  EA EA      NOP   LOCATIONS 247 TO 24F ARE NOT
24A      EA  EA EA            USED IN THIS PROGRAM.
24D      EA  EA EA
250      A9  05         LDA
252      85  03         STA   STORE 05 IN LOCATION 03
254      C6  03         DEC   DECREMENT LOCATION 03 BY 1
256      D0  05         BNE   CHECK FOR 00 IN LOCATION 03
258      00  00 00      BRK   STOP PROGRAM, THE PULSES HAVE
                              BEEN GENERATED
25B      EA  EA         NOP   NO OPERATION
25D      4C  12 02      JMP   JUMP TO 0212 AND START NEXT
                              PULSE.
```

NOTES: A. This program is started at location 0212.
B. To change the pulse width and frequency, change the hex data in locations 202, 205, 222, and 225.
C. Load the number of pulses (In Hex) to be generated into location 251.
D. The number of pulses that are generated will be one less than the hex number entered in location 0251.

Table 5-18. A KIM-1 Pulse-Generating Routine.

A. This routine can be used to generate up to 255 pulses on any output port A bit. The pulse width can programmed to be between 50 microseconds and 1/2 second wide, and the time between pulses can be programmed also to be between 50 microseconds and 1/2 second.
B. This program will run on a KIM-1.

```
Address--Instructions--Mnemonic--Description
Location B1--B2--B3
200        A9  30        LDA
202        85  00        STA    STORE 30 IN LOCATION 00
204        A9  30        LDA
206        85  01        STA    STORE 30 IN LOCATION 01
208        C6  01        DEC    DECREMENT LOCATION 01
20A        DO  FC        BNE    IF LOCATION 01 IS NOT ZERO,
                                BRANCH BACK TO LOCATION 208.
20C        C6  00        DEC    DECREMENT LOCATION 00
20E        D0  F4        BNE    IF LOCATION 00 IS NOT ZERO,
                                BRANCH BACK TO LOCATION 204.
210        60            RTS    RETURN TO PROGRAM
211        00                   THIS LOCATION NOT USED
212        A9  FF        LDA
214        8D  01  17    STA    MAKE PORT A AN OUTPUT PORT
217        A9  00        LDA
219        8D  00  17    STA    SET OUTPUT PORT TO ZERO
21C        4C  34  02    JMP    JUMP TO LOCATION 0234
21F        00                   NOT USED
220        A9   30        LDA    THIS TIME LOOP IS  THE SAME AS
                                ONE AT LOCATION 200
222        85  00        STA
224        A9  30        LDA
226        85  00        STA
228        C6  01        DEC
```

The square-wave programs, which are presented in Tables 5-21 and 5-22, will run on the KIM-1, the SYM-1, and the AIM-65 single-board computers. The program contains two double-nested timing loops which control the on and off times of the pulses. Other various load and store instructions are used that will turn the I/O port bits off and on to form the square waves. This is a closed-loop program, so you will have to interrupt the computer by using the reset button or some other method to stop the program after it has been started. When the program is running, the output waveform can be observed if you connect an oscilloscope to the EXP-6522 as shown in Fig. 5-3.

A nested-loop timing routine is shown in Table 5-23. Just about every programming book that you read will discuss nested loops or subroutines. Most of the nested loops use some form of advanced programming, but the routine that is shown in Table 5-23 uses only user RAM memory locations, simple programming methods, and can be located anywhere in the operating RAM memory that you wish. You can jump into and out of this routine using the JUMP instruction (4C) or you can use it as a

```
22A     D0  FC       BNE
22C     C6  00       DEC
22E     D0  F4       BNE
230     60           RTS
231     00  EA EA          THESE LOCATIONS ARE NOT USED
234     A9  01       LDA
236     8D  00 17    STA   SET PA0 TO A LOGIC-ONE STATE.
239     20  00 02    JSR   JUMP TO SUBROUTINE AT 200
23C     A9  00       LDA
23E     8D  00 17    STA   SET PA0 TO A LOGIC-ZERO STATE
241     20  20 02    JSR   JUMP TO SUBROUTINE AT 220
244     4C  54 02    JMP   JUMP TO 0254
247     EA  EA EA    NOP   LOCATIONS 247 TO 24F ARE NOT
24A     EA  EA EA          USED IN THIS PROGRAM.
24D     EA  EA EA
250     A9  05       LDA
252     85  03       STA   STORE 05 IN LOCATION 03
254     C6  03       DEC   DECREMENT LOCATION 03 BY 1
256     D0  05       BNE   CHECK FOR 00 IN LOCATION 03
258     00  00 00    BRK   STOP PROGRAM, THE PULSES HAVE
                           BEEN GENERATED
25B     EA  EA       NOP   NO OPERATION
25D     4C  12 02    JMP   JUMP TO 0212 AND START NEXT
                           PULSE.

NOTES: A. This program is started at location 0212.
       B. To change the  pulse width and  frequency,  change
the hex data in locations 202, 205, 222, and 225.
       C. Load the number of pulses (In Hex) to be generated
into location 251
.      D. The  number of pulses  that are generated  will be
one less than the hex number entered in location 0251.
```

subroutine with the JSR instruction (20) and RTS instruction (60). You can couple these routines together to increase the time delays if needed. If for some reason, you need longer time delays, it might be better to use some other form of time delay such as an external 555 timer with the bit-test function to check on the timer circuit time-out. With an external timer circuit, the computer can do other things while the needed time delay is timing out. When you learn how to use the timers that are located in the 6522 VIA chips, you perform similar software functions but they will require a more advanced understanding of the computer system than is required to use the nested-loop or external timer methods.

The last three routines will show how to use some of the 6522 VIA timer functions. The routines of Tables 5-24, 5-25, and 5-26 only touch on a few of the many ways in which you can use the programmable timers. If you learn what these routines do and how they do it, you will have no trouble moving on to the more advanced functions of the 6522 VIA timers. You should briefly read the portion of your computer instruction manual which describes the operation of the programmable timers that are

Table 5-19. A Pulse-Counting Routine for the SYM-1 or AIM-65.

```
A. This routine can  be  used to count up  to  256  positive
pulses that are applied to port bit PA7.
B. This routine will run on a SYM-1 and the AIM-65.
C. Use DDRA at address A003 and I/O DRA at A001.

Address--Instructions--Mnemonic--Description
Location B1--B2--B3
200       A9  00       LDA  LOAD 00 INTO THE ACCUMULATOR
202       8D  03  A0   STA  STORE IN DDRA AT A003
205       A9  05       LDA  LOAD THE NUMBER OF PULSES TO BE
                            COUNTED IN LOCATION 206.
207       8D  1F  02   STA  STORE 05 IN LOCATION 021F
20A       2C  01  A0   BIT  TEST FOR POSITIVE PULSE ON PA7
20D       10  FB       BPL  IF NO PULSE, BRANCH BACK TO 020A
20F       CE  1F  02   DEC  DECREMENT 021F BY 1
212       D0  03       BNE  CHECK FOR A ZERO IN 021F, IF NO
                            ZERO, GO TO LOCATION 0217
214       00  00  00   BRK  STOP PROGRAM, THE COUNT IN 021F
                            IS ZERO.  SEE NOTES
217       2C  01  A0   BIT  CHECK FOR END OF PULSE AT PA7
21A       30  FB       BMI  IF PULSE IS ON PA7, GO TO 0217
21C       4C  0A  02   JMP  JUMP TO 020A AND CHECK FOR THE
                            NEXT PULSE TO BE COUNTED.

NOTES: A. The  hexadecimal  data  representing  number  of
pulses  that are  to be counted  is stored in  location 206.
       B. This  program will  count  five positive pulses on
PA7,  and then stop  at  location  214 or jump  to  the  new
location  that is set by a JUMP instruction in 214, 215, and
216. If you wanted to go  to location 230 after you  counted
five pulses,  location 214,  215,  and  216  would  read  as
follows:

216       4C  30  02    JMP   JUMP TO LOCATION 0230

       C. This  program  will count pulses  at the  rate  of
10,000  pulses  per  second. Special effort must be  made to
insure that noise is eliminated on  input  port PA7, because
noise will be counted as pulses.
       D. Start this program at location 200
```

Table 5-20. A Pulse-Counting Routine for the KIM-1.

```
A. This routine can  be  used to count up  to  256  positive
pulses that are applied to port bit PA7.
B. This routine will run on a KIM-1.
C. Use DDRA at address 17Ø1 and I/O DRA at 17ØØ.

Address--Instructions--Mnemonic--Description
Location B1--B2--B3
2ØØ        A9   ØØ        LDA   LOAD ØØ INTO THE ACCUMULATOR
2Ø2        8D   Ø1   17   STA   STORE IN DDRA AT AØØ3
2Ø5        A9   Ø5        LDA   LOAD THE NUMBER OF PULSES TO BE
                                COUNTED IN LOCATION 2Ø6.
2Ø7        8D   1F   Ø2   STA   STORE Ø5 IN LOCATION Ø21F
2ØA        2C   ØØ   17   BIT   TEST FOR POSITIVE PULSE ON PA7
2ØD        1Ø   FB        BPL   IF NO PULSE, BRANCH BACK TO Ø2ØA
2ØF        CE   1F   Ø2   DEC   DECREMENT Ø21F BY 1
212        DØ   Ø3        BNE   CHECK FOR A ZERO IN Ø21F, IF NO
                                ZERO, GO TO LOCATION Ø217
214        ØØ   ØØ   ØØ   BRK   STOP PROGRAM, THE COUNT IN Ø21F
                                IS ZERO.  SEE NOTES
217        2C   ØØ   17   BIT   CHECK FOR END OF PULSE AT PA7
21A        3Ø   FB        BMI   IF PULSE IS ON PA7, GO TO Ø217
21C        4C   ØA   Ø2   JMP   JUMP TO Ø2ØA AND CHECK FOR THE
                                NEXT PULSE TO BE COUNTED.

NOTES:  A. The  hexadecimal  data  representing  number  of
pulses that are to be counted is stored in location 2Ø6.
        B. This program  will count five positive pulses  on
PA7,  and  then  stop  at  location  214 or jump to the new
location that is set  by a JUMP instruction in 214, 215, and
216. If  you wanted to go to location  23Ø after you counted
five  pulses, location  214,  215,  and  216 would read  as
follows:

216        4C   3Ø   Ø2    JMP   JUMP TO LOCATION Ø23Ø

        C. This program will  count pulses  at the  rate  of
1Ø,ØØØ  pulses per second.  Special  effort must be  made to
insure that noise is  eliminated on  input port PA7, because
noise will be counted as pulses.
        D. Start this program at location 2ØØ
```

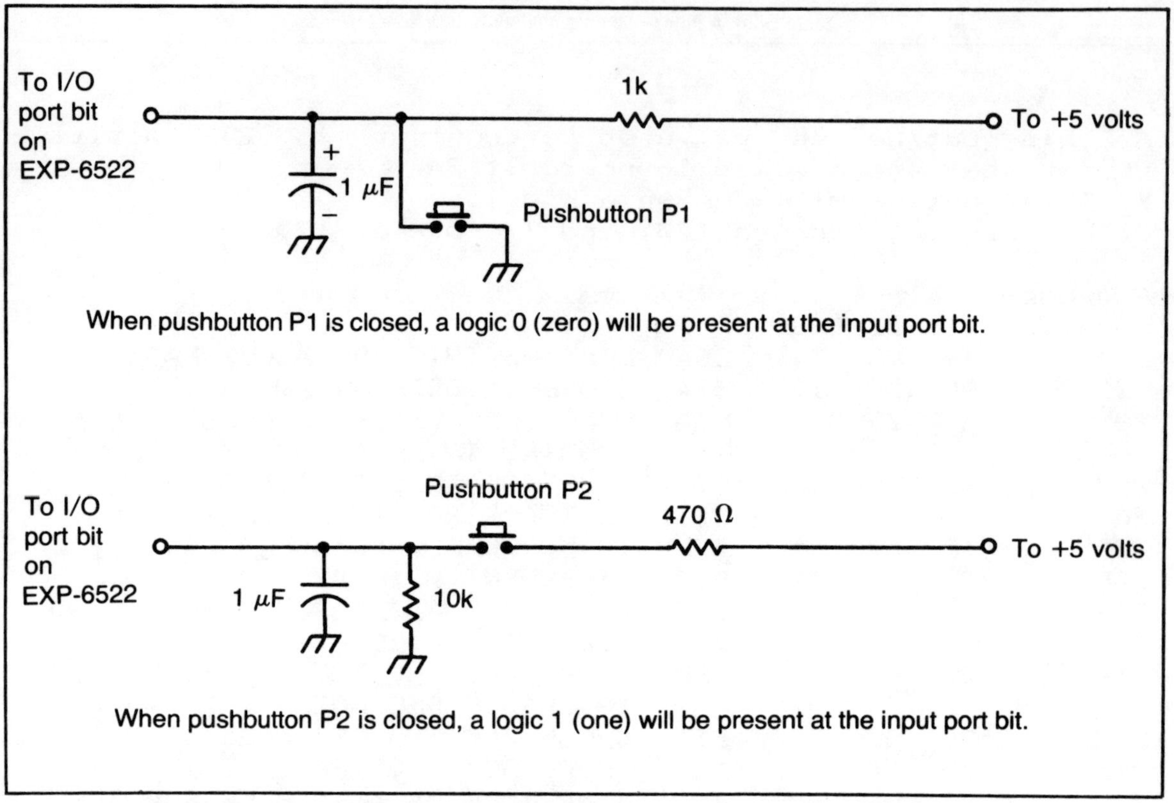

Fig. 5-2. The pushbutton connection diagram for experimenting with the pulse-counting routines.

Table 5-21. A Square-Wave Generating Program for the SYM-1 or AIM-65.

```
A. This is  a  software  program that will  generate  square
waves or pulses of different widths.  The output frequencies
that can be  produced  with  this program will  vary  between
1 Hz to 10,000 Hz.
B. This program uses port  "A"  and  outputs the square waves
or pulses on output line PA0.
C. The program can be run on a SYM-1 or the AIM-65.


 Address--Instructions--Mnemonic--Description
 Location B1--B2--B3
 200       A9  10         LDA
 202       85  00         STA   STORE 10 IN LOCATION 00
 204       A9  10         LDA
```

Table 5-21. A Square-Wave Generating Program for the SYM-1 or AIM-65 (continued from page 66).

```
206     85  01          STA    STORE 10 IN LOCATION 01
208     C6  01          DEC    DECREMENT LOCATION 01
20A     DO  FC          BNE    IF LOCATION 01 IS NOT ZERO,
                               BRANCH BACK TO LOCATION 208.
20C     C6  00          DEC    DECREMENT LOCATION 00
20E     D0  F4          BNE    IF LOCATION 00 IS NOT ZERO,
                               BRANCH BACK TO LOCATION 204.
210     60              RTS    RETURN TO PROGRAM
211     00                     THIS LOCATION NOT USED "*"
212     A9  FF          LDA
214     8D  03  A0      STA    MAKE PORT A AN OUTPUT PORT
217     A9  00          LDA
219     8D  01  A0      STA    SET OUTPUT PORT TO ZERO
21C     4C  34  02      JMP    JUMP TO LOCATION 0234
21F     00                                                "*"
220      A9  10          LDA    THIS  TIME LOOP IS THE SAME AS
                               ONE AT LOCATION 200
222     85  00          STA
224     A9  10          LDA
226     85  00          STA
228     C6  01          DEC
22A     D0  FC          BNE
22C     C6  00          DEC
22E     D0  F4          BNE
230     60              RTS
231     00  EA  EA             THESE LOCATIONS ARE NOT USED
234     A9  01          LDA
236     8D  01  A0      STA    SET PA0 TO A LOGIC-ONE STATE.
239     20  00  02      JSR    JUMP TO SUBROUTINE AT 200
23C     A9  00          LDA
23E     8D  01  A0      STA    SET PA0 TO A LOGIC-ZERO STATE
241     20  20  02      JSR    JUMP TO SUBROUTINE AT 220
244     4C  12  02      JMP    JUMP BACK TO STARTING LOCATION


NOTES: A. This program is started at location 0212.
          (GO-0212)
       B. To change frequency or pulse widths, change the
          hex data in locations 202, 205, 222, and 225.
       C. Push the reset button to stop the program.
```

Table 5-22. A Square-Wave Generating Program for the KIM-1.

```
A. This is a software program that will generate square
waves or pulses of different widths. The output frequencies
that can be produced with this program will vary between
1 Hz to 10,000 Hz.
B. This program uses port "A" and outputs the square waves
or pulses on output line PA0.
C. The program can be run on a KIM-1.

Address--Instructions--Mnemonic--Description
Location B1--B2--B3
200      A9  20        LDA
202      85  00        STA   STORE 20 IN LOCATION 00
204      A9  20        LDA
206      85  01        STA   STORE 20 IN LOCATION 01
208      C6  01        DEC   DECREMENT LOCATION 01
20A      DO  FC        BNE   IF LOCATION 01 IS NOT ZERO,
                             BRANCH BACK TO LOCATION 208.
20C      C6  00        DEC   DECREMENT LOCATION 00
20E      D0  F4        BNE   IF LOCATION 00 IS NOT ZERO,
                             BRANCH BACK TO LOCATION 204.
210      60            RTS   RETURN TO PROGRAM
211      00                  THIS LOCATION NOT USED "*"
212      A9  FF        LDA
214      8D  01  17    STA   MAKE PORT A AN OUTPUT PORT
217      A9  00        LDA
219      8D  00  17    STA   SET OUTPUT PORT TO ZERO
```

located in the 6522 VIA chips before using these routines. Then when you have these program routines up and running, you can study them a little more deeply.

Table 5-24 shows a routine which will measure the length of a positive logic pulse that is applied to port bit PA7 of a SYM-1 or the AIM-65 using timer 1 of the 6522 VIA. The routine simply uses the bit-test function to check when a logic one pulse is on PA7. When a logic-one pulse is applied to PA7, the routine starts timer 1 functioning. While timer 1 is timing down, the routine looks for the end of the logic one pulse using another bit-test routine which watches for a logic zero. When the logic-zero condition is detected, the program reads the timer 1 data and stores it in a memory location for future use. The timer 1 data plus any machine cycle time that is required to run the program is the total positive pulse width duration time, You can observe the operation of the program by using the 555 timer circuit shown in Fig. 5-4 and the EXP-6522.

The 6522 has a very useful square wave function using port PB7. You can program the 6522 VIA to output continuous square waves from port PB7 while the computer is going about its business doing other functions. You can update the square function any time to change the frequency of the output waveform which will give you the ability to generate a wide variety of waveforms and frequencies under software control. A program routine for using the PB7 square wave function is given in Table 5-25.

The last routine that is presented in Chapter 5 will

```
21C        4C  34 02      JMP   JUMP TO LOCATION 0234
21F        00                                              "*"
220         A9  20         LDA   THIS  TIME LOOP IS THE SAME AS
                                ONE AT LOCATION 200
222        85  00         STA
224        A9  20         LDA
226        85  00         STA
228        C6  01         DEC
22A        D0  FC         BNE
22C        C6  00         DEC
22E        D0  F4         BNE
230        60             RTS
231        00  EA EA            THESE LOCATIONS ARE NOT USED
234        A9  01         LDA
236        8D  00  17     STA   SET PA0 TO A LOGIC-ONE STATE.
239        20  00  02     JSR   JUMP TO SUBROUTINE AT 200
23C        A9  00         LDA
23E        8D  00  17     STA   SET PA0 TO A LOGIC-ZERO STATE
241        20  20  02     JSR   JUMP TO SUBROUTINE AT 220
244        4C  12  02     JMP   JUMP BACK TO STARTING LOCATION

NOTES: A. This program is started at location 0212.
          (GO-0212)
       B. To change frequency or pulse widths, change the
          hex data in locations 202, 205, 222, and 225.
       C. Push the reset button to stop the program.
```

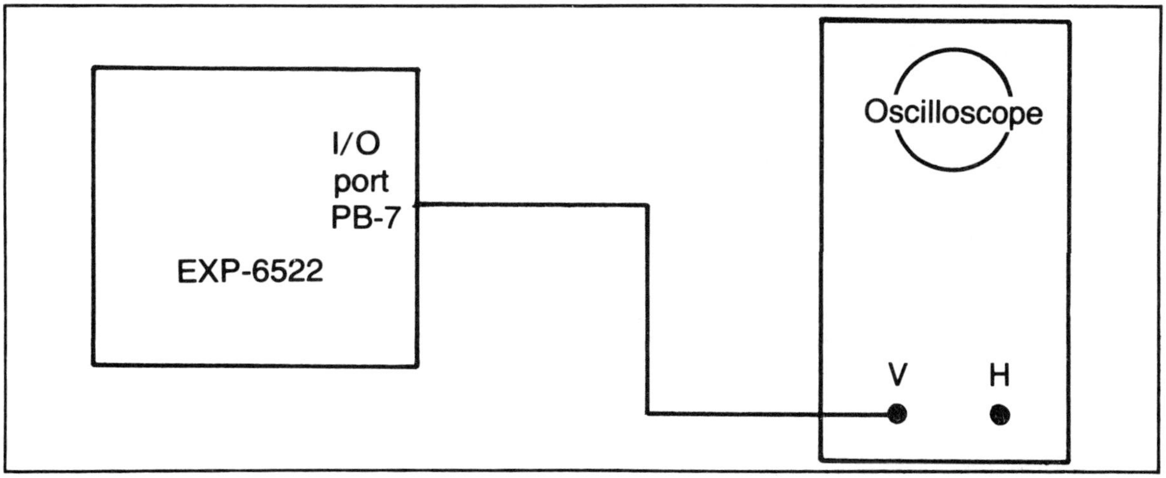

Fig. 5-3. An easy method for using an oscilloscope to observe the square-wave output of the single-board computer.

Table 5-23. A Time-Delay Routine for the SYM-1 and AIM-65.

```
A. This routine can be used to generate software  controlled
time delays of between 50 microseconds and one-half second.
B. This routine can be used on a SYM-1 or the AIM-65.
C. Use DDRA at address A003 and I/O DRA at address A001.
D. This time loop is called a double nested loop.

Address--Instructions--Mnemonic--Description
Location B1--B2--B3
200       A9   FF          LDA   LOAD FF INTO THE ACCUMULATOR.
202       85   00          STA   STORE FF IN LOCATION 00.
204       A9   FF          LDA.
206       85   01          STA   STORE FF IN LOCATION 01.
208       C6   01          DEC   DECREMENT LOCATION 01 BY 1.
20A       D0   FC          BNE   IF LOCATION 01 IS ZERO, GO TO
                                 NEXT INSTRUCTION. IF LOCATION
                                 01 IS NOT ZERO, BRANCH BACK TO
                                 LOCATION 208 AND DECREMENT
                                 UNTIL LOCATION 01 IS ZERO.
20C       C6   00          DEC   DECREMENT LOCATION 00 BY 1.
20E       D0   F4          BNE   IF LOCATION 00 IS ZERO, GO TO
                                 NEXT INSTRUCTION. IF LOCATION
                                 00 IS NOT ZERO, BRANCH BACK
                                 TO LOCATION 204 AND START
                                 NEXT INTER TIMING LOOP.
210       00               BRK   STOP, TIME DELAY IS OVER.

NOTE:     The time  delay  is  controlled  by  the  data  in
locations 00  and 01. a  "01"  in location  00 and  01  will
generate  about  a fifty microsecond time  delay. A  "FF" in
location 00 and  01  will generate  about a 1/2 second  time
delay.
```

Table 5-24. A Pulse-Length Measuring Program for the SYM-1 or AIM-65.

```
A. This program will measure the length of a  positive pulse
   in microseconds which is applied to input port PA7.
B. Pulses between 25 and 65000 microseconds can  be measured
   with this program.
C. This program uses Timer 1 in the 6522 VIA. on the SYM-1
   or the AIM-65.

Address--Instructions--Mnemonic--Description
Location B1--B2--B3
200        A9  00      LDA
202        8D  03  A0  STA  STORE 00 IN DDRA AT A003
205        8D  2E  02  STA  SET LOCATION 022E TO ZERO
208        8D  2F  02  STA  SET LOCATION 022F TO ZERO
20B        A9  FF      LDA
20D        8D  06  A0  STA  SET LOW ORDER LATCH
210        8D  07  A0  STA  SET HIGH ORDER LATCH
213        2C  01  A0  BIT  TEST FOR POSITIVE PULSE
216        10  FB      BPL  LOOP AND WAIT FOR PULSE
218        8D  05  A0  STA  START TIMER 1
21B        2C  01  A0  BIT  TEST FOR END OF PULSE
21E        30  FB      BMI  LOOP AND WAIT FOR END OF PULSE
220        AD  04  A0  LDA  READ TIMER 1  "LOW ORDER"
223        8D  2F  02  STA  STORE LOWER ORDER T1 IN 022F
226        AD  05  A0  LDA  READ TIMER 1  "HIGH ORDER"
229        8D  2E  02  STA  STORE HIGH ORDER T1 IN 022E
22C        00  00  00  BRK  PULSE IS MEASURED - STOP

NOTE:  As the  pulse becomes shorter,  you  must count  the
       machine cycles  used in  the BIT test and the timer 1
       load   routine  to  secure  an  accurate  reading  in
       microseconds.
```

Table 5-25. A Square-Wave Program Using the Free-Running Function of the 6522 VIA Timer #1 on the SYM-1 or AIM-65.

```
A. This routine will generate square waves on PB7  using the
   Timer 1 free running mode of a 6522 VIA.
B. This routine can be used to generate square wave
   frequencies from about 8 Hz to 250,000 Hz.
C. This routine does not require a software  program to keep
   it  running. Once  you  have  started  this program,  the
   computer is free to do other functions.

Address--Instructions--Mnemonic--Description
Location B1--B2--B3
200       A9  C0        LDA
202       8D  0B  A0    STA   STORE C0 IN THE 6522  ACR
205       A9  FF        LDA
207       8D  06  A0    STA   SET LOW ORDER LATCH
20A       A9  FF        LDA
20C       8D  07  A0    STA   SET HIGH ORDER LATCH
20F       8D  05  A0    STA   START SQUARE-WAVE GENERATION
                              WRITING TO LOCATION A005
212       00  00  00    BRK   STOP INSTRUCTION OR PLACE A
                              JUMP INSTRUCTION HERE TO THE
                              NEXT PROGRAM ROUTINE

TO CHANGE  SQUARE-WAVE FREQUENCY, RUN THIS ROUTINE WHILE THE
SQUARE-WAVE GENERATOR IS RUNNING.

215       A9  01        LDA
217       8D  06  A0    STA   LOAD NEW DATA INTO LATCH
21A       A9  01        LDA
21C       8D  07  A0    STA   LOAD NEW DATA INTO LATCH
21F       00  00  00    BRK   STOP OR JUMP TO NEXT ROUTINE
NOTE:     The hex numbers that are located in locations 216
          and 21B are loaded into the low order and high
          order latches which control the output frequency
          of the square generation circuit in the 6522 VIA.

TO  STOP  THE  SQUARE-WAVE  FUNCTION OF  THE 6522,  RUN THIS
ROUTINE.

220       A9  00        LDA
222       8D  0B  A0    STA   RESET ACR TO 00 WHICH WILL
                              STOP THE SQUARE-WAVE FUNCTION

NOTES: A.  The  routine  at location  200  will  generate  a
frequency of about 8 Hz.
       B.  The  routine   at  215  will  change  the  output
frequency to about 250,000 Hz.
       C.  By  using the  routine at  215  and a time delay
routine, you can generate very complex waveforms.
```

Table 5-26. A Program Routine which Uses the 6522 VIA Timer #2 in the One-Shot Mode on a SYM-1 or AIM-65.

```
A. This routine gives you an example of how to use
   Time 2 of the 6522 VIA in the one-shot mode. Then we
   will give a second routine which will use the one-shot
   mode routine in a square-wave generation program.
B. The square-wave signal will be available on any Port A
   output bit.

Address--Instructions--Mnemonic--Description
Location B1--B2--B3
THIS IS THE ONE-SHOT TIMER 2 ROUTINE
200       A9  00        LDA
202       8D  0B  A0    STA   SET UP THE ACR
205       A9  BB        LDA
207       8D  08  A0    STA   LOAD THE LOW ORDER LATCH
20A       A9  01        LDA
20C       8D  09  A0    STA   LOAD THE HIGH ORDER LATCH
20F       A9  20        LDA
211       2C  0D  A0    BIT   CHECK FOR TIME OUT
214       F0  FB        BEQ   GO TO 211 IF NO TIME OUT
216       AD  08  A0    LDA   CLEAR INTERRUPT FLAG
219       00  00  00    BIT   STOP OR JUMP OR RTS
NOTE: LOCATION 206 AND  20A CONTAIN THE TIME DELAY  DATA  IN
HEX FORM. MEMORY  LOCATION 20A IS THE HIGH  ORDER LATCH DATA
WHICH EXHIBITS THE MAJOR TIME  DELAY CONTROL. THE  ABOVE DATA
IN  LOCATIONS   206  AND  20A  WILL  GENERATE  ABOUT  A  1/2
MILLISECOND TIME DELAY.

21A       A9  FF        LDA
21C       8D  03  A0    STA   MAKE PORT A AN OUTPUT PORT
21F       A9  00        LDA
221       8D  01  A0    STA   SET OUTPUT PORT A "LOW"
224       20  00  20    JSR   JUMP TO SUBROUTINE FOR A 1/2
                              MILLISECOND TIME DELAY.
227       A9  FF        LDA
229       8D  01  A0    STA   SET OUTPUT PORT A "HIGH"
22C       20  00  02    JSR   JUMP TO SUBROUTINE FOR A 1/2
                              MILLISECOND TIME DELAY
22F       4C  1A  02    JMP   JUMP BACK TO START LOCATION

NOTES: A. Start this program at location 021A.
       B. Location  0219 must contain  the hex number  of 60
which is a return from subroutine instruction code.
       C. The output frequency of this  square-wave  program
is  about  1000  Hz. The  output  frequency  can  easily  be
changed  by  changing  the  Timer  2  time  delay  data   in
locations 206 and 20A.
```

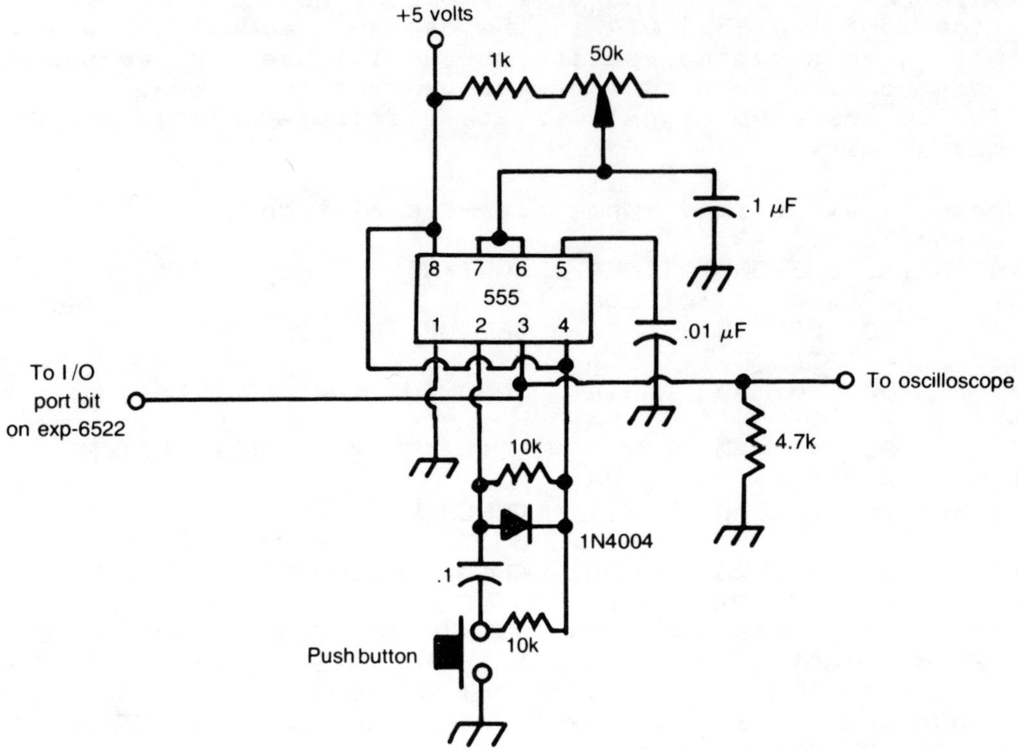

Fig. 5-4. A 555 timer circuit that can be used to experiment with the pulse width measuring routines.

show you how to use timer 2 in the 6522 VIA chip in the one-shot mode of operation. After the one-shot timer function of Table 5-25 is presented, a short routine is given so you can set up a 1,000 Hz oscillator using timer 2 and some JSR instructions. The oscillator routine is only given to help you understand the timer 2 operation because, after you have discovered the PB7 square wave abilities of the routine in the above paragraph, you will not be too impressed with this square-wave program.

CONCLUSION

We have used the phrase several times "simple routines or simple program", but they really are not simple until you understand what the machine-language instructions are doing for you. The fifteen machine-language instructions that have been used in the 6502 single-board computer programs will be explained for you in Tables 5-27 through 5-41. There is no way you can completely use a single-board computer system if you do not have the ability to use the basic building block machine-language instructions for that system.

Chapter 5 has presented some useful 6502 computer routines that can transform any one of the 6502 single-board computers into quite an elaborate system controller. Once you have learned how to program a single-board computer, you will be able to do a lot more with a low-cost computer than you can do with a lot of the expensive programmable controllers because the computer can do math and other high-level logical functions while programmable control systems generally perform only control system functions. Programmable controllers do have their advantages in that they will come equipped with ready to use interface circuits and terminal strips for easy connections.

A special note on the following machine-language explanations:

Table 5-27. Op-Code - FO ---- BEQ.

Machine Language Instruction--BEQ--"Branch Instruction"

Machine Language Op Code -------- FØ

Required Number of Bytes ------------ 2

Require Machine Time ----------------- 2 Cycles

Description: The BEQ instruction, with the op code FØ, will cause the computer program to branch to a location that is dictated by the BEQ instruction if the results of the last computer operation was zero. This instruction is very handy for branching to various computer routines, if the results of a logical operation such as an AND operation was zero, in order to complete the computer's program objectives. The machine operation which is shown in the example below means that the computer will branch to a routine at memory location 355, if the results of a previous logical operation was zero, when the microprocessor executes the instruction at location 350.

Address--Instructions--Mnemonic--Description
Location B1--B2--B3

```
350     FØ  Ø3      BEQ     BRANCH TO LOCATION 355H IF
                            THE RESULT OF THE LAST
                            OPERATION WAS ZERO
```

Table 5-28. Op-Code - 2C ---- BIT.

Machine Language Instruction--BIT--"Memory BIT Test"

Machine Language Op Code -------- 2C

Required Number of Bytes ------------ 3

Require Machine Time ----------------- 4 Cycles

Description: The BIT instruction, with the op code 2C, will test the bit contents of a specified memory location in the ram memory. This instruction is very handy for checking the logic level (One or Zero) of data bits 6 and 7 in any ram memory location. The BIT instruction will set the V flag of the flag register to the logic value of bit 6 and the N flag to the logic value of bit 7 of the tested memory byte. The machine operation which is shown in the example below means that the computer will test the bit contents of memory location A001 when the microprocessor executes the instruction at location 200. The results of the BIT-test instruction can be used to control the program operation of the single-board computer with one of the 6502 BRANCH instruction.

Address--Instructions--Mnemonic--Description
Location B1--B2--B3

```
200     2C  Ø1  AØ  BIT     BIT TEST LOCATION A001
203     BRANCH INSTRUCTION
```

Table 5-29. Op-Code - 30 ---- BMI.

Machine Language Instruction--BMI--"Branch Instruction"

Machine Language Op Code -------- 3Ø

Required Number of Bytes ------------ 2

Require Machine Time ----------------- 2 Cycles

Description: The BMI instruction, with the op code 3Ø, will cause the computer program to branch to a location that is dictated by the BMI instruction if the results of the last computer operation sets the N bit of the flag register to a "1". This instruction is very handy for branching to various computer routines, if the results of a BIT-test operation showed that bit 7 was a logic one, in order to complete the computer's program objectives. The machine operation which is shown in the example below means that the computer will branch back to memory location 200, if the results of a previous BIT instruction showed that bit 7 of address location A001 was a "1". If bit 7 is a "1", the routine will stay in a closed loop until bit 7 becomes a zero.

Address--Instructions--Mnemonic--Description
Location B1--B2--B3

```
200     2C  Ø1  AØ   BIT      BIT TEST A001
203     3Ø  FB       BMI      BRANCH BACK TO 200H IF
                              BIT 7 IS A "1"
```

Table 5-30. Op-Code - DO ---- BNE.

Machine Language Instruction--BNE--"Branch Instruction"

Machine Language Op Code -------- DØ

Required Number of Bytes ------------ 2

Require Machine Time ----------------- 2 Cycles

Description: The BNE instruction, with the op code DØ, will cause the computer program to branch to a location that is dictated by the BNE instruction if the results of the last computer operation sets the Z flag of the flag register to a "Ø". This instruction is very handy for indicating a zero condition when using a DEC instruction to decrement a memory location to zero. The machine routine which is shown in the example below will branch back to memory location 200 and decrement location 300 again if location 300 was not decremented to zero during the last machine operation.

Address--Instructions--Mnemonic--Description
Location B1--B2--B3

```
200     CE  ØØ  03   DEC      DECREMENT LOCATION 300H
203     DØ  FB       BNE      BRANCH BACK TO 200H IF
                              LOCATION 300H WAS NOT ZERO
                              DURING LAST OPERATION
205     NEXT INSTRUCTION
```

Table 5-31. Op-Code - 10 ---- BPL.

Machine Language Instruction--BPL--"Branch Instruction"

Machine Language Op Code -------- 1Ø

Required Number of Bytes ------------ 2

Require Machine Time ----------------- 2 Cycles

Description: The BPL instruction, with the op code 1Ø, will cause the computer program to branch to a location that is dictated by the BPL instruction if the results of the last computer operation sets the N bit of the flag register to a "0". This instruction is very handy for branching to various computer routines, if the results of a BIT-test operation showed that bit 7 was a logic zero, in order to complete the computer's program objectives. The machine operation which is shown in the example below means that the computer will branch back to memory location 200, if the results of a previous BIT instruction showed that bit 7 of address location A001 was a "0". If bit 7 is a "0", the routine will stay in a closed loop until bit 7 becomes a logic one.

Address--Instructions--Mnemonic--Description
Location B1--B2--B3

```
200     2C Ø1  AØ   BIT       BIT TEST A001
203     1Ø FB       BMI       BRANCH BACK TO 200H IF
                              BIT 7 IS A "0"
```

Table 5-32. Op-Code - 50 ---- BVC.

Machine Language Instruction--BVC--"Branch Instruction"

Machine Language Op Code -------- 5Ø

Required Number of Bytes ------------ 2

Require Machine Time ----------------- 2 Cycles

Description: The BVC instruction, with the op code 5Ø, will cause the computer program to branch to a location that is dictated by the BVC instruction if the results of the last computer operation sets the V flag of the flag register to a "Ø". This instruction is very handy for branching to various computer routines, if the results of a BIT test operation showed that bit 6 was a logic 0. The machine operation which is shown in the example below means that the computer will branch back to memory location 200, if the results of a previous BIT instruction showed that bit 6 of address location A001 was a "0". If bit 6 is a "0", the routine will stay in a closed loop until bit 6 becomes a logic one.

Address--Instructions--Mnemonic--Description
Location B1--B2--B3

```
200     2C Ø1  AØ   BIT       BIT TEST A001
203     5Ø FB       BVC       BRANCH BACK TO 200H IF
                              BIT 6 IS A "0"
205     NEXT INSTRUCTION
```

Table 5-33. Op-code - 70 ---- BVS.

Machine Language Instruction--BVS--"Branch Instruction"

Machine Language Op Code -------- 70

Required Number of Bytes ------------ 2

Require Machine Time ----------------- 2 Cycles

Description: The BVS instruction, with the op code 70, will cause the computer program to branch to a location that is dictated by the BVS instruction if the results of the last computer operation sets the V flag of the flag register to a "1". This instruction is very handy for branching to various computer routines, if the results of a BIT-test operation showed that bit 6 was a logic one. The machine operation which is shown in the example below means that the computer will branch back to memory location 200, if the results of a previous BIT instruction showed that bit 6 of address location A001 was a "1". If bit 6 is a "1", the routine will stay in a closed loop until bit 6 becomes a logic zero.

Address--Instructions--Mnemonic--Description
Location B1--B2--B3

```
200    2C Ø1  AØ  BIT    BIT TEST A001
203    7Ø FB      BVC    BRANCH BACK TO 200H IF
                         BIT 6 is A "0"
205    NEXT INSTRUCTION
```

Table 5-34. Op-Code - CE ---- DEC.

Machine Language Instruction--DEC--"Decrement Memory"

Machine Language Op Code ------------------------CE

Required Number of Bytes -----------------------------3

Require Machine Time -------------------------6 Cycles

Description: The DEC instruction, with the op code CE, will decrement the contents of a specified memory location in the ram memory by 1 (One). This instruction is very handy for decrementing data in any ram memory location. The machine operation which is shown in the example below means that the computer will decrement the contents of memory location 0550 by 1 (One) when the microprocessor executes the instruction at location 200.

Address--Instructions--Mnemonic--Description
Location B1--B2--B3

```
200    CE  5Ø  Ø5  STA    DECREMENT 0550
                          BY 1 (ONE)
```

Table 5-35. Op-code - C6 ---- DEC Page ZERO.

Machine Language Instruction--DEC--"Decrement Memory, Zero Page"

Machine Language Op Code ---------------------------C6

Required Number of Bytes --------------------------------2

Require Machine Time ----------------------------5 Cycles

Description: The DEC instruction, with the op code C6, will decrement the contents of a specified memory location in page ZERO of the ram memory by 1 (One). This instruction is very handy for decrementing data in memory using a minimum amount of machine time and memory space. The machine operation which is shown in the example below means that the computer will decrement the contents of memory location 0050 by 1 (One) when the microprocessor executes the instruction at location 200.

Address--Instructions--Mnemonic--Description
Location B1--B2--B3

```
200    C6  5Ø    STA    DECREMENT 0050
                        BY 1 (ONE)
```

Table 5-36. Op-Code - 20 ---- JSR.

Machine Language Instruction--JSR--"Jump To Subroutine"

Machine Language Op Code -------- 20

Required Number of Bytes ----------- 3

Require Machine Time ---------------- 6 Cycles

Description: The JSR instruction, with the op code 20, will cause the computer program to jump to a subroutine location that is dictated by the JSR instruction and then return to the original program execution when the subroutine is completed. This instruction is very handy for calling up various computer routines in order to complete the computer's program objectives. The machine operation which is shown in the example below means that the computer will jump to a subroutine at memory location 430 when the microprocessor executes the instruction at location 200. After the subroutine is completed, the program will then continue on at memory location 203.

Address--Instructions--Mnemonic--Description
Location B1--B2--B3

200	2Ø 3Ø Ø4	JSR	JUMP TO SUBROUTINE AT 430H
203	NEXT PROGRAM INSTRUCTION		

Table 5-37. Op-Code - 4C ---- JMP.

Machine Language Instruction--JMP--"Jump To Location"

Machine Language Op Code -------- 4C

Required Number of Bytes ----------- 3

Require Machine Time ---------------- 3 Cycles

Description: The JMP instruction, with the op code 4C, will cause the computer program to jump to the memory location which is dictated by the JUMP instruction. This instruction is very handy for connecting various computer routines together in order to form a complete computer program. The machine operation which is shown in the example below means that the computer will jump to memory location 430 when the microprocessor executes the instruction at location 200.

Address--Instructions--Mnemonic--Description
Location B1--B2--B3

200	4C 3Ø Ø4	JMP	JUMP TO LOCATION 430H

Table 5-38. Op-code - AD ---- LDA.

Machine Language Instruction--LDA--"Load The Accumulator"

Machine Language Op Code -------- AD

Required Number of Bytes ----------- 3

Require Machine Time ---------------- 4 Cycles

Description: The LDA instruction, with the op code AD, will load the hex data which is in a specified memory location into the accumulator. This instruction is very handy when you want to work with data that has been placed into a given memory location by another program operation. The machine operation which is shown in the example below means that the computer will load the hex data from memory location 330 into the accumulator when the microprocessor executes the instruction at location 200.

Address--Instructions--Mnemonic--Description
Location B1--B2--B3

200	AD 3Ø Ø3	LDA	PLACE THE DATA IN LOCATION 330H IN THE ACCUMULATOR

NOTE: Low address byte first and high address byte second of address 330H.

Table 5-39. Op-Code - A9 ---- LDA.

Machine Language Instruction--LDA--"Load The Accumulator"

Machine Language Op Code -------- A9

Required Number of Bytes ----------- 2

Require Machine Time ---------------- 2 Cycles

Description: The LDA instruction, with the op code A9, will load the hex data which is in the next memory location into the accumulator. This instruction is very handy when you want to work with a specific hex number. The machine operation which is shown in the example below means that the computer will load the hex number 30 into the accumulator when the microprocessor executes the instruction at location 200.

Address--Instructions--Mnemonic--Description
Location B1--B2--B3

200	A9 3Ø	LDA	PLACE 30H IN ACCUMULATOR

Table 5-40. Op-Code - 8D ---- STA.

Machine Language Instruction--STA--"Store the Accumulator"

Machine Language Op Code -------- 8D

Required Number of Bytes ------------ 3

Require Machine Time ----------------- 4 Cycles

Description: The STA instruction, with the op code 8D, will store the contents of the accumulator into a specified memory location. This instruction is very handy for storing data into a specified location in memory to perform a required function. The machine operation which is shown in the example below means that the computer will store the contents of the accumulator into memory location 501 when the microprocessor executes the instruction at location 200.

Address--Instructions--Mnemonic--Description
Location B1--B2--B3

200	8D 01 05	STA	STORE THE ACCUMULATOR INTO LOCATION 501H

Table 5-41. Op-Code - 85 ---- STA.

Machine Language Instruction--STA--"Store the Accumulator"

Machine Language Op Code -------- 85

Required Number of Bytes ------------ 2

Require Machine Time ----------------- 3 Cycles

Description: The STA instruction, with the op code 85, will store the contents of the accumulator into a specified memory location in page ZERO of the ram memory. This instruction is very handy for storing data in memory using a minimum amount of machine time and memory space. The machine operation which is shown in the example below means that the computer will store the contents of the accumulator into memory location 0050 when the microprocessor executes the instruction at location 200.

Address--Instructions--Mnemonic--Description
Location B1--B2--B3

200	85 50	STA	STORE THE ACCUMULATOR INTO LOCATION 0050H

The explanations of the preceding 6502 machine-langauge instructions are not complete in-depth explanations. The explanations only indicate how these instructions are used in this chapter to create the intended end results. A complete machine-language presentation of the 6502 op-codes is presented in Chapter 13.

Continuity Checks and Resistance Measurements

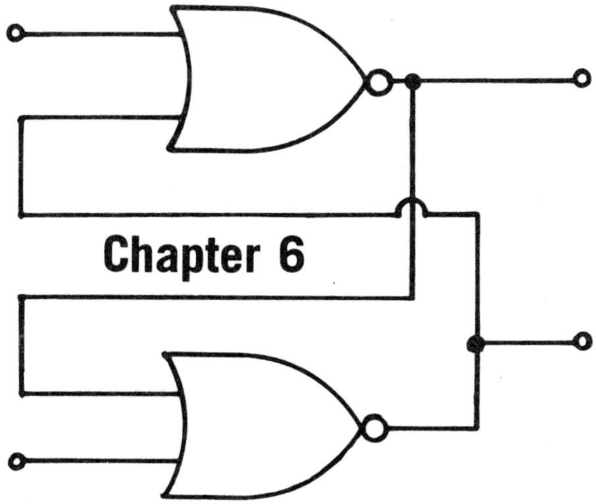

Chapter 6

Resistance measurements and continuity checks are a very important area of production testing. Just about everything that has something to do with electricity needs a continuity check or resistance measurement sometime during its trip down the production line. You may need only a continuity check at some point during the production of the product to verify that the production process is functioning correctly. But when the product item is finished, you will need a complete resistance measurement to verify the product's integrity. These continuity checks and resistance measurements will add to the cost of production. So, the faster you can do the measurements, the lower the cost of producing the item. It is the job of the test-system engineer to secure faster continuity checks and resistance measurements while maintaining or improving the accuracy of these measurements. In this chapter you will be given examples of several fast and accurate methods of making these continuity checks and resistance measurements.

CONTINUITY CHECKS

A continuity check only verifies that a complete electrical circuit exists between two points. It does not show whether the electrical path is a high resistance or low resistance, but only that an electrical current path for electricity does exist. Most of the time a continuity check will completely satisfy an in-process type of production line resistance measurement.

A continuity test is really not too involved. Why not just use some type of ohmmeter and two test leads to make the electrical contacts to the two points that need checked? Well that is ok if the production rate is not too high or only a few electrical circuits need checked. But, if you are operating a high volume production line or producing a product which has several electrical paths which need to be checked, you can easily pay for a continuity inspection system in a very short time with the labor savings from using an automated continuity tester. We will investigate two methods of continuity testing using a single-board computer which should solve most of the continuity testing problems you will encounter in production.

A continuity test circuit is shown in Fig. 6-1 which is simple and does a very good job. The circuit uses a 4049 hex inverter IC which detects the voltage drop through the 1 k resistor R1. If you are using a five volt power supply, the resistance value of resistor R1 should be at least ten times larger than the resistance of the circuit being tested. Two other factors which determine the resistance value of resistor R1 are the maximum current which can be handled by the circuit being tested and the current that is available from the power supply for the continuity test. The resistance value of R1 must limit the

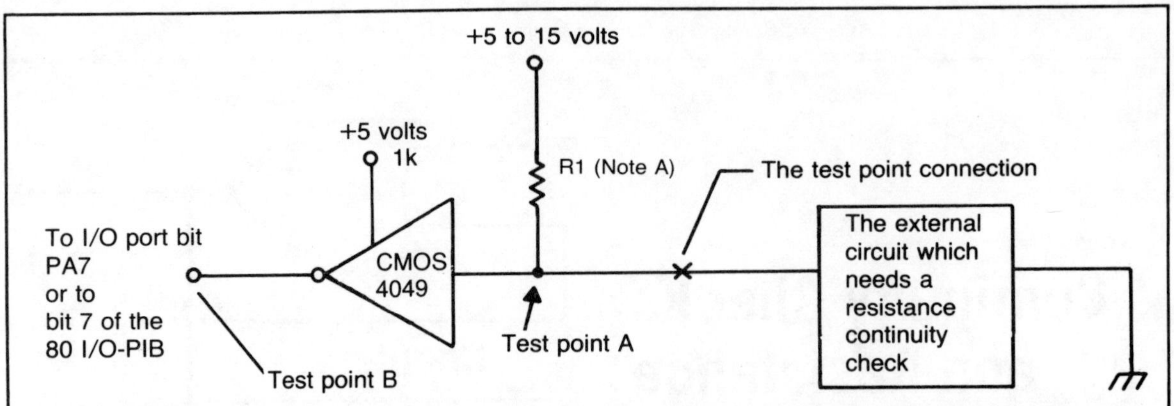

NOTE: The resistor R1 determines what dc current will flow through the external circuit which is receiving the continuity check. The current that flows through the external circuit must be enough to cause a voltage drop across R1 that leaves no more than 1 volt at test point A. If the external circuit has the required continuity, a logic one will be generated at test point B.

Fig. 6-1. The dc-continuity test circuit.

two dc currents to a safe value while permitting a voltage drop across itself which will set up a voltage at test point A of no more than 0.5 volt. When a voltage at test point A is 0.5 volt or lower, the 4049 CMOS inverter circuit will generate a logic one signal at test point B. This logic one signal can then be used by a single-board computer to determine if the circuit is ok. If only one circuit is being tested in a manual-type situation, you can place a LED at test point B which will indicate a *go* or *no-go* condition.

If you have a production situation where you need several continuity checks in a very short period, naturally a single-board computer can do the job in very fine style. Table 6-1 and Table 6-2 show two program routines which can be used on the SYM-1 and KIM-1 to indicate if a continuity test is good or bad. Table 6-3 presents a program routine for the AIM-65 which will print-out on the system printer if the circuit continuity is good or bad. This AIM-65 program uses both BASIC and machine-language programming.

If you have a test sequence to run which will be measuring several different parameters which includes a continuity check, you can hook up a pushbutton as shown in Fig. 6-2 which can actually be used as a "push-to-test" button to start your test sequence. If the continuity check is not ok, the test sequence will simply not run when the push-to-test button is pressed. A customer is generally very impressed when he sees that the product that you are producing does not pass through the final test system if a ground bracket or something similar is not made correctly. A push-to-test program routine is shown in Tables 6-4 to 6-8 for each of the four computers that we have been using in this book.

AN EIGHT CIRCUIT CONTINUITY TEST SYSTEM PROGRAM

It is very easy to use a single-board computer like the SYM-1 and the AIM-65 as a continuity tester without making any modifications to the computer system at all. It is possible to use both of the PA and PB ports of a 6522 VIA to make a continuity test system which can test the continuity of eight independent circuits while also checking to see if there are any shorts between the independent circuits. This program is great for checking cables and small circuit boards.

The 6522 VIA uses pull-up resistors on all of the PA port lines. The pull-up resistors will give you a full logic one voltage on any of the PA I/O lines when they are in the input mode or when they are in the output mode and set to a logic one level. You can use the logic one voltage from the PA ports to drive your continuity checks. Since you have eight PA ports, you can check eight lines at once.

Figure 6-3 shows how to connect a cable or some other circuit system to the PA and PB ports so you can run the continuity check program. To secure the continuity check, set up all of the PA ports as input ports and set up all of the PB ports as output ports. The PA input ports will supply a +5 volts to all of the port lines which are connected to the PB ports through the external circuits. When you set all of the PB ports to a logic zero, all

Table 6-1. This Is a Continuity-Test Program which can be used with the Circuit in Fig. 6-1 with a SYM-1.

```
A. This is a continuity test program routine.
B. This program routine is written for a SYM-1
C. The program uses port bit PA7 as an input.

Address--Instructions--Mnemonic--Description
Location B1--B2--B3
200        A9  00         LDA
202        8D  03  A0     STA    MAKE PORT A AN INPUT PORT
205        2C  01  A0     BIT    BIT TEST LOCATION A001
208        10  03         BPL    IF PA7 IS A ZERO, BRANCH TO
                                 LOCATION 20D
20A        4C  10  02     JMP    IF PA7 IS A ONE, JUMP TO
                                 LOCATION 210
20D        4C  UU  UU     JMP    JUMP TO ROUTINE FOR A BAD TEST
210        UU  UU  UU            SEE NOTES

NOTES: A. "UU" means some unknown data that must be filled
in by the user at a later time.
       B. If the continuity test is ok, the program will
jump to location 210 where the next program routine should
start.
       C. If you are experimenting with this program, load
the BREAK instruction into locations 20D and 210. When the
program is executed, it will stop at location 20D for a bad
test and location 210 for a good test.
```

of the PA ports should also be zero because the PB ports will be placing a zero logic load on them. If any PA port bit is not zero, there is no continuity between that PA port bit and the corresponding PB port bit of the 6522 VIA. You can also set one of the PA-PB port bit sets to a logic one state and all other PA and PB port bits to a logic zero. If the PA-PB port set that is at logic one level goes to a logic zero, there is a short between the circuit elements somewhere in the circuit system that is being tested.

Two computer programs which will set up the SYM-1 and the AIM-65 to do multiple continuity checks are presented in Tables 6-9 and 6-10. The programs that are presented in Tables 6-11 and 6-12 will check for shorts between the different circuits paths of the system being tested. When all the programs are put together to make a complete test system, you will be able to check for circuit path continuity and inter-circuit shorts in a very short period of time.

The AIM-65 has only one 6522 VIA in the system, so you will only be able to test eight lines unless you add on some 6522 VIAs. The SYM-1 has the ability to use three 6522 VIA chips on the single-board systems, so you will be able to test a maximum of 23 circuit paths without adding any off-board items to the computer system. You will be pleasantly surprised with the speed and accuracy that can be achieved using the single-board computer to do a simple task such as continuity testing. There are two main points to consider about these testing methods. One point is that the 6522 VIA can only supply a dc current of about 0.6 mA per circuit path. The second point to remember is that your 6522 VIA can not drive a high capacity circuit load with any speed. If you are going to test any system in which the stray capacitances may be over 100 pF per circuit path, beware of the possible slow rise-times you may be generating with the 6522 VIA when switching from a logic zero to a logic one state.

Table 6-2. This Is a Continuity-Test Program which can be used with the Circuit in Fig. 6-1 with a KIM-1.

```
A. This is a continuity test program routine.
B. This program routine is written for a KIM-1
C. The program uses port bit PA7 as an input.

Address--Instructions--Mnemonic--Description
Location B1--B2--B3
200       A9  00         LDA
202       8D  01  17     STA    MAKE PORT A AN INPUT PORT
205       2C  00  17     BIT    BIT TEST LOCATION A001
208       10  03         BPL    IF PA7 IS A ZERO, BRANCH TO
                                LOCATION 20D
20A       4C  10  02     JMP    IF PA7 IS A ONE, JUMP TO
                                LOCATION 210
20D       4C  UU  UU     JMP    JUMP TO ROUTINE FOR A BAD TEST
210       UU  UU  UU            SEE NOTES

NOTES: A. "UU" means  some unknown data that must  be filled
in by the user at a later time.
       B. If the continuity  test is  ok,  the  program will
jump  to location 210 where the next program routine  should
start.
       C. If  you are  experimenting with this program, load
the  BREAK instruction into locations  20D and 210. When the
program is  executed, it will stop at location 20D for a bad
test and location 210 for a good test.
```

Table 6-3. This Is a Continuity-Test Program which can be used with the Circuit in Fig. 6-1 with an AIM-65.

```
A. This is a continuity test program for the  AIM-65 using a
small BASIC program with a USR (1) machine-language routine
B. Locate the BASIC  program in the lower  3K  of the 4K ram
by entering  3072 when the  AIM-65 requests the  MEMORY SIZE
for the BASIC program.
C. The USR (1) machine-language routine will start at 0FE0H

The machine  language routine  using  the AIM-65 disassembly
format.
OFE0  A9  LDA  #00
0FE2  8D  STA  A003
0FE5  2C  BIT  A001
0FE8  10  BPL  0FED
0FEA  4C  JMP  0FF3
OFED  A9  LDA  #00
0FEF  8D  STA  0FFF
```

Table 6-3. This Is a Continuity-Test Program which can be used with the Circuit in Fig. 6-1 with an AIM-65 (continued from page 84)

```
0FF2  60  RTS
0FF3  A9  LDA  #FF
0FF5  8D  STA  0FFF
0FF8  60  RTS
0FF9  00  BRK

THE AIM-65 BASIC PROGRAM  (LIMIT THE MEMORY SIZE TO 3072)

10 PRINT "CONTINUITY TEST"
20 POKE 04, 224: POKE 05, 15
30 X=USR (1): PRINT X
40 IF PEEK (4095)=255 THEN 100
50 PRINT "TEST IS BAD"
60 END
100 PRINT "TEST IS GOOD"
110 END
```

NOTES: A. Line 20 gives the BASIC program the starting point information for the USR (1) instruction. 224 is the decimal number for E0 (HEX) and 15 is the decimal number for 0F (HEX). Remember, the low address byte is first and the high address byte is second.

B. The program is started by the RUN command.

WINDOW COMPARATORS

Most of the testing problems that you will encounter in a production operation will be the go no-go type of tests. One of the most useful circuits that you can have in your arsenal of test circuit weapons to fight the go no-go problem is the window comparator circuit. This circuit is built around two operational-amplifier circuits which are arranged so they will turn off and on at specific voltage levels. You can adjust the two operational amplifiers so both amplifiers will put out a logic one signal when the same input signal to both amplifiers is in between two given voltage levels which forms the voltage window. The window comparator circuit can be used for a large number of applications some of which are checking resistance, pulse measurements, linear slope measurements, and a thermistor temperature-controller and so on.

The window comparator circuit, shown in Fig. 6-4, is designed to detect a voltage window which can be adjusted anywhere between 2.1 to 2.9 volts with a five volt supply voltage. The narrowest window voltage which can be reasonably detected is about .010 volts. The circuit uses a UA358 dual operational amplifier IC (U1A and U1B) which can operate from a single supply voltage source. The logic circuits are all CMOS chips, so you can use a supply voltage of 5 to 15 volts with this comparator circuit. The circuit is designed for a voltage window which is in the middle of the supply voltage range, but you can adjust the resistors RA, RB, RC, RD, RE, and RF to operate a voltage window about anywhere within the supply voltage range. You should stay about one-half volt away from the rail voltages.

The upper window-voltage limit is controlled by minipot RA and the lower voltage limit is controlled by minipot RB. When the input voltage is within the voltage window limits, both operational amplifiers will generate logic one output signals which are inverted by the two

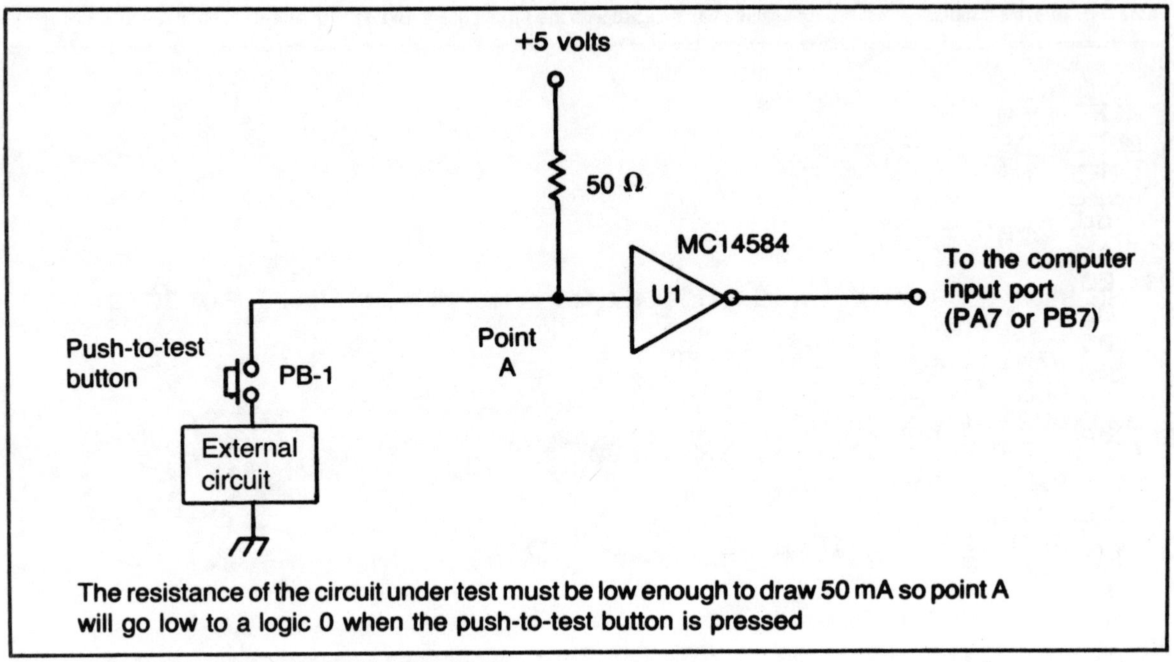

Fig. 6-2. The push-to-test continuity checking circuit.

Table 6-4. A Push-to-Start Program for the SYM-1.

```
A. This is a PUSH TO START program routine.
B. This program routine is written for a SYM-1
C. The program uses port bit PA7 as an input.

Address--Instructions--Mnemonic--Description
Location B1--B2--B3
200        A9   00         LDA
202        8D   03   A0    STA   MAKE PORT A AN INPUT PORT
205        2C   01   A0    BIT   BIT TEST LOCATION A001
208        10   FB         BPL   IF PA7 IS A ZERO, BRANCH BACK
                                 TO LOCATION 205
20A        UU   UU   UU          IF PA7 IS A ONE, GO ON WITH
                                 THE TEST SEQUENCE ROUTINE


NOTES: A. "UU" means  some unknown data that must  be filled
in  by the  user  at  a  later  time.  Location  20A is  the
starting point for the next test routine.
       B. If you are experimenting with  this program,  load
the  BREAK  instruction  (00)  into location 20A.  When  the
program  is executed, it  will  stop at  location 20A if the
continuity  check  for the PUSH TO  START  routine is  good.
```

Table 6-5. A Push-to-Start Program for the KIM-1.

```
A. This is a PUSH TO START program routine.
B. This program routine is written for a KIM-1
C. The program uses port bit PA7 as an input.

Address--Instructions--Mnemonic--Description
Location B1--B2--B3
200        A9  00        LDA
202        8D  01  17    STA   MAKE.PORT A AN INPUT PORT
205        2C  00  17    BIT   BIT TEST LOCATION 1700
208        10  FB        BPL   IF PA7 IS A ZERO, BRANCH BACK
                               TO LOCATION 205
20A        UU  UU  UU          IF PA7 IS A ONE, GO ON WITH
                               THE TEST SEQUENCE ROUTINE


NOTES: A. "UU" means some unknown data that must be filled
in by the user at a later time. Location 20A is the
starting point for the next test routine.
       B. If you are experimenting with this program, load
the BREAK instruction (00) into location 20A. When the
program is executed, it will stop at location 20A if the
continuity check for the PUSH TO START routine is good.
```

Table 6-6. A Push-to-Test Program for the AIM-65.

```
A. This is a PUSH TO TEST program for the AIM-65 using a
short BASIC program with a USR (1) machine language routine
B. Locate the BASIC program in the lower 3K of the 4K RAM
by entering 3072 when the AIM-65 requests the MEMORY SIZE
for the BASIC program.
C. The USR (1) machine language routine will start at 0FE0H

The machine - language routine using the AIM-65 disassembly
format.
OFE0  A9  LDA  #00
0FE2  8D  STA  A003
0FE5  2C  BIT  A001
0FE8  10  BPL  0FE5
0FEA  60  RTS

THE AIM-65 BASIC PROGRAM  (LIMIT THE MEMORY SIZE TO 3072)
```

Table 6-6. A Push-to-Test Program for the AIM-65 (continued from page 87).

```
10 PRINT "PUST START BUTTON"
20 POKE 04, 224: POKE 05, 15
30 X=USR (1): PRINT X
40 PRINT"CONTINUITY OK-START TEST SEQUENCE"
50 END
      (THE NEXT PROGRAM SEQUENCE WILL START AT LINE 50)
```

NOTES: A. Line 20 gives the BASIC program the starting point information for the USR (1) instruction. 224 is the decimal number for E0 (HEX) and 15 is the decimal number for 0F (HEX). Remember, the low address byte is first and the high address byte is second.

B. The program is started by the RUN command.

C. The next test instruction will start on line 50.

Table 6-7. A Push-to-Start Program for the AIM-65.

A. This is a PUSH TO START program routine.
B. This program routine is written for the AIM-65
C. The program uses port bit PB7 as an input.

```
Address--Instructions--Mnemonic--Description
Location B1--B2--B3
300      A9  00         LDA
302      8D  02  A0     STA   MAKE PORT B AN INPUT PORT
305      2C  00  A0     BIT   BIT TEST LOCATION A000
308      10  FB         BPL   IF PA7 IS A ZERO, BRANCH BACK
                              TO LOCATION 305
30A      UU  UU  UU           IF PA7 IS A ONE, GO ON WITH
                              THE TEST SEQUENCE ROUTINE
```

NOTES: A. "UU" means some unknown data that must be filled in by the user at a later time. Location 30A is the starting point for the next test routine.

B. If you are experimenting with this program, load the BREAK instruction (00) into location 30A. When the program is executed, it will stop at location 30A if the continuity check for the PUSH TO START routine is good.

Table 6-8. A Push-to-Test Program for the Model III.

```
A. This is a PUSH TO TEST program for  the Model III using a
BASIC  program with  a  USR (1)  instruction  and  a machine
language subroutine.
B. This program must be used with the 80-I/O-PIB.
C. The machine language routine will start at 7F00H.
D. Limit the Basic memory size to 32245. SEE NOTES

THE MODEL III MACHINE LANGUAGE ROUTINE
Address--Instructions--Mnemonic--Description
Location B1--B2--B3
7F00      F3              DI        DISABLE INTERRUPTS
7F01      3E   10         LD        LOAD 10H INTO REGISTER A
7F03      D3   EC         OUT       PLACE 10H IN PORT ECH
7F05      DB   6F         IN        PLACE CONTENTS OF PORT 6F
                                    INTO REGISTER A
7F07      32   FF   7F    LD        LOAD REGISTER A IN 7FFFH
7F0A      C9              RET       RETURN TO BASIC PROGRAM

THE MODEL III BASIC PROGRAM (LIMIT MEMORY SIZE TO 32245)

10 PRINT "PUSH START BUTTON TO TEST"
20 POKE 16526,00:POKE 16257,127
30 X=USR (1)
40 IF PEEK (32767)=255 THEN 100
50 GO TO 20
100 PRINT "CONTINUITY TEST IS OK - STARTING TEST"
110 END

NOTES: A.  Load the machine language routine in first  using
the DEBUG  program and  then  reset the machine and bring up
the BASIC program limiting the memory size to 32245.
       B.  Line 20 is  the subroutine RAM  starting location
data. See the Model III reference manual, page 191 and 192.
       C.  The BASIC  program  will loop  at line 50 back to
line 20 until the PUSH TO START push button is pressed.
```

inverter circuits of U2A and U2B (4584). The inverted output signals will both be logic zeros which are then applied to the two inputs of the NOR circuit of U3A. When both inputs to U3A are zeros, the output will be a logic one which indicates that the input voltage is within the window-voltage limits. If the input voltage is outside either one of the window-voltage limits, the output of one of the operational amplifiers will be a logic zero. That logic zero will be inverted to a logic one which will turn off the NOR circuit indicating that the input voltage is outside of the window voltage limits. The logic one signal will also be sent on to one of the input voltage high or input voltage low output pins by the noninverting buffer circuits U4A or U4B (4050). The construction of the

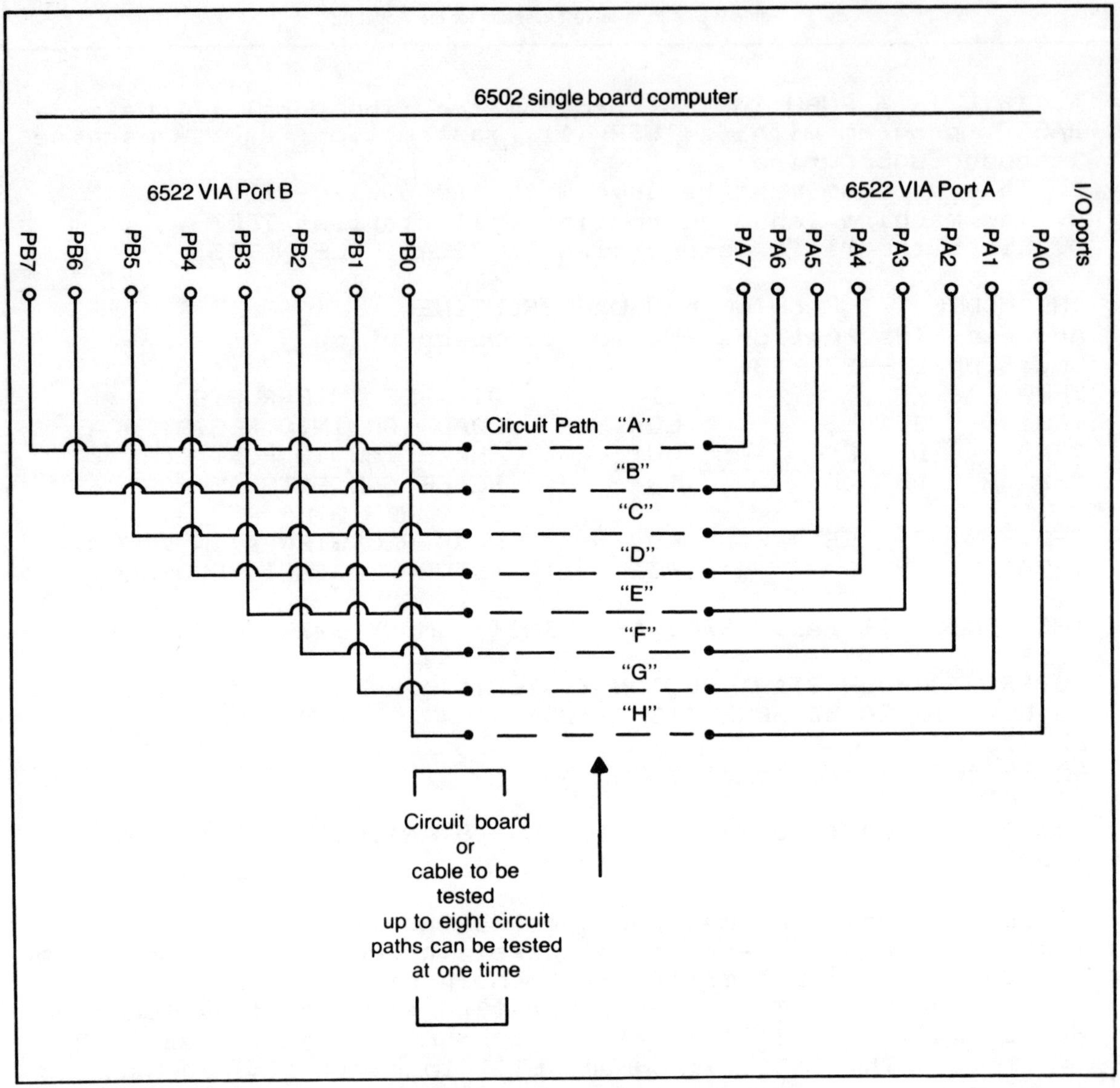

Fig. 6-3. The eight circuit continuity test schematic.

window comparator circuit is not critical and one circuit layout is shown in Fig. 6-5.

It is very easy to interface the voltage comparator to a single-board computer. The comparator circuits will give you one of three logic output signals which are high, low, or ok. These three logic signals can be connected directly to the input-port bit lines. Tables 6-13 to 6-16 present four computer programs that will run on either the KIM-1, the SYM-1, the AIM-65, or the Model III computer system. The KIM-1 and the SYM-1 programs are pure machine-language routines with locations set up for JUMPS to other routines that are dictated by the outcome of the voltage test. The locations that are set up are for four possible test conditions which are *voltage high, voltage low, voltage ok,* and *check test circuits* in case no logic signals are received if the circuitry fails. The AIM-65 and the Model III programs work about the same, but with these two computer systems, you can let the

BASIC program do your thinking and then print out voltage too high, voltage too low, voltage ok, or check test circuits. All our programs assume that your voltage comparator circuit is connected and supplying the logic signals when the programs are executed. The four programs that are presented here are examples of how you can test the product and verify that your test is functioning at the same time.

Using the Window Comparator to Check Resistance

The window comparator's main objective is to inform you when the input voltage is at a given voltage level. If you connect two resistors as a voltage divider on the input, as shown in Fig. 6-6, you can set up the window comparator circuit to inform you when both resistors have the same resistance value. A standard resistor or a decade resistor box can be connected between the comparator input and ground and when an unknown resistance is connected between the input and the positive supply voltage which is equal to the standard resistance, the voltage at the input of the comparator will be one-half of the supply voltage. The window comparator circuit can be set up to detect that one-half supply voltage point plus whatever tolerance level you may wish to adjust into the test system. The test resistance can be about anything like a coil of wire, a heating element, or a resistor, because you are comparing the unknown test resistance with a known standard resistance in a voltage divider circuit which does not care about anything but dividing the voltage as per the values of resistance in the circuit and Ohm's law.

Using the resistance-checking window comparator

Table 6-9. An Eight Circuit Continuity Checking Program for the SYM-1.

```
A. This is a  continuity test program that  will  test  from
one to eight separate circuits at one time.
B. This program will run on a SYM-1.
C. This program  uses port PA as  an  input port and port PB
as an output port.

Address--Instructions--Mnemonic--Description
Location B1--B2--B3

200        A9  00          LDA
202        8D  03  A0      STA
205        A9  FF          LDA
207        8D  02  A0      STA
20A        A9  00          LDA
20C        8D  00  A0      STA
20F        A9  FF          LDA
211        2C  01  A0      BIT     TEST FOR ZEROS
214        F0  03          BEQ
216        4C  UU  UU      JMP     BAD TEST SUBROUTINE ADDRESS
219        4C  UU  UU      JMP     GOOD TEST SUBROUTINE ADDRESS

NOTES: A.  Any input port  bit  which is  not used  must  be
connected to the logic system ground.
       B.  UU  indicates  the next subroutine  address  data
which must be supplied by the user.
       C.  If you are going to experiment with this routine,
fill locations 216 and 219 with 00 to stop the program.
```

Table 6-10. An Eight Circuit Continuity Checking Program for the AIM-65.

```
A. This is a  test program that will test  from one to eight
separate circuits at one time.
B. This program will run on an 4K AIM-65 with BASIC.
C. This program uses  port PA as an  input  port and port PB
as an output port.

The  machine-language routine using  the AIM-65  disassembly
format.
0FC0    A9    LDA    #00
0FC2    8D    STA    A003
0FC5    A9    LDA    #FF
0FC7    8D    STA    A002
0FCA    2C    BIT    A001
0FCD    F0    BEQ    0FD5
0FCF    A9    LDA    #00
OFD1    8D    STA    0FFF
0FD4    60    RTS
0FD5    A9    LDA    #FF
0FD7    8D    STA    0FFF
0FDA    60    RTS

THE AIM-65 BASIC PROGRAM (LIMIT MEMORY SIZE TO 3072)

10 PRINT "EIGHT CIRCUIT CONTINUITY TEST"
20 POKE 04,192:POKE 05,15
30 X=USR (1): PRINT X
40 IF PEEK (4095)=255 THEN 100
50 PRINT "TEST BAD"
60 END
100 PRINT "TEST GOOD"
110 END

NOTE: A. Any  input  port  bit  which is not used  must be
connected to the logic system ground.
```

with one of the four computers that we are using in this book is not too different from what we did with the voltage-comparator circuit. The BASIC programs are a little different, so two new programs for the resistance window comparator circuit will be presented for the AIM-65 and the Model III. The same programs can be used for the SYM-1 and the KIM-1 that were used for the voltage comparator. Just make sure that you observe which port bits are used for the high and low resistance connections. They are the opposite of the high and low voltage comparator connections that were used in Fig. 6-4. The two new computer programs are presented in Tables 6-17 and 6-18.

The window comparator circuits that are shown in Figs. 6-4 and 6-6 can be built with very inexpensive components and the circuits will function accurately, but

Table 6-11. An Eight Circuit Test Program which will Check for Shorts between Circuit Elements with a SYM-1.

```
A. This is a  continuity test program that will  test one to
eight separate circuits at  one time for shorts  between the
circuit elements.
B. This program will run on a SYM-1.
C. This program uses port PA as an input port and port PB
as an output port.

Address--Instructions--Mnemonic--Description
Location B1--B2--B3

200       A9   00          LDA
202       8D   03   A0     STA
205       A9   FF          LDA
207       8D   02   A0     STA
20A       A9   80          LDA
20C       8D   00   A0     STA
20F       A9   80          LDA
211       2C   01   A0     BIT     TEST FOR ZEROS
214       F0   03          BEQ
216       UU   UU   UU     JMP     BAD TEST SUBROUTINE ADDRESS
219       UU   UU   UU     JMP     GOOD TEST SUBROUTINE ADDRESS

NOTES: A. Any  input port bit  which is not  used  must  be
connected to the logic system ground.
       B. UU  indicates  the  next  subroutine  address  data
which must be supplied by the user.
       C. The  program data that is in locations 20B and 210
chooses the circuit that  will be  checked for shorts to the
other  circuit lines. Program data for  circuit  8 (PA7)  is
given in the program  above and data for checking  the other
lines follows.
CIRCUIT 1 ---- 01
CIRCUIT 2 ---- 02
CIRCUIT 3 ---- 04
CIRCUIT 4 ---- 08
CIRCUIT 5 ---- 10
CIRCUIT 6 ---- 20
CIRCUIT 7 ---- 40
CIRCUIT 8 ---- 80
       D. In order to check all eight circuits,  the program
routine will have to  be repeated  eight times by connecting
the routines together with JUMP  instructions. If a  circuit
element  checks out bad,  jump to the  BAD TEST  routine and
terminate the  test sequence. If all eight circuit  routines
run  ok,  jump  to the GOOD  TEST subroutine after the  last
check is finished, and then set up for the next test.
       E.  If all of the connectors and other common circuit
elements  of the  system being tested  are connected to  the
test  system ground  or common point, the program  will also
check for shorts to ground.
```

Table 6-12. An Eight Circuit Test Program which will Check for Shorts between Circuit Elements with an AIM-65.

A. This is a test program that will test from one to eight separate circuits for shorts between the circuit elements.
B. This program will run on an 4K AIM-65 with BASIC.
C. This program uses port PA as an input port and port PB as an output port.

The machine-language routine using the AIM-65 disassembly format.

```
ØFCØ    A9    LDA    #ØØ
ØFC2    8D    STA    AØØ3
ØFC5    A9    LDA    #FF
ØFC7    8D    STA    AØØ2
ØFCA    A9    LDA    #8Ø
ØFCC    8D    STA    AØØØ
ØFCF    2C    BIT    AØØ1
ØFD2    FØ    BEQ    ØFDA
ØFD4    A9    LDA    #ØØ
OFD6    8D    STA    ØFFF
ØFD9    6Ø    RTS
ØFDA    A9    LDA    #FF
ØFDC    8D    STA    ØFFF
ØFDF    6Ø    RTS
```

THE AIM-65 BASIC PROGRAM (LIMIT MEMORY SIZE TO 3Ø72)

```
1Ø PRINT "TESTING FOR CIRCUIT ELEMENT SHORTS"
2Ø POKE Ø4,192:POKE Ø5,15
3Ø X=USR (1): PRINT X
4Ø IF PEEK (4Ø95)=255 THEN 1ØØ
5Ø PRINT "TEST BAD"
6Ø END
1ØØ PRINT "TEST GOOD"
11Ø END
```

NOTES: A. Any input port bit which is not used must be connected to the logic system ground.

B. The program data that is in location ØFCB chooses the circuit that will be checked for shorts to the other circuit lines. Program data for circuit 8 is given in the program above and data for checking the other lines follows.

CIRCUIT 1 --- Ø1
CIRCUIT 2 --- Ø2
CIRCUIT 3 --- Ø4
CIRCUIT 4 --- Ø8

CIRCUIT 5 --- 10
CIRCUIT 6 --- 20
CIRCUIT 7 --- 40
CIRCUIT 8 --- 80

C. In order to check all eight circuits, the program routine will have to be repeated eight times by connecting the BASIC program routines together and POKING the new circuit testing data into location ØFCB for each routine. If a circuit element checks out bad, go to the BAD TEST routine and terminate the test sequence. If all eight routines run ok, go to the GOOD TEST routine after the last check is finished, and then set up for the next test.

D. If all of the connectors and other common circuit elements of the system being tested are connected to the test system ground or common point, the program will also check for shorts to ground.

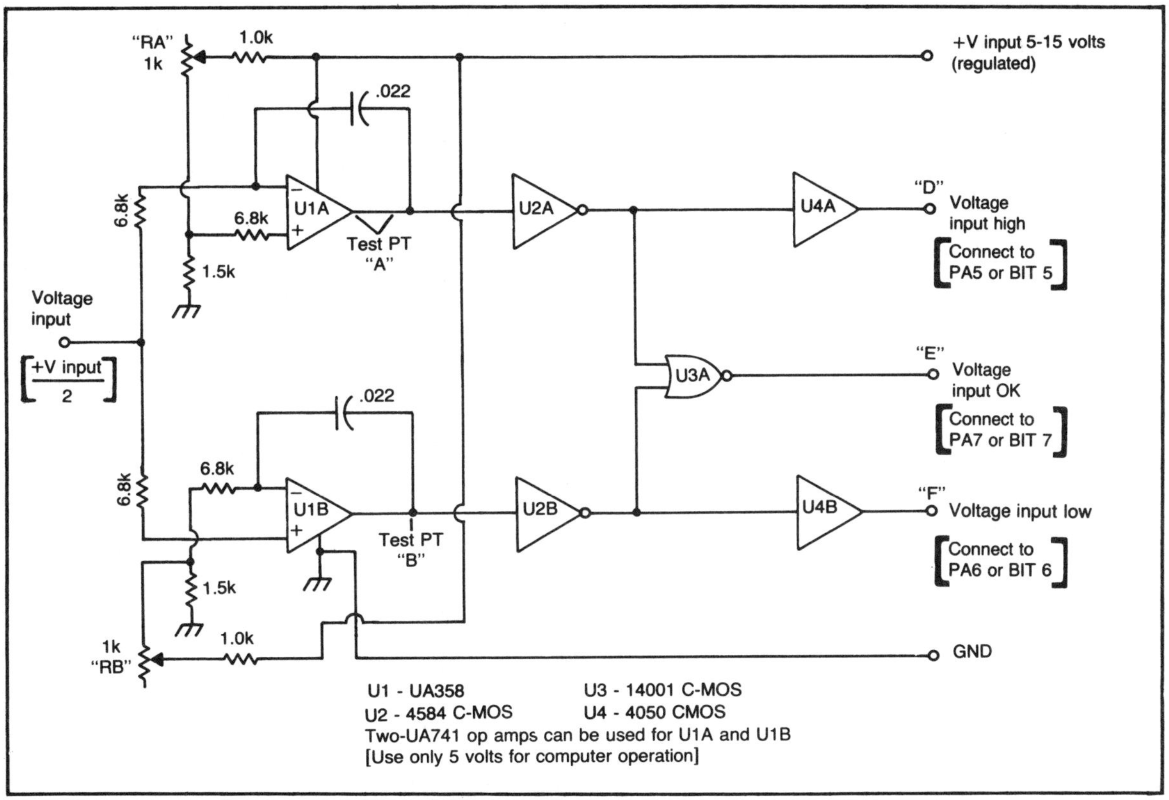

Fig. 6-4. The voltage-window comparator circuit schematic.

Fig. 6-5. The voltage comparator circuit.

Table 6-13. A Voltage-Comparator Program for the KIM-1.

```
A. This program will  interface  the voltage  comparator  of
Fig. 6-4  to a KIM-1 single board computer.
B. This program uses PA6, PA7, and PB7 as inputs.

Address--Instructions--Mnemonic--Description
Location B1--B2--B3
200        A9  00          LDA
202        8D  03   17     STA        MAKE PORT B AN INPUT PORT
205        8D  01   17     STA        MAKE PORT A AN INPUT PORT
208        2C  02   17     BIT        TEST PORT B
208        10  03          BPL        BRANCH IF PA7 IS ZERO
20D        UU  UU   UU     JMP        JUMP TO NEW LOCATION IF
                                      PB7 IS A LOGIC ONE FOR
                                      VOLTAGE TEST OK.
210        2C  00   17     BIT        TEST PORT A
213        50  03          BVC        BRANCH IF PA6 IS ZERO
215        UU  UU   UU     JMP        JUMP TO NEW LOCATION IF
                                      PA6 IS A LOGIC ONE FOR
                                      VOLTAGE HIGH
218        2C  00   17     BIT        TEST PORT A
21B        10  03          BPL        BRANCH IF PA7 IS A ZERO
21D        UU  UU   UU     JMP        JUMP TO NEW LOCATION IF
                                      PA7 IS A LOGIC ONE FOR
                                      VOLTAGE LOW
220         START A ROUTINE TO THE STOP TEST SYSTEM  AND CHECK
THE TEST CIRCUITS. SEE NOTES.

NOTES:  A. If  all  of  the  test circuits are  working,  you
should   never  reach   location   220.   If   location  220  is
reached, you  are not generating  any   logic one  signals in
your test circuits.
        B. Connect PB7 to the voltage OK terminal.
        C. Connect PA6 to the voltage high terminal.
        D. Connect PA7 to the voltage low termainal.
        E.  Make sure that your input  voltage is  connected
and stable before you execute this program.
```

Table 6-14. A Voltage-Comparator Program for the SYM-1.

```
A. This program will  interface  the voltage  comparator  of
Fig. 6-4  to a SYM-1 single board computer.
B. This program uses PA6, PA7, and PB7 as inputs.



Address--Instructions--Mnemonic--Description
Location B1--B2--B3
200         A9   00          LDA
202         8D   02   A0     STA       MAKE PORT B AN INPUT PORT
205         8D   03   A0     STA       MAKE PORT A AN INPUT PORT
208         2C   00   A0     BIT       TEST PORT B
208         10   03          BPL       BRANCH IF PA7 IS ZERO
20D         UU   UU   UU     JMP       JUMP TO NEW LOCATION IF
                                       PB7 IS A LOGIC ONE FOR
                                       VOLTAGE TEST OK.
210         2C   01   A0     BIT       TEST PORT A
213         50   03          BVC       BRANCH IF PA6 IS ZERO
215         UU   UU   UU     JMP       JUMP TO NEW LOCATION IF
                                       PA6 IS A LOGIC ONE FOR
                                       VOLTAGE HIGH
218         2C   01   A0     BIT       TEST PORT A
21B         10   03          BPL       BRANCH IF PA7 IS A ZERO
21D         UU   UU   UU     JMP       JUMP TO NEW LOCATION IF
                                       PA7 IS A LOGIC ONE FOR
                                       VOLTAGE LOW
220          START A ROUTINE TO THE STOP TEST SYSTEM  AND CHECK
THE TEST CIRCUITS. SEE NOTES.



NOTES:  A. If  all  of  the  test circuits are  working,  you
should   never  reach  location  220.  If  location  220  is
reached, you  are not generating  any  logic one  signals in
your test circuits.
        B. Connect PB7 to the voltage OK terminal.
        C. Connect PA6 to the voltage high terminal.
        D. Connect PA7 to the voltage low termainal.
        E. Make sure that your input  voltage is  connected
and stable before you execute this program.
```

Table 6-15. A Voltage-Comparator Program for the AIM-65.

```
A.   This program  will  interface  the  voltage  comparator
circuit of Fig. 6-4 to a 4K AIM-65 with BASIC.
B.   This program uses Port A as an input port.

The machine-language routine using the  AIM-65 disassembley
format.

0FC0 A9 LDA #00
0FC2 8D STA A003
0FC5 AD LDA A001
0FC8 8D STA 0FFF
0FCB 60 RTS
0FCC 00 BRK

THE AIM-65 BASIC PROGRAM (LIMIT MEMORY SIZE TO 3072)

10 PRINT "CHECKING VOLTAGE COMPARATOR"
20 POKE 04,192: POKE 05, 15
30 X=USR (1) : PRINT X
40 IF PEEK (4095)=32 THEN 100
50 IF PEEK (4095)=64 THEN 150
60 IF PEEK (4095)=128 THEN 200
70 PRINT "CHECK TEST CIRCUITS"
100 PRINT "VOLTAGE CHECK LOW"
110 END
150 PRINT "VOLTAGE CHECK HIGH"
160 END
200 PRINT "VOLTAGE CHECK OK"
210 END

NOTES:  A.  If  all  of  the test  circuit are working,  you
should never reach line 70.  If line  70  is printed, you're
test circuits are not generating any logic ONE pulses.
        B. Connect PA7 to voltage OK terminal.
        C. Connect PA6 to the voltage high terminal.
        D. Connect PA5 to the voltage low terminal.
        E. Make sure that  your input  voltage is connected
and stable before you execute this program.
        F. All unused  input  port bits  must  be tied to  a
logic system ground point.
```

Table 6-16. A Voltage-Comparator Program for the Model III.

```
A.  This is a  program  for the  Model  III  using  a  BASIC
program with  a USR  (1) instruction and  a machine-language
subroutine which will interface with the voltage  comparator
circuit of Fig. 6-4.
B.  This program must be used with the 80-I/O-PIB.
C.  The machine-language routine will start at 7F00H.
D.  Limit the BASIC memory size to 32245. SEE NOTES

THE MODEL III MACHINE LANGUAGE ROUTINE
Address--Instructions--Mnemonic--Description
Location B1--B2--B3
7F00      F3              DI       DISABLE INTERRUPTS
7F01      3E  10          LD       LOAD 10H INTO REGISTER A
7F03      D3  EC          OUT      PLACE 10H IN PORT ECH
7F05      DB  6F          IN       PLACE CONTENTS OF PORT 6F
                                   INTO REGISTER A
7F07      32  FF  7F      LD       LOAD REGISTER A IN 7FFFH
7F0A      C9              RET      RETURN TO BASIC PROGRAM

THE MODEL III BASIC PROGRAM (LIMIT MEMORY SIZE TO 32245)

10 PRINT "CHECKING VOLTAGE COMPARATOR"
20 POKE 16526,00:POKE 16257,127
30 X=USR (1)
40 IF PEEK (32767)=32 THEN 100
50 IF PEEK (32767)=64 THEN 150
60 IF PEEK (32767)=128 THEN 200
70 PRINT "CHECK TEST CIRCUITS"
100 PRINT "VOLTAGE CHECK IS LOW"
110 END
150 PRINT "VOLTAGE CHECK IS HIGH"
160 END
200 PRINT "VOLTAGE CHECK IS OK"
210 END

NOTES: A. Load  the machine-language routine in first using
the  DEBUG program and then  reset the  machine and bring up
the BASIC program limiting the memory size to 32245.
       B. Line 20  is  the subroutine  ram starting location
data. See the Model III reference manual, page 191 and 192.
       C.  If  all of the test  circuits  are  working,  you
should never reach line  70. If  line 70 is  printed, you're
test circuits are not generating any logic ONE pulses.
```

Table 6-16. A Voltage-Comparator Program for the Model III (continued from page 99).

```
        B. Connect the input bit 7 to voltage OK terminal.
        C.  Connect  the input  bit  6  to  the  voltage high
terminal.
        D. Connect  the  input  bit  5  to  the  voltage  low
terminal.
        E. Make  sure that your  input  voltage is  connected
and stable before you execute this program.
        F.  All unused input  bits  must  be connected  to  a
logic zero or grounded.
```

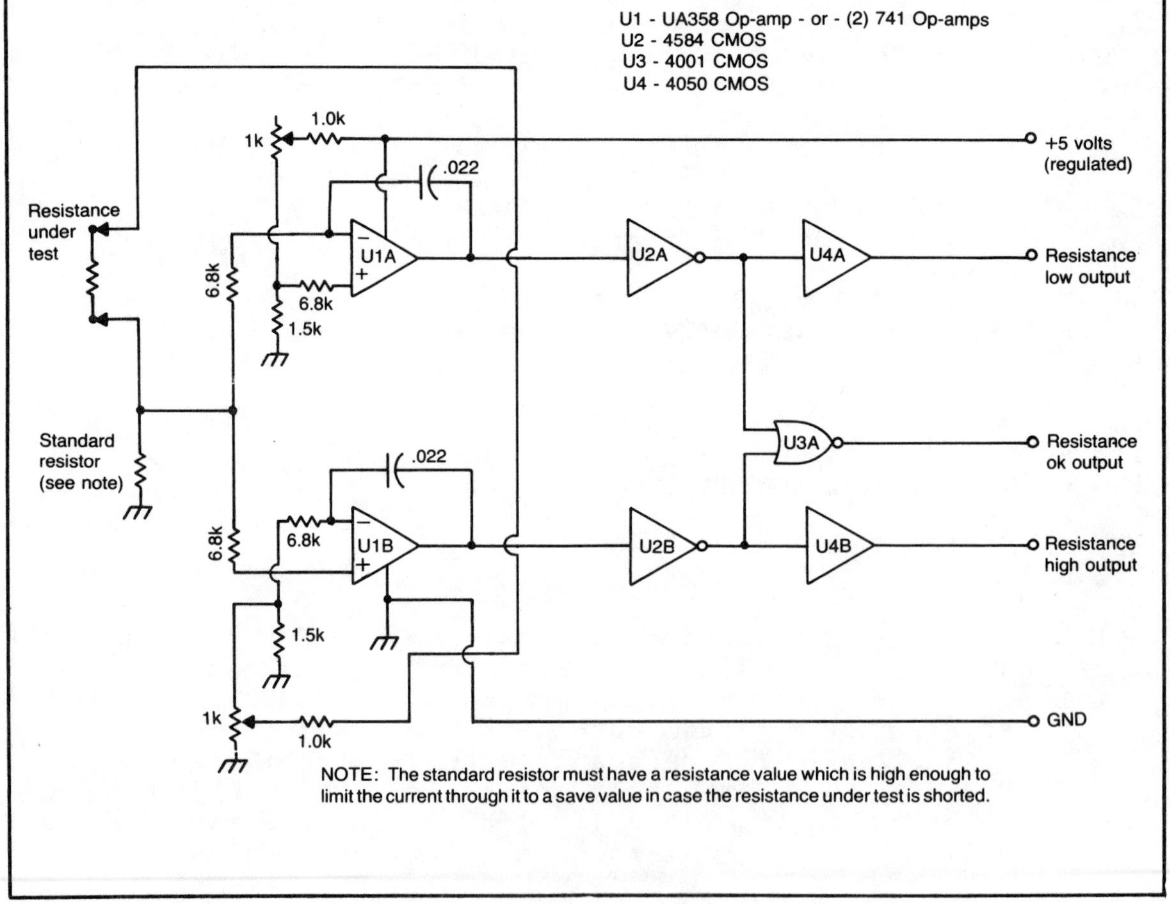

Fig. 6-6. A voltage-comparator circuit designed for checking resistance.

Table 6-17. A Resistance-Comparator Program for the AIM-65.

A. This is a program that will interface the resistance comparator circuit of Fig. 6.6 to a 4K AIM-65 with BASIC.
B. This program uses Port A as an input port.
C. Limit the BASIC memory size to 3072.

The machine-language routine using the AIM-65 disassembly format.

```
0FC0  A9  LDA  #00
0FC2  8D  STA  A003
0FC5  AD  LDA  A001
0FC8  8D  STA  0FFF
0FCB  60  RTS
```

THE AIM-65 BASIC PROGRAM (LIMIT MEMORY SIZE TO 3072)

```
10 PRINT "CHECKING RESISTANCE"
20 POKE 04,192: POKE 05,15
30 X-USR (1) : PRINT X
40 IF PEEK (4095) = 32 THEN 100
50 IF PEEK (4095) = 64 THEN 150
60 IF PEEK (4095)=128 THEN 200
70 PRINT "CHECK TEST CIRCUITS"
100 PRINT "RESISTANCE HIGH"
110 END
150 PRINT "RESISTANCE LOW"
160 END
200 PRINT "RESISTANCE OK"
210 END
```

NOTES: A. If all of the test circuit are working, you should never reach line 70. If line 70 is printed, you're test circuits are not generating any logic ONE pulses.
B. Connect PA7 to the resistance OK terminal.
C. Connect PA6 to the resistance low terminal.
D. Connect PA5 to the resistance high terminal.
E. Make sure that your input voltage divider is connected and the input voltage is stable before you execute this program.
F. All unused input port bits must be tied to a logic system ground point.

Table 6-18. A Resistance-Comparator Program for the Model III.

A. This is a program for the Model III (16K) using a BASIC program with a USR (1) instruction and a machine language subroutine which will interface to the resistance comparator circuit of Fig. 6-6.
B. This program must be used with the 80-I/O-PIB.
C. The machine-language routine will start at 7F00H.
D. Limit the BASIC memory size to 32245. SEE NOTES

THE MODEL III MACHINE-LANGUAGE ROUTINE

```
Address--Instructions--Mnemonic--Description
Location B1--B2--B3
7F00     F3              DI      DISABLE INTERRUPTS
7F01     3E  10          LD      LOAD 10H INTO REGISTER A
7F03     D3  EC          OUT     PLACE 10H IN PORT ECH
7F05     DB  6F          IN      PLACE CONTENTS OF PORT 6F
                                 INTO REGISTER A
7F07     32  FF  7F      LD      LOAD REGISTER A IN 7FFFH
7F0A     C9              RET     RETURN TO BASIC PROGRAM
```

THE MODEL III BASIC PROGRAM (LIMIT MEMORY SIZE TO 32245)

```
10 PRINT "CHECKING RESISTANCE"
20 POKE 16526,00:POKE 16257,127
30 X=USR (1)
40 IF PEEK (32767)=32 THEN 100
50 IF PEEK (32767)=64 THEN 150
60 IF PEEK (32767)=128 THEN 200
70 PRINT "CHECK TEST CIRCUITS"
100 PRINT "RESISTANCE CHECK IS HIGH"
110 END
150 PRINT "RESISTANCE CHECK IS LOW"
160 END
200 PRINT "RESISTANCE CHECK IS OK"
210 END
```

NOTES: A. Load the machine-language routine in first using the DEBUG program and then reset the machine and bring up the BASIC program limiting the memory size to 32245.

B. Line 20 is the subroutine ram starting location data. See the Model III reference manual, page 191 and 192.

C. If all of the test circuits are working, you should never reach line 70. If line 70 is printed, you're test circuits are not generating any logic ONE pulses.

B. Connect the input bit 7 to resistance OK terminal.

C. Connect the input bit 6 to the resistance lowterminal.

D. Connect the input bit 5 to the resistance high terminal.

E. Make sure that your input voltage divider is connected and the voltage is stable before you execute this program.

F. All unused input bits must be connected to a logic zero or grounded.

G. The machine-language routine could also be poked into memory if you do not have a DEBUG program.

then they are a bit slow and cannot be used where high speed comparisons are required. By slow, I mean that the two circuits cannot function in nanoseconds and should not be used where the comparison times are shorter than one-half millisecond. A faster window comparator circuit which can function with comparison times as short as 100 nanoseconds is presented in Chapter 11.

CONCLUSION

The window comparators presented in this chapter can function very nicely as go no-go test circuits. You must keep the fact in mind that they are only as accurate as you make them. The temperature considerations for the parts that are used to build the comparators and the resistance standards that are used for the comparison must be closely observed if close tolerance measurements are going to be attempted. It would be very useful to draw some graphs representing the various comparator testing characteristics, such as window drift, tolerance drift, standard resistance value drift, of the window comparator versus the complete range of ambient temperatures in which it must function. Remember, when it comes to test circuits, no surprises are the best surprises.

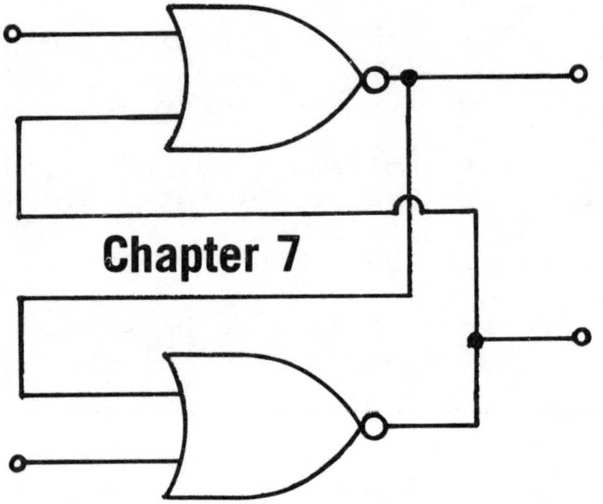

Chapter 7

Interfacing Ac and Dc Bridge Circuits

You can only do so much testing by measuring dc and ac voltages and currents. When it comes time to measure other electrical quantities, such as resistance, inductance, and capacitance, the test systems engineer will need to resort to more advanced testing methods which will characterize the component in question by securing the required technical data. The basic circuit that is used to secure this type of technical data is called the *bridge circuit*. The theory of the bridge circuit can vary from simple to very complicated. In this chapter we will assume that you have a basic idea of what a bridge is, how it works, and continue on from there.

Dc and ac bridge circuits have been used in the electrical world for about the last 125 years or so. Bridge circuits can also be used in electronic functions other than just testing resistance, inductance, and capacitance. The object of this chapter is to demonstrate the use of a bridge circuit with a single-board computer.

Bridge circuits usually function with very low currents and voltages while the single-board computers require the use of logic ones and zeros at a level of five volts and zero volts (respectively) which does not make too good of a match up. So, we will have to build some type of amplifier circuit to increase the voltages and currents and then build a detector circuit to tell the computer when the bridge circuit is in a *null* condition by generating a logic one or zero to indicate the given condition. All of the test circuits that will be described in this chapter will have one common function which is to indicate when the bridge circuit is in the required null condition. The circuits will not tell you if you are above or below the null point, but only that you are in or out of the null condition of the bridge. You will be able to adjust the circuits to indicate different levels of the null point so you can detect a specific null point plus or minus a given percentage. When you use these bridge circuits in a high-speed test system with a single-board computer, you will be able to secure highly accurate and expedient test measurements. The detection circuits are fast enough that, if you include a null meter in your system, the null meter's needle will not have time to indicate the null condition because the detection circuits will have already told the single-board computer that the null condition is okay and the computer will have started the next test function.

In this chapter we will only discuss a few typical bridge circuit applications, but it will be very easy for you to expand these circuit's applications with a little technical understanding and ingenuity.

INTERFACING TO A DC BRIDGE CIRCUIT

The bridge circuit that is shown in Fig. 7-1 is used to measure dc resistance values. The actual bridge circuit is made up of resistances R1, R2, R_x, and R_s which are connected in the form of a rectangle. Test point A is

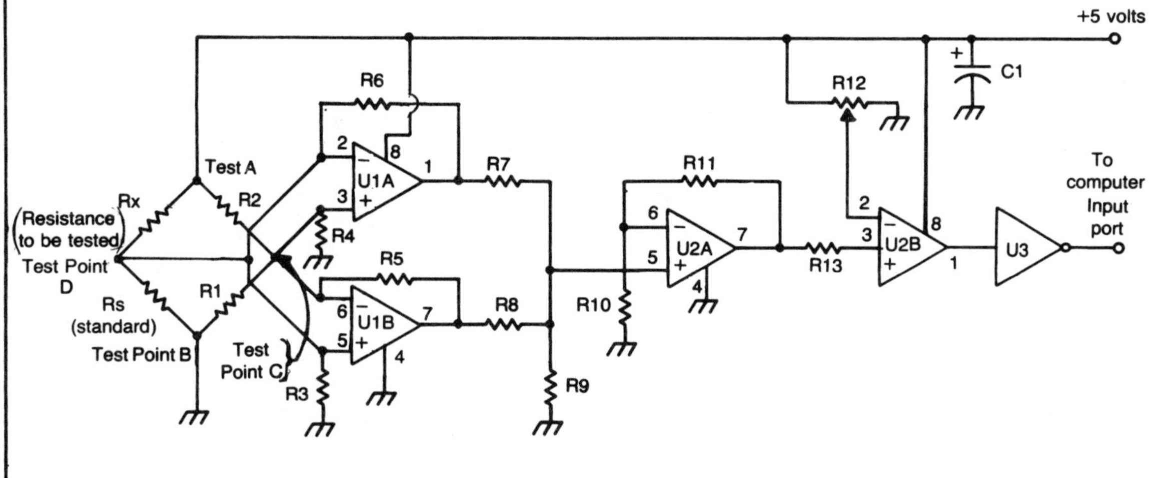

Parts List for the dc bridge amplifier and detector circuit

Rx - Resistance to be tested
Rs - Standard resistance value
R1, R2, R13 - 1k resistors (matched as close as possible)
R3, R4, R5, R6, R11 - 100k resistors
R7, R8 - 4.7k resistor
R9 - 1.5k resistor
R10 - 10k resistor
R12 - 5k trim pot
U1, U2 - LM 358 Op-amp
U3 - 4584 CMOS
C1 - 470 μF

Fig. 7-1. The dc bridge-amplifier circuit.

where the +V voltage is applied to the circuit, and test point B is where the bridge is connected to the ground or common circuit point. Resistors R1 and R2 are chosen so their resistances are equal or as close to equal as you can obtain. Resistor R_s is the *standard* resistor which is the resistance that you are comparing R_x to. R_x is the resistor under test which is an unknown quantity. Since resistor R1 and R2 are equal, the voltage at test point C will be exactly one-half of the +V voltage. If the resistance of the unknown resistance R_x is equal to the resistance of the standard resistor R_s, the voltage at test point D will be equal to one-half of the +V voltage. Now if both voltages at test point C and D are equal, the outputs of both op amps (U1A and U1B) will be zero which will indicate that the bridge circuit is in a null condition. The null condition will tell you that R_x and R_s are equal resistances.

When the R_x and R_s resistances are not equal, the voltage at test point D will no longer be one-half of the +V voltage because of the different voltage drops across the R_x and R_s resistances. The voltage difference that will exist between test points C and D will be detected by the op-amps and one of them will increase its output voltage. The increased output voltage will be amplified by op amp U2A and applied to the noninverting input of op amp U2B, which is a voltage detector circuit. If the voltage at pin 3 of op amp U2B is higher than the voltage at pin 2, the output of U2B will go high. If the voltage at pin 3 is lower than pin 2, the op amp's output will go low. U3 is a 4584 CMOS Schmitt trigger inverter which will take out any noise or slow rise and fall times from the op-amp circuits and permit easy connection to the input port of the single-board computer.

In a nutshell, the operation of the circuit can be described as generating a logic one if the bridge circuit is in a null condition or generating a logic zero if the bridge circuit is not in a null condition. Trim pot R12 is used to control the voltage-detector circuit's trip point. By setting the trip point low, you can detect a very sharp null point, and by setting the trip point high, you will detect a wide null point. The trip-point setting can be used to control a given amount of tolerance on each side of the standard resistance, such as testing for the standard resistance value plus or minus 10 percent.

AC BRIDGE CIRCUITS AND AC SINE-WAVE SOURCES

Ac bridge circuits are much more complicated than dc bridge circuits because you are dealing with many more variables than you are with dc bridge circuits. The variables that are in your ac bridge circuits do not really cause a lot of trouble until your ac frequencies go into the high audio frequency range and on into the rf frequency range. The ac bridge circuits that are described in this chapter can be used at frequencies between 60 and 1500 Hz quite easily. However, if you try and measure high inductances or low capacitance values, the situation will become a bit tricky. The best instructor on bridge circuits is experience, so, get out the experimenter's boards and go to it.

In order to experiment with an ac bridge circuit, you will need a sine-wave generator. There are three ways to secure a sine-wave signal. Way number one is to go out and buy a sine-wave generator. Way number two is to build a sine-wave generator such as the one shown in Fig. 7-2. Way number three is to simply use the 60 Hz sine wave frequency that is available from your friendly power company as shown in Fig. 7-3. If you are going to use an ac bridge circuit, you will need an ac signal from some source, so you might as well decide which method you intend to use.

Figure 7-3 is quite simple and does a fine job of giving you a 60-Hz sine wave which is variable between about 6.3 volts and zero volts depending upon the load that the bridge circuits place on it. Do not use this sine-wave signal source if the ac or dc resistance of the total bridge circuit is less than 50 ohms because the high output current requirements can damage the output con-

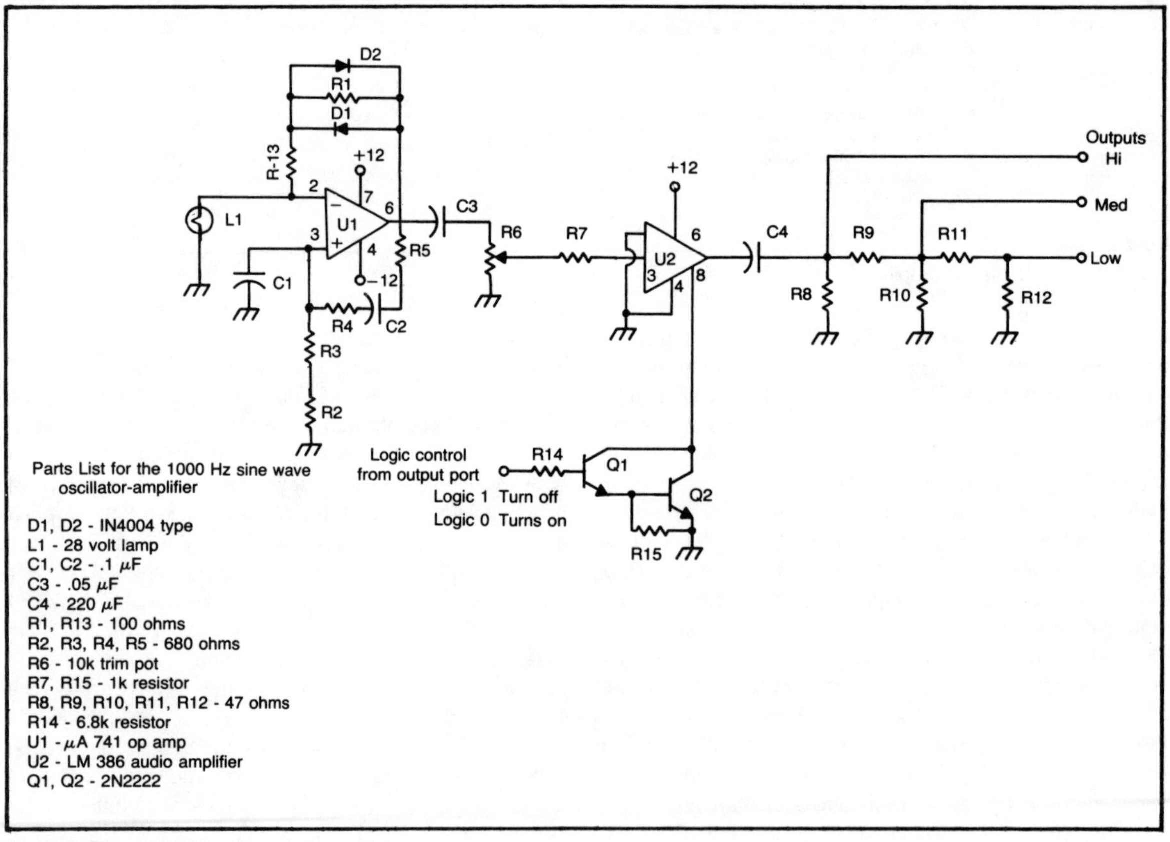

Fig. 7-2. The 1000 Hz sine-wave oscillator.

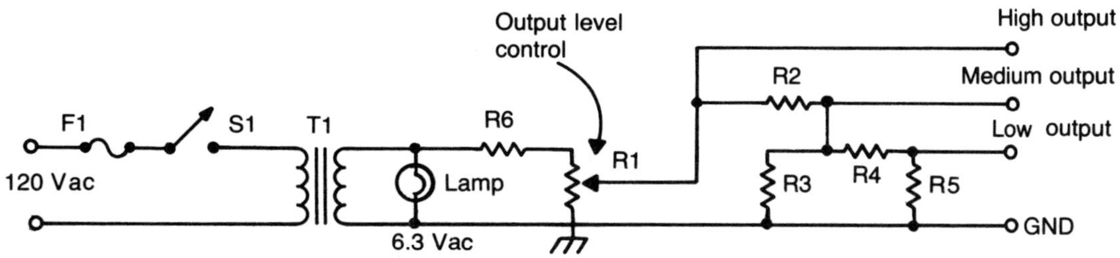

Parts list for the 60 Hz sine wave source

F1 - ½ amp fuse
S1 - 3 amp ac switch
T1 - Radio Shack 273-1384
Lamp - 6.3 volt lamp
R6 - 49 ohms, 1 watt resistor
R1 - 500 ohms, 2 watt control pot
R2. R3. R4, R5 - 68 ohm, ½ watt resistor

Fig. 7-3. The 60 Hz sine-wave source.

trol pot (R1). This means that you had better keep a watchful eye on your circuit if you try and measure high capacitance values or low inductance values.

Figure 7-2 shows a 1,000-Hz sine-wave generator that can be built on a very limited budget. The nice point about this sine-wave generator is the fact that it can be turned off and on by the computer by sending a logic one or zero to transistor Q1. This type of off and on operation is advantageous in situations where you must do both ac and dc measurements on the same device. There is nothing critical about this circuit. You can change the operating frequency of the circuit by changing the values of capacitors C1 and C2 or resistors R2, R3, R4, and R5. If at any time the waveform becomes distorted, try adjusting the values of resistors R1 and R13 one way or another but not too much.

The bridge circuit that is presented in Fig. 7-4 can be used to compare inductor coils. Most of the time a coil will have to be manufactured to a certain inductance specification (measured in henrys). But, when you wind this coil, you will find that you can have a great difference in coil turns and still have an adequate amount of inductance. Naturally you will not want to wind any more copper wire on the coil than is needed in order to keep the price of the coil low. This fact means that you will need some method of testing the number of turns on the coil to insure that a given inductance is being produced with the least amount of copper in the coil. The bridge circuit in Fig. 7-4 will give you the ability to compare coil A with coil B and that the number of turns on coil A is within .005 % of the number of turns on coil B. Of course, the tighter you try to measure the coil turns the more difficult it will become. You will just have to keep experimenting with different fixturing, probes, and bridge-circuit values until you find the combination that will work. You can start out by winding coil "L" over the entire length of the 12-inch steel rod. Place the rod with coil "L" through the coil A and B cores and place coils A and B together in the center of the rod. You should now be able to null out the bridge circuit by adjusting the 500 ohm fine-balance control.

The bridge circuit in Fig. 7-5 can be used to compare the capacitance value of one capacitor to a standard capacitor. The circuit is not as critical as the inductance comparison circuit, so, you should not have any trouble getting this circuit working. This bridge circuit is easier to experiment with because you can easily buy capacitors of the same value.

AC BRIDGE CIRCUIT AMPLIFIER AND LEVEL DETECTOR

Once you have built the ac bridge circuit and have it working, you must find a method to detect the null point of the bridge circuit and then convert that null point into a

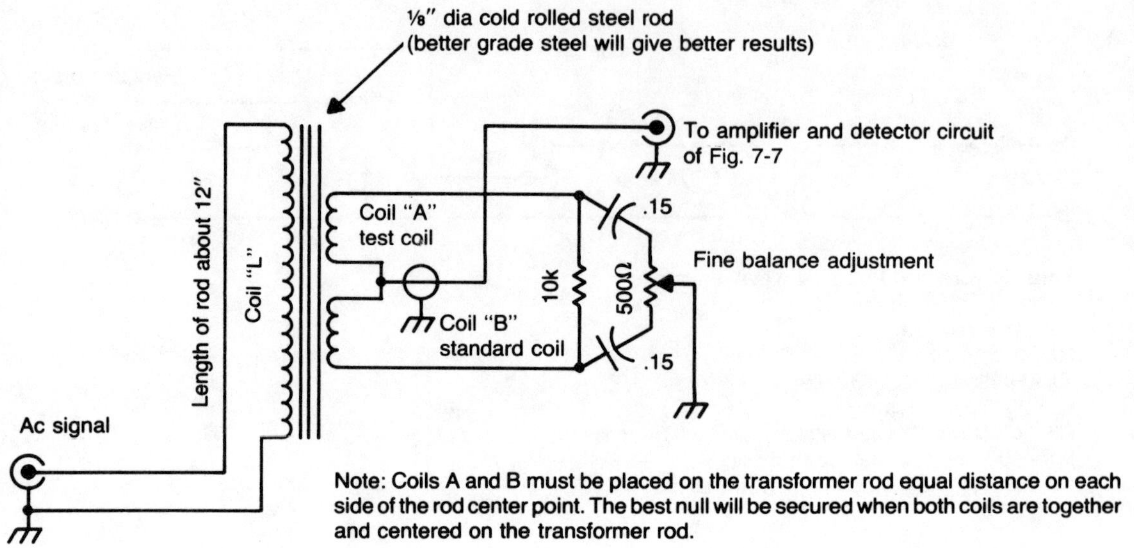

Fig. 7-4. The inductor-comparison bridge circuit.

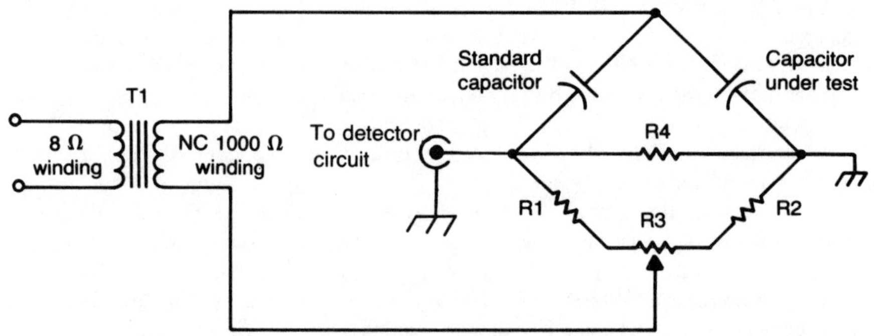

Parts list for the capacitor comparison bridge

T1 - Radio Shack 273-1380
R4 - 47k resistor
R3 - 100 ohm ten turn trim pot
R1, R2 - 1k resistors

Note: Control pot R3 should be adjusted for the bridge null condition with two matched capacitors of the same value.

Fig. 7-5. The capacitor-comparison bridge circuit.

logic signal that can be used by a computer. The ac bridge circuit interfacing system is not as simple as the dc bridge system because the ac circuits are not linear functions, and as the ac sine-wave driving signal increases in frequency, the stray capacitances and inductances of the circuit wiring can play tricks on you if you are not careful.

To start off, you will have to build an ac amplifier circuit to amplify the ac output signal from the bridge circuit so you can observe the null point and then you will need an ac detector circuit so you can tell the computer when the null has been found. The ac output signal from the bridge circuit will be very low (less than 200 microvolts) at the null point, so the amplifiers will have to have a very low internal noise factor to accurately yield a good amplified null-point signal. A good low noise op-amp circuit can be hard to build from low priced op amps. The solution is to build a low noise ac amplifier from dual gate MOSFETs.

A good low-noise amplifier is shown in Fig. 7-6. This amplifier has a complete set of control pots so you can adjust every circuit amplification factor required for your interface system. You can adjust this circuit to be a low-gain amplifier or you can adjust it to be a very high gain compression amplifier. The only sneaky thing about this amplifier is the diode combination of D3 and D4. After you have gained a little ac bridge experience, you will find that you will need a very high gain amplifier if you are going to be attempting any high quality detection work around the bridge null point. For example, let's say that you are attempting to detect a .01 μF capacitor at a tolerance of plus or minus a few percent. You will observe that it is easy to find the .01 μF capacitor at 1% but the null points at the 2, 3, 4, and 5 percentage point are all scrunched together because of the high gain of the amplifier. The diodes D3 and D4 will give you a dead band in the area of the null point which will give you the ability

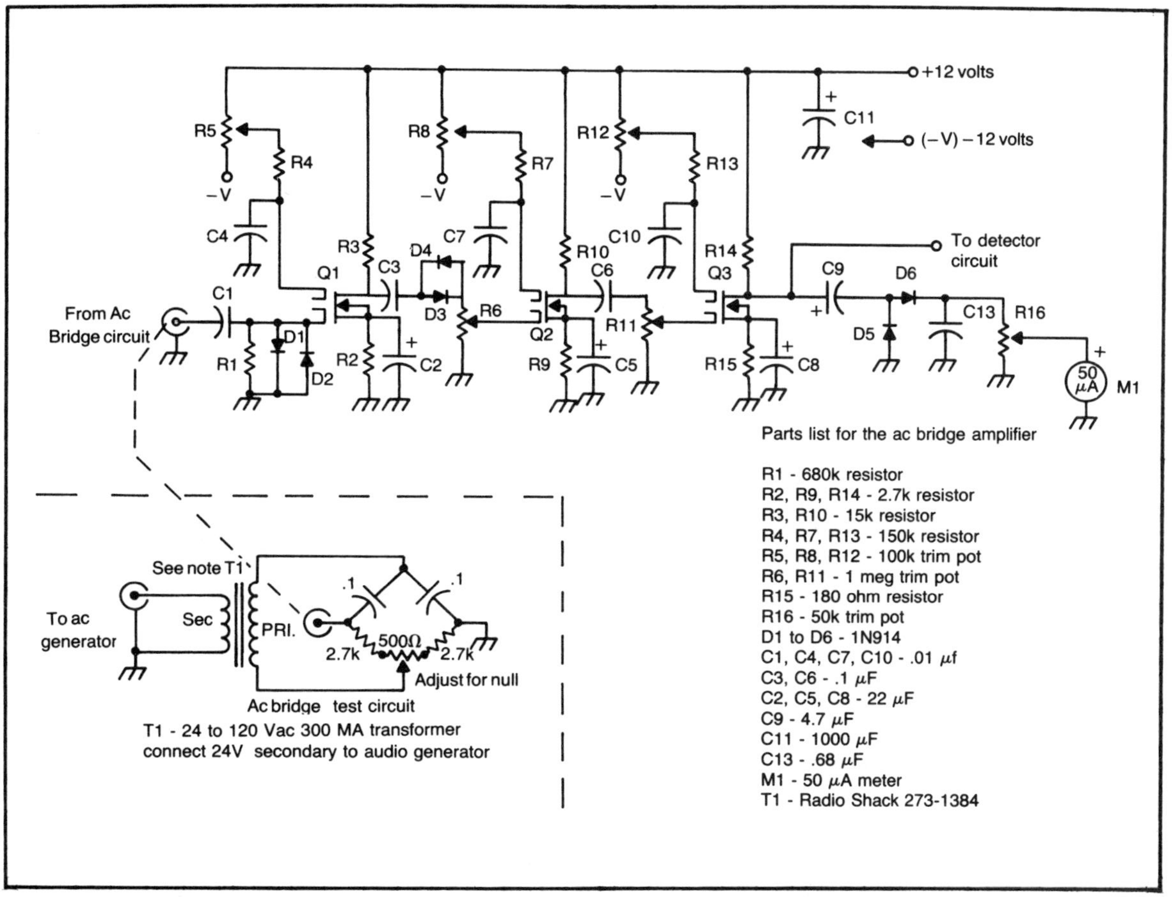

Fig. 7-6. The ac bridge amplifier.

to discriminate between the 2, 3, 4 and 5 percentage tolerance points a little easier. This ability to discriminate between the 2, 3, 4 and 5 percentage points is really what makes this bridge-circuit interface system usable in the go no-go type of test circuit work.

After the amplifier in Fig. 7-6 is working, you can build the detection circuit in Fig. 7-7. This circuit is a straightforward voltage detector circuit using op-amp U1 as a noninverting buffer circuit, and op-amp U2 as a voltage detector circuit. The voltage doubler circuit of D1 and D2 develops a dc voltage from the ac output signal of op-amp U1. This dc voltage level will be proportional to the ac signal at the input of the detection circuit. When the bridge circuit is in a null condition, there will be a very low ac input signal which will yield a low dc voltage level. By adjusting trim pot R2, you will be able to detect about any voltage level between 0.5 volts to 8 volts which will give you the ability to detect various levels of null points. Trim pot R3 is used to control the time constant of the rectifier filter circuit. The output of the voltage detector circuit goes to the three CMOS circuits and then on to your computer.

It will take you a little time to learn how to use the ac bridge interfacing circuits, but after you have solved the start-up problems, you will find that you can do some really outstanding high speed ac bridge testing using this method.

CONNECTING THE HEATHKIT MODEL IB-5281 RLC BRIDGE TO YOUR SINGLE-BOARD COMPUTER

This little project is the experimenter's delight. The Heath RLC Bridge is an inexpensive but a very useful piece of experimenter's lab equipment. It is really very easy to connect the Heath RLC Bridge to your computer

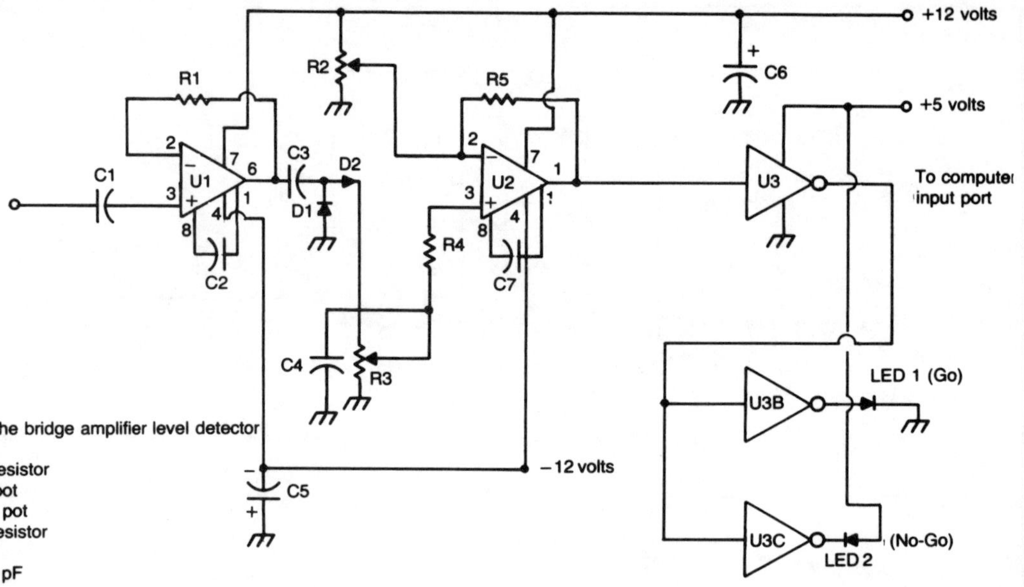

Parts list for the bridge amplifier level detector

R1, R4 - 1k resistor
R2 - 5k trim pot
R3 - 50k trim pot
R5 - 1 meg resistor
C1 - .05 μF
C2, C7 - 150 pF
C3 - 10 μF
C4 - .5 μF
C5, C6 - 220 μF
U1 - CA-3140 CMOS op amp
U2 - CA-3130 CMOS op amp
Note: If CMOS op amps can not be secured, try using two μA 741 op amps.

U3 - 4049 CMOS hex inverter
LED-1 - green LED
LED-2 - red LED
All capacitors are rated at 16 volts or higher.
All resistors are ¼ watt or bigger.

Fig. 7-7. The ac bridge-amplifier level detector.

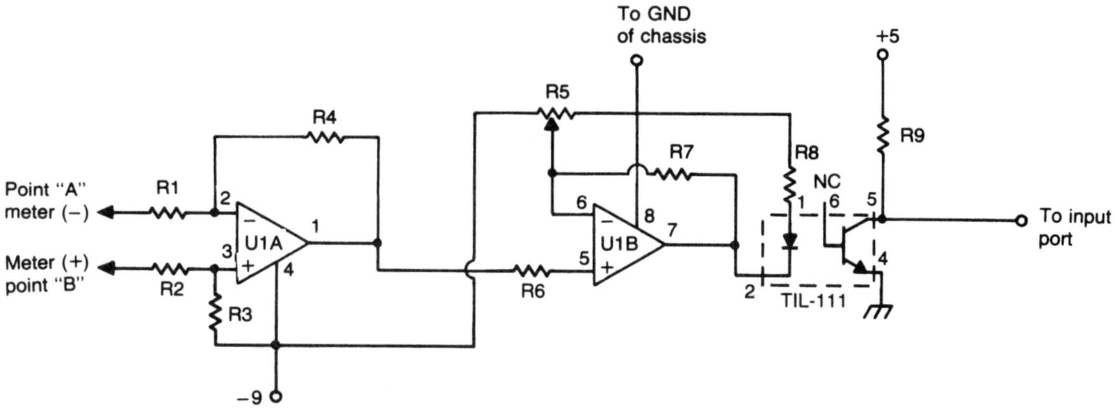

Parts list for the Heathkit RLC bridge and computer interface circuit for Heath Model 1B-5281

R1, R2 - 10k resistor
R3, R4 - 100k resistor
R6, R8, R9 - 1k resistor
R5 - 10k trim pot
R7 - 1 meg resistor
U1 - μA 358 dual single supply op amp
TIL-111 - Optocoupler Radio Shack 276-132

Fig. 7-8. The interface circuit for the Heathkit IB-5281 RLC bridge.

by using the circuit that is shown in Fig. 7-8.

This circuit is really nothing more than a voltage detector circuit which drives an optocoupler IC. The interface circuit is connected to the null-meter terminals of the Heath RLC Bridge as shown in Fig. 7-9. The trim pot R5 is adjusted to give you the desired null detection point, and the output of the optocoupler is connected to the computer input port bit line. You will find that when you have this circuit up and running that your computer will be able to detect the null point before the null meter starts to dip. Tables 7-1 through 7-4 present the single-board computer routines which can be used with the Heath interface circuit or any of the other previously described bridge-interface units.

USING THE AC BRIDGE AMPLIFIER SYSTEM WITH AN R-X NOISE BRIDGE FOR RADIO FREQUENCY MEASUREMENTS

The ac bridge amplifier system will not function too well above about 10,000 Hz. So, if you need to do some rf measurements from about 2 MHz and on up to over 30 MHz, you might try using a R-X noise bridge. The R-X noise bridge can be connected to a communications receiver which will convert the R-X noise reading into an audio frequency noise that can be used by the ac bridge amplifier. A method for setting up this type of test system is shown in Fig. 7-10. You should be able to make reasonable go no-go type of measurements in the rf frequency spectrum with this type of equipment.

A few words of caution should be in order now. If you are using a single-board computer, it will not be enclosed in any type of metal cabinet unless you have put it in one yourself. The crystal-controlled clock circuit on the single-board computer does a very good job of emitting radio frequency signals all the way up into the hundreds of megahertz range if it is not enclosed and still does a good job when it is enclosed. Keep a watchful eye on this problem so you do not secure bad test readings due to rf interference.

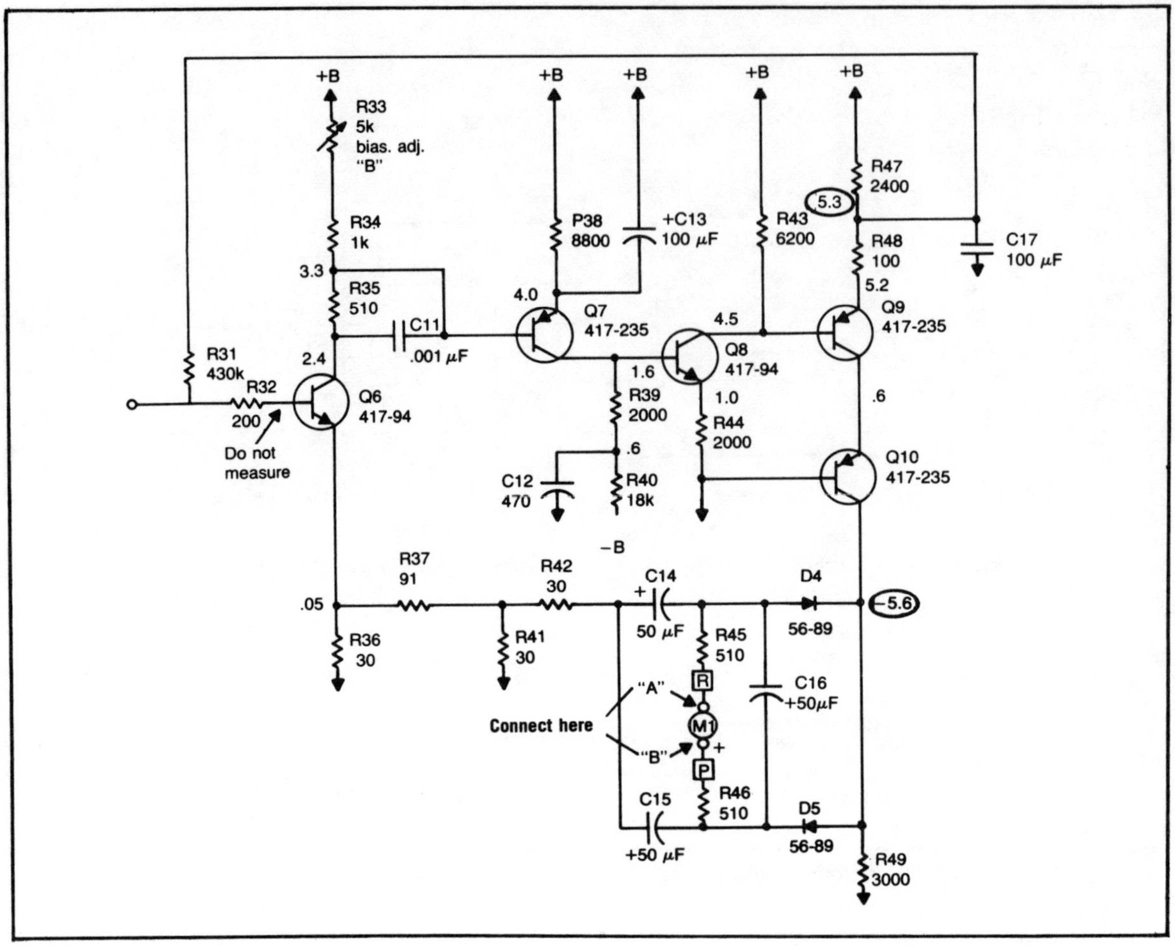

Fig. 7-9. Interface circuit connecting points on the Heathkit RLC Bridge circuit board (Reprinted by Permission of Heath Company).

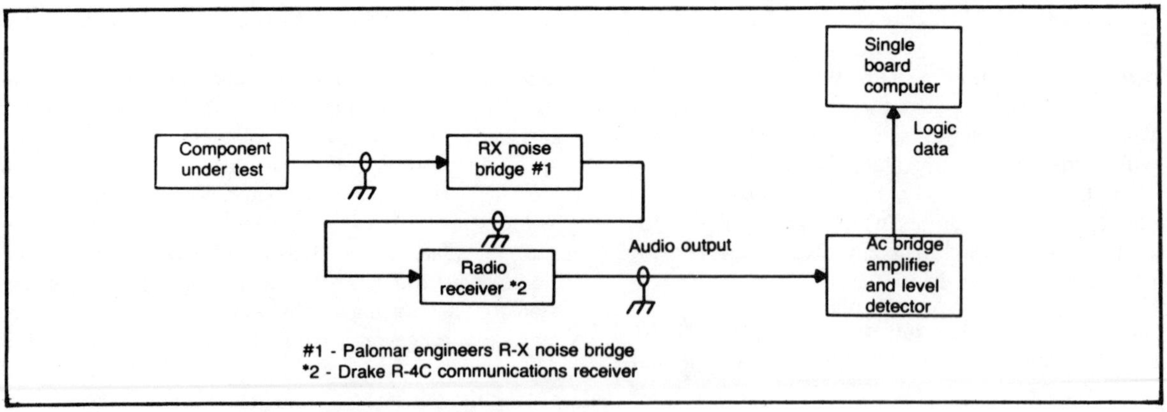

Fig. 7-10. A method of making rf impedance measurements.

Table 7-1. A Machine-Language Program for the KIM-1 which can be used with any of the Bridge-Detector Circuits.

```
A. This program will  provide the software that  is  needed
to interface a KIM-1 to any of the bridge  circuits that are
described in Chapter 7.
B. This program uses PA7 as an input port.

Address--Instructions--Mnemonic--Description
Location B1--B2--B3
200        A9  00           LDA
202        8D  01   17      STA    MAKE PORT A AN INPUT PORT
205        2C  00   17      BIT    BIT TEST LOCATION A001
208        10  03           BPL    IF PA7 IS A ZERO, BRANCH TO
                                   TO LOCATION 20D
20A        UU  UU   UU      JMP    IF PA7 IS A ONE, THE NULL
                                   IS OK - GO ON WITH THE
                                   TEST SEQUENCE ROUTINE
20D        UU  UU   UU      JMP    IF PA7 IS A ZERO, THE NULL
                                   IS BAD, JUMP TO NEXT ROUTINE

NOTES: A. "UU" means some unknown data that must be  filled
in by  the  user at a later  time. Location  20A is the JUMP
instruction that points  to  the next  test  routine  if the
bridge  null  condition is  OK.  Location 20D  is  the  JUMP
instruction which  points to the next routine if  the bridge
was not in a null condition.
       B. If you  are experimenting with this  program, load
the BREAK instruction (00)  into location  20A and 20D. When
the program is executed, it  will stop at  location  20A  if
the null condition is ok and location 20D if  the bridge was
not in a null condition.
```

Table 7-2. A Machine-Language Program for the SYM-1 which can be used with any of the Bridge-Detector Circuits.

```
A. This program will provide the software that is needed
to interface a SYM-1 to any of the bridge  circuits that are
described in Chapter 7.
B. This program uses PA7 as an input port.

Address--Instructions--Mnemonic--Description
Location B1--B2--B3
200        A9  00           LDA
202        8D  03   A0      STA    MAKE PORT A AN INPUT PORT
205        2C  01   A0      BIT    BIT TEST LOCATION A001
208        10  03           BPL    IF PA7 IS A ZERO, BRANCH TO
                                   TO LOCATION 20D
```

Table 7-2. A Machine-Language Program for the SYM-1 which can be used with any of the Bridge-Detector Circuits (continued from page 113).

```
20A       UU  UU  UU    JMP   IF PA7 IS A ONE, THE NULL
                              IS OK - GO ON WITH THE
                              TEST SEQUENCE ROUTINE
20D       UU  UU  UU    JMP   IF PA7 IS A ZERO, THE NULL
                              IS BAD, JUMP TO NEXT ROUTINE
```

NOTES: A. "UU" means some unknown data that must be filled in by the user at a later time. Location 20A is the JUMP instruction that points to the next test routine if the bridge null condition is OK. Location 20D is the JUMP instruction which points to the next routine if the bridge was not in a null condition.

B. If you are experimenting with this program, load the BREAK instruction (00) into location 20A and 20D. When the program is executed, it will stop at location 20A if the null condition is ok and location 20D if the bridge was not in a null condition.

Table 7-3. This Software Program can be used to Interface the AIM-65 to any of the Bridge-Detector Circuits.

A. This program will provide the required software to interface the AIM-65 to any of the bridge interface circuits that are described in Chapter 7 using a short BASIC program with a USR (1) machine-language routine.
B. Locate the BASIC program in the lower 3K of the 4K ram by entering 3072 when the AIM-65 requests the MEMORY SIZE for the BASIC program.
C. The USR (1) machine-language routine will start at 0FE0H.

The machine-language routine using the AIM-65 disassembly format.

```
OFE0  A9  LDA  #00
0FE2  8D  STA  A003
0FE5  2C  BIT  A001
0FE8  10  BPL  0FF0
0FEA  A9  LDA  #FF
0FEC  8D  STA  0FFF
OFEF  60  RTS
0FF0  A9  LDA  #00
0FF2  8D  STA  0FFF
0FF5  60  RTS
```

Table 7-3. This Software Program can be used to Interface the AIM-65 to any of the Bridge-Detector Circuits (continued from page 114).

```
THE AIM-65 BASIC PROGRAM  (LIMIT THE MEMORY SIZE TO 3072)

10 PRINT "CHECKING FOR A NULL CONDITION"
20 POKE 04, 224: POKE 05, 15
30 X=USR (1): PRINT X
40 IF PEEK (4095)= 255 THEN 60
50 IF PEEK (4095)= 00  THEN 80
60 PRINT "NULL CONDITION IS PRESENT"
70 END
80 PRINT "NULL CONDITION IS NOT PRESENT"
90 END
```

NOTES: A. Line 20 gives the BASIC program the starting point information for the USR (1) instruction. 224 is the decimal number for E0 (HEX) and 15 is the decimal number for 0F (HEX). Remember, the low address byte is first and the high address byte is second.

B. The program is started by the RUN command.

Table 7-4. This Software Program can be used to Interface the Model III to any of the Bridge-Detector Circuits.

A. This program will provide the required software to interface the Model III to any of the bridge interface circuits of Chapter 7 using a BASIC program with a USR (1) instruction and a machine-language subroutine.

B. This program must be used with the 80-I/O-PIB.

C. The machine language routine will start at 7F00H.

D. Limit the BASIC memory size to 32245. SEE NOTES

E. Connect the bridge interface unit to input bit 7.

THE MODEL III MACHINE-LANGUAGE ROUTINE

```
Address--Instructions--Mnemonic--Description
Location B1--B2--B3
7F00      F3                DI      DISABLE INTERRUPTS
7F01      3E   10           LD      LOAD 10H INTO REGISTER A
7F03      D3   EC           OUT     PLACE 10H IN PORT ECH
7F05      DB   6F           IN      PLACE CONTENTS OF PORT 6F
                                    INTO REGISTER A
7F07      32   FF   7F      LD      LOAD REGISTER A IN 7FFFH
7F0A      C9                RET     RETURN TO BASIC PROGRAM
```

Table 7-4. This Software Program can be used to Interface the Model III to any of the Bridge-Detector Circuits (continued from page 115).

```
THE MODEL III BASIC PROGRAM (LIMIT MEMORY SIZE TO 32245)

10 PRINT "CHECKING BRIDGE NULL CONDITION"
20 POKE 16526,00:POKE 16257,127
30 X=USR (1)
40 IF PEEK (32767)=255 THEN 100
50 PRINT "NULL CONDITION IS NOT PRESENT"
60 END
100 PRINT "NULL CONDITION IS PRESENT"
110 END

NOTES: A.  Load  the machine-language routine in first using
the DEBUG program and  then reset  the machine and  bring up
the BASIC program limiting the memory size to 32245.
       B.  Line 20  is the subroutine RAM starting  location
data. See the Model III reference manual, page 191 and 192.
```

CONCLUSION

In this chapter, we have mainly worked with only simple bridge circuits, but even the more advanced circuits must be approached in a similar manner because only the complexity of the bridge circuits will differ. You will discover that when you try to interface to a commercial bridge system that you will only be looking for a logic one or zero which will be brought out to one of the application terminals on the commercially manufactured bridge.

Digital-to-Analog Converter Circuits and Programs

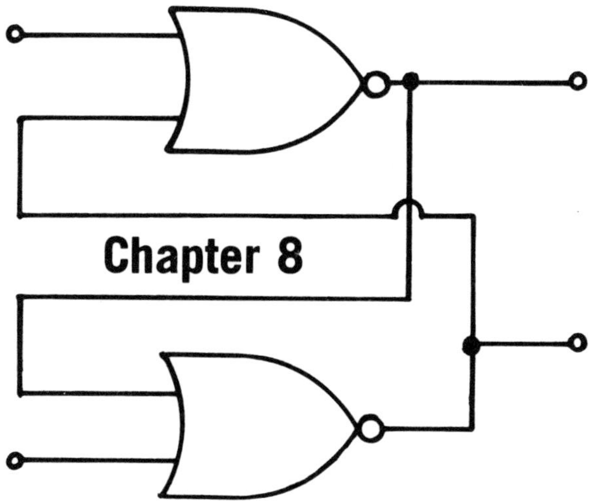

Chapter 8

In this chapter we will present two functional digital-to-analog circuits that you can build and run with a single-board computer. The topic of A/D and D/A converters is a large area and one can easily write a whole book on the subject. We will only be concerned with the two given circuits and how to make these circuits work. After you have built and operated the D/A converters, you may want to learn more about other data converting circuits. One book which has a very good presentation of D/A and A/D basics is: *Microcomputer Interfacing Handbook A/D & D/A, by: Joseph J Carr published by: TAB Books Inc.*

The D to A converter circuit can be used very ingeniuously in test equipment circuits if you put your mind to work thinking. The two circuits that are presented in this chapter are designed to generate different output signals. One circuit will generate an output signal between zero and ten volts and the other will generate an output signal of plus or minus five volts. You can operate these D/A converter circuits with a single-board computer or use the SBC simulator to drive them.

THE ZERO TO TEN VOLTS OUTPUT D/A CONVERTER CIRCUIT

The D/A converter that is shown in the schematic diagram of Fig. 8-1 is designed to generate an output between zero and ten volts dc. The circuit is built around the DAC-801 (Radio Shack 276-1791) D/A converter IC. The circuit can generate various waveform functions at frequencies up to 5 kHz.

The D/A circuit that is connected to the single-board computer I/O port uses all eight port bit lines. The output voltage resolution between zero and ten volts is about .039 volts per step because an eight port will give you 255 steps. Resistor trim pot "RA" is used to adjust the maximum output voltage which can be adjusted from a little above ten volts down to zero. The resistor trim pot "RB" is used to adjust the zero voltage reference point. Outputs A and B are opposite of each other so if you have a positive going sawtooth waveform on output A, you will have a negative going sawtooth waveform on output B. The low cost, simplicity, and easy availability of parts will make this D/A circuit a very good lab project. Another good use is with voltage detector circuits and window comparator circuits because you can make these circuits programmable if you use a programmable voltage reference source such as a D/A converter. If you don't have a single-board computer, the D/A circuit can be operated by using the SBC simulator circuit of Chapter 4.

Table 8-1 presents a program which will generate a sawtooth waveform with the D/A converter circuit and a SYM-1. Table 8-2 gives a program which will generate a simple sinewave-style waveform using the AIM-65. Table 8-3 is a simple voltage-reference program for the

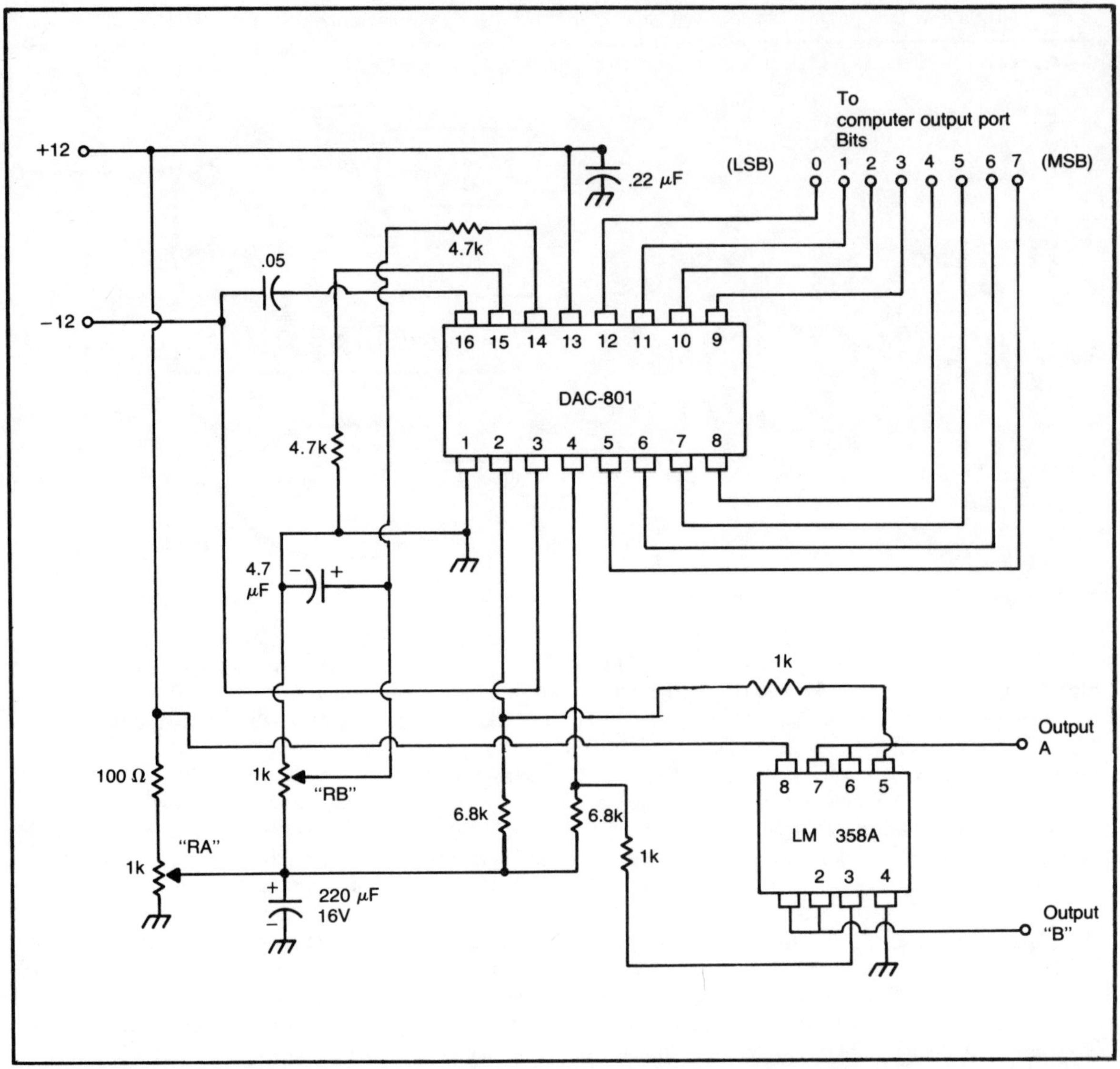

Fig. 8-1. This circuit uses easy to find parts in a D/A circuit that will generate zero to ten volts output.

Model III. Table 8-4 gives some approximate output voltages for a given hexadecimal input data.

THE ± FIVE VOLTS D/A CONVERTER CIRCUIT

Figure 8-2 presents a schematic diagram of a D/A converter circuit that uses a NE5018 D/A IC. This circuit is a little more complex than the previous circuit, but you can do more with it. The NE5018 contains a latch circuit that will retain the last data present when the latch is set. The D/A output will remain unchanged until the latch is released and new data presented to the NE5018. The latching function of the NE5018 gives you the ability to operate more than one D/A converter from the same I/O port bus by placing the hex data on the I/O port bus and then latching the data in the chosen D/A circuit.

The D/A operation of the NE5018 is not much different from the previous circuit and with the exception of the latching function, the same programs will run the NE5018 that were used for the DAC-801. The

Table 8-1. This Program has been Run on a SYM-1 but it can be used on any of the 6502 SBCs.

```
A. This is a  D to A waveform program  which will generate a
sawtooth waveform.
B. This program is  a machine-language  program  which will
work  on SYM-1  and the  AIM-65  with  the DAC-801  D  to  A
circuit.

Address--Instructions--Mnemonic--Description
Location B1--B2--B3
200        A9   FF        LDA
202        8D   03   A0   STA       MAKE  PORT  A  AN  OUTPUT  PORT
205        A9   00        LDA
207        8D   01   A0   STA       SET  I/O  PORT  A  TO  ZEROs
20A        8D   11   02   STA       SET  LOCATION  0211  TO  ZEROs
20D        EA   EA   EA   NOP
210        A9   00        LDA
212        8D   01   A0   STA       STORE  DATA  IN  I/0  PORT   A
215        EE   11   02   INC       INCREMENT  LOCATION  0211
218        4C   10   02   JMP       LOOP  BACK  TO  210
NOTE:   This  program  will   generate   a   sawtooth   waveform
        with 256 voltage steps.
```

Table 8-2. This Is a General Purpose D/A Program. By Placing the Proper Data in Page Three of an AIM 65 Memory, You can Generate a Sine Wave, Triangle Wave, or almost any Low-Frequency Waveform Function.

A. This is a D to A waveform program which uses the program data that is stored in page 300 (300 to 3FF).
B. This program is a machine language program which will work in a KIM-1, SYM-1, and the AIM-65 with the DAC-801 D to A circuit.
C. The entire page 300 must be loaded with waveform data.

```
Address--Instructions--Mnemonic--Description
Location  B1--B2--B3

200       A9   FF       LDA
202       8D   03   A0  STA       MAKE PORT A AN OUTPUT PORT
205       A9   00       LDA
207       8D   01   A0  STA       SET I/O PORT A TO ZEROs
20A       8D   11   02  STA       SET LOCATION 0211 TO ZEROs
20D       EA   EA   EA  NOP
210       AD   00   03  LDA       LOAD DATA FROM LOCATION 300
213       8D   01   A0  STA       STORE DATA IN I/O PORT A
216       EE   11   02  INC       INCREMENT LOCATION 0211
219       4C   10   02  JMP       LOOP BACK TO 210
```

Notes: A. This program will sequence through page 300 and place the data in the memory locations in output port A. The first location that will be loaded into port A is location 300. The program will sequence completely through page 300 and when location 3FF is used, the program will loop back to location 300 and start over again.

B. A sawtooth waveform can be generated by loading 00 into location 300 and adding "1" to the next location and "1" more to the next (300-00, 301-01, 302-02->-3FE-FE and 3FF-FF) until you have loaded all of page 300. After you have generated a saw tooth waveform, you have no problems generating a triangle or sine wave function.

C. Use Table 8-1 to help you choose the hex data for the proper output voltage.

Table 8-3. This Program can be used with a Model III to Generate Programmable-Reference Voltages.

A. This is a program for the Model III using a BASIC program with a USR (1) instruction and a machine-language subroutine which can control the output of the A to D converter of Fig. 8.10
B. This program must be used with the 80-I/O-PIB.
C. The machine-language routine will start at 7F00H.
D. Limit the Basic memory size to 32245. SEE NOTES

THE MODEL III MACHINE-LANGUAGE ROUTINE

```
Address--Instructions--Mnemonic--Description
Location B1--B2--B3
7F00     F3             DI      DISABLE INTERRUPTS
7F01     3E   10        LD      LOAD 10H INTO REGISTER A
7F03     D3   EC        OUT     PLACE 10H IN PORT ECH
7F05     3E   7C        LD      PLACE HEX 7C IN REGISTER A
7F07     D3   6F        OUT     PLACE HEX 7C IN PORT 6FH
7F0A     C9             RET     RETURN TO BASIC PROGRAM
```

THE MODEL III BASIC PROGRAM (LIMIT MEMORY SIZE TO 32245)

```
10 PRINT "PROGRAM OUTPUT VOLTAGE TO 5 VOLTS"
20 POKE 16526,00:POKE 16257,127
30 X=USR (1)
40 PRINT "D to A OUTPUT VOLTAGE IS NOW 5 VOLTS"
50 END
```

NOTES: A. Load the machine-language routine in first using the DEBUG program and then reset the machine and bring up the BASIC program limiting the memory size to 32245.

B. Line 20 is the subroutine ram starting location data. See the Model III reference manual, page 191 and 192.

C. A 7C in memory location 7F06 will set the D to A converter output voltage to 5 volts.

D. Use Table 8-4 to choose the hex data for other output voltages.

The DAC-801 D to A
Converter Output Voltage Chart

Hexadecimal Input Data From I/O Port	Output Voltage Output A	Output Voltage Output B
00 --------------	0 V	10 V
19 --------------	1 V	9 V
34 --------------	2 V	8 V
4C --------------	3 V	7 V
65 --------------	4 V	6 V
7C --------------	5 V	5 V
95 --------------	6 V	4 V
B0 --------------	7 V	3 V
CA --------------	8 V	2 V
E4 --------------	9 V	1 V
FF --------------	10 V	0 V

Table 8-4. This Table Presents the Corresponding Output Voltage for a Given Hexadecimal Input Data to the D/A Converter Circuit in Fig. 8-1.

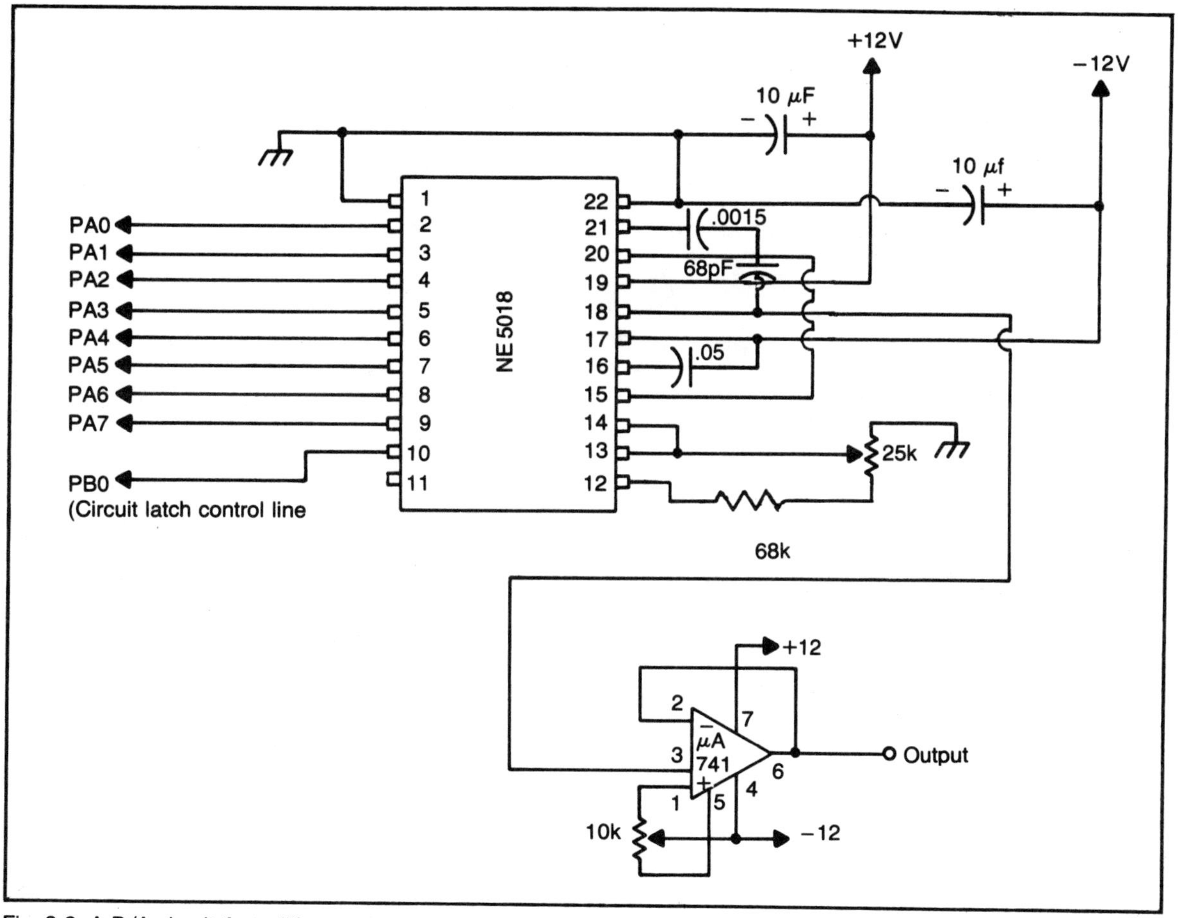

Fig. 8-2. A D/A circuit that will generate a plus or minus five volts output.

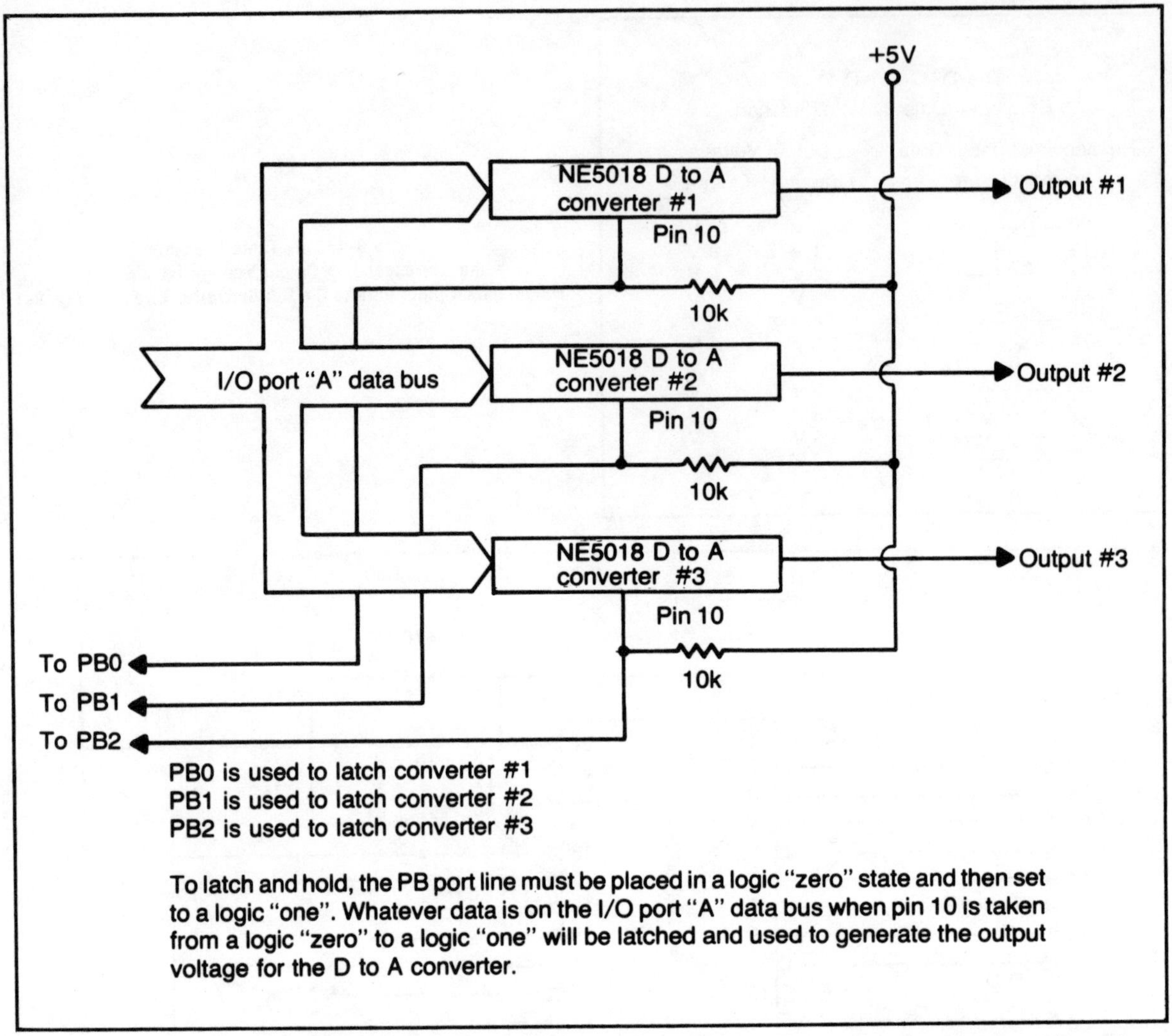

Fig. 8-3. This method may be used to operate two or more D/A circuits (like the circuit shown in Fig. 8-2) from one I/O port bus.

latching pulse is applied to pin 10 of the NE5018, and the data that is present on the data bus pins when pin 10 is taken from logic zero (zero volts) to a logic one will be latched and held. Pin 10 must be held at the logic one level to maintain the latched state. When pin 10 is lowered to logic zero, the output of the D/A converter will again follow whatever data appears at the data bus pins. Figure 8-3 shows how you would connect three D/A converters to the same I/O port.

CONCLUSION

D/A converters are really simple circuits to build, but the software programs that are used to operate them can become quite complex. The application of D/A circuits is also an area where the circuit usually must be customized to the application. Once you have learned how to operate the D/A circuits in this chapter, you will have no problems applying these circuits to your applications.

Small Motor Speed Control for Test Systems

Chapter 9

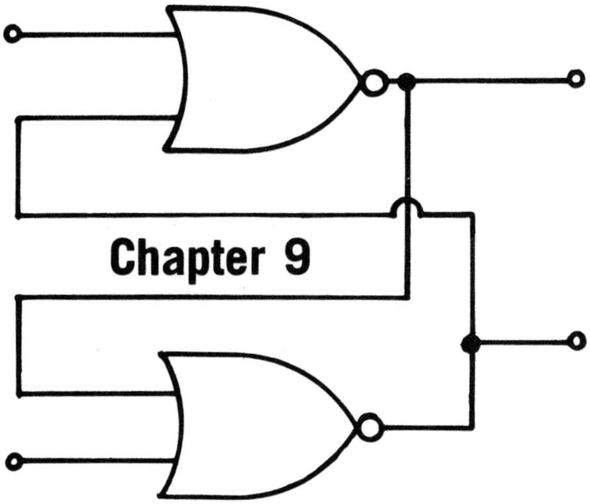

Sometime, sooner or later, you will need to build a test system which will require some type of rotating mechanism that must spin at a given speed or move a given number of degrees. When you enter the area of functional small motor system control, you are left pretty well alone with very little outside help. Try calling a company that sells small motors or small gear motors and try to buy a 250 rpm or 295 rpm synchronous motor; you can't find one. Next, try to purchase an inexpensive stepper motor which will work with your computer; that will be a lot of fun too. There are a lot of applications in test system construction where you will need a special motor rpm speed which will really present a problem. In this chapter you will be presented with a few methods of motor speed control which will solve most of the small motor speed requirements.

I can just hear someone saying, "Why don't you use a dc motor with a SCR speed control?" Well, the first part of my answer is "What happens when you are stuck with a speed specification of about 275 rpm plus or minus 3 rmp and the ac line voltage varies about plus or minus 3 or 4 volts when the air conditioner turns on? What happens is that your SCR controller is not regulated and the motor rpm drops. If the motor rpm drops during a critical portion of an rpm, the test system will reject the part being tested. The second part of my answer is to use a small synchronous gear motor and vary the frequency of the ac driving voltage to secure the proper output rpm. It is quite easy to take a 200 rpm shaded-pole gear motor and vary its output speed between 100 rpm to 350 rpm by controlling the ac frequency of the driving voltage.

If you can remember back to the time when you studied ac machines (and what a boring time it was) you will recall that a synchronous motor's speed is controlled by the ac line frequency and not the ac line voltage. If you do lower the ac line voltage, a synchronous motor will slow down, but that is due to a condition called slipping because the circulating magnetics fields of the field windings are no longer strong enough to keep the motor rotor moving at a synchronous motor speed. So, if your motor load is fairly constant, the motor speed will remain constant when you set the ac driving voltage to a given ac frequency. For a shaded-pole motor, that driving voltage frequency will be between 25 Hz and 120 Hz. The motors will run at frequencies outside this area, but it will be hard to control the motor start-up.

The main design point that you will need to keep in mind is that the shaded-pole motor (and other synchronous motors) is designed for an ac line voltage of 120 Vac. If you reduce the operating ac frequency, the motor winding impedance will be lowered and thus you will need to reduce the ac input voltage to maintain the same ac driving current. The opposite is true if you increase the ac driving voltage frequency above 60 Hz, the motor winding impedance will increase and you will need more than 120 Vac to maintain the proper driving current. This problem is handled easily in the following motor control systems, but it was mentioned here so you will not overheat the motor and smoke the windings the first time that you try to reduce the motor's output speed.

The shaded-pole motor is not the only ac motor that you can control with these methods. The same systems can be used to control the small split-capacitor motors which will go both directions. Small fan motors will also work with these control systems. Probably the best point of all of this is the fact that you can use your computer to control the motor speed and the start and stop motor functions.

A COMPUTER CONTROLLED STEPPER-MOTOR SYSTEM

A stepper motor is an electromechanical rotating device which is used to convert electrical pulses into discrete mechanical rotational movements with a degree of accuracy which is unobtainable with other methods using equal capital investments. The stepper-motor system that is described in this chapter is constructed from components manufactured by the AIRPAX Corporation.[1] This corporation manufactures a complete line of stepper motors and control circuitry which is easily controlled by a single-board computer. The cost of these components will not send your test department's budget through the roof either. The actual cost of the stepper-motor system described here could easily fall within a student's senior lab project funding ability.

The stepper motor that we will use is a two-phase permanent-magnet motor which will provide a discrete angular movement every time the polarity of the motor windings are changed. The construction of the stepper motor is shown in Fig. 9-1. It is constructed with two coils (A and B) which are each contained in a metal cup assembly that sets up the correct magnetic fields, polarities, and poles for motor operation. A permanent-magnet rotor is used which has the same number of pole pairs as the stator coil assemblies. The magnetic interaction between the rotor assembly and the stator assembly causes the rotor to move a given amount of degrees each time the winding polarity is changed. The two-phase motor that we will be using has twelve pole-pairs per stator coil section and will move 7.5 degrees per step which means that it will require forty-eight steps for one complete 360 degree revolution.

The stepping accuracy of the North American Phillips stepper motor is plus or minus 6.5 percent per step and is noncumulative. This accuracy will give you the ability to step to within plus or minus 0.5 degree of a position no matter if you step ten steps or ten revolutions plus five steps.

The torque characteristics of a stepper motor are a little more involved than the torque characteristics of a standard motor. The torque which is produced by a stepper motor is really a function of the step rate, the drive current supplied to the windings, and the drive design. The stepper-motor torque paramenters are further divided into the characteristics of holding torque, residual torque, and dynamic torque.

The holding torque is the amount of torque that is required to force the motor to skip one step when it is stopped (that is zero steps/second at the rated winding current). The normal holding torque is higher than the running torque and will perform the function of a very strong brake when the motor is stopped. A strong holding torque will give you good positioning accuracy when you stop your motor because it will over ride the deflection forces that are torquing the motor one way or the other.

The residual torque is the nonenergized detent torque caused by the permanent magnet when the motor is shut-off. The residual torque is approximately 1/10 of the holding torque and will give you the ability to hold your position when the motor is deenergized; although not with the same accuracy as you can secure with the holding torque.

The dynamic torque characteristics of the stepper motor are the actual motor running torque and the start without error torque. The graph in Fig. 9-2 shows the torque characteristics for the stepper motor that is specified in this book. The dashed line is the start-without-error torque curve which shows what torque the motor can start and stop without losing a step. The solid line is the running torque that shows what torque is available from the motor if it is slowly accelerated to its operating speed. The speed torque characteristics curves are main points that must be considered when you are selecting the stepper motor and the motor drive system for your application.

Table 9-1 presents some very informative stepper motor terminology. For more information on stepper motors and the stepper motor components that are used in this chapter, contact: AIRPAX, North American Phillips Corporation, Cheshire Division, Cheshire Industrial Park, Cheshire, CT 06410.

BUILDING A SMALL SYNCHRONOUS MOTOR CONTROLLER

The synchronous motor controller circuit which will be presented now will run almost any motor which does

1. Stepper Motor Handbook, Airpax Corporation, 1981.

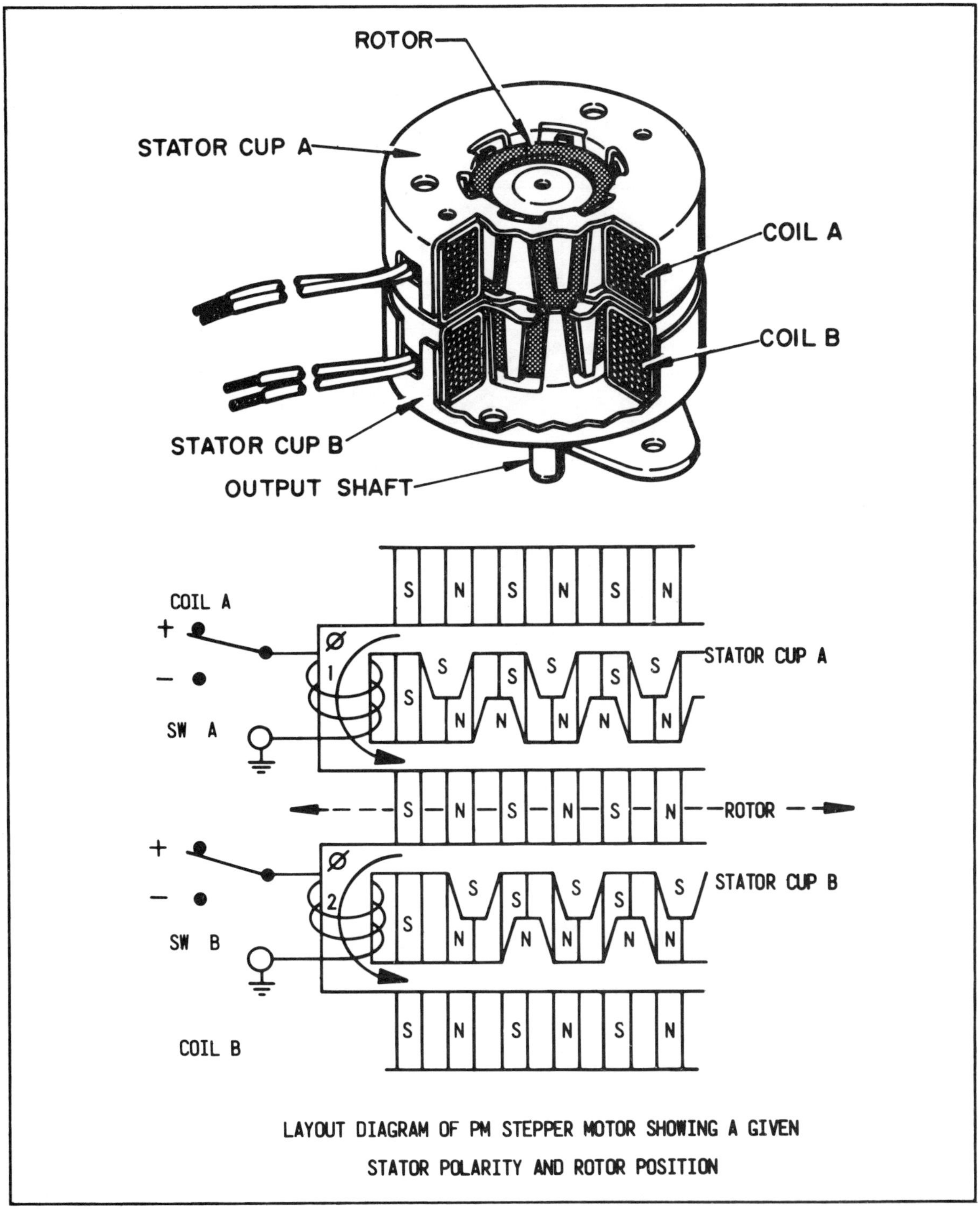

Fig. 9-1. A cutaway view of a two phase permanent-magnet stepper motor.

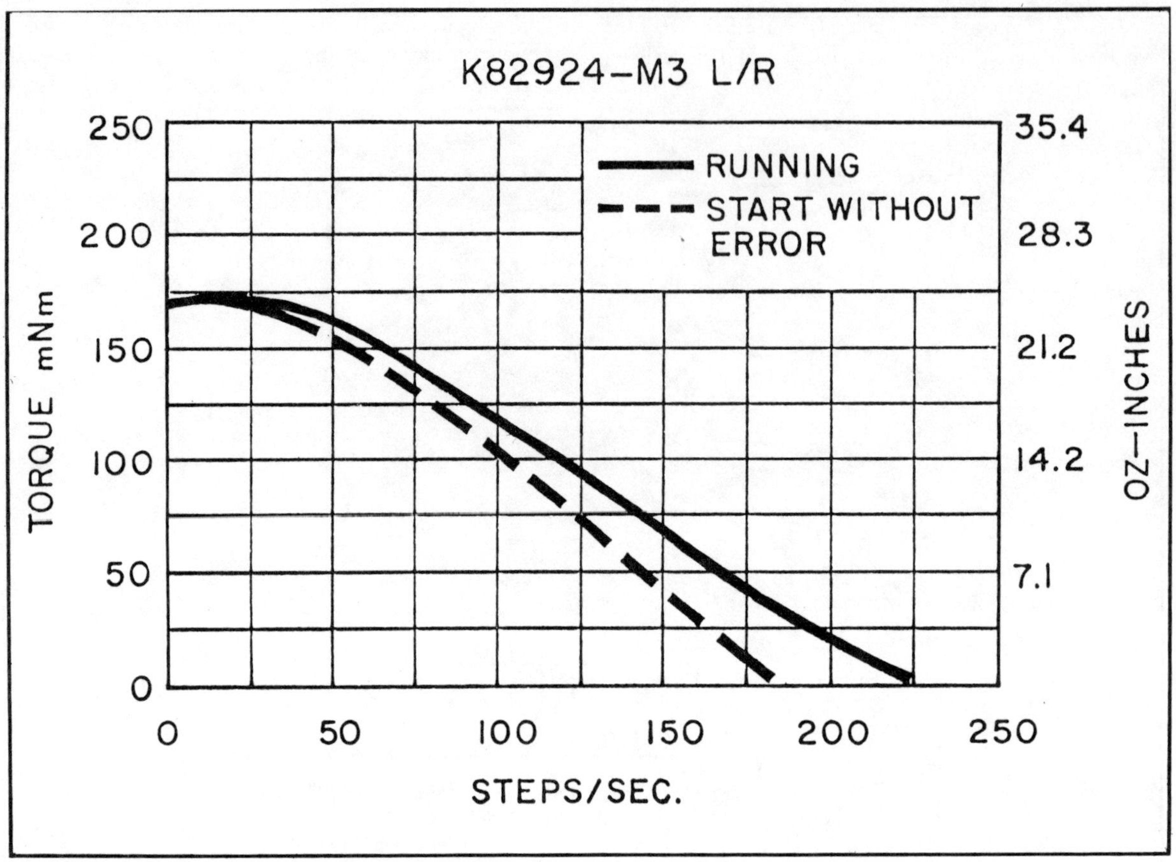

Fig. 9-2. The stepper-motor speed/torque graph.

not require more than about one ampere of ac current at 120 Vac. This will include most if not all shaded-pole motors, small split-capacitor three-wire reversible motors, and a lot of the small fan motors. There are three methods given to control the speed of the driven motors which are a simple 555-oscillator circuit, a very stable square-wave generator circuit, and the square wave output from PB-7 of a 6522 VIA on a 6502 single-board computer. You will most likely want to use the stable square-wave generator circuit with a Model III and the 6522 VIA method with a 6502 system. The control circuit can operate continuously with the small motors without heating up the heatsink of the amplifier module.

The main circuit of the motor controller is shown in Fig. 9-3. The heart of this circuit is an ECG-1148 which is a standard 50-watt replacement amplifier module that is sold for the home entertainment electronics market. The amplifier is not called on to do any linear amplification because square waves are being used, so there is very little heat generated since the output transistors are either completely turned on or turned off. The amplifier is operated from a +35 volt and a −35 volt dc power source which does not have to be regulated. The generated 70 volt square-wave signal is coupled to the ac motor through two capacitors (C1 and C2) which block the flow of dc current and a variac autotransformer which is used to perform a voltage and impedance match between the motor and amplifier module. If you observe the output signal waveform at test point "A" on a properly adjusted system, you will find a nice looking triangle waveform.

A μA741 op amp (U1) is used to drive the power amplifier. This circuit is designed to be a high-gain amplifier which will turn all the way on or off according to whether the input signal at pin 2 is above or below 2.5 volts which is on pin 3. The op-amp circuit can be driven by any TTL compatible output IC.

The 555-oscillator circuit that is shown in Fig. 9-3 is used only for testing because the output frequency is not very stable. If you are not planning on driving the control circuit with a computer signal, you should plan on using the square-wave generator of Fig. 9-4. The 555 oscillator in this circuit operates in a frequency range of 4 kHz to 15 kHz. When this frequency is divided by 128 in the CMOS 4024 binary-counter circuit, any oscillator frequency drift is also divided by the same amount. The frequency drift of the 555 oscillator then becomes insignificant and the output of the generator is very stable. This frequency stability factor will give you a very close and constant rpm control.

The main point that you must understand in order to use this system is how the motor winding impedance is affected by the input driving frequency. The motor will have a designed ac impedance which will limit the ac current to the proper running value when it is operating at 120 Vac. If the input driving frequency is reduced, the motor winding impedance is reduced. If the input driving frequency is increased, the motor winding impedance will be increased. These two facts mean that you will have to adjust the autotransformer to maintain the proper ac driving current as you increase or decrease the input driving frequency to adjust the motor speed.

When operating the control system, the lowest motor speed that you will be able to use will be determined by how much jumping you can live with. As the motor speed drops, you will reach a point where the ac motor will start acting like a stepper motor and it will start stepping around its rotations if the speed is slow enough. The upper rpm speed point is reached when the motor pull-out torque causes the motor to stop. On a small motor that is unloaded, this upper rpm speed point can be three to four times its normal operating speed if the motor rotor is well balanced.

Table 9-1. A Stepper-Motor Glossary (courtesy Airpax Corporation).

STEPPER-MOTOR TERMINOLOGY

Step Angle: The nominal angle that the motor shaft rotates for each winding polarity change.

Step Accuracy: The per step deviation from the nominal step angle of an unloaded motor. May be expressed as a percent or in degrees.

Holding Torque: The torque required to deflect the rotor a full step with the motor energized and in a standstill condition.

Residual Torque: The non-energized detent torque due to the effects of the permanent magnet and bearing friction.

Running Torque: The torque produced by a stepper motor after it has been accelerated to a running rate (sometimes called slew or pull-out torque).

Start Without Error Torque: The torque produced by a stepper motor when started at a fixed frequency or step rate. Also called pull-in torque.

Start Without Error Rate: The stepping rate at which a motor with no external load inertia can start and stop without losing a step.

Ramping: A control method used to vary the pulse rate to accelerate from zero steps per second to the running rate or from any step rate to a different rate whether it is accelerating or decelerating.

Torque-To-Inertia Ratio: The holding torque of a motor divided by the rotor inertia. This ratio is sometimes used to relate the step response of one motor size or design to another.

Step Response: The motor shaft rotational response to a step command related to time.

Overshoot: The amount the motor shaft may rotate beyond the step angle before it comes to rest at the step angle position.

Drive: The switching circuitry which controls the stepper motor.

Pulse Rate: The rate, pulses per second, which pulses are fed to a drive. In most cases, the pulse rate is the stepping rate or running rate.

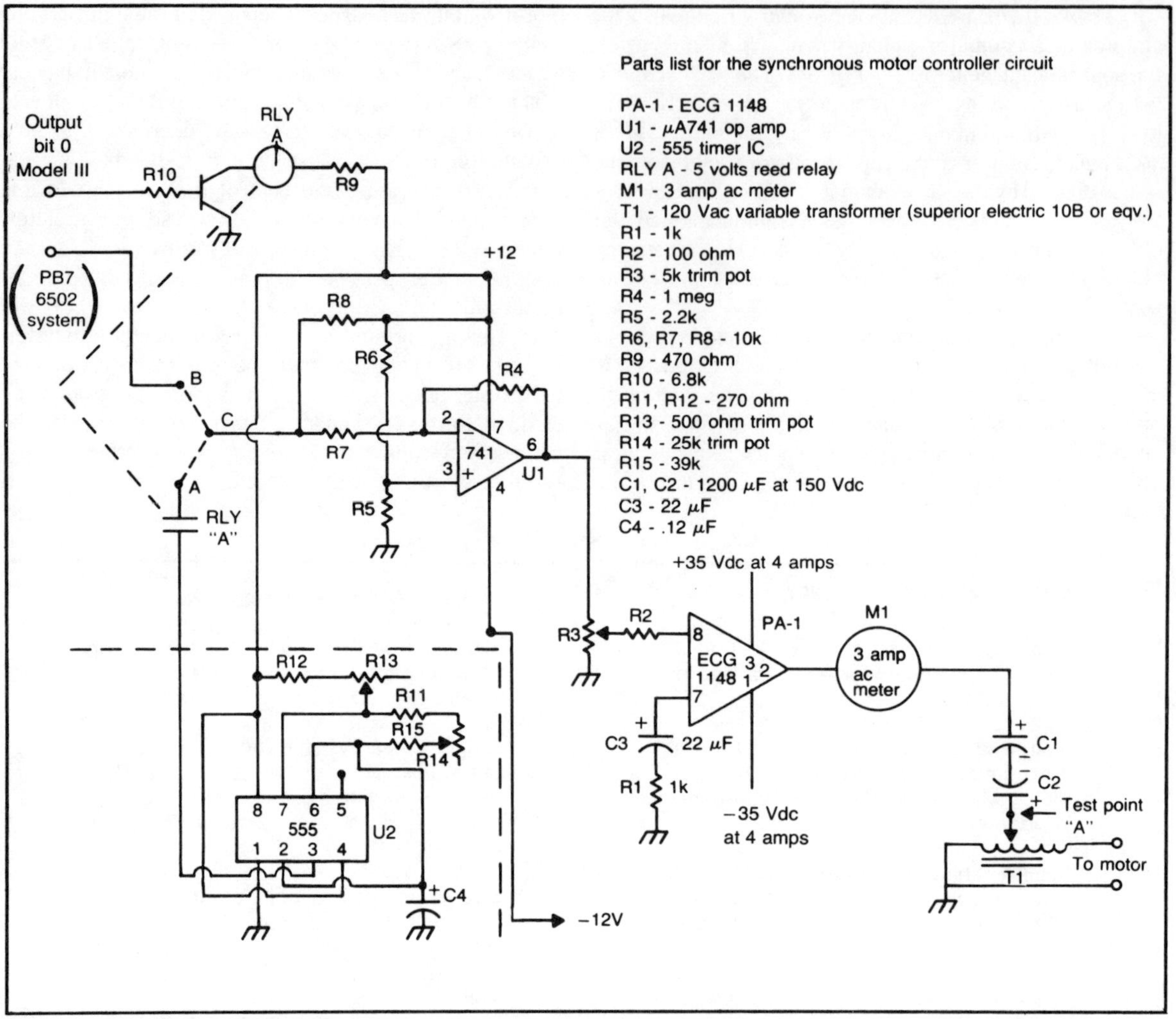

Fig. 9-3. A computer-controlled synchronous motor-speed-controller circuit.

Table 9-2 presents a single-board computer program which will run the motor control system. Although it is not shown here, you can automatically reverse the direction of rotation of a split-capacitor three-wire reversible motor under computer program control by using a relay and connecting it as per the motor connection specifications.

ASSEMBLING A SIMPLE BUT ACCURATE STEPPER-MOTOR CONTROLLER

Building a stepper-motor system is quite a bit easier than building the synchronous-motor controller because most of the system described here is already done. The main circuit that you will need to construct is the interface circuit that will connect the Airpax stepper-motor system to your single-board computer.

The Airpax stepper-motor components are used here because I have used them for several years and have found them to be reliable and affordable which is what I look for when I buy electronic parts. The two Airpax components that are used are the stepper motor P/N K82924 and a K33504 pulse to step-circuit-board drive card. With these two Airpax components, the interface circuit, two power supplies, and a single-board computer, you can perform the rotational functions that will be required in a small test system which needs some type of rotational control.

The circuit shown in Fig. 9-5 is the interface circuitry that is required so you can control the Airpax stepper motor with a single-board computer. This interface card will give you ability to step continuously or for only a given number of steps. You will be able to stop or start the stepper motor or change the rotational direction.

If you are using a 6502 system you will be able to control the speed of the stepper motor by using the free-running square-wave mode of the 6522 VIA chip. You can also use one of the single-board computer programs in Tables 9-3 through 9-5 to do various control functions.

If you are using a Model III computer, you will want to use the 555 oscillator that is on board the K33505 card to control the stepper motor speed while you use the computer output ports to control the stopping and starting and directional control of the stepper motor. Figures

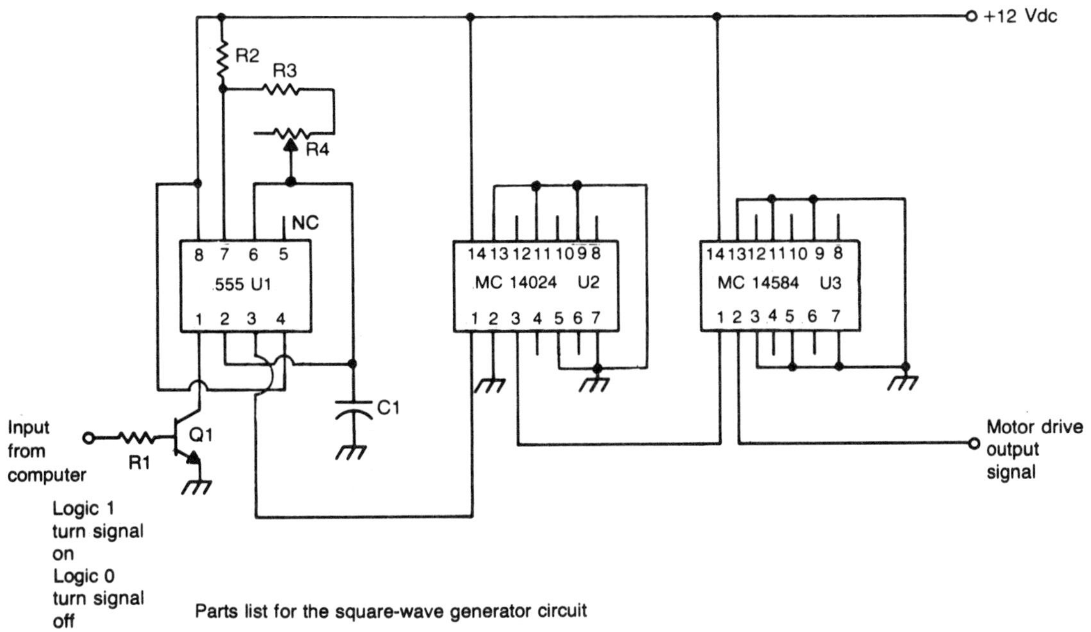

Parts list for the square-wave generator circuit

Q1 - 2N2222
U1 - 555 timer IC
U2 - CMOS 4024
U3 - CMOS 14584
R1 - 6.8k
R2 - 330 ohm
R3 - 1k
R4 - 25k control pot
C1 - .05 μF

Fig. 9-4. A square-wave generator circuit which can be used to control the synchronous motor speed.

Table 9-2. This Computer Program can be used to Control the Synchronous-Motor-Controller Circuit.

A. Use this program routine to control the synchronous motor control system of Fig. 9-3 with a SYM-1 or an AIM-65.
B. Set up PB7 for generating square waves.
C. This is a machine language program only.

```
Address--Instructions--Mnemonic--Description
Location  B1--B2--B3
200       A9  C0         LDA
202       8D  0B  A0     STA      SET UP PB7 TO GENERATE
                                  SQUARE WAVES.
205       A9  FF         LDA
207       8D  04  A0     STA      LOAD RPM DATA INTO LOW
                                  ORDER LATCH
20A       A9  20         LDA
20C       8D  05  A0     STA      LOAD RPM DATA INTO HIGH
                                  ORDER LATCH
20F       00             BRK

USE THIS ROUTINE TO CHANGE THE SPEED OF THE MOTOR WHILE
RUNNING

210       A9  UU         LDA      LOW ORDER SPEED DATA
212       8D  04  A0     STA      LOAD INTO LATCH
215       A9  UU         LDA      HIGH ORDER SPEED DATA
217       8D  05  A0     STA      LOAD INTO LATCH

TO STOP MOTOR USE THIS ROUTINE

21C       A9  00         LDA
21E       8D  0B  A0     STA     RESET ACR REGISTER TO STOP
                                 SQUARE-WAVE GENERATION
221       BRK
```

NOTES: A. UU is the data which the user must supply.
B. A HEX FF loaded into A005 will give you about 6 RPM. A HEX 10 loaded into A005 will give you about 130 RPM and a HEX 07 will give you about 300 RPM from a 200 RPM gearmotor.
C. The motor will not start or change speed until the high order latch is loaded.

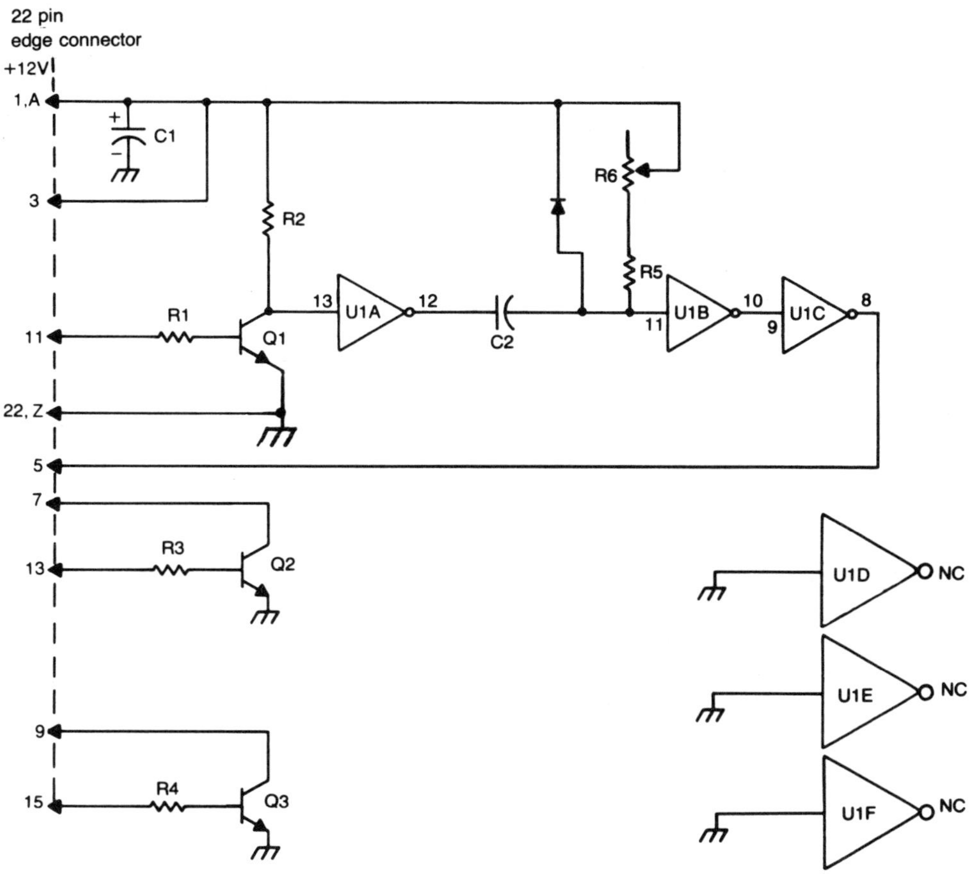

Parts list for the stepper-motor interface circuit

Q1, Q2, Q3 - 2N2222
U1 - MC14584
R1, R2, R3, R4 - 6.8k
R5 - 27k
R6 - 250k trim pot
C1 - 1000 μF at 16 Vdc
C2 - .0033 μF

Fig. 9-5. The stepper-motor interface circuit.

9-6 through 9-8 show how to connect the stepper-motor circuits together for the presented computer programs.

After you have learned how to control rotational movement with a stepper motor, you will be pleased to learn of another device which is called a *bidirectional linear actuator*. A bidirectional linear actuator is a stepper motor that is designed to deliver a very accurate incremental linear motion. The linear motion is generated by a stepper motor that has been modified by incorporating an internally threaded rotor and fitting it with a lead screw shaft. Linear motion increments of .002 inches per step can be achieved by using a bidirectional linear actuator

Table 9-3. This Machine-Language Program can be used to Control the Stepper-Motor Systems Using a SYM-1 or an AIM-65.

```
A. This program will interface a SYM-1 with the stepper
motor system of Fig. 9-6.
B. Set up PB7 to generate square waves.

Address--Instructions--Mnemonic--Description
location  B1   B2   B3
200       A9   FF        LDA
202       8D   02   A0   STA
205       A9   01        LDA
207       8D   00   A0   STA
20A       A9   C0        LDA
20C       8D   0B   A0   STA
20F       A9   FF        LDA
211       8D   04   A0   STA
214       A9   10        LDA
216       8D   05   A0   STA      START MOTOR
219       00   00        BRK
USE THIS ROUTINE TO STOP THE MOTOR
21B       A9   02        LDA
21D       8D   00   A0   STA
220       00   00        BRK
USE THIS ROUTINE TO RESTART MOTOR IN CW DIRECTION
222       A9   00        LDA
224       8D   00   A0   STA
227       00   00        BRK    SEE NOTE #1
USE THIS ROUTINE TO RESTART MOTOR IN CCW DIRECTION
229       A9   01        LDA
22B       8D   00   A0   STA
22E       00   00        BRK    SEE NOTE #1
USE THIS ROUTINE TO  CHANGE THE SPEED OF THE  MOTOR WHILE IT
IS RUNNING
230       A9   UU        LDA
232       8D   04   A0   STA
235       A9   UU        LDA
237       8D   0F   A0   STA
23A       00   00        BRK    SEE NOTE #2

NOTES:  1.  This routine can also be used to change the
direction of rotation while the motor is running.
        2.  This routine can be used to change to speed of
rotation.
        3.  UU is data that must be supplied by the user.
```

Table 9-4. This Program will Control the Stepper-Motor Systems with a 4K AIM-65 with BASIC.

A. This program will interface a 4K AIM-65 with the stepper with BASIC to the motor system of Fig. 9-7

The machine-language routine using the AIM-65 disassembly format.

```
ØFAØ   A9   LDA   #FF        MOTOR START ROUTINE
ØFA2   8D   STA   AØØ2
ØFA5   A9   LDA   #Ø1
ØFA7   8D   STA   AØØØ
ØFAA   A9   LDA   #CØ
ØFAC   8D   STA   AØØB
ØFAF   A9   LDA   #FF
ØFB1   8D   STA   AØØ4
ØFB4   A9   LDA   #1Ø
ØFB6   8D   STA   AØØ5
ØFB9   6Ø   RTS
ØFBA   ØØ   BRK
ØFBB   A9   LDA   #Ø2        MOTOR STOP ROUTINE
ØFBD   8D   STA   AØØØ
ØFCØ   6Ø   RTS
ØFC1   ØØ   BRK
ØFC2   A9   LDA   #ØØ        START MOTOR  --  CW
ØFC4   8D   STA   AØØØ
ØFC7   6Ø   RTS
ØFC8   ØØ   BRK
ØFC9   A9   LDA   #Ø1        START MOTOR  --  CCW
ØFCB   8D   STA   AØØØ
ØFCE   6Ø   RTS
ØFCF   ØØ   BRK
ØFDØ   A9   LDA   #21        CHANGE MOTOR SPEED
ØFD2   8D   STA   AØØ4
ØFD5   A9   LDA   #16
ØFD7   8D   STA   AØØ5
ØFDA   6Ø   RTS
ØFDB   ØØ   BRK
```

Table 9-4. This Program will Control the Stepper-Motor Systems with a 4K AIM-65 with BASIC (continued from page 133).

```
THE AIM-65 BASIC PROGRAM (LIMIT MEMORY TO 3999)

10 PRINT "STEPPER-MOTOR CONTROL PROGRAM"
20 PRINT "TO START STEPPER MOTOR, TYPE (RUN 100 - RETURN)"
30 PRINT "TO STOP STEPPER MOTOR, TYPE (RUN 150 - RETURN)"
40 PRINT "TO RUN MOTOR CW, TYPE (RUN 200 - RETURN)"
50 PRINT "TO RUN MOTOR CCW, TYPE (RUN 300 - RETURN)"
60 PRINT "TO CHANGE SPEED, TYPE (RUN 350 - RETURN)"
70 END
100 POKE 04,160: POKE 05,15
110 X=USR(1)
120 END
150 POKE 04,187: POKE 05,15
160 X=USR (2)
170 END
200 POKE 04,194: POKE 05,15
210 X=USR (3)
220 END
300 POKE 04,201: POKE 05,15
310 X=USR (4)
320 END
350 PRINT "SPEED CHANGE ROUTINE"
360 INPUT "INPUT SPEED DATA  HI, LO"
370 INPUT A,B
380 POKE 4049,B: POKE 4054,A
390 POKE 04,208: POKE 05,15
400 X=USR (5)
410 END

NOTES: A.  The initial motor speed data is stored in
locations 0FB0 and 0FB5.  The data in 0FB5 has the most
control over the motor speed.
       B.  The initial motor direction data is stored in
location 0FA6.
```

Table 9-5. This Program can be used to Step the Stepper Motor a Given Number of Degrees Using a 4K AIM-65.

```
A. This program will interface a 4k AIM-65 with the stepper-
motor system of Fig. 9-7.
B. This program uses the free running square function of
PB7.
C. Port B is set up as an output port.
D. The machine language routines are called for by the
BASIC program.
E. Limit the BASIC memory size to 3999 or lower.

The machine-language routine using the AIM-65 disassembly
format.

0FA0   A9 LDA #FF        THIS ROUTINE BETWEEN 0FA0 AND 0FB9
0FA2   8D STA A002       SETS UP THE SQUARE FUNCTION OF PB7,
0FA5   A9 LDA #01        SETS PORT B AS AN OUTPUT PORT, AND
0FA7   8D STA A000       INPUTS THE STARTING MOTOR SPEED AND
0FAA   A9 LDA #C0        DIRECTION DATA.
0FAC   8D STA A00B
0FAF   A9 LDA #FF
0FB1   8D STA A004
0FB4   A9 LDA #10
0FB6   8D STA A005
0FB9   60 RTS
0FBA   00 BRK
0FBB   A9 LDA #02       STOP MOTOR
0FBD   8D STA A000
0FC0   60 RTS
0FC1   00 BRK
0FC2   A9 LDA #00       RESTART MOTOR -- CW
0FC4   8D STA A000
0FC7   60 RTS
0FC8   00 BRK
0FC9   A9 LDA #01       RESTART MOTOR -- CCW
0FCB   8D STA A000
0FCE   60 RTS
0FCF   00 BRK
0FD0   A9 LDA #21       CHANGE MOTOR SPEED
0FD2   8D STA A004
0FD5   A9 LDA# 16
0FD7   8D STA A005
0FDA   60 RTS
0FDB   00 BRK
```

Table 9-5. This Program can be used to Step the Stepper Motor a Given Number of Degrees Using a 4K AIM-65 (continued from page 135.)

```
THE AIM-65 BASIC PROGRAM  (REMEMBER,  LIMIT MEMORY  SIZE  TO
3999 OR LOWER)
10 PRINT "STEPPER-MOTOR CONTROL PROGRAM"
20 PRINT "TO START STEPPER MOTOR, TYPE RUN 100-RETURN"
30 PRINT "TO STOP STEPPER MOTOR, TYPE RUN 150-RETURN"
40 PRINT "TO RESTART MOTOR-CW, TYPE RUN 200-RETURN"
50 PRINT "TO RESTART MOTOR-CCW, TYPE RUN 300-RETURN"
60 PRINT "TO CHANGE SPEED, TYPE RUN 350-RETURN"
70 END
100 POKE 04,160:POKE 05,15
110 X=USR(1): PRINT X
120 END
150 POKE 04,187: POKE 05:15
160 X=USR(2): PRINT X
170 END
200 POKE 04,194: POKE 05,15
210 X=USR(3): PRINT X
220 END
300 POKE 04,201: POKE 05,15
310 X=USR(4): PRINT X
320 END
350 PRINT "SPEED CHANGE ROUTINE"
360 PRINT "INPUT SPEED DATA-HI,LO"
370 INPUT A,B
380 POKE 4049,B: POKE 4054,A
390 POKE 04,208: POKE 05,15
400 X=USR(5): PRINT X
410 END

NOTES: A. The initial motor  speed is  stored in  locations
0FB0 and 0FB5. The data in 0FB5 has the most control
       B. The initial  motor direction  data  is stored  in
location 0FA6.
       C. The BASIC  speed program  requires  that the speed
data be entered in  decimal form  of aaa,bbb when  the input
data is requested.  The data that is entered for the aaa and
bbb  data request will be between  30 and 255.  The data  of
30,30 will give you a very fast speed  (about 300+ RPM)  and
the  data of 255,255  will give  you a  very  slow  stepping
motion (about 6 RPM).
```

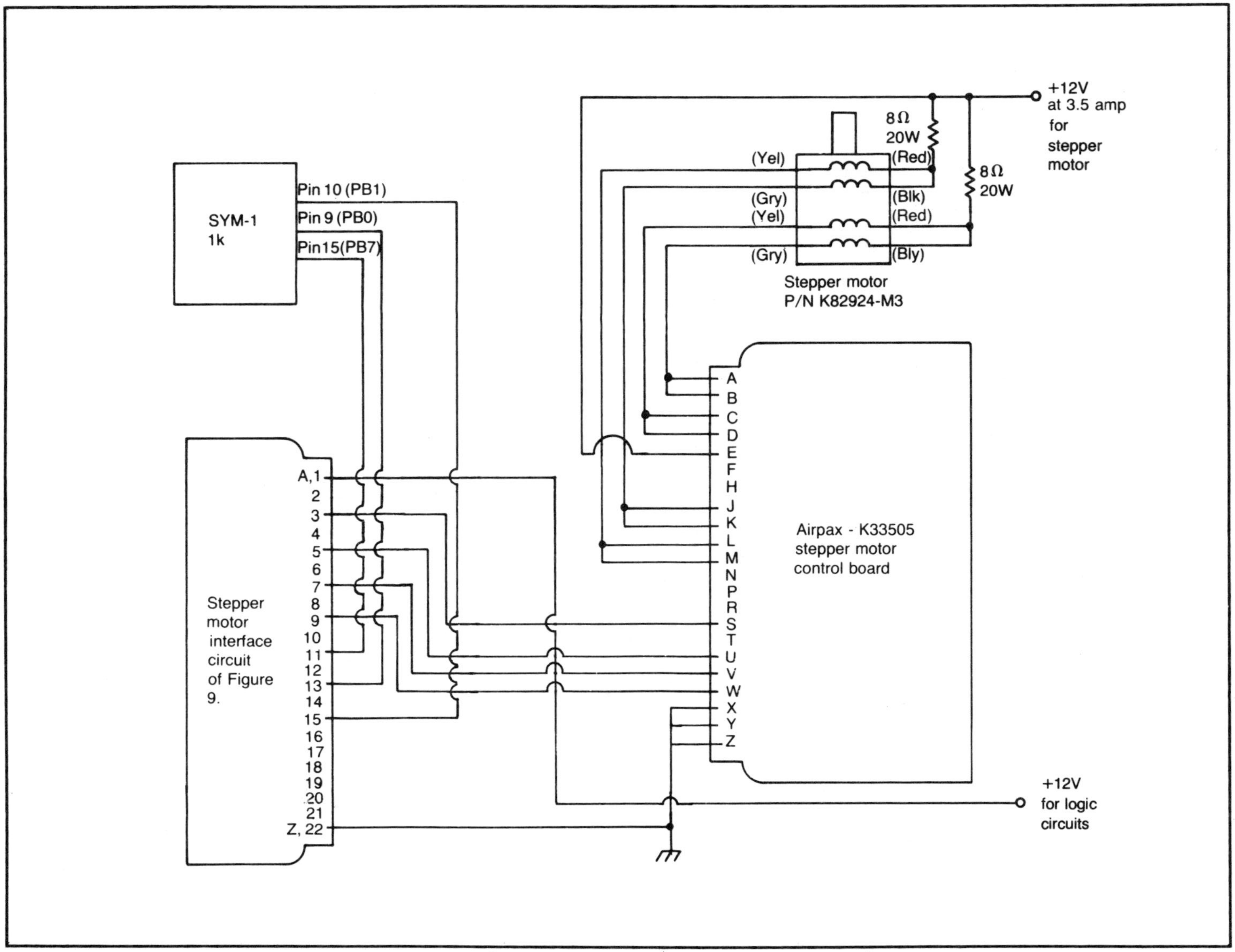

Fig. 9-6. The stepper-motor connection diagram for operation with a SYM-1.

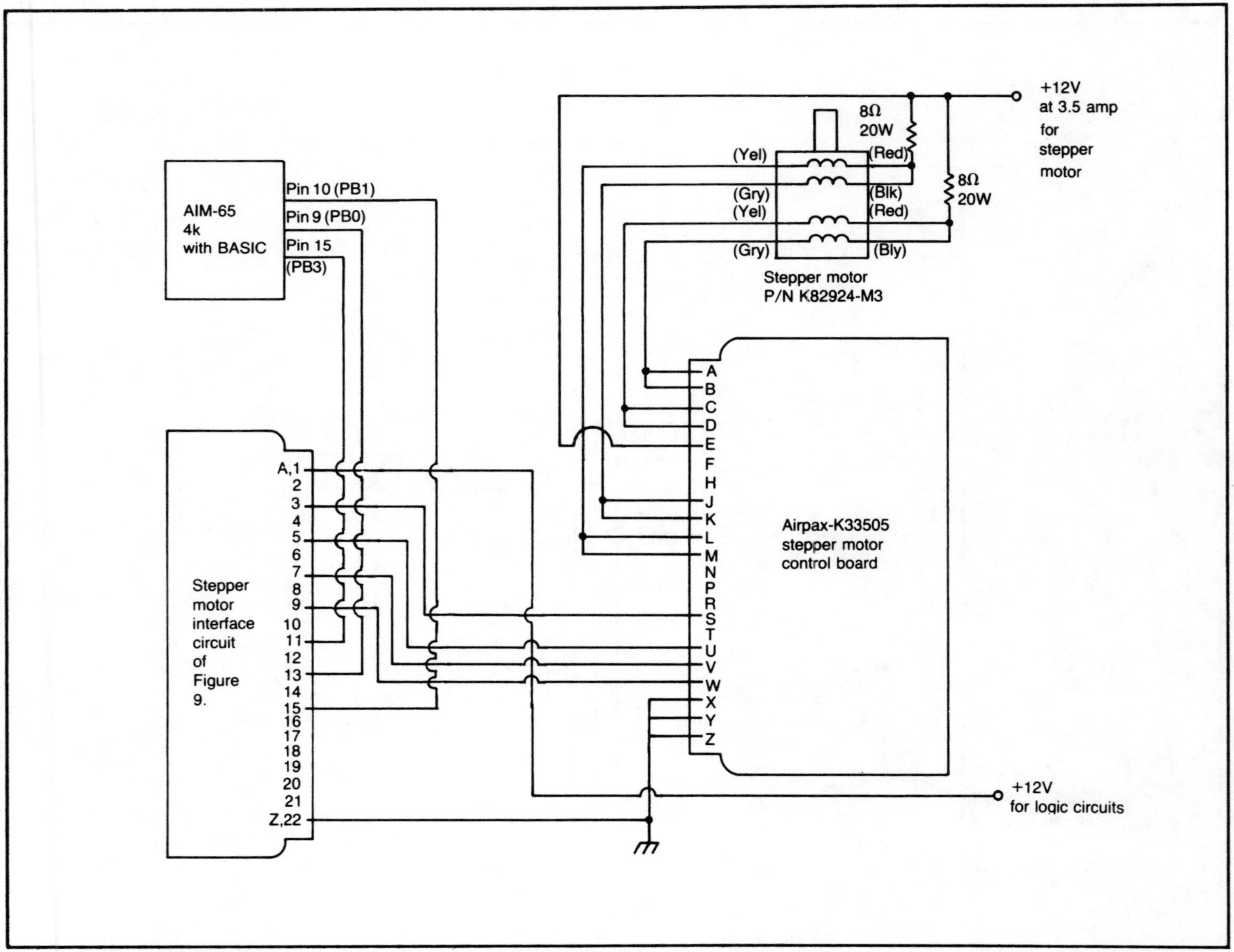

Fig. 9-7. The stepper-motor connection diagram for operation with the AIM-65.

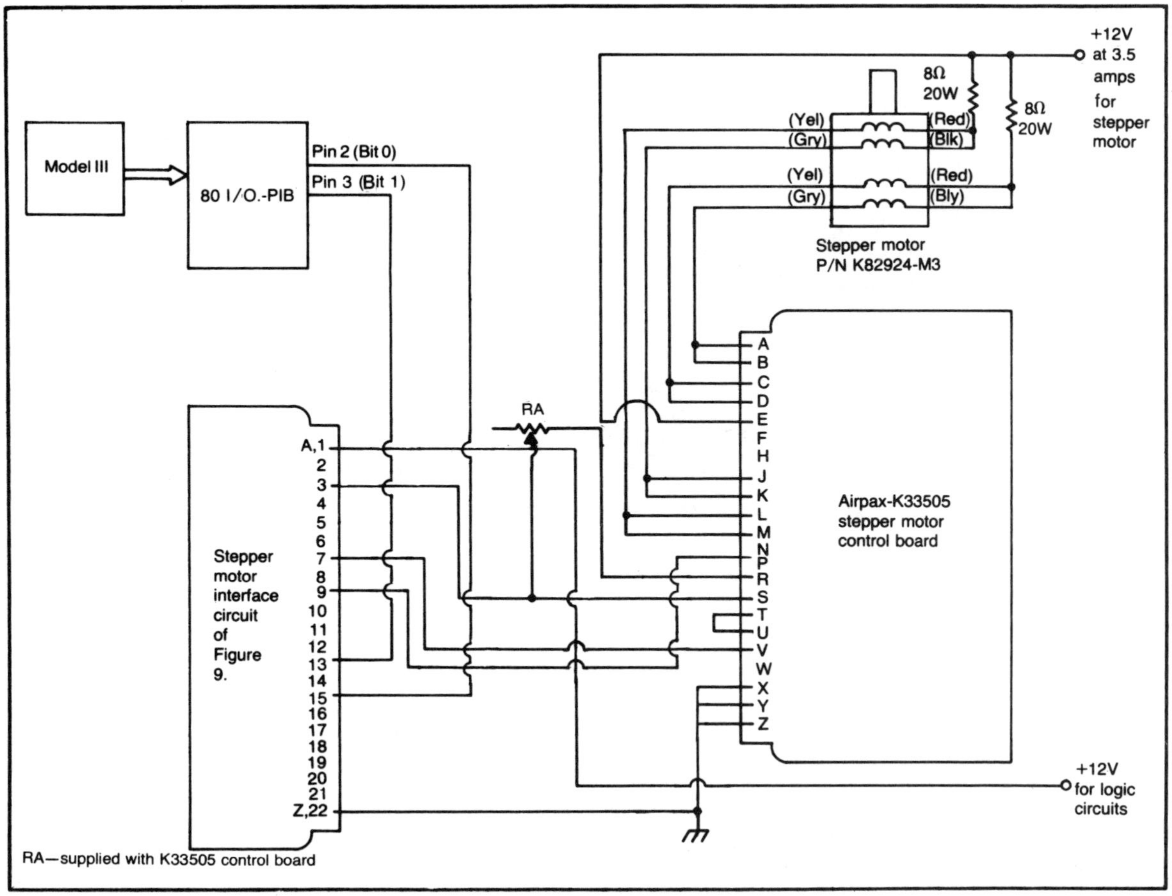

Fig. 9-8. The stepper-motor connection diagram for operation with the Model III.

Fig. 9-9. A view of a bidirectional linear-actuator stepper motor (courtesy Airpax Corporation).

Fig. 9-10. A view of three standard-rotational stepper motors (courtesy Airpax Corporation).

stepper motor. A bidirectional linear actuator is shown in Fig. 9-9 and a standard stepper motor is shown in Fig. 9-10.

CONCLUSION

The motor control circuits that are presented here will not solve all of your motor control problems, but they will work in a lot of the applications that require some form of rotational control or movement. The motor control systems do not have a lot of horsepower, but if you need horsepower, there are many good three-phase control systems that are presently being marketed. Also, the construction of higher power ac control systems is a little beyond the scope and ability of the small test sytems department.

If you are interested in more information about this subject I recommend the book: *How To Design, Build & Use Electronic Control Systems*, by Frank P. Tedeschi, TAB Books, Inc., 1981.

Chapter 10

Test Equipment Construction Style

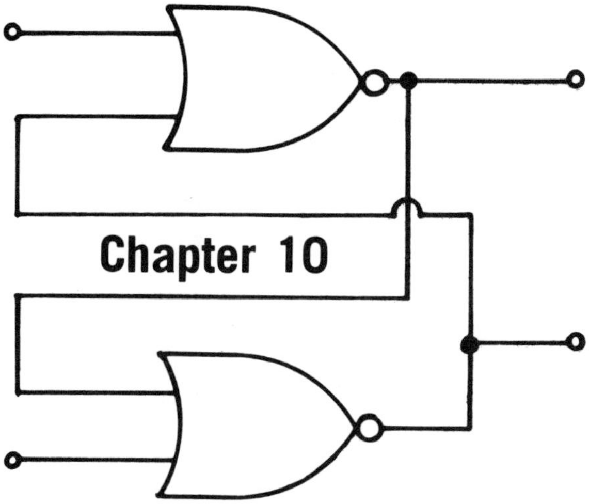

There are many factors which dictate how you will build a test system. Some of the factors in descending order of importance are money, how fast must the system be built, how long must the system last, portability, and efficiency. Factors such as accuracy, dependability, and stability are generally given in the engineering specifications of the product you are going to manufacture and must be designed into the test system that is to be built.

There are two construction methods which I use when assembling a test system. First, in a large test system that will use a lot of commercially built test equipment, you generally will use a standard 19-inch rack-mount assembly that is selected from a catalog. If this method is going to be used, you can make a few telephone calls and have three dozen salesmen pounding on your door in a couple of days trying to sell you their rack system assemblies. Well, buy the one that suits your fancy and budget and proceed on. The second method is to build something from scratch. I generally use this method since it gives me the maximum amount of design freedom. The figures that are presented in this chapter show how I like to put a test system together. There are no outstanding features to brag about when assembling a test system this way, but it is the easiest and fastest method I have found for building a test system and secure acceptable results.

Figures 10-1 through 10-6 show how to use standard chassis boxes to assemble a test system which is portable, rugged, shielded, and easy to maintain. I call this the chassis box method. The chassis-box method uses all standard stock items which most of the larger electronic supply houses and hardware stores keep on hand. You can build a chassis-box assembly with the minimum amount of time and effort when compared to other methods.

Figure 10-1 shows a system that is being built using six chassis boxes. Three large chassis (17×13×4) are connected together using 8-32 machine screws for the bottom, and the three chassis (17×13×2) are connected together in a similar manner to form a top. As shown in Fig. 10-2, the six chassis are connected together with a long piano hinge. For this chassis-box assembly, a plywood top was placed over the top three chassis and then covered with a hard tabletop material that was purchased from a lumberyard. As shown in Fig. 10-3, a large working area on top of the chassis box assembly is available for production functions. If you observe Fig. 10-1 closely, you will note that two card-table leg locks are used at the two chassis box ends to lock open the chassis-box assembly so you can work inside. The whole chassis-box assembly can be built using no more than standard shop tools.

In the test system that is shown in Figs. 10-1, 10-2, and 10-3. An AIM-65 is located in a small compartment on top of the chassis-box assembly, as shown in Figs. 10-4

Fig. 10-1. A three compartment chassis-box assembly under construction. Note the motor, motor controls, and power supplies are in the left compartment. The middle compartment contains the system electronics, and the right compartment contains the computer system. This type of separation prevents noise from being introduced into the system from circuits that operate at different voltage and power levels.

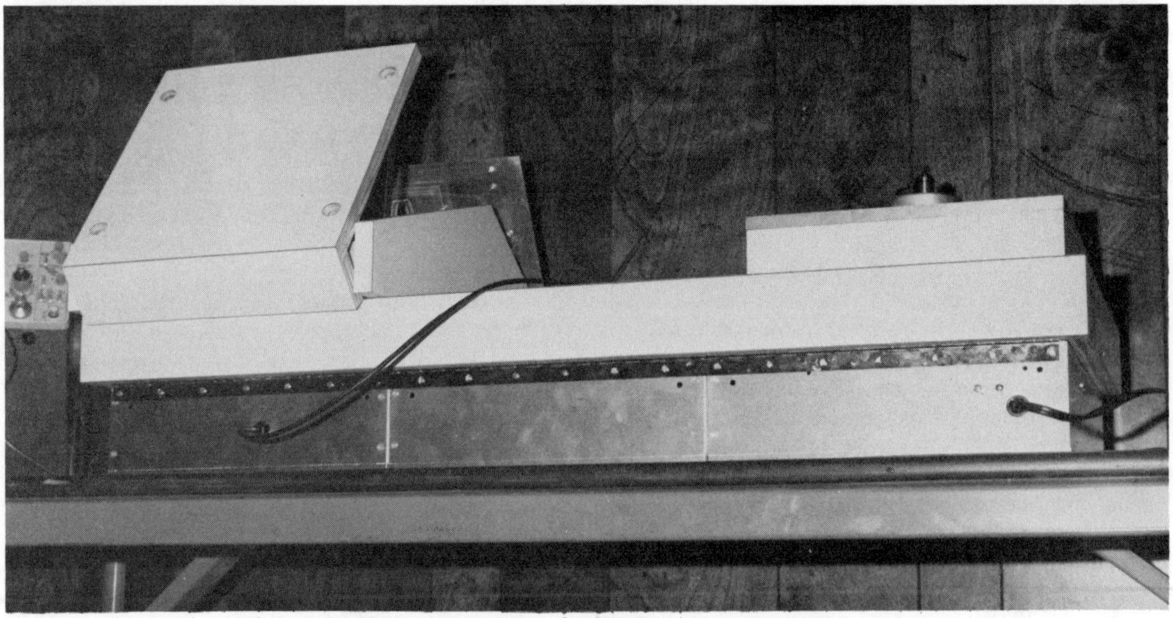

Fig. 10-2. The backside of the chassis-box assembly which shows the long piano hinge.

Fig. 10-3. The chassis-box assembly with the top closed will give you plenty of room for the test system fixtures and control panels.

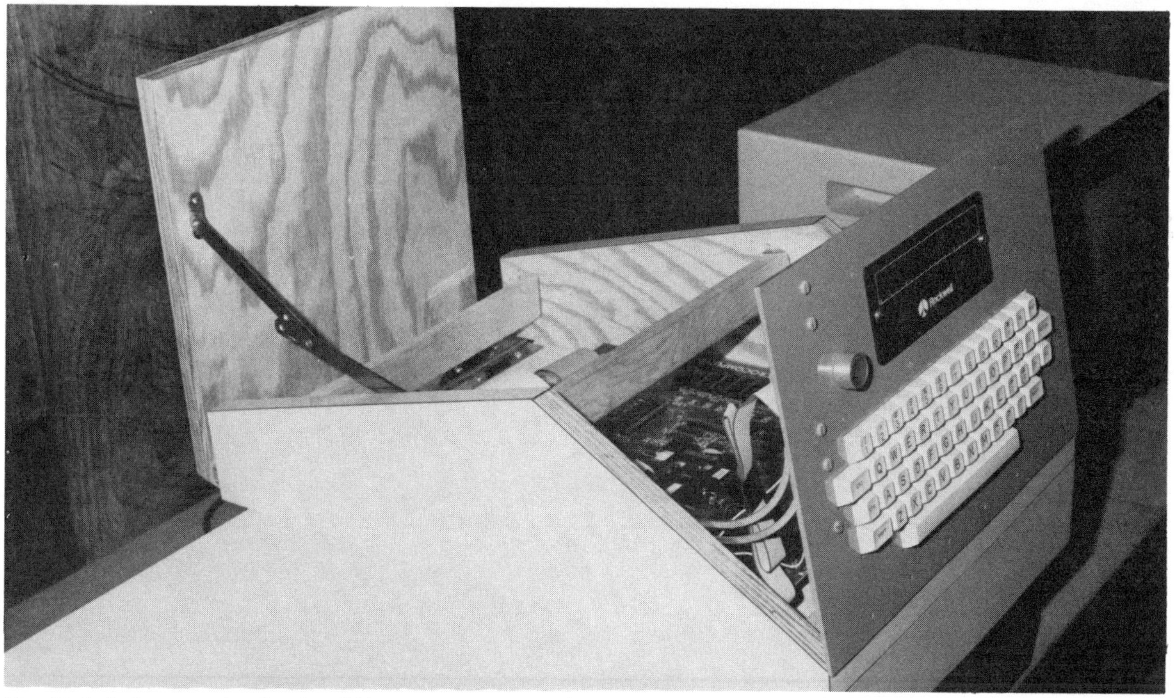

Fig. 10-4. A close-up showing the AIM-65 compartment.

Fig. 10-5. Another close-up showing the assembly mounting of the AIM-65. In this system, the printer will not be used after the system development is completed.

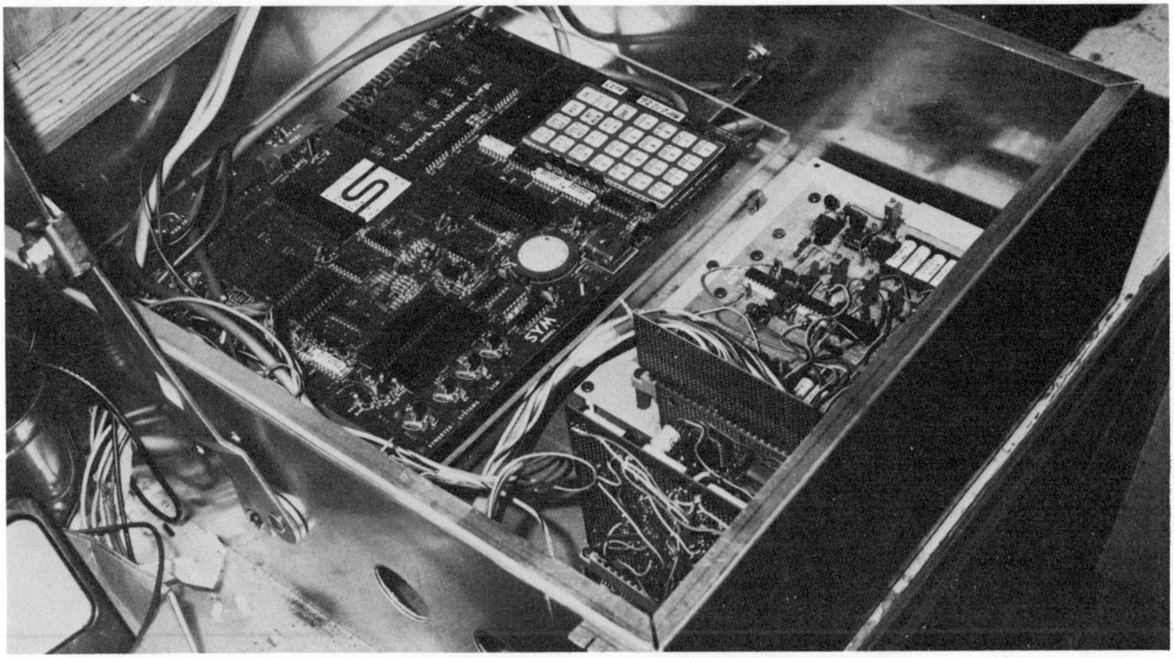

Fig. 10-6. A SYM-1 mounted in a chassis-box assembly along with the support electronics.

and 10-5, and the RM-65 Card Cage is shown mounted in the assembly bottom. There have been no noticeable effects on the single-board computer from outside electrical interference sources using this type of set-up.

If you believe that electrical shielding is needed, you can easily locate a single-board computer inside the chassis-box assembly as was done with the SYM-1 that is shown in Fig. 10-6. In this chassis-box system, the single-board computer, the A/D and D/A electronics, along with the electronics which controls all the lights and audio alarms are located in the right chassis with the power supplies and motor controls located in the left chassis. Note the card-table leg lock on the left side of the picture which locks up the top when you must work on the inside of the box. If you observe Fig. 10-1 again, you will note that the motor and power supplies are located in the left chassis box, the electronic components are being installed in the center box, and the microprocessor equipment is being installed in the right chassis box. The intercompartment wiring is passed between the chassis-box compartments through a couple of two-inch diameter holes in the back of the chassis-box compartments. This style of assembly will generally provide the required electrical noise isolation to secure proper system operation.

The chassis-box assembly method is presented here to show how you might construct a complete test system. I have used this method for about ten years now, and I have always enjoyed building the successful test systems that this method has given me.

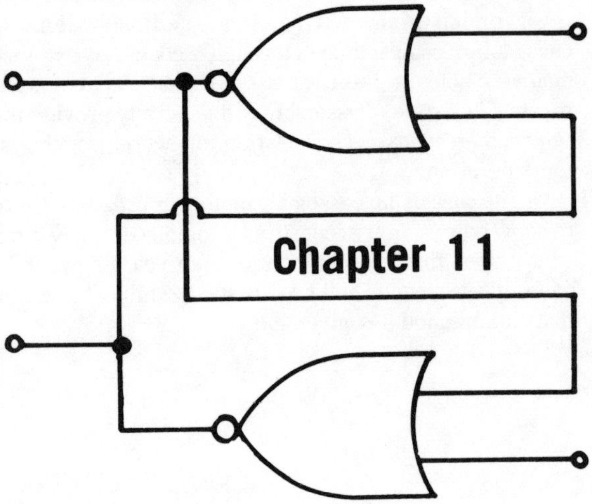

Chapter 11

Useful Testing and Control Circuits

This chapter presents various circuits that are not related to the circuits in the other chapters of this book. All of these circuits are very useful in the field of testing and control functions. These circuits have been designed for a specific function and research references are given which should help you to redesign these circuits for your own applications as needed. See Figs. 11-1 through 11-30.

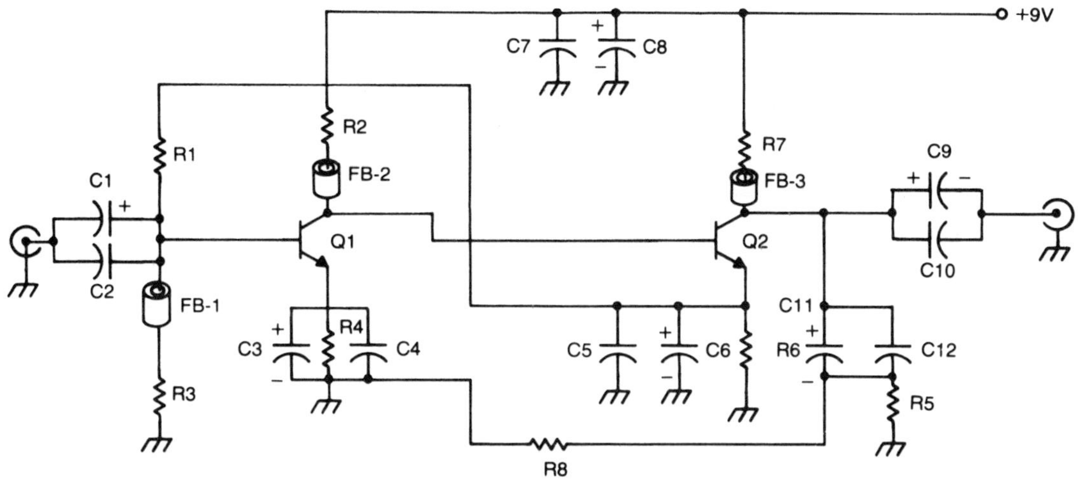

Parts List For The Wide Bandwidth Amplifier

C1, C3, C6, C9, C11 - 100 μF capacitor at 16 volts
C2, C4, C5, C10, C12 - 470 pF capacitor
C7 - 1000 pF capacitor
C8 - 1000 μF capacitor at 16 volts
R1 - 27k resistor
R2 - 6.8k resistor
R3 - 1.5k resistor
R4 - 1k resistor
R5 - 100 ohm resistor
R6 - 270 ohm resistor
R7, R8 - 4.7k resistor
FB-1, FB-2, FB-3 - Ferrite Bead, Radio Shack 273-1571
Q1, Q2 - Radio Shack 276-2015

Fig. 11-1. This is a wide-bandwidth amplifier (video amplifier) which can be used as an oscilloscope preamplifier for most of the 5 MHz bandwidth hobby oscilloscopes that have limited vertical or horizontal amplification ability.

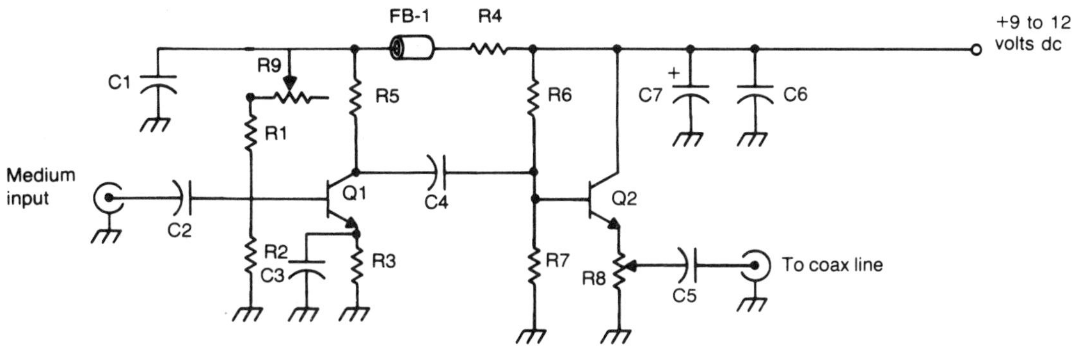

Parts List For Rf Amplifier-Buffer Circuit

R1, R2 - 10k resistor
R3 - 1.0k resistor
R4 - 270 ohm resistor
R5 - 1.5k resistor
R6, R7 - 6.8k resistor
R8 - 500 ohm trim pot (carbon or cermet)
R9 - 50k trim pot
C1 to C6 - .1 μF Mylar capacitor
C7 - 22 μF, 16 volts capacitor
FB-1 Ferrite Bead, Radio Shack 273-1571
Q1, Q2 - 2N2222 transistor

Fig. 11-2. This circuit is a broadband rf amplifier and buffer circuit which can be used to pick-up, amplify and feed a broadband of rf signals into a low impedance coaxial cable for transmission to another test instrument such as an rf voltmeter (which may be located some distance from the pick-up point).

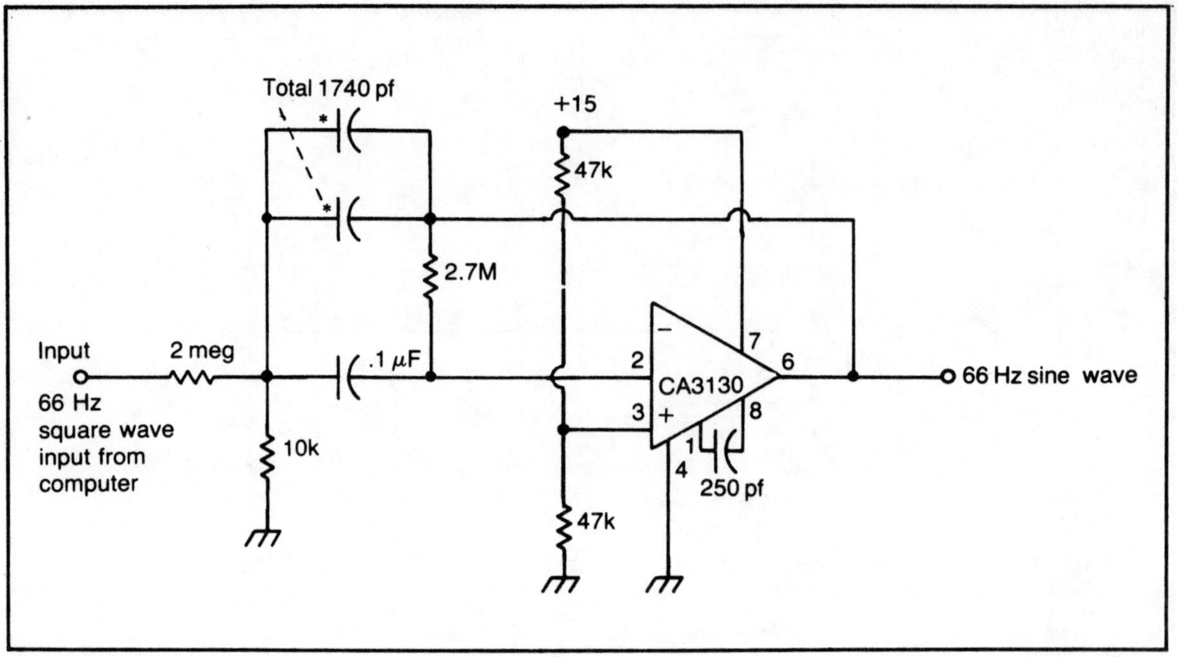

Fig. 11-3. This circuit is a square-wave to sine-wave converter circuit. It can be used to transform a square-wave signal from PB7 of a VIA 6522 into a sine wave at a specific frequency. This circuit is really a bandpass Butterworth filter circuit.

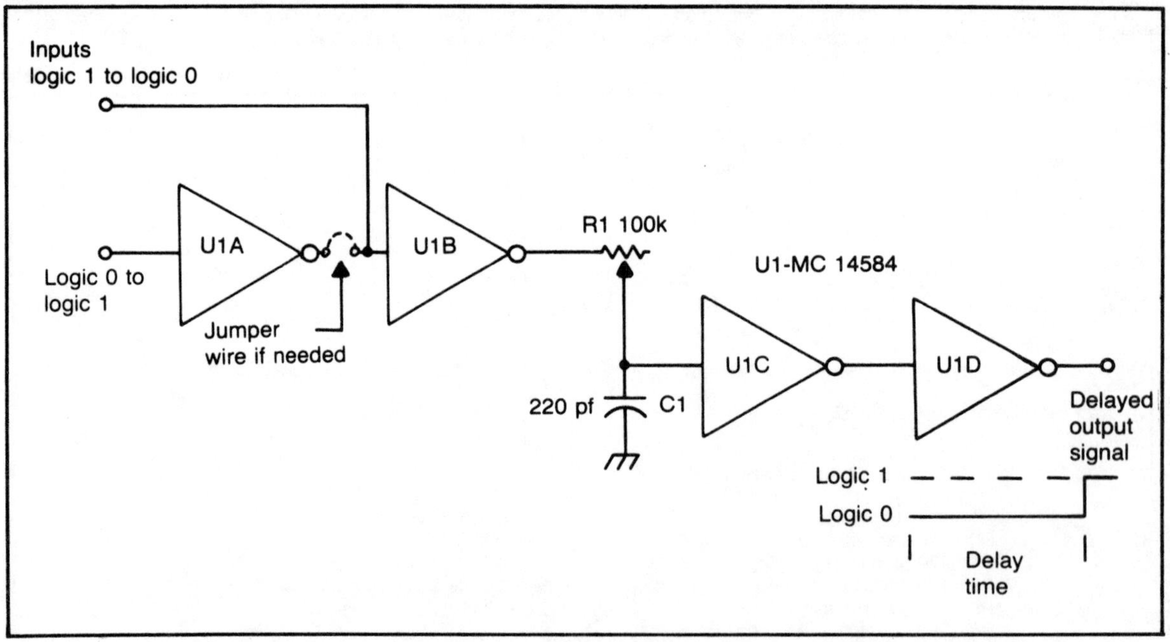

Fig. 11-4. This is a pulse-delay circuit which can be used in conjunction with a single-board computer. It is sometimes a problem generating logic pulses which are closer than about 10 microseconds of each other. Using this circuit, you can generate a pulse delay from .250 microseconds to 12.5 microseconds after the computer has generated its pulse.

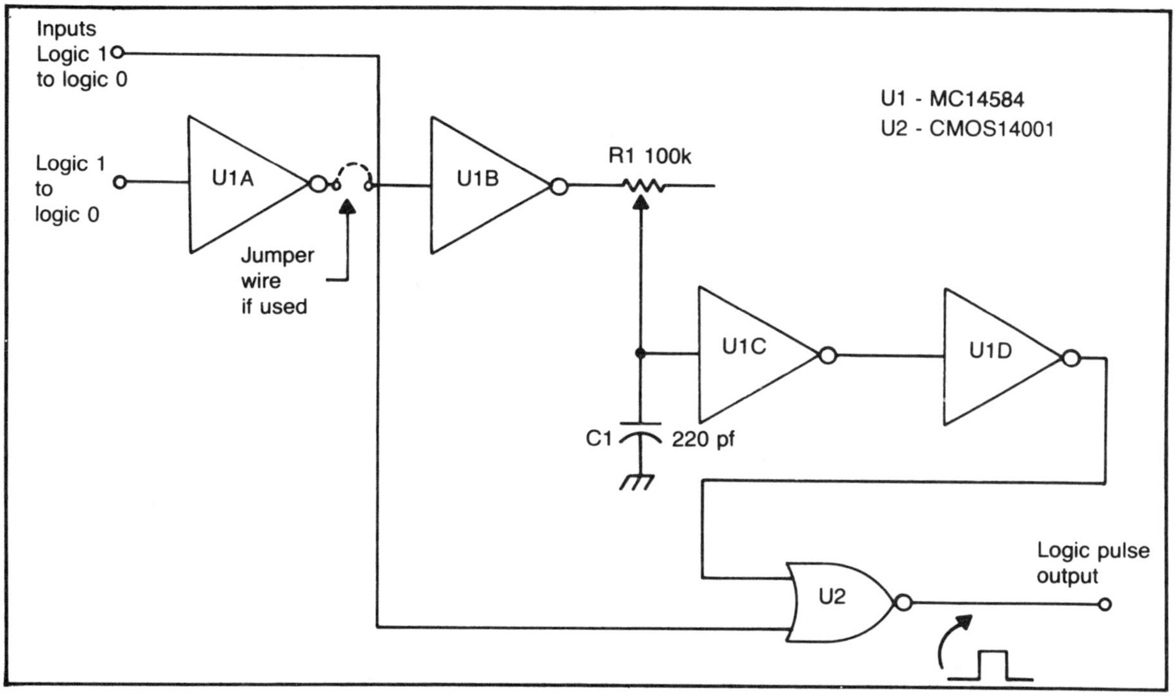

Fig. 11-5. This circuit is similar to the one in Fig. 11-4. This circuit will generate a complete pulse and not just a pulse delay. You will not be able to generate short duration pulses with a single-board computer shorter than about eight to ten microseconds. Using this circuit, you will be able to generate a pulse with a duration of .250 microseconds to 12.5 microseconds.

Notes: Output goes high for the time delay duration when the circuit is triggered by a logic zero pulse which is more than 100 microseconds long.

555 Timer — Single Shot Time Delay Circuit Parts List
R1 - See chart
R2 - Trim pot (see chart)
R3, R4, 6.8k resistor
R5 - 270 ohm resistor
C1 - 1000 μF, 16 volts capacitor
C2, C5 - .05 μF capacitor
C3 - See chart
C4 - 1.0 μF capacitor

Time delay -	(5 sec)	(1 sec)	(.5 sec)	(.1 sec)	(.001 sec)
R1 -	3.9 meg	2 meg	1 meg	330k	68k
C3-μF	1.0	.47	.47	.05	.01
R2 -	250k	250k	100k	50k	25k

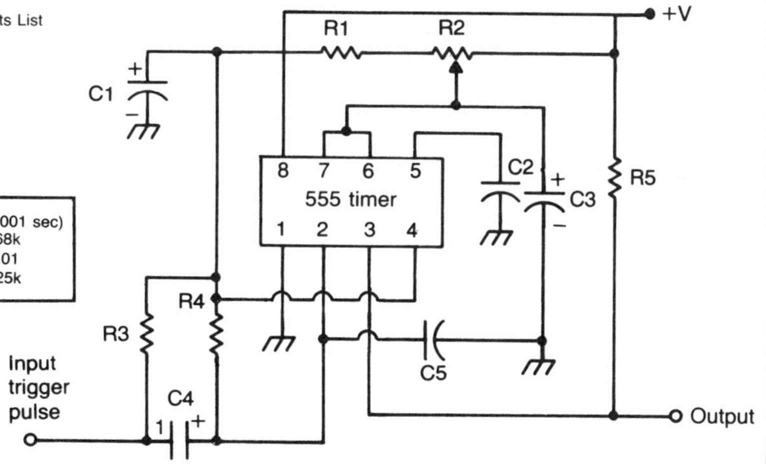

Fig. 11-6. This circuit is a standard 555 time-delay circuit. Other 555 IC circuits can be found by consulting pages 201 to 207 of *The Master Handbook of IC Circuits* by Thomas R. Powers and published by TAB Books Inc.

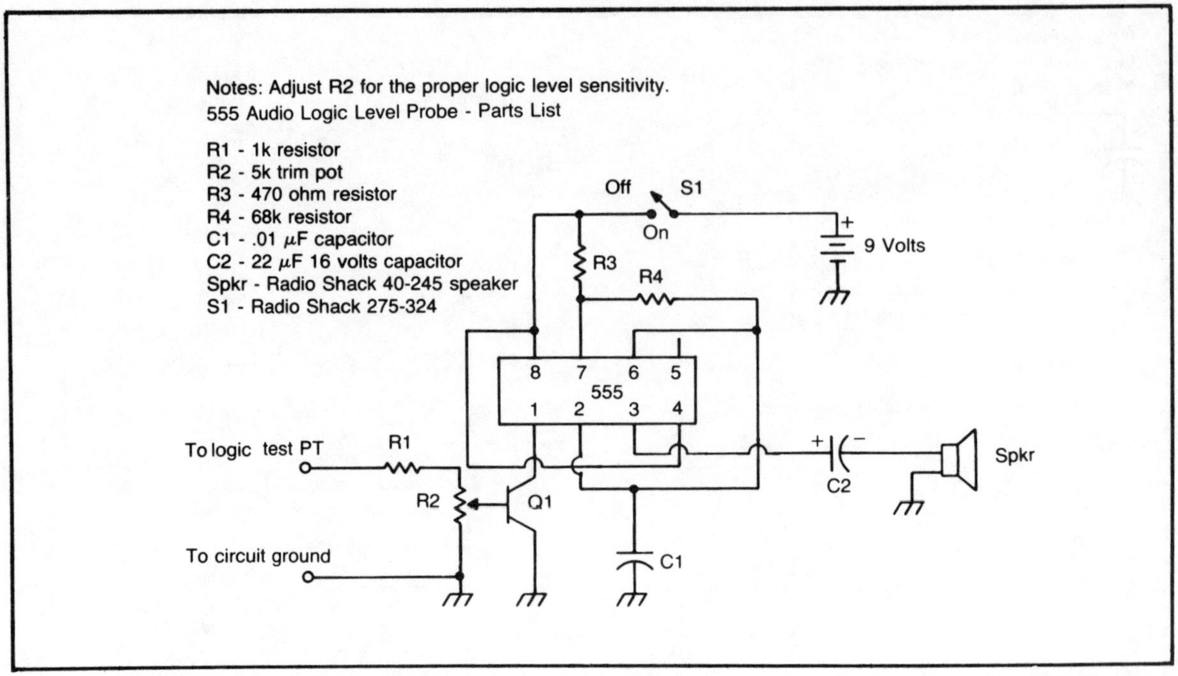

Fig. 11-7. This circuit shows an audio logic probe that can be used to detect logic voltage levels between 3 and 25 volts. It can be very handy when checking 24-volt relays and other control elements.

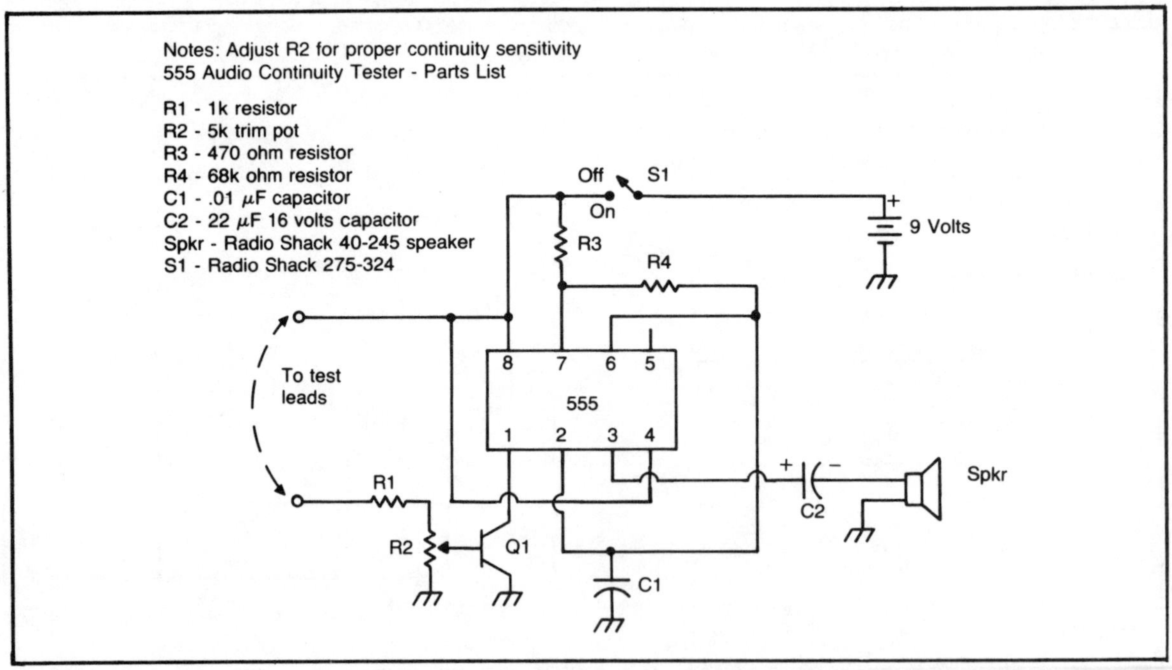

Fig. 11-8. This circuit is a continuity tester which generates an audio sound if the circuit under test is complete. R2 can be adjusted for different levels of circuit resistance.

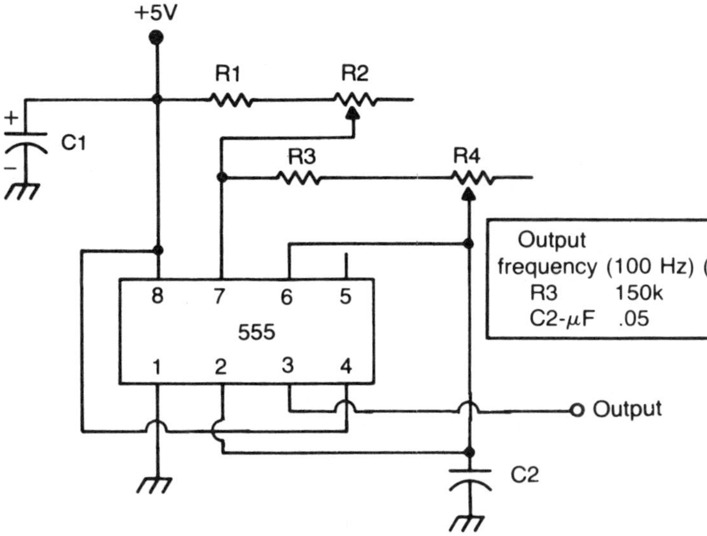

Output frequency	(100 Hz)	(500 Hz)	(1000 Hz)	(5000 Hz)	(10 kHz)
R3	150k	150k	68k	150k	33k
C2-μF	.05	.01	.01	.001	.001

Notes: Adjust R2 for 50% duty cycle and R4 for frequency output.

555 Timer - Free Running Oscillator Circuit - Parts List

C1 - 1000 μF at 16 volts
C2 - See chart
R1 - 150 ohms
R2 - 500 ohms
R3 - See chart
R4 - 50k trim pot

Fig. 11-9. This circuit is a free-running 555 IC oscillator that will oscillate the specified audio frequencies for various values of R3 and C2. The 555 IC can be made to oscillate at frequencies above 1 MHz.

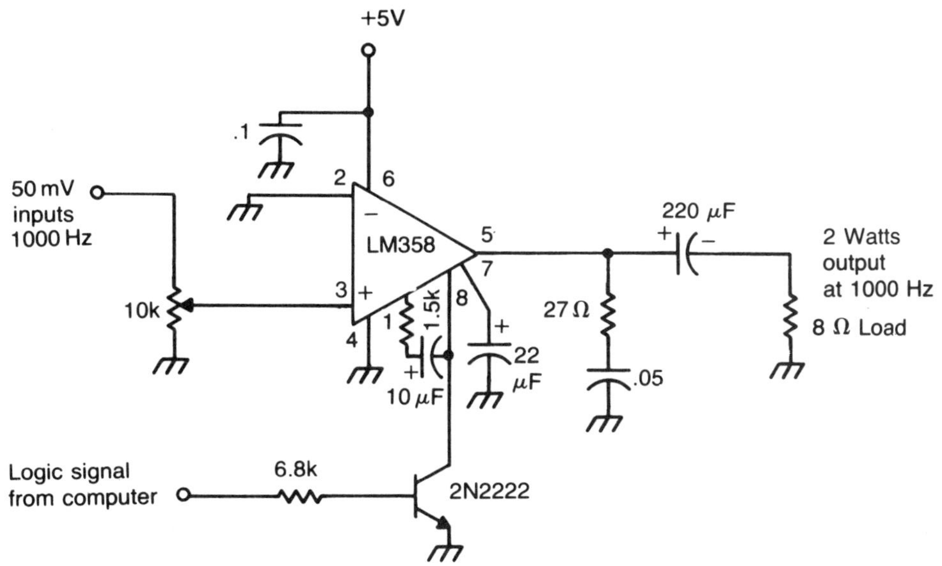

Fig. 11-10. This audio amplifier will provide a clean 2 watts of audio into 8 ohms at 1000 Hz with an input drive of only 50 mV. The nice part about this amplifier is that you can turn it off and on with your computer by applying logic one and zero signals to transistor Q1.

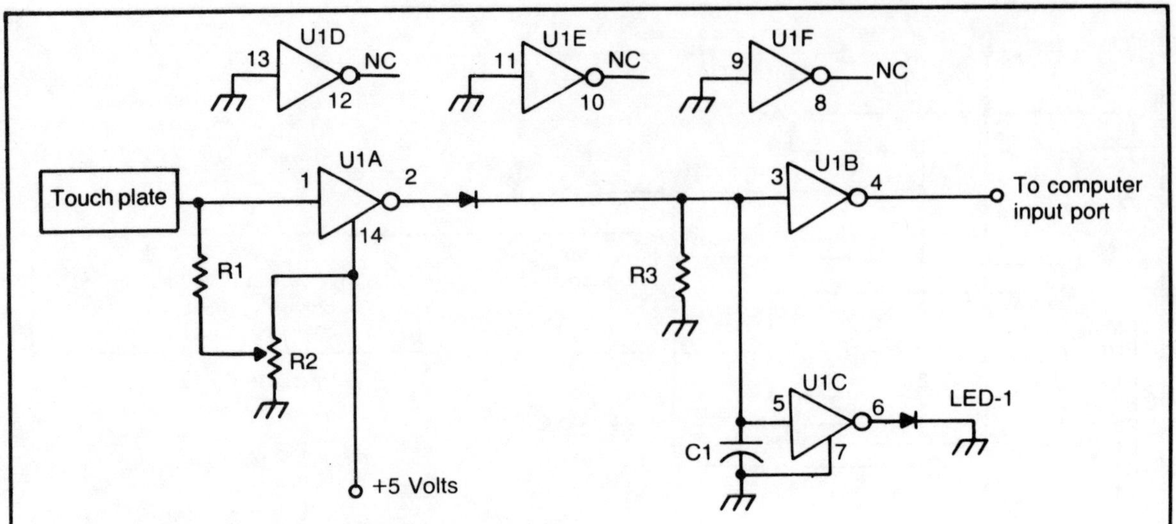

CMOS MC14584 Touch Plate Control Circuit - Parts List

R1 - 22 meg
R2 - 5k trim pot
R3 - 1 meg
D1 - 1N914
C1 - .05 μF
LED - Radio Shack 276-1622
U1 - MC14584 CMOS IC

Fig. 11-11. This is a CMOS touch plate control circuit which can be used with a computer. Adjust R2 for the proper touch plate trigger level.

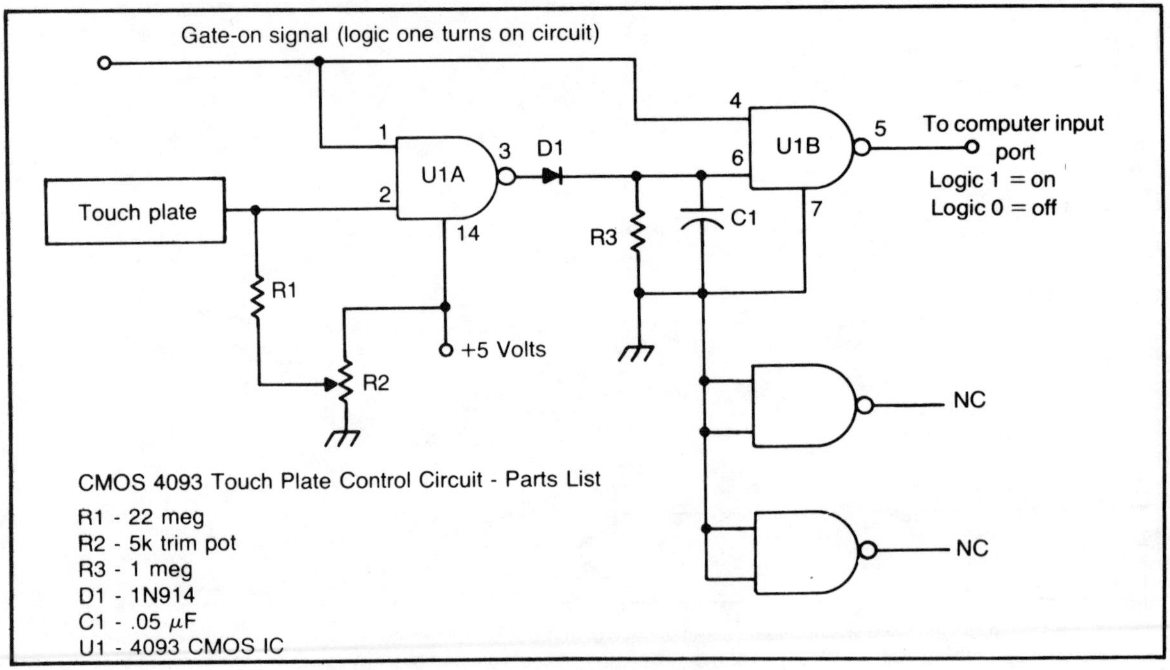

CMOS 4093 Touch Plate Control Circuit - Parts List

R1 - 22 meg
R2 - 5k trim pot
R3 - 1 meg
D1 - 1N914
C1 - .05 μF
U1 - 4093 CMOS IC

Fig. 11-12. This touch plate circuit can be gated off and on by the computer.

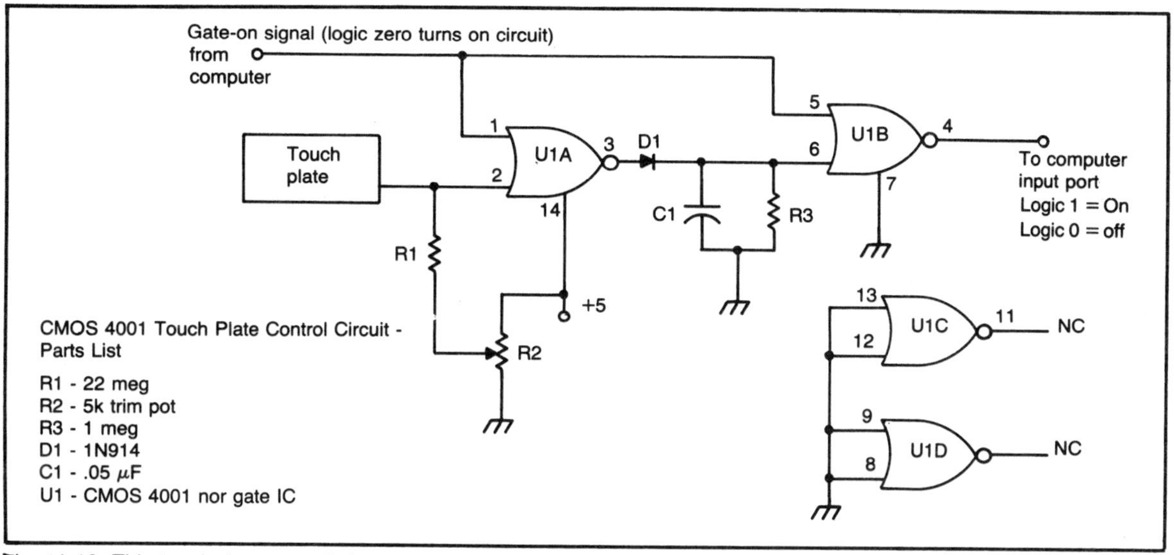

Fig. 11-13. This touchplate control circuit uses the 4001.

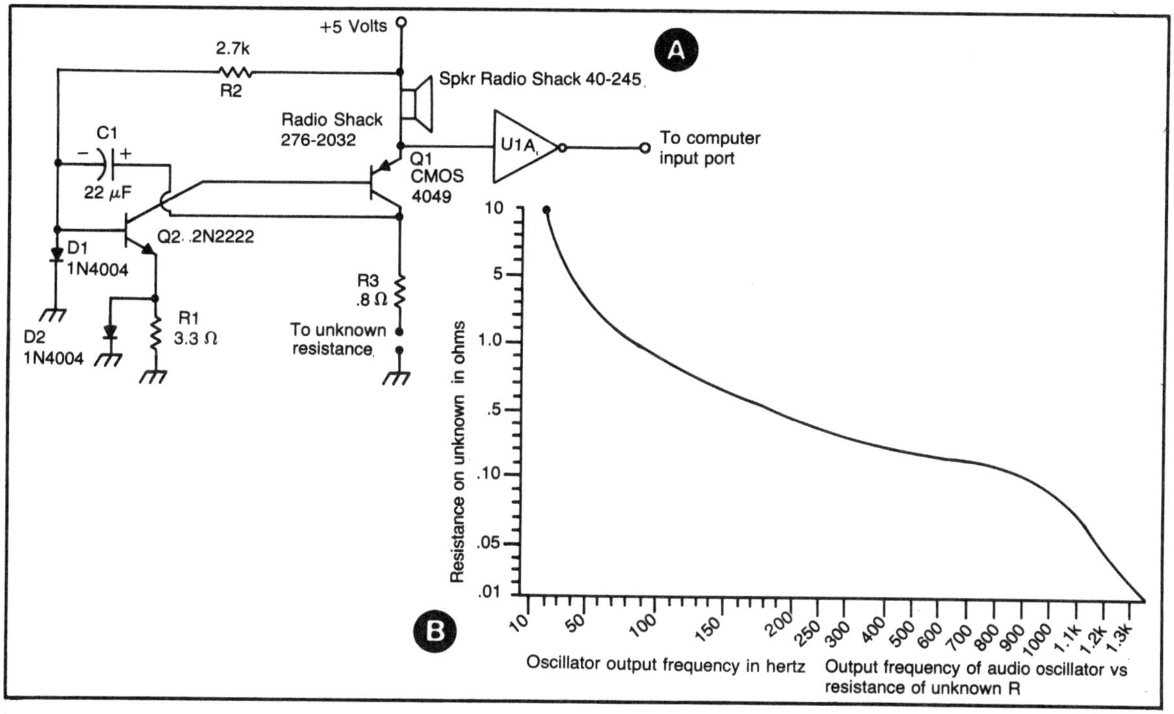

Fig. 11-14. This is an audio-oscillator circuit which can be interfaced to a single-board computer to measure very low resistance values with your computer. As shown in the graph (Fig. 11-14B) resistance values between .01 ohms and 10 ohms will generate different audio frequencies. You can measure these audio frequencies with your computer by counting the number of audio pulses per second or measuring the generated pulse width. This measured data can then be inputted into a BASIC program which will determine the value of unknown resistance. Every circuit of this type that is built will have its own frequency characteristics, so you will have to build the circuit first and then experimentally determine what frequencies are generated for a given resistance value.

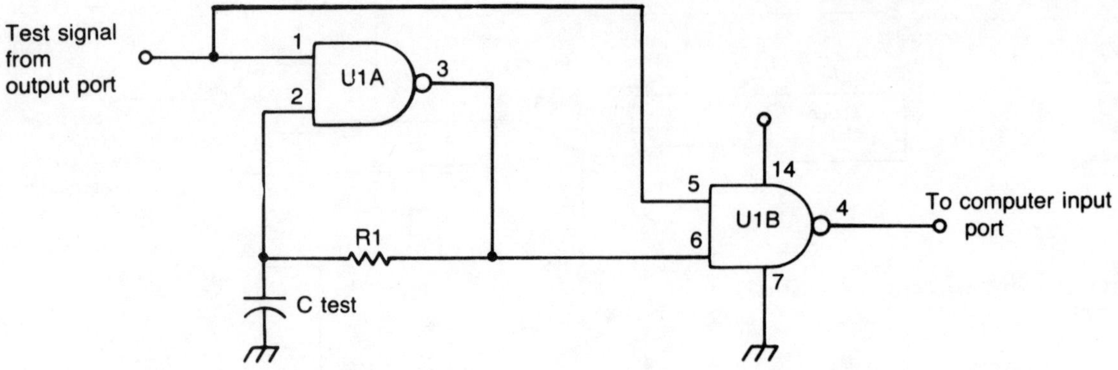

Notes: Positive output pulses of "XX" seconds long will be generated by this circuit when the following capacitors are connected as the C-Test capacitor.

.5 μF ---------- 12.5 milliseconds long pulse
.1 μF ---------- 3.1 milliseconds
.05 μF ---------- 1.4 milliseconds
.01 μF ---------- 225 microseconds
.001 μF ---------- 30 microseconds
Single IC Capacitor Testing Circuit - Parts List
R1 - 100k
U1A and U1B - CMOS 4093

Fig. 11-15. This circuit will measure unknown values of capacitance and works in the same fashion as the one in Fig. 11-14. The CMOS circuit will oscillate at some frequency that is determined by the value of the "C Test" capacitor. The frequency of oscillation can be used to compute the value of the unknown capacitance.

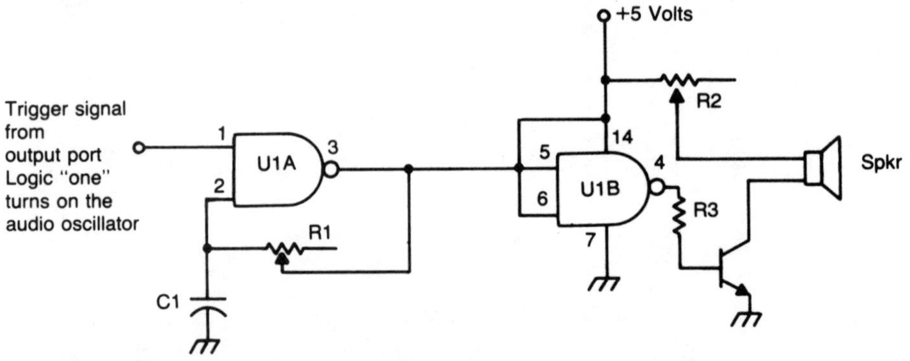

Computer Controlled Audio Oscillator - Parts List

R1 - 50k trim pot	C1 - .22 μF capacitor
R2 - 500 ohm trim pot	U1A and U1B - CMOS 4093
R3 - 6.8k resistor	Spkr - Radio Shack 40-245

Fig. 11-16. This circuit is a simple audio oscillator which can be turned off and on by a single-board computer. There are many programs published on generating audio sounds with the computer. But, why tie-up an expensive computer to generate a simple audio tone when three dollars worth of electronic parts will do the job and free the computer for other more important jobs?

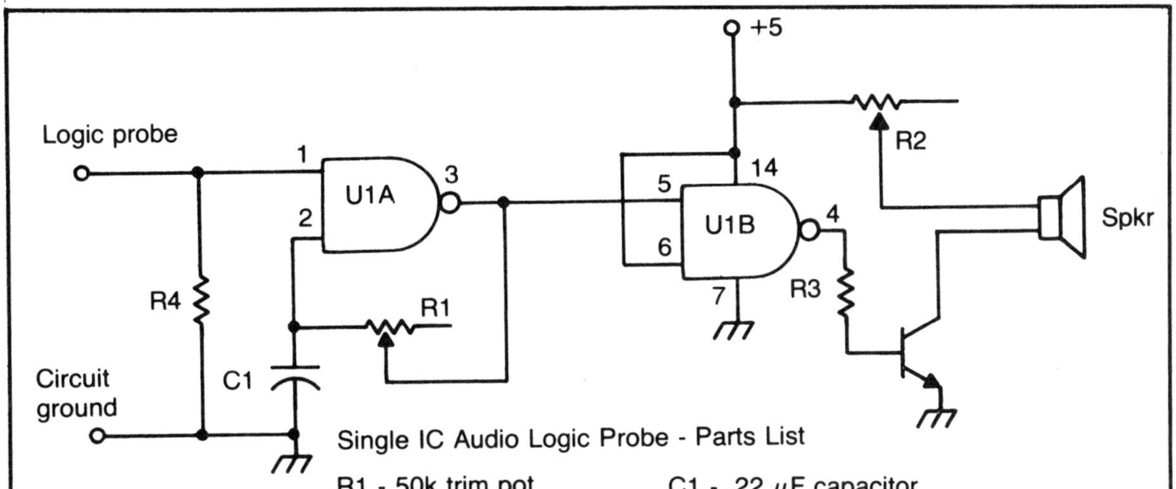

Single IC Audio Logic Probe - Parts List

R1 - 50k trim pot
R2 - 500 ohm trim pot
R3 - 6.8k resistor
R4 - 100k resistor
C1 - .22 μF capacitor
U1A and U1B - CMOS 4093
SPKR - Radio Shack 40-245

Fig. 11-17. This circuit presents another method of using CMOS ICs to make a simple audio logic probe. You ask, "Why use an audio logic probe?" Well, some logic probes that you can buy use an LED to indicate if a logic one or zero is present. If the logic level is pulsing at more than 30 Hz per second, the LED logic probe will most likely indicate a continuous logic one level because the eye can not detect the pulses. If you use an audio logic probe, you can detect logic pulse rates up to around 19 kHz.

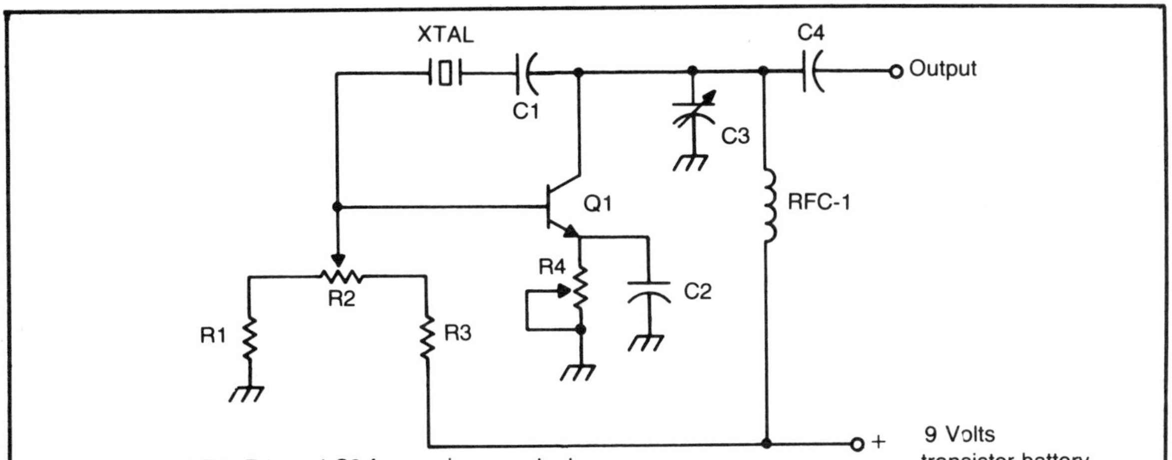

Notes: Adjust R2, R4, and C3 for maximum output

Transistor Crystal Oscillator - Parts List

R1 - 4.7k resistor
R2 - 25k cermet trim pot
R3 - 33k resistor
R4 - 1k cermet trim pot
C1, C2, C4 - .01 μF ceramic capacitor
C3 - 300 pF mica compression trimmer capacitor
XTAL - 1 to 20 MHz transmitting crystal
RFC-1 - 2.5 mH choak

Fig. 11-18. This circuit is a Pierce crystal oscillator which will oscillate at the fundamental frequency of a transmitting crystal. If the crystal that you are going to test is good, it should function at some setting of the three controls R2, R4, and C3. If a small transistor battery is used, this circuit cannot be damaged by adjusting any of the controls.

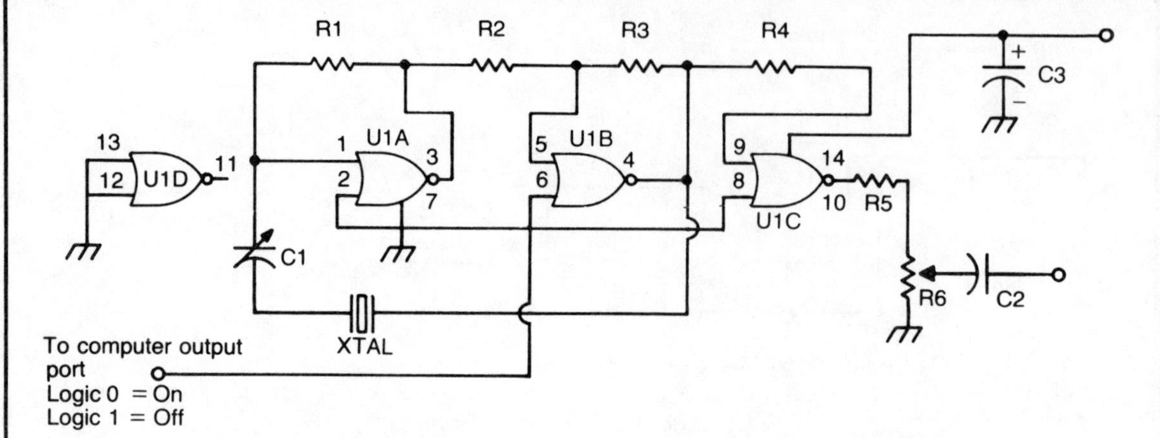

Crystal Clock Oscillator - Parts List

R1, R3, R4 - 10k resistor
R2, R5 - 2.7k resistor
R6 - 5k cermet trim pot
C1 - 60 pF mica compression capacitor
C2 - .001 μF ceramic capacitor
C3 - 1000 μF 16 volt capacitor
XTAL - 1 to 5 MHz clock crystal

Fig. 11-19. A gated crystal-clock oscillator is presented in this figure. The harmonic content of this oscillator will make it a good frequency-calibrator circuit

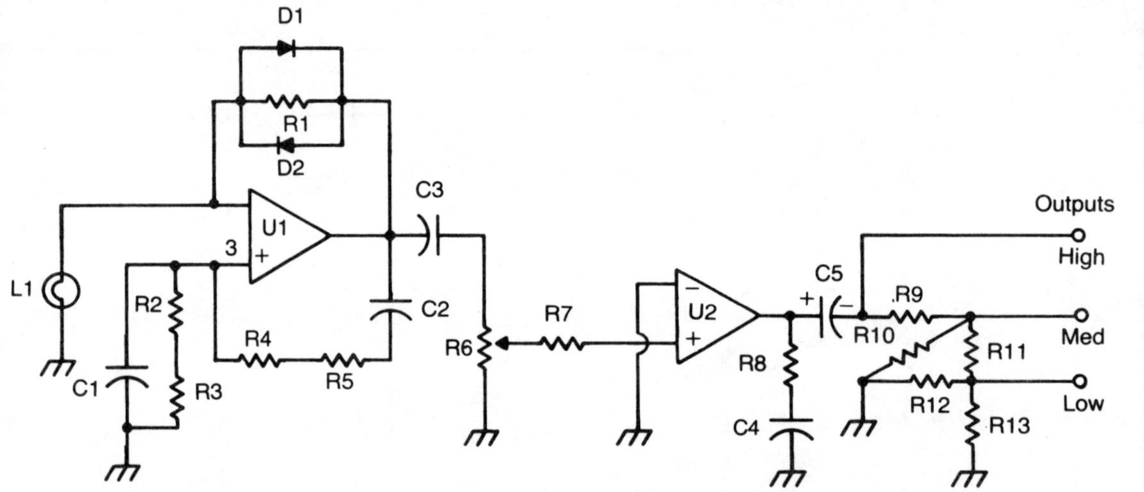

1 kHz Audio Oscillator - Parts List

L1 - 24 lamp
C1, C2 - .1 μF
C3 - .22 μF
C4 - .05 μF
C5 - 220 μF at 16 volts
D1, D2 - 1N4004 or equiv.
R1 - 100 ohms
R2, R3, R4, and R5 - 680 ohms
R6 - 10k trim pot
R7 - 1k
R8 - 15 ohms
R9, R10, R11, R12, R13 - 100 ohm ½ watt

Fig. 11-20. This is a 1kHz audio power oscillator which can be used to drive an ac bridge circuit. The stability of this circuit is very dependent upon the regulation of the circuit's power supply.

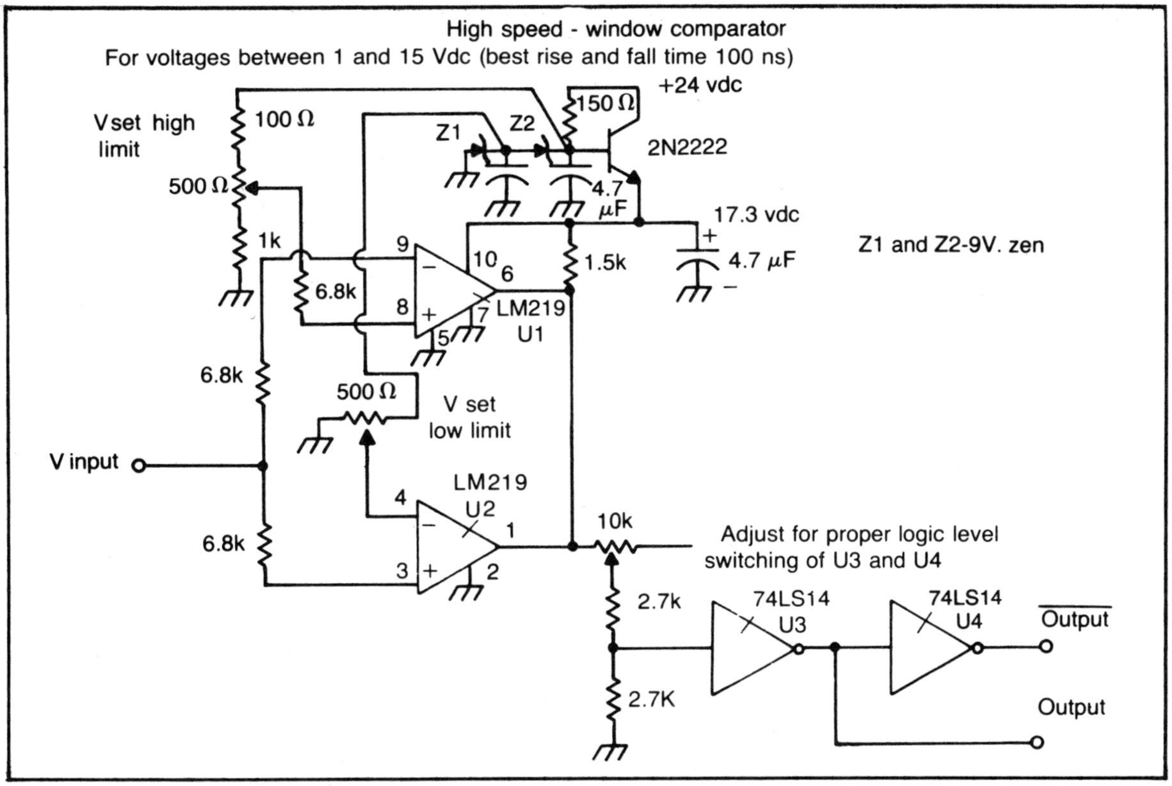

Fig. 11-21. The window comparator in this circuit is very nigh speed circuit. It is possible to use this circuit to generate a logic pulse whose width is equal to the rise and fall time of a lot of solid-state devices. This generated logic pulse can then be inputted into the digital logic circuitry as a representation of the solid-state device's rise of fall time for computation purposes.

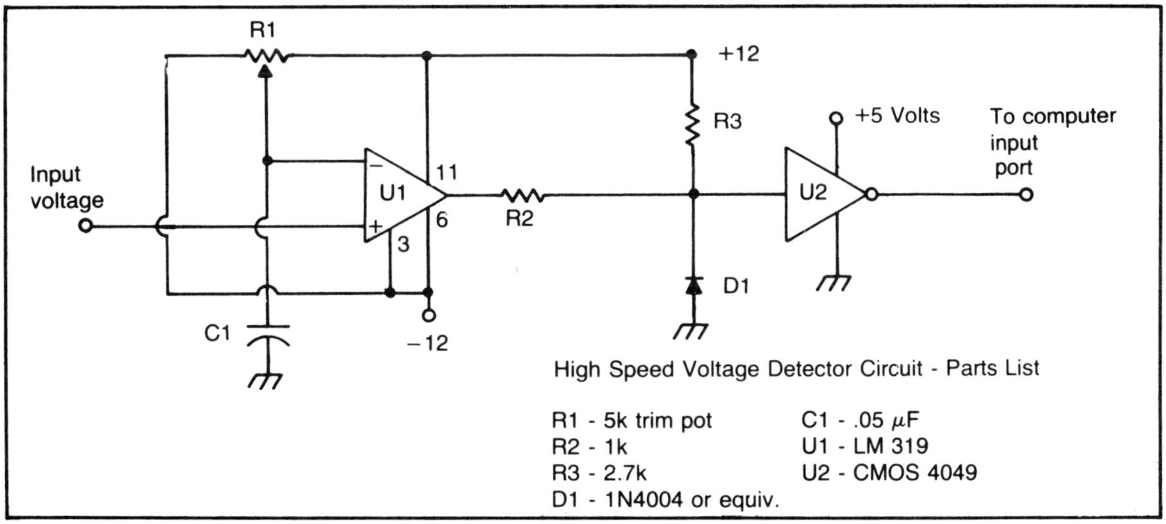

Fig. 11-22. This circuit is a high-speed voltage detector. It is possible to use this circuit to detect voltage levels of electrical pulses as short as 250 nanoseconds.

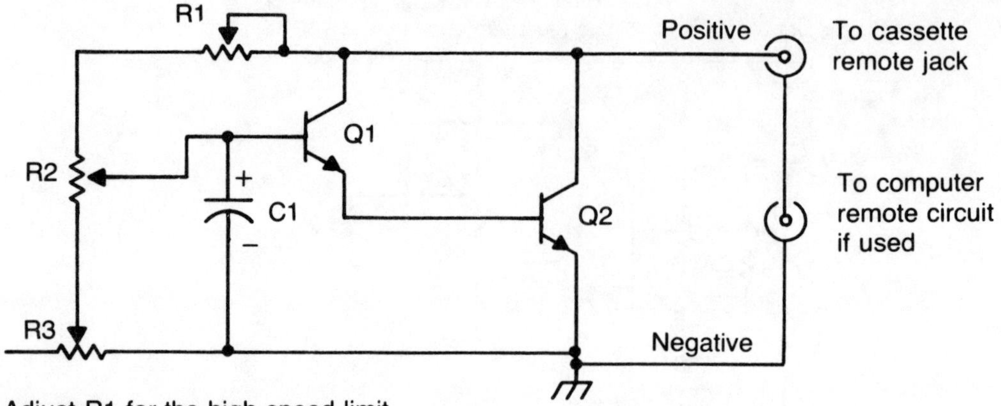

Notes: Adjust R1 for the high speed limit
Adjust R3 for the low speed limit
Adjust R2 for proper speed

Cassette Recorder Speed Controller - Parts List

R1, R3 - 10k trim pots
R2 - 5k trim pot
C1 - 10.0 μF at 16 volts
Q1, Q2 - 2N2222

Fig. 11-23. This circuit is a speed controller for a cassette tape recorder. You can use this circuit to slow your cassette tape unit when you are saving a software program and you will only be able to reload the tape into the computer at the slower tape speed. This is an easy way to protect your software from being used when you don't want it to be used.

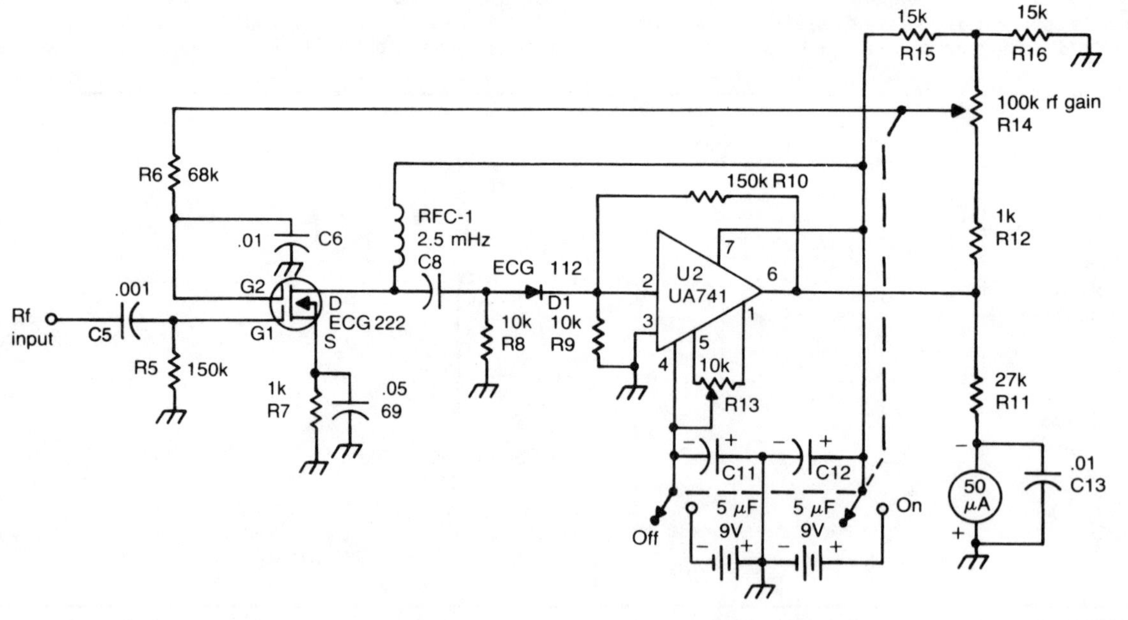

Fig. 11-24. This circuit is a wide-band rf detector circuit.

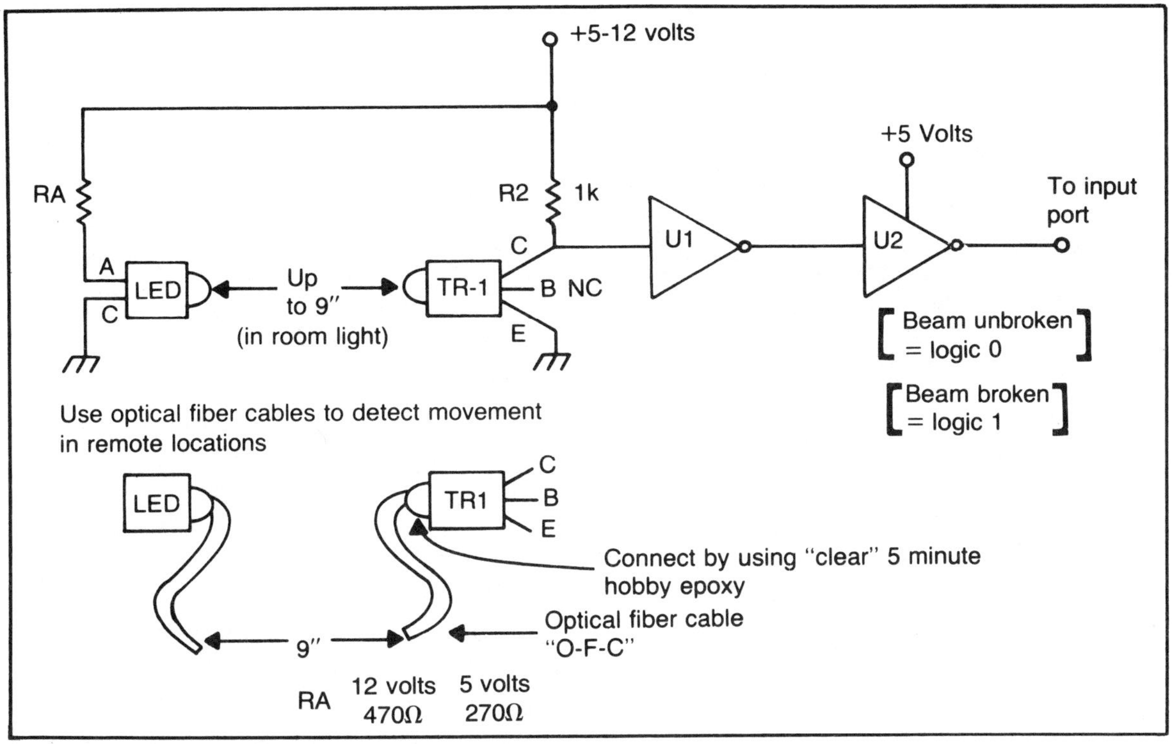

Fig. 11-25. This circuit is an optical-position sensing circuit. It will input logic data into the computer anytime the beam of light between the LED and TR1 is broken.

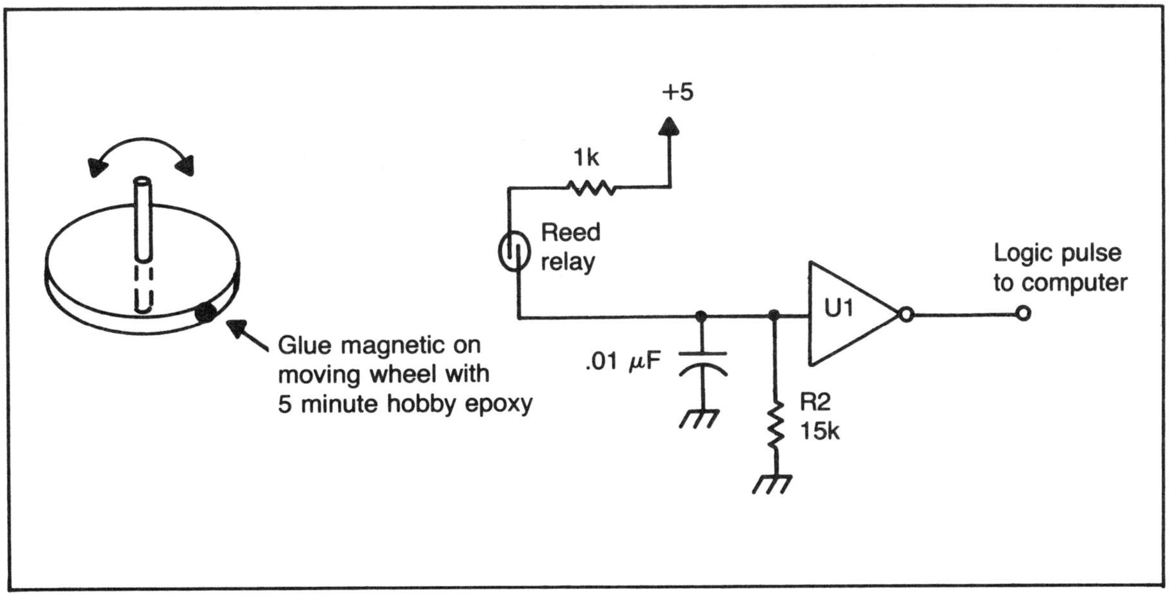

Fig. 11-26. This figure shows how a magnet and reed relay can be used to input rotational-position information into a single-board computer.

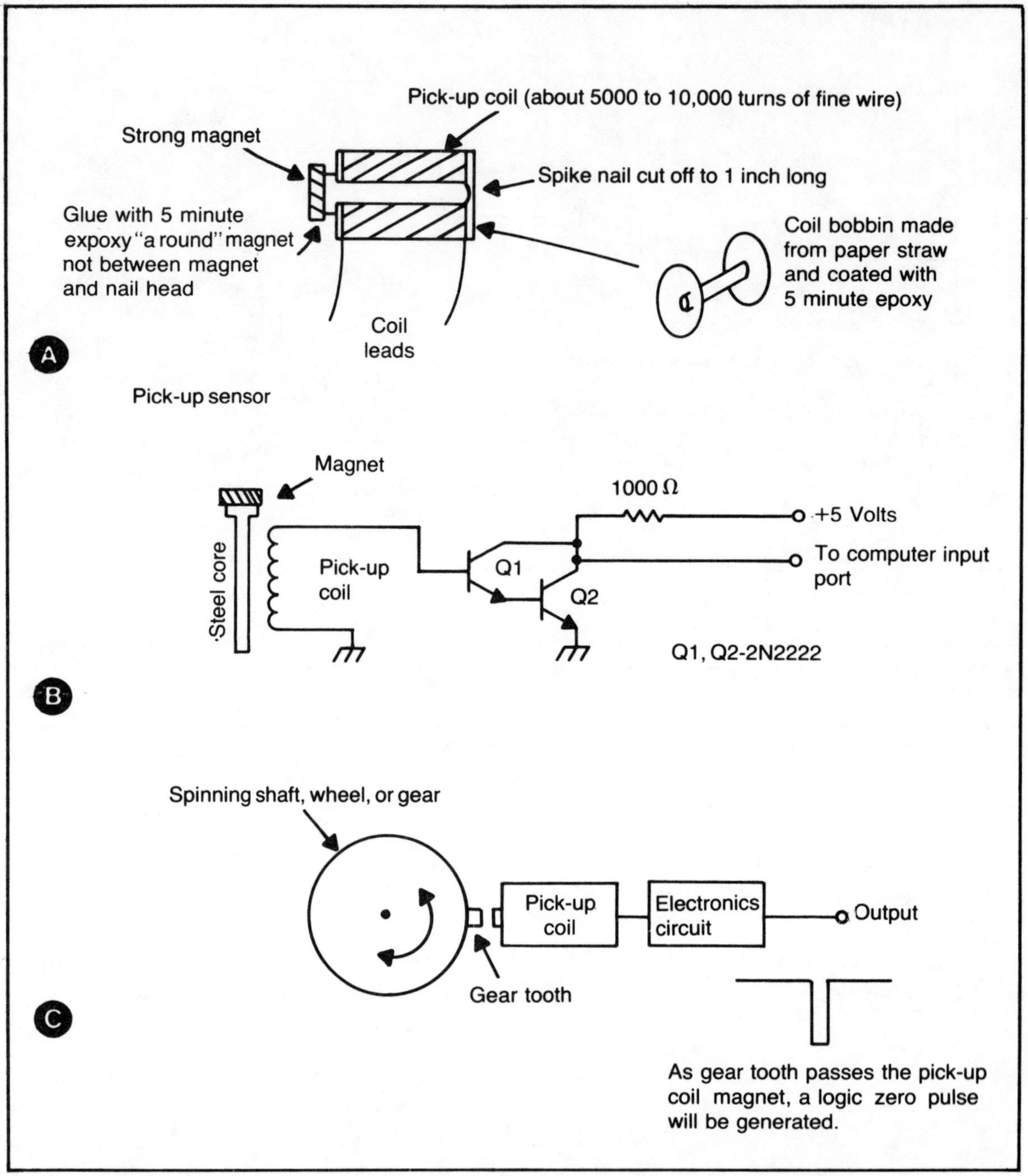

Fig. 11-27. This is a magnetic pick-up coil gear tooth sensor. When a gear tooth passes by the magnet, a change in the magnetic field flux around the magnet causes a voltage to be developed in the pick-up coil. The pick-up coil voltage is then used to turn-on the transistor circuit and generate a logic pulse everytime a gear tooth passes by the magnet. Figure 11-27A shows the physical construction of the sensor assembly, B shows the electrical circuit, and C shows the practical application method. This sensor requires a very strong magnet to generate logic pulses at slow gear speeds.

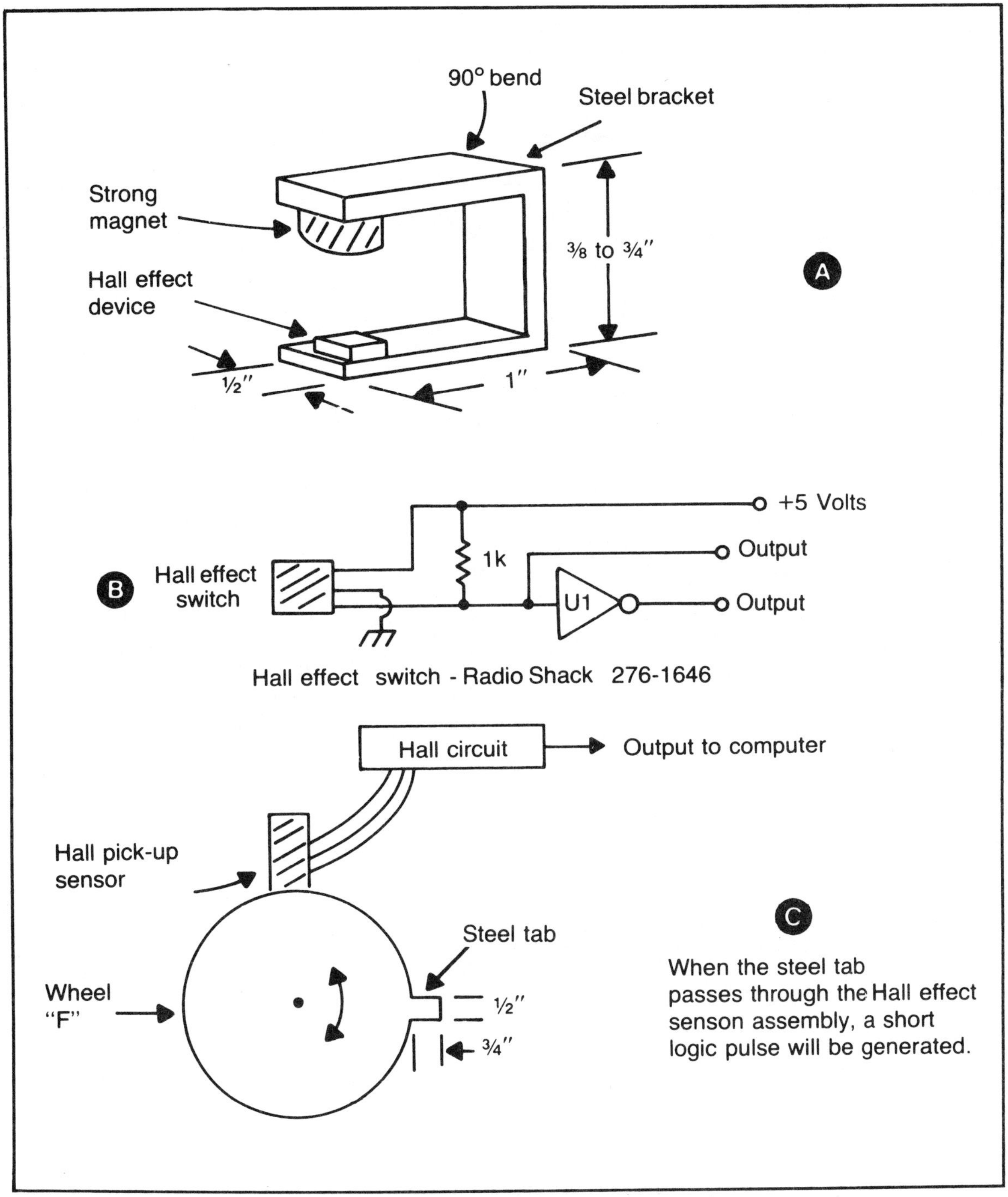

Fig. 11-28. This is a method of using a Hall-effect switch to input rotational position information into a computer. When the steel tab interrupts the magnetic circuit between the magnet and the Hall device, the Hall-effect switch will change logic states. Some Hall devices will have switching times of less than one microsecond which will supply very accurate data to the computer.

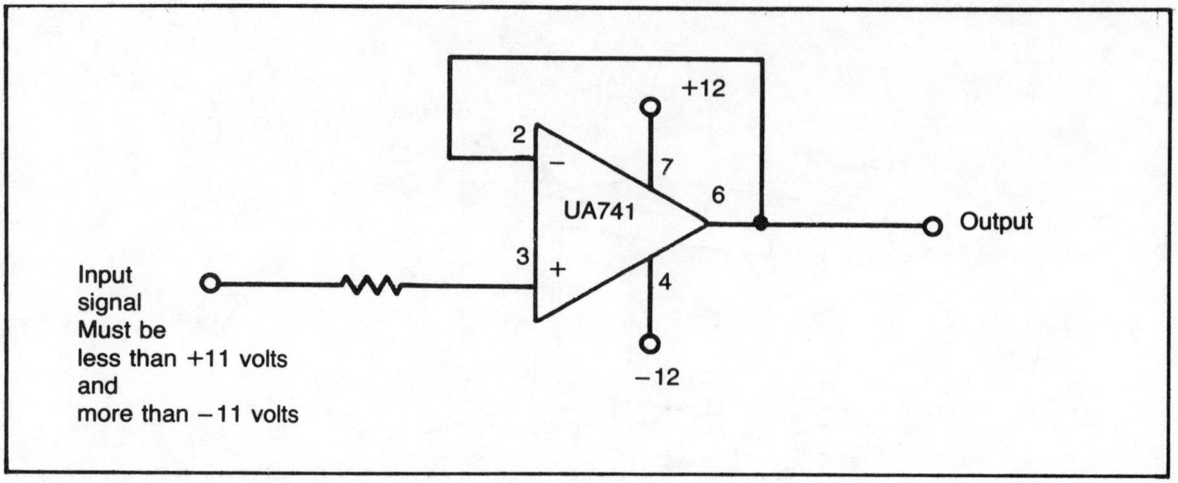

Fig. 11-29. This circuit is a standard noninverting op-amp circuit.

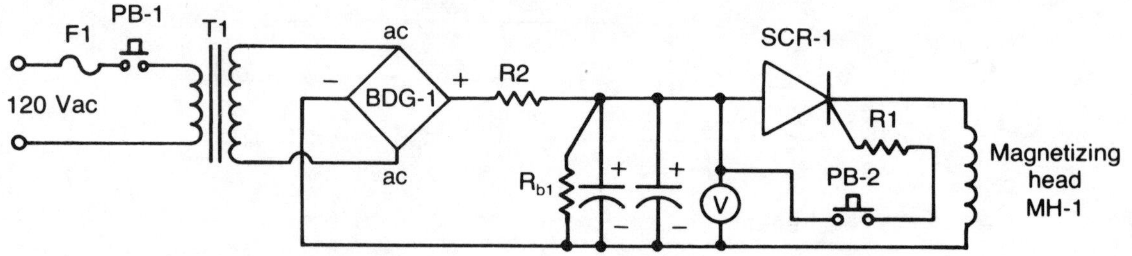

Work Bench Magnetizer - Parts List

T1 - Transformer, Primary - 120 Vac.
Secondary - 300 Vac.
F1 - Fuse 5 Amps
PB-1, PB-2 - 120 Vac push button switches
R1 - 1k at 1 watt (must limit gate current to safe value)
R2 - 100 ohms 20 watts
BDG-1 - 600 volts dc bridge at 6 amps
C1, C2 - 1250 μF at 450 volts (should be rated for capacitor discharge operation if used very much.)
SCR-1 - Should be at least a 150 amp SCR at 600 Vdc.
MH-1 - Magnetizing head, start with at least 300 turns of heavy copper wire. The impedance of magnetizing head must limit the capacitor discharge current to below the peak current of the SCR-1.
Voltage Meter "v" - 500 Vdc meter (must be a high resistance meter)
Rb1 - Bleeder resistor - 500k 20 watt

Fig. 11-30. This circuit is a workbench magnetizer. You must be very careful with this circuit. When capacitors C1 and C2 are fully charged, they can zap you out and that is all the way out! Do not place loose objects like screwdrivers, pliers, steel nuts, etc. in the magnetizing head because they will simply be thrown at you or somewhere else in the room when the magnetizer fires. Also, do not place any test instruments like a vom, a voltmeter, or an ammeter close to the magnetizing head because the magnetic flux around the head is quite strong when the unit fires and it will permanently damage any meter in the nearby area.

Chapter 12

Advanced Test Systems

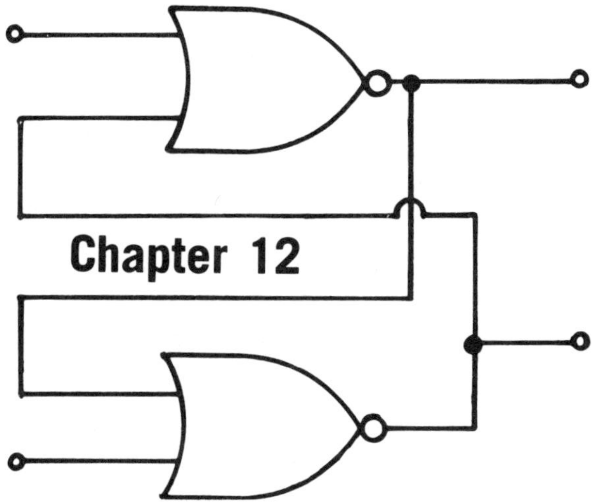

Up to this point in the book, we have only discussed simple test and control circuits for a single specific function. In this chapter, we will give you some suggestions on how to put them together to form a multifunction test or control system which will use both BASIC- and machine-language routines to secure an end result. We will mainly discuss using the AIM-65 and the AIM-65/40 which is manufactured by Rockwell International for the single-board computer market. Tables and charts will be presented for both the AIM-65 and the Model III which will help you to use these two systems with BASIC and USR called machine-language routines.

PROGRAM CONTROL METHODS AND SYSTEMS

It will probably not be anything new when I tell you that there are generally three ways for your computer programs to run your control functions and test circuits. Your programs can use (A) all machine-language routines, (B) nothing but BASIC language, or (C) a combination of both BASIC and machine language. Up to this chapter, we have given all programs for the SYM-1 in 6502 machine language and all AIM-65 and Model III programs in a combination of BASIC and machine language. The reasons for this is that the bare bones SYM-1 is a machine-language machine and it will use machine language a lot easier than the other two machines, but that is my opinion and I guess that statement can be debated. I like to use 6502 machine language, and so I like the SYM-1.

As the test system becomes larger, the need for high level math becomes very important. The AIM-65 is usually purchased with BASIC programming capability and BASIC is all that the model uses unless you buy the *assembly language DEBUG program* from Radio Shack. Since machine-language math routines can be very hard for the new computer programmer or the test engineer who programs only two or three test systems a year, we will only discuss using BASIC with USR functions in this chapter. This will limit us to using only the AIM-65 or the Model III. Now, when you must expand the computer to handle a larger test system, Rockwell International has a broad line of RM-65 system expansion components for their AIM-65 and AIM-65/40 which makes it easy to assemble a complete computer that is no larger than you need for a specific test system. So, in this chapter, we will be discussing a lot of AIM-65 and RM-65 technical data.

USING BASIC AND USR MACHINE-LANGUAGE ROUTINES (MODEL III)

The Model III has a very good BASIC language program which includes editing functions plus a whole lot more. We have shown in Chapter 3 how to use the 80

Table 12-1. This Table Presents a Hexadecimal-to-Decimal Memory Location Conversion for the Upper 96 Memory Locations of the 16K Memory in a Model III. This Table may be used to Locate PEEK and POKE Addresses Easily.

7FA0-32672	7FC0-32704	7FE0-32736
7FA1-32673	7FC1-32705	7FE1-32737
7FA2-32674	7FC2-32706	7FE2-32738
7FA3-32675	7FC3-32707	7FE3-32739
7FA4-32676	7FC4-32708	7FE4-32740
7FA5-32677	7FC5-32709	7FE5-32741
7FA6-32678	7FC6-32710	7FE6-32742
7FA7-32679	7FC7-32711	7FE7-32743
7FA8-32680	7FC8-32712	7FE8-32744
7FA9-32681	7FC9-32713	7FE9-32745
7FAA-32682	7FCA-32714	7FEA-32746
7FAB-32683	7FCB-32715	7FEB-32747
7FAC-32684	7FCC-32716	7FEC-32748
7FAD-32685	7FCD-32717	7FED-32749
7FAE-32686	7FCE-32718	7FEE-32750
7FAF-32687	7FCF-32719	7FEF-32751

I/O-PIB which requires the user of the USR command to operate the I/O port. Now, let us look into this operation a little deeper.

In order for you to use a USR function in a BASIC program, you must allocate some memory space for the machine-language routine. If you do not allocate a given memory space for your machine-language routine, the BASIC program will simply write-over what ever you load into the RAM memory during program execution. To allocate a given memory area for your machine-language routines, all you need to do is input the correct data into the computer when it requests MEMORY SIZE at the start of the BASIC program. Table 12-1 is set-up to give you the decimal and hexadecimal numbers for the last 96 memory locations in a 16K Model III computer. As shown in the table, if you need only twenty memory locations for your routine, you would input 32726 after MEMORY SIZE and the MODEL III will not use the last twenty memory locations in its BASIC program operations.

How do you use these reserved memory spaces? You can use these locations by using the USR (X) and the PEEK and POKE special features of the Model III BASIC

7FB0-32688	7FD0-32720	7FF0-32752
7FB1-32689	7FD1-32721	7FF1-32753
7FB2-32690	7FD2-32722	7FF2-32754
7FB3-32691	7FD3-32723	7FF3-32755
7FB4-32692	7FD4-32724	7FF4-32756
7FB5-32693	7FD5-32725	7FF5-32757
7FB6-32694	7FD6-32726	7FF6-32758
7FB7-32695	7FD7-32727	7FF7-32759
7FB8-32696	7FD8-32728	7FF8-32760
7FB9-32697	7FD9-32729	7FF9-32761
7FBA-32698	7FDA-32730	7FFA-32762
7FBB-32699	7FDB-32731	7FFB-32763
7FBC-32700	7FDC-32732	7FFC-32764
7FBD-32701	7FDD-32733	7FFD-32765
7FBE-32702	7FDE-32734	7FFE-32766
7FBF-32703	7FDF-32735	7FFF-32767

program. If you have only reserved a few memory locations, you can POKE the machine-language data into the locations, but if your program is very big, you should purchase a DEBUG program from your local Radio Shack Store which will make it easy to use machine language on your Model III.

To POKE data into a specific memory location, all you need to do is to type a program line like the one that follows.

```
10    POKE 32672.255
```

This program line tells the computer to place the decimal number 255 (hexadecimal FF) into memory location 32672 (hexadecimal location 7FA0). The following program line will place 00 into memory location 7FA1 (Check Table 12-1 and verify this).

```
20    POKE 32673, 00
```

When you have POKED your machine language program into the memory, you will next want to call up that short program. To do this, you must tell the computer where this program is located when the USR (X) function is called. In the Model III you will need to POKE this data into memory locations 16526 and 16527. In the above examples, we started the program at hexadecimal location 7FA0. To tell the computer that your program starts at memory location 7FA0, you will have to POKE "A0" (LSB of the location) into memory location 16526 and then POKE "7F" (MSB) into location 16527. But, the BASIC program can not POKE hexadecimal data, so you must look up the decimal equivalent to "A0" and "7F" in Table 12-2. The decimal equivalent to "A0" and "7F" in Table 12-2. The decimal equivalent of "A0" is 160 and "7F" is 127 which will be used in a BASIC program line as follows:

```
30  POKE 16526, 160: POKE 16527, 127
```

Now that you have told the computer where to go if a USR (X) function is called, let's write a USR (X) program line as follows:

```
40  X=USR (1)
```

The data in program line 40 will tell the computer to execute the machine-instruction code that is located in memory location 7FA0. Every time that you call a USR (X) function, you will need to precede that program line with the POKE data that will tell the computer where to go. Once you have jumped from your BASIC program into a machine-language routine you will have to jump back into the BASIC program using a RETURN machine-language instruction. The machine language code for RETURN is "C9".

A BASIC program is presented in Table 12-3 which will give you a simple demonstration of a USR (1) function. If you try to poke very many locations with machine language, the operation becomes boring. The simple monitor program that is presented in Table 12-4 will help you enter and check machine language easily.

USING THE AIM-65 IN ADVANCED TEST SYSTEMS (AIM-65)

The AIM-65 is a complete microcomputer which has everything you need to run a test system when it is purchased. A brief description was given in Chapter 2 when we were generally discussing the various operational single-board computers that are available for the test system engineer. At that time we pointed out that the AIM-65 has a printer, a keyboard, and a LED character display which will make it very easy to operate a test system and display and record the results. Everything on the AIM-65 is ready to go when the power is supplied to the board and all you need to do is to learn how to operate the system. At this time, I know of no other competitive system which offers similar features in the same price range, so we will apply the rest of this chapter to running advanced test systems with Rockwell International computer equipment.

The BASIC language that is in the AIM-65 is very similar to the BASIC that is in the Model III. If you can operate one, you can operate the other one also. The AIM-65 can have a maximum of 4K of on-board RAM memory which will control a small test system easily. Table 12-5 shows the hexadecimal to decimal location data for the top 96 locations in the 4K RAM. This table is presented so you can easily learn how to use the PEEK, POKE, and USR (X) functions of the AIM-65 BASIC. If you are going to use Table 12-5, you must limit the BASIC memory size to 3999 when the BASIC program is started. This will leave the top 96 memory locations free for machine language use which is much easier with the AIM-65.

The PEEK and POKE functions operate just like the Model III functions as shown in the following examples:

```
10  Print PEEK (4005)
20  POKE 4010,255
```

Line 10 will print-out the data that is in memory location 0FA5 in decimal form which then may be converted into hexadecimal form by using Table 12-2. Line 20 will POKE the hexadecimal data FF (255) into memory location 0FAA. The USR (X) function in the AIM-65 must be handled a little differently than the Model III USR (X) function as shown in the following example:

```
30  X=USR (1) : PRINT X
```

When line 30 is run, the BASIC program will turn the program control over the machine-language instruction which is located in the first memory location of the USR (1) routine. The first memory location data of the USR (1) routine is placed in memory locations 04 and 05 with the LSB placed in 04 and the MSB placed in 05. As an example, let us say that our first memory location is 0FB4. You would POKE B4 into location 04 and 0F into location 05. But you must change the hexadecimal data to decimal so the BASIC program can use the information, so the POKE statement would look like this example:

```
50  POKE 04,180: POKE 05,15
60  X=USR (1): PRINT X
```

The above example will tell the BASIC program to run the machine-language routine that starts at memory location 0FB4. Remember to end the machine-language routine with a RTS instruction (60) so the machine-language program will return control back to the BASIC program. If you do not use the RTS instruction, your

Table 12-2. This Table Gives the Cross-Reference between Hexadecimal and Decimal Numbers from 0 to 255 (00 to FF) which will make the Task of Choosing the Right USR (X) Address Memory (POKE) Data Easy.

00-00	50-32	100-64	150-96	200-C8	250-FA
01-01	51-33	101-65	151-97	201-C9	251-FB
02-02	52-34	102-66	152-98	202-CA	252-FC
03-03	53-35	103-67	153-99	203-CB	253-FD
04-04	54-36	104-68	154-9A	204-CC	254-FE
05-05	55-37	105-69	155-9B	205-CD	255-FF
06-06	56-38	106-6A	156-9C	206-CE	
07-07	57-39	107-6B	157-9D	207-CF	
08-08	58-3A	108-6C	158-9E	208-D0	
09-09	59-3B	109-6D	159-9F	209-D1	
10-0A	60-3C	110-6E	160-A0	210-D2	
11-0B	61-3D	111-6F	161-A1	211-D3	
12-0C	62-3E	112-70	162-A2	212-D4	
13-0D	63-3F	113-71	163-A3	213-D5	
14-0E	64-40	114-72	164-A4	214-D6	
15-0F	65-41	115-73	165-A5	215-D7	
16-10	66-42	116-74	166-A6	216-D8	
17-11	67-43	117-75	167-A7	217-D9	
18-12	68-44	118-76	168-A8	218-DA	
19-13	69-45	119-77	169-A9	219-DB	
20-14	70-46	120-78	170-AA	220-DC	
21-15	71-47	121-79	171-AB	221-DD	
22-16	72-48	122-7A	172-AC	222-DE	
23-17	73-49	123-7B	173-AD	223-DF	
24-18	74-4A	124-7C	174-AE	224-E0	

Table 12-2. This Table Gives the Cross-Reference between Hexadecimal and Decimal Numbers from 0 to 255 (00 to FF) which will make the Task of Choosing the Right USR (X) Address Memory (POKE) Data Easy (continued from page 167).

25-19	75-4B	125-7D	175-AF	225-E1
26-1A	76-4C	126-7E	176-B0	226-E2
27-1B	77-4D	127-7F	177-B1	227-E3
28-1C	78-4E	128-80	178-B2	228-E4
29-1D	79-4F	129-81	179-B3	229-E5
30-1E	80-50	130-82	180-B4	230-E6
31-1F	81-51	131-83	181-B5	231-E7
32-20	82-52	132-84	182-B6	232-E8
33-21	83-53	133-85	183-B7	233-E9
34-22	84-54	134-86	184-B8	234-EA
35-23	85-55	135-87	185-B9	235-EB
36-24	86-56	136-88	186-BA	236-EC
37-25	87-57	137-89	187-BB	237-ED
38-26	88-58	138-8A	188-BC	238-EE
39-27	89-59	139-8B	189-BD	239-EF
40-28	90-5A	140-8C	190-BE	240-F0
41-29	91-5B	141-8D	191-BF	241-F1
42-2A	92-5C	142-8E	192-C0	242-F2
43-2B	93-5D	143-8F	193-C1	243-F3
44-2C	94-5E	144-90	194-C2	244-F4
45-2D	95-5F	145-91	195-C3	245-F5
46-2E	96-60	146-92	196-C4	246-F6
47-2F	97-61	147-93	197-C5	247-F7
48-30	98-62	148-94	198-C6	248-F8
49-31	99-63	149-95	199-C7	249-F9

Table 12-3. A Model III BASIC Program which demonstrates the use of a USR (X) in a BASIC Program.

```
A. This is a Model III BASIC program
   which shows an example of using a
   USR (X) function in a BASIC program.
B. Limit the Model III memory size to
   32671

10 PRINT"THIS PROGRAM IS A USR
(X) PROGRAM WHICH WILL ADD 1 TO
THE VALUE OF INPUT A IN A MACHINE
LANGUAGE ROUTINE. INPUT A MUST
BE BETWEEN 0 AND 255"
20 PRINT"INPUT A":INPUT A
30 POKE 32704,A
40 POKE 16526,160:POKE16527,127
50 POKE32672,58:POKE32673,
   192:POKE32674,127:POKE
   32675,60:POKE32676,50:POKE
   32677,208:POKE32678,127:
   POKE32679,201
60 X=USR(1)
70 PRINT"THE VALUE OF INPUT A
WHICH HAS BEEN INCREMENTED BY
ONE IN THE USR(X) R OUTLINE IS";
80 PRINTPEEK(32720)
90 END

This is how the program looks when it is
RUN.

READY
>RUN
THIS PROGRAM IS A USR (X) PRO-
GRAM WHICH WILL ADD 1 TO THE
VALUE OF INPUT A IN A MACHINE
LANGUAGE ROUTINE. INPUT A MUST
BE BETWEEN 0 AND 255
INPUT A
? 200
THE VALUE OF INPUT A WHICH HAS
BEEN INCREMENTED BY ONE IN THE
USR(X) ROUTINE IS 201
READY
>S.
```

computer program control will wander off into no-man's land and plow-up memory locations plus other unwanted happenings. An easy way to learn how to use the USR (X) routines in a BASIC program is to use some of the machine-language routines that were shown in Chapter 5 with some BASIC print commands which will tell an observer what the machine-language program is doing. The ability to intermix a BASIC program and USR (X) machine-language routines is really a must if you are going to attempt to do any test system operation which will require some type of math functions.

A COMPLETE FUNCTIONAL DESCRIPTION OF THE AIM-65

The following description of the AIM-65 is from the AIM-65 data sheet. The AIM-65 memory map is shown in Table 12-6. The block diagram is shown in Fig. 12-1.

The AIM-65 microcomputer is a complete, assembled microcomputer system featuring a 20-column thermal printer, a 20-character alphanumeric display, and a full size terminal style keyboard. On-board memory sockets accept up to 20K bytes of PROM/ROM and 4K bytes of static RAM. A user R6522 Versatile Interface Adapter (VIA) dedicates 16 parallel I/O data lines and four handshaking control lines to application usage. The address, data, and control lines are also accessible for off-board memory, peripheral and I/O expansion. An 8K-byte ROM-resident debug monitor and text editor provides immediate interactive operation upon power turn-on.

With its self-contained printer and display, the AIM-65 microcomputer is ideal for educational and industrial desk-top applications. The on-board printer, unique to single-board microcomputers in its class, make the AIM-65 microcomputer a natural for any control and monitor application requiring hard copy output—such as equipment performance monitoring, data logging, test and evaluation, specialized data acquisition and reduction, laboratory measurements and analysis, and untold others.

Features

☐ Single Board Computer with on-board RAM, ROM, and I/O.

— Powerful and Popular 6502 CPU
— Up to 4K bytes of 2114 Static RAM
— Up to 20K bytes of 2532 PROM or R2332 ROM
— User Dedicated Application Parallel I/O Interface
— Low-Cost Audio Cassette Recorder Interface with 2 Recorder Remote Control Lines
— 20 mA Current Loop Serial Interface

Table 12-4. A Simple Model III Machine-Language Monitor Program.

```
 10 PRINT"A SIMPLE MODEL III MACHINE LANGUAGE MONITOR PROGRAM"
 12 PRINT
 15 PRINT"          WHEN REQUESTED"
 20 PRINT"INPUT THE STARTING ADDRESS LOCATION IN DECIMAL"
 30 PRINT"INPUT ALL MEMORY DATA IN DECIMAL"
 35 PRINT
 40 INPUT"THE STARTING ADDRESS LOCATION -----";A
 45 PRINT"                   LOCATION----DATA"
 50 Z=PEEK(A)
 70 PRINT"MEMORY ADDRESS LOCATION---";A;"---";Z;"---";:INPUT B
 80 POKE A,B
 90 A=A+1
100 GOTO50
```

NOTE: For a 16K Model III, limit the memory size to 32672
Start your machine language routine at location 32673

This is what the program looks like when it is ran.

```
A SIMPLE MODEL III MACHINE LANGUAGE MONITOR PROGRAM
                                WHEN REQUESTED
INPUT THE STARTING ADDRESS LOCATION IN DECIMAL
INPUT ALL MEMORY DATA IN DECIMAL
THE STARTING ADDRESS LOCATION-----? 32672
                                  LOCATION----DATA
MEMORY ADDRESS LOCATION--- 32672 --- 0 ---?
MEMORY ADDRESS LOCATION--- 32673 --- 0 ---? 255
MEMORY ADDRESS LOCATION--- 32674 --- 0 ---? 00
MEMORY ADDRESS LOCATION--- 32675 --- 0 ---? 120
MEMORY ADDRESS LOCATION--- 32676 --- 0 ---?
```

NOTE: If you do not enter any data into the memory location, the program will enter 00. If you do not want to change the memory location, then reenter the same memory data.

- — Expansion Bus Interface
- ☐ 20-Column Thermal Printer
- — 64 Character ASCII Format
- — 120 Lines per Minute
- — 5 × 7 Dot Matrix Character Font
- ☐ 20-Character Display
- — 64-Character ASCII Format
- — 16-Segment Font
- — High Contrast Monolithic Characters
- ☐ Full-Size 54-key Terminal Style Keyboard
- — 26 Alphabetic, 10 Numeric, and 22 Special Characters
- — 9 Control Functions and 3 User-Defined Functions
- ☐ ROM-Resident Interactive Debug Monitor
- — Monitor-Generated Prompts and Single Keystroke Commands
- — Single-Step Execution with Tracing and Breakpoints
- — Memory and Register Examine and Alter
- — Mnemonic Instruction Entry and Disassembly

☐ Text Editor
— Line Oriented Commands (Read, Insert, Delete, List)
— Character String Find and Change

☐ Parallel Application Interface
— R6522 Versatile Interface Adapter (VIA)
— Two 8-bit Parallel Bidirectional Data Ports
— Two 2-bit Handshake Control Ports
— Two Programmable 16-bit Counter/Timers
— 8-bit Serial Interface

Functional Description

The AIM-65 microcomputer consists of a Master Module (which includes the central processing and control circuitry, decoders, memory, I/O and printer control circuit), an attached Display Module and a separate Keyboard Module. A thermal print is mounted directly on the Master Module while the Display Module is mounted on angle brackets which are fastened to the Master Module.

Central Processing and Control

The R6502 8-bit microprocessor, the central processing unit (CPU) of the AIM-65 microcomputer, provides the overall control and monitoring of all AIM-65 operations. The R6502 communicates with other AIM-65 elements on three separate buses. A 16-bit address bus allows the CPU to directly address 65,536 memory locations. An 8-bit bidirectional data bus carries data from the CPU to/from memory and interface devices. The control bus carries various timing and control signals between the CPU and interfacing peripherals, devices, and off-board elements.

The CPU operates at 1 MHz, which is derived from a 4MHz crystal-controlled oscillator. The 02 system clock and read/write control signals are generated by the CPU, and are buffered and routed to other devices on-board and to the expansion connector.

A decoder circuit provides chip select signals to the on-board PROM/ROM and RAM sockets and to the I/O devices. 4K-byte chip selects are sent to the PROM/ROM sockets ($BXXX-$FXXX) while 1K-byte select signals are routed to the RAM sockets ($00XX-$XCXX). Onboard I/O is also decoded to 1K-byte selects ($A0XX-$ACXX).

A pushbutton switch initiates RESET to the on-board devices and to interfacing equipment through the expansion connector. Installed terminal posts allow connection to a remote RESET switch. The STEP/RUN switch selects program execution in either the single-step mode or the run mode. In single-step mode, execution of all instructions in the address range 0-$9FFF can be traced or can be stopped at any of four specified breakpoints. The KB/TTY switch selects operation using the AIM-65 keyboard and display or using a teletypewriter attached to the 20 mA current loop interface.

Table 12-5. This Table is a Hexadecimal-to-Decimal Table for the Upper 96 Memory Locations of a 4K AIM-65 which will make the Task of Choosing PEEK and POKE Addresses Easy.

0FA0-4000	0FB0-4016	0FC0-4032	0FD0-4048	0FE0 -4064	0FF0-4080
0FA1 4001	0FB1-4017	0FC1-4033	0FD1-4049	0FE1-4065	0FF1-4081
0FA2 4002	0FB2-4018	0FC2-4034	0FD2-4050	0FE2-4066	0FF2-4082
0FA3-4003	0FB3-4019	0FC3-4035	0FD3-4051	0FE3-4067	0FF3-4083
0FA4-4004	0FB4-4020	0FC4-4036	0FD4-4052	0FE4-4068	0FF4-4084
0FA5-4005	0FB5-4021	0FC5-4037	0FD5-4053	0FE5-4069	0FF5-4085
0FA6-4006	0FB6-4022	0FC6-4038	0FD6-4054	0FE6-4070	0FF6-4086
0FA7-4007	0FB7-4023	0FC7-4039	0FD7-4055	0FE7-4071	0FF7-4087
0FA8-4008	0FB8-4024	0FC8-4040	0FD8-4056	0FEB-4072	0FF8-4088
0FA9-4009	0FB9-4025	0FC9-4041	0FD9-4057	0FE9-4073	0FF9-4089
0FAA-4010	0FBA-4026	0FCA-4042	0FDA-4058	0FEA-4074	0FFA-4090
0FAB-4011	0FBB-4027	0FCB-4043	0FDB-4059	0FEB-4075	0FFB-4091
0FAC-4012	0FBC-4028	0FCC-4044	0FDC-4060	0FEC-4076	0FFC-4092
0FAD-4013	0FBD-4029	0FCD-4045	0FDD-4061	0FED-4077	0FFD-4093
0FAE-4014	0FBE-4030	0FCE-4046	0FDE-4062	0FEE-4078	0FFE-4094
0FAF-4015	0FBF-4031	0FCF-4047	0FDF-4064	0FEF-4079	0FFF-4095

Table 12-6. The AIM-65 Memory Map (courtesy of Rockwell International Corp.).

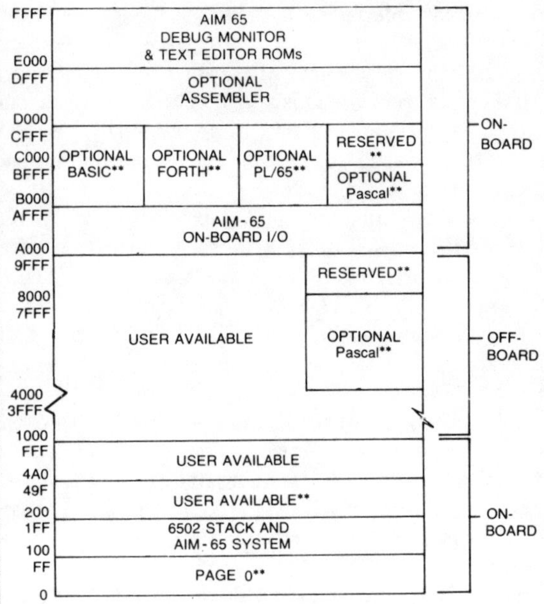

NOTES: *USER AVAILABLE IF MONITOR/EDITOR IS NOT USED.
**USER AVAILABLE IF OPTIONAL LANGUAGE IS NOT USED.

LANGUAGE	PAGE 0	PAGE 2-4
Assembler	0-DE	NOT USED
BASIC	0-D6	200-211
FORTH	0-A4	200-30A
PL/65	0-04	200-49F
Pascal	06-B4,FC-FF	200-2FF
Monitor/Editor	DF-FF	NOT USED

Memory

Two 1024 × 4 2114 static RAM devices are required for each 1K-byte of installed RAM. Both 1K and 4K versions are available. The 1K version may be expanded on-board in 1K increments up to 4K using the spare RAM sockets.

Five PROM/ROM sockets accept installation of the 4K-byte R2332 ROM, 2532 PROM, or smaller devices with compatible pinouts, e.g., 2K-byte 2516 PROM. The AIM-65 microcomputer comes with two R2332 ROMs containing the Debug Monitor/Text Editor installed at addresses $E000-$FFFF.

I/O

The 16 bidirectional data lines and 4 handshake control lines of the user-dedicated R6522 VIA are routed directly to the application connector. The high current capacity of the VIA's eight "B" port lines can directly drive many industry-standard devices, such as solid-state relays. One of the lines can be used as either a serial input or output line.

The audio recorder interface connects to one or two low-cost audio cassette recorders. Two remote control lines can control two separate recorders independently during read and write operations using the AIM-65 blocked audio recording format.

Peripherals

The printer prints on heat-sensitive roll paper by means of ten thermal elements, mounted on a movable head, each of which can print two 5×7 matrix dot characters. The printed characters are formed by dot patterns stored in the AIM-65 Monitor/Editor ROMs. A motor-driven platen advances the paper after each row of horizontal dots is printed. The motor and thermal element driver voltages are derived from an external +24V power supply. The printing is controlled by subroutines resident in the Monitor/Editor ROMs.

The AIM-65 display consists of five four-digit 16-segment alphanumeric, displays and an R6520 Peripheral Interface Adapter (PIA) mounted on the Display Module which connects to the Master Module through two short solid-conductor ribbon cables. Each display quad contains internal memory, decoder, and driver circuitry. The display quads interface with the Master Module through the PIA. Data may be sent to the display using Monitor ROM subroutines.

The Keyboard Module connects to the Master Module by a removable 16-conductor flat ribbon cable. The interface is through an R6532 RAM, I/O, and Timer (RIOT) device which supports the Monitor with the RAM and timer. The key matrix is strobed by eight lines output through the RIOT with the matrix returns routed back through eight R6532 input lines.

A FUNCTIONAL DESCRIPTION OF THE AIM-65/40

The following description of the AIM-65/40 repeats some of the previous data that was presented about the AIM-65, but is presented so that you may read only the AIM-65/40 data without having to read about the AIM-65 first. The AIM-65/40 is shown in Fig. 12-2. The system memory map is shown in Table 12-7. The functional block diagram is shown in Fig. 12-3.

The AIM-65/40 microcomputer system integrates the AIM-65/40-modular components—Single Board Computer, 40 Character Display, Graphics Printer and Standard Keyboard—into a couple self-contained system including an application-oriented I/O ROM and a ROM resident operator-oriented Debug Monitor/Text Editor. The display and printer modules are mounted onto the

SBC while the keyboard is detached—all peripherals are connected through removable 40 conductor ribbon cables. The peripherals can easily be relocated to other positions to satisfy unique installation requirements

In its integrated form, a desk-top installation of the AIM-65/40 microcomputer system can perform a wide range of specialized data acquisition, data reduction, control, and monitor functions in either OEM or end-user configurations. As a development tool, the system can support software developed in either assembly or high level language for operation in AIM-65/40 or RM 65 based microcomputers at a fraction of the cost of other systems.

As an advanced generation of the popular AIM-65

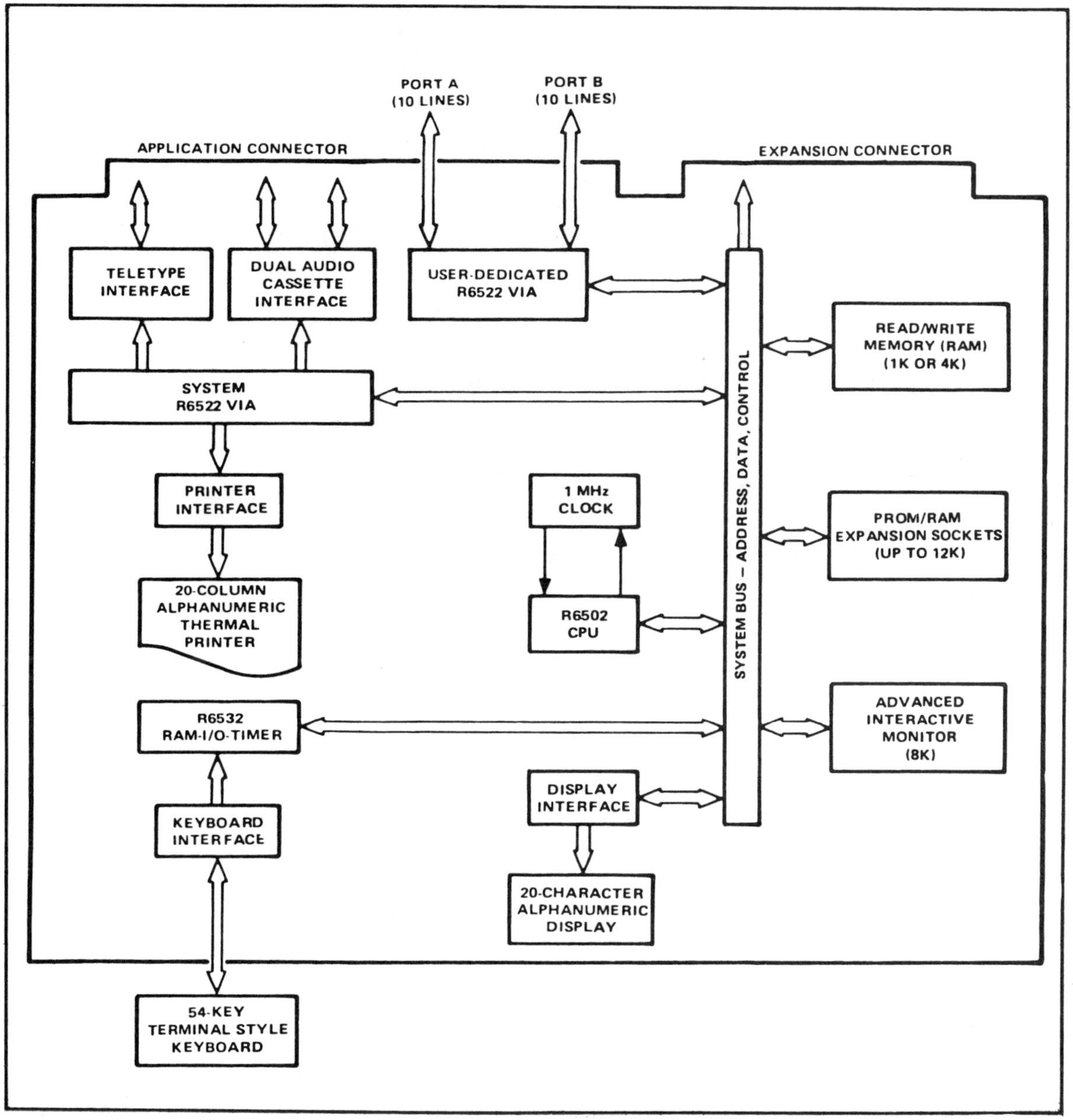

Fig. 12-1. This is the functional block diagram of the AIM-65 computer system (courtesy of Rockwell International Corp.).

Fig. 12-2. The AIM-65/40 is an advanced version of the AIM-65 which can be considered the elite of the single-board computers (courtesy of Rockwell International Corp.).

microcomputer, the separate AIM-65/40 assemblies provide increased processing throughout, improved keyboard, display and printer modules, and expanded application interfaces. The 6502 CPU-based AIM-65 Single-Board Computer, with a full address complement of memory capacity on-board, extremely flexible I/O, and interrupt driven I/O handlers in firmware, is the heart of the AIM 65/40 microcomputer system. The AIM-65 Graphics Printer, with its separate microcomputer controller, prints 40 columns of characters using a complete set of upper and lower case alphabetic, numeric, semigraphic, and special characters in the text mode at 240 lines per minute, and also provides a full graphics mode of 280 dots by n rows. The AIM-65/40-Character Display, with its own microprocessor-based controller, features an easy-to-read fluorescent display, and provides a full complement of alphanumeric and special characters as well as internal editing, scrolling, and blinking functions. The terminal-style AIM-65 Standard Keyboard contains a full-size main keyboard plus a separate row of eight dedicated function keys and isolated RESET and ATTN keys.

Features

- ☐ Single Board Computer with Extensive Memory and I/O
- — 6502 CPU
- — 131K Addressing, in Two 65K-Byte Banks
- — Up to 48K Bytes of On-Board RAM, with Write-Protect
- — Up to 32K Bytes of On-Board PROM or ROM

Table 12-7. The AIM-65/40 Memory Map (courtesy of Rockwell International Corp.).

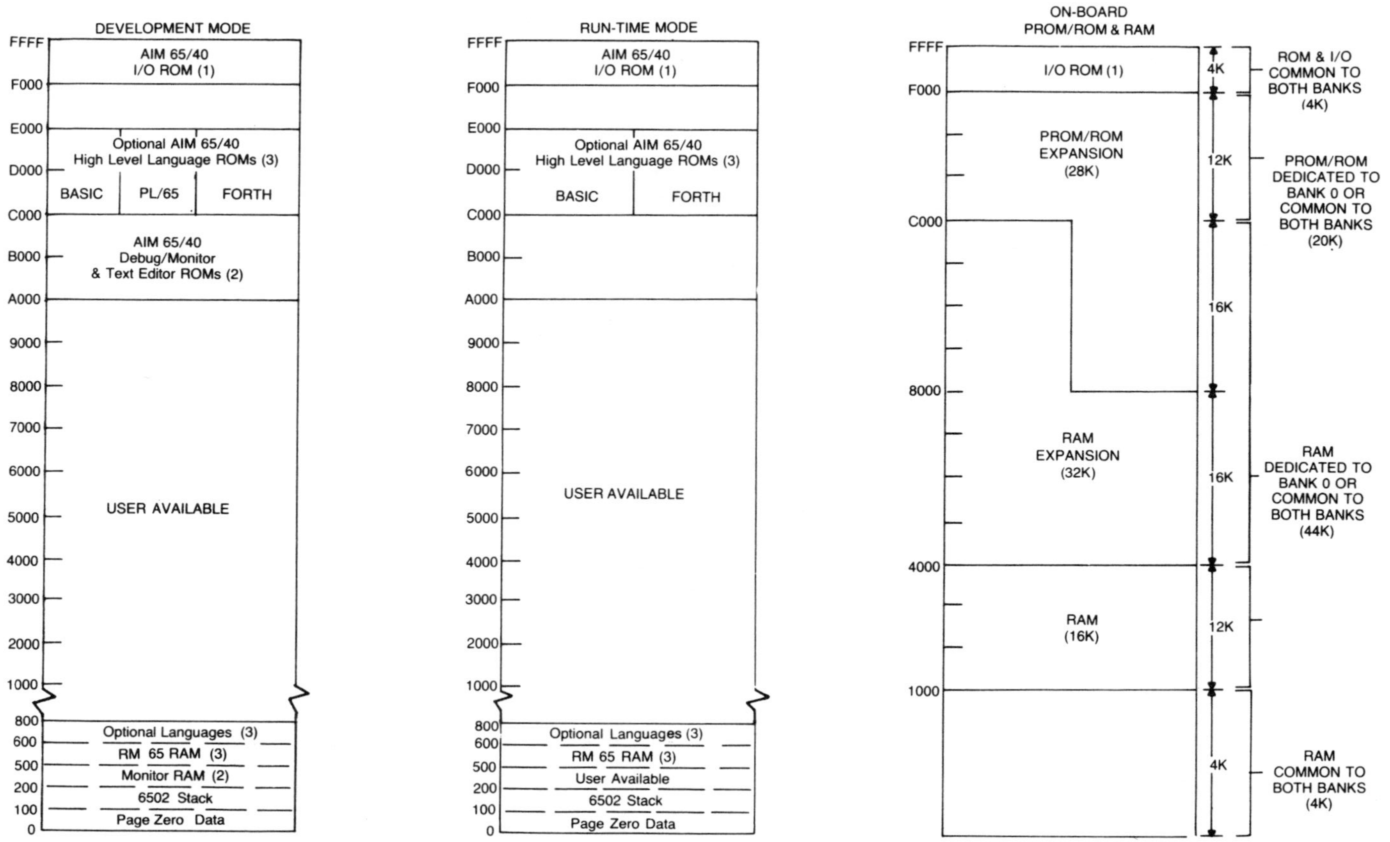

Notes: (1) AIM 65/40 System peripheral I/O addresses are assigned to FF80 - FFDF.
(2) User available during application program operation if the debug and text editor functions are not used.
(3) User available if the optional language and the RAM 65 expansion module ROMs are not used.

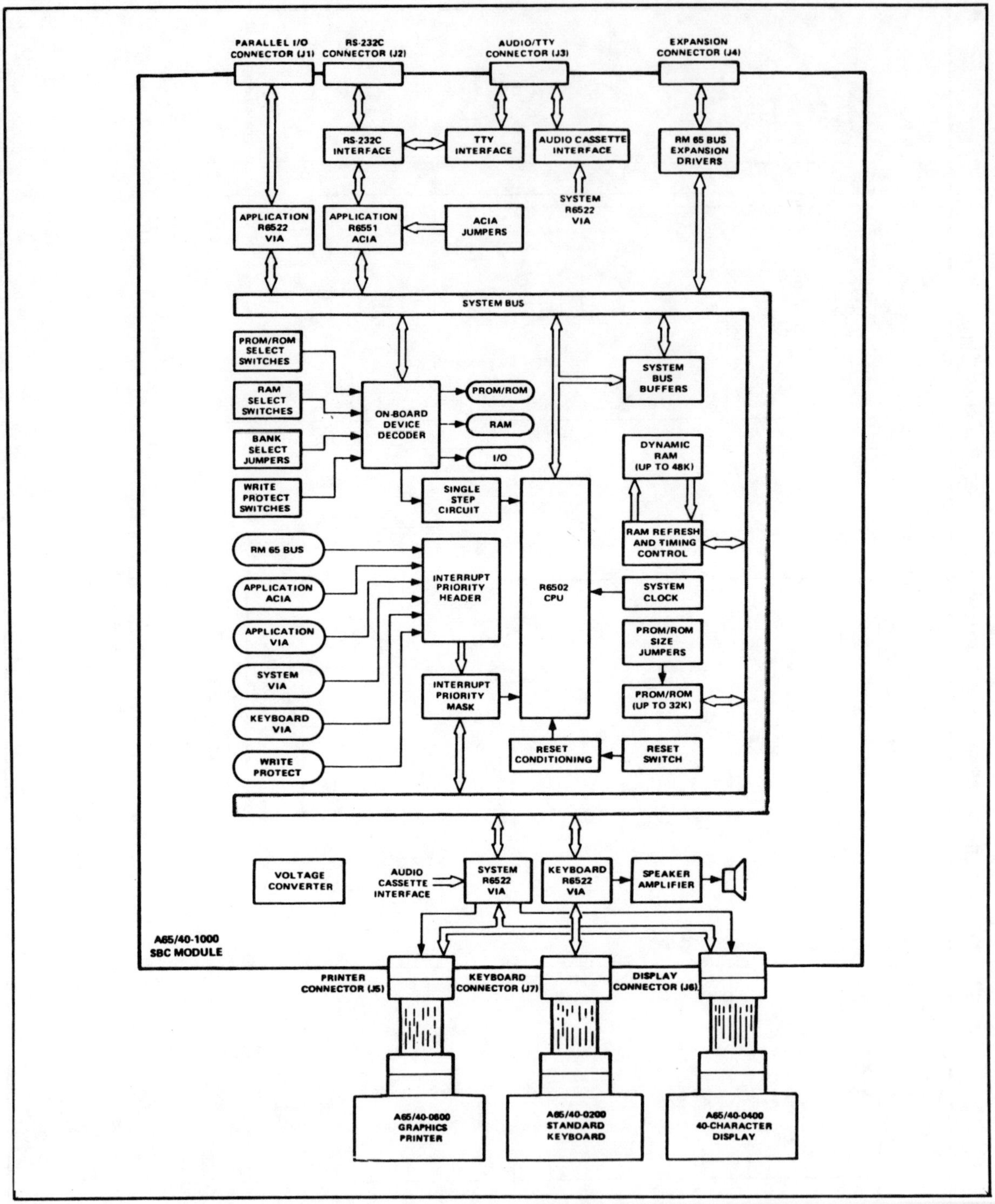

Fig. 12-3. This is the functional block diagram of the AIM-65/40 advanced single-board computer system (courtesy of Rockwell International Corp.).

— User-Prioritized Interrupts, Up to Six Levels
— User-Dedicated Parallel I/O Interface
— User-Dedicated RS-232C Serial Interface
— Audio Cassette/TTY (20 mA Current) Interface
— RM 65 Bus Expansion Interface

☐ Graphics Printer
— Text Mode Provides Upper/Lower Case Alphanumerics, Math, and Special Characters at 240 Lines/Minute
— Full Graphics Mode Provides 280-Dot Resolution
— Quiet, Reliable Thermal Operation

☐ 40-Character Display
— Full Upper Case Alphanumeric and Special Characters
— Bright, Crisp Vacuum Fluorescent Display
— Display, Edit, Auto-Scroll, and Character Blinking Functions

☐ Full-Size Terminal-Style Standard Keyboard
— 57 Keys, Including Locking ALL CAPS Key
— Eight User Function Keys, Plus ATTN and RESET

☐ I/O ROM
— Auto-Start Initialization
— Interrupt-Driven Peripheral I/O Handling
— RAM Vectored I/O with Expansion Hooks
— General Purpose I/O and Utility Subroutines

☐ ROM-Resident Interactive Debug Monitor
— Accepts Instructions in Mnemonic Form
— Machine Level Debug Functions
— Command File for Automatic Command Execuion

☐ ROM-Resident Interactive Debug Monitor
— Line and Screen Oriented Commands
— Read, List, Insert, Delete Functions
— Cursor Control Functions
— Automatic and Manual Block Change Functions

Functional Description

SBC Module

The SBC module contains an R6502 CPU, a 1 MHz clock circuit, onboard device decoders, interrupt request priority circuit, reset conditioning, and both PROM/ROM and RAM memory. On-board sockets accept up to 65K bytes of read-only and read/write memory. Up to 32K bytes of PROM/ROM and up to 48K bytes of RAM may be installed. All on-board memory may be enabled in 4K-byte blocks, yielding an optimal mix of on-board/off board memory and I/O to be addressed. The RAM may also be write-protected in 8K byte segments. Dual bank addressing allows an additional 56K bytes of memory or I/O to be accessed off-board.

The SBC module is connected by removable cables to the 40-Character Display and the Graphics Printer over identical Centronics type parallel handshaking interfaces. The SBC is also connected to the Standard Keyboard through a removable interface cable. These peripheral ports may be also used as general purpose bi-directional data ports with parallel, serial, interrupt, and timer capabilities controlled by user programming of two onboard R6522 Versatile Interface Adapter (VIA) devices.

A separate user-dedicated R6522 VIA interfaces with the Parallel I/O Connector. The high current drive capacity of the VIA's eight "B" port lines can directly drive many industry-standard devices, such as solid state relays. The RS-232C connector provides an interface that allows the SBC to function as a data set or data terminal. An Audio/TTY Connector interfaces to one or two audio cassette recorders and to a 20 mA current loop serial interface.

An Expansion Connector extends the system bus to Rockwell RM 65 bus compatible memory, I/O, or peripheral controller modules. Up to six levels of interrupt priority may be assigned to on-board and off-board peripherals.

GRAPHICS PRINTER

The Graphics Printer includes a dot matrix thermal printer mechanism, a microcomputer controller, thermal head drivers, and motor/strobe timing circuitry.

The printer mechanism includes a thermal head, platen, motor drive linkage, and associated wiring. There are 40 thermal elements on the thermal head, each of which spans seven dot fields; each element is a discrete point which rides against heat sensitive paper. Control logic turns on the thermal head drivers to heat the sensitized paper when a dot is to be printed. During a print cycle, the thermal head moves horizontal across the paper; when an entire row of dots has been printed, the printer motor advances the platen by one horizontal row of dots.

The printer controller includes an R6504 CPU, 4K-byte ROM, RAM, I/O, timer, clock, and reset circuitry. The ROM contains both the CPU instructions and the individual character bit patterns. The controller performs printer motor and thermal head timing and control functions to enable the printer to operate independently from the SBC module.

Data and control commands are transmitted to the printer over the Centronics type parallel handshake interface. An internal buffer accepts up to 80 bytes for printing. The controller automatically prints the first 40 7 ×8 dot-matrix characters in the text mode or after receiving a row of 280 dots in the grahics mode. The paper can also be advanced with a paper feed command, or manually using the paper feed switch.

40-CHARACTER DISPLAY

The 40-Character Display contains a vacuum fluorescent display, a microprocessor-based controller, a 2K-byte character font/program ROM, character and segment drivers, and a dc/dc power converter.

The vacuum fluorescent display is a single sealed unit containing 40 separately controllable digits. Each digit is composed of a 16-segment font which allows a full set of upper case alphabetics, numerics, and special characters to be displayed. In the semi-graphics mode, the 16 segments of each digit are individually controlled. In addition, each digit includes a separate decimal point. When energized, the digits form bright, crisp characters in a blue-green color.

The display controller includes an R6504 CPU, RAM, I/O, timer, clock and reset circuitry. The 2K-byte ROM contains both the CPU controller instructions and the individual character segment patterns. The controller performs all communications interfacing, display refreshing, and control functions—enabling the display to operate independently from the SBC module.

STANDARD KEYBOARD

The AIM 65/40 Standard Keyboard assembly is a full-size terminal style alphanumeric keyboard containing 66 momentary contact single pole single throw (SPST) keys and one locking SPST key.

The keyboard has a complement of 63 momentary contact keys in an 8 × 9 matrix; with nine positions unused. An ALL CAPS locking key is also in this matrix. Nine strobe and eight return lines are used to determine which key is pressed. Three momentary contact keys—RESET, ATTN, and PAPER FEED are outside of the keyboard matrix. These key switches have dedicated returns.

All keyboard lines are brought out to a 40-pin keyboard interface connector, which connects to the AIM-65/40 SBC module through a short interface cable.

I/O ROM

The I/O ROM includes preprogrammed auto-start initialization, interrupt, input/output and utility functions which support user-defined programs as well as AIM-65/40 optional firmware/software. Auto-start initialization jumps to predetermined PROM/ROM addresses during RESET processing. The application program can assume direct control of the system for continued operation, or it can just initialize required functions, then return control back to the I/O ROM for continued auto-star of other functions. I/O drivers directly support AIM 65/40 intelligent display and printer peripherals. Othei drivers support the RS-232C/TTY interfaces, the audio cassette ports and control the on-board speaker.

DEBUG MONITOR/TEXT EDITOR

The Debug Monitor/Text Editor includes a wide selection of functions to simplify computer program entry and checkout. Text can be easily entered, edited, saved, and retrieved using either line or screen oriented commands in the Text Editor. A character cursor can be positioned left, right, up, or down to aid character insertion, addition, and deletion. Automatic and selective character string change capability makes block changes as desired. Multiple text buffers can easily be maintained for separate program and data files.

The Debug Monitor controls program execution in single step and run modes and allows convenient examination and altering of memory and registers. Single step operation allows instruction and register trace for detail examination of executed instructions. Symbol level debugging reduces dependence on absolute addresses and simplifies program checkout.

Command string capability allows command sequences to be chained and easily repeated.

Object code may be output, input, and verified in binary or ASCII format to maximize mass storage performance or to display/print data.

EXPANDING A SINGLE-BOARD COMPUTER FOR ADVANCED TEST SYSTEMS

As you progress along in your understanding and operation of the single-board computers, there will be a time when the single-board computer will not be able to handle all the functions that will be needed in an advanced test system. Again, an advanced test system is defined in this book as any test system that performs more than two or three functions and requires some control operations to run the testing functions. If you are using a Model III, you can expand your 80 I/O-PIB to handle more inputs and outputs. If you have a SYM-1 or AIM-65, the job is a lot simpler because you can use the Rockwell International RM-65 product line of plug-in computer system cards. Although these RM-65 products are designed for the AIM-65 and AIM-65/40, some of the cards will work

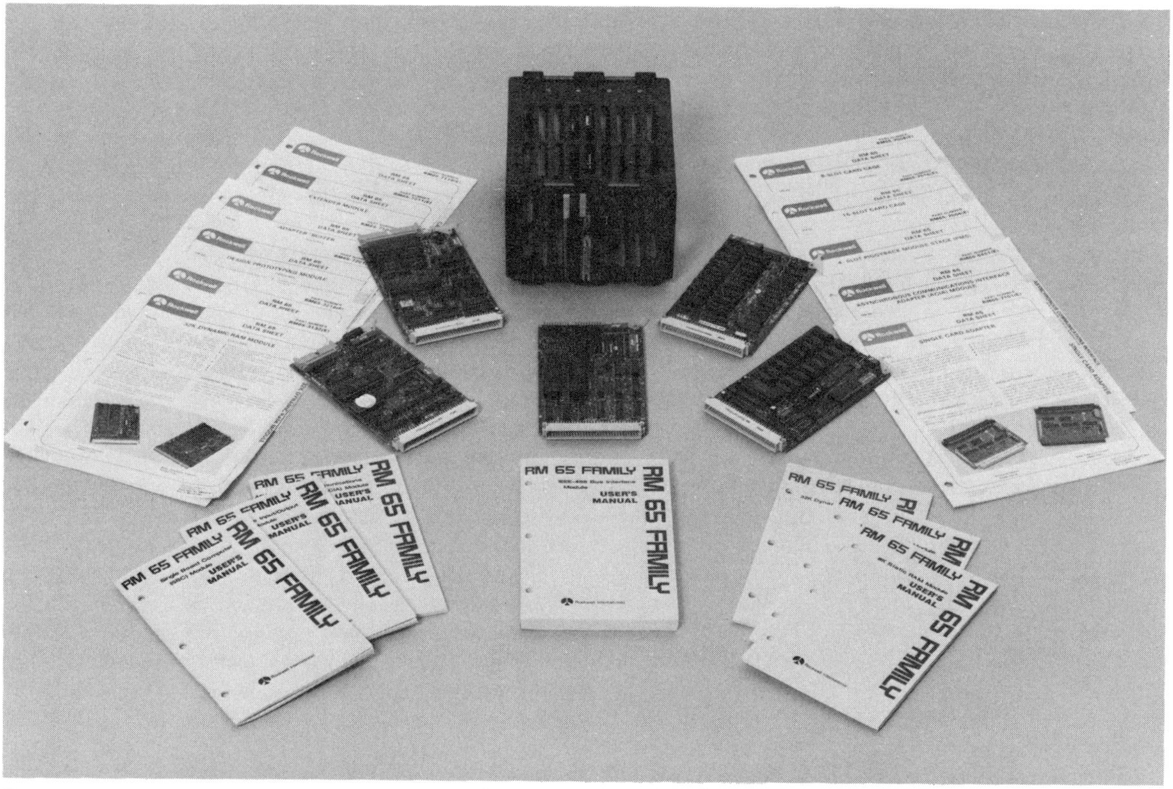

Fig. 12-4. This shows a few of the RM 65 computer system cards and the documentation that is supplied with each system component (courtesy of Rockwell International Corp.).

with the SYM-1 which makes the addition of more memory and I/O ports to either single-board computer an easy task. I have used the RM-65 components in a lot of my test systems, so I will present some general information on a few of the RM-65 products. This information has been obtained from the RM-65 product data sheets.

THE RM-65 COMPUTER PRODUCTS FOR SBC EXPANSION

We will start our RM-65 exploration with the 8K static RAM module which is probably one of the first cards that one would need. When you build an advanced test system, you will generally always need more memory and I/O ports than the single-board computer you are using contains. Figure 12-4 shows a RM-65 product line layout.

8K Static RAM Module (RM65-3108)

The RM-65 8K Static RAM Module contains 8192 8-bit bytes of Random Access Memory (RAM), in sixteen 2114 static RAM devices. The memory is arranged as two separately addressable 4K memory sections. The starting address of each 4K section is selectable by on-board address switches. A Bank Select switch allows the RAM module to be assigned to one of two 64K memory banks. 8K bytes of static 2114 RAM are divided into two separately addressable 4K blocks. Two devices per 1K bytes are required since each device is 1K × 4 bits.

The Data Transceivers invert and transfer 8-bits of parallel data between the RAM devices and the RM-65 Bus, based on data direction signals from the Data Transceiver Control Circuit.

The Address Buffers invert and transfer 16 address bits from the RM-65 Bus to the RAM devices, to the Base Address Decoders and to the Chip Select Decoder.

The Control Buffers invert and transfer phase 2 clock and read/write control signals from the RM-65 Bus onto the RAM module, and drive the bus active signal onto the RM-65 Bus.

The Bank Select Controller detects when the RAM module's assigned memory bank is addressed, by comparing the bank address signal from the RM 65 Bus to the settings of the Bank Select and Bank Select Enable switches. If the addressed bank is the same as the selected memory bank, an enable signal is sent to the Chip Select Decoder.

Two Base Address Decoders detect when either 4K RAM Section (1 or 2) is addressed, by comparing the address lines to Base Address Select switch settings. When a match occurs, an enable signal is sent to the Chip Select Decoder. The Chip Select Decoder uses outputs from the Bank Select Control circuit, the Base Address Decoders, and the PROM/ROM size jumpers as well as address lines A11 and A10 to generate one of eight chip select lines to the RAM devices. A signal indicating that a chip select line is active is also sent to the Write Control and Data Transceiver Control circuits.

The Write Control circuit generates the write enable signals to the RAM devices and to the Data Transceiver Control circuit. If the corresponding write protect switch is off, the write enable signal is activated. If the Write Protect switch is on, the Data Transceivers are disabled.

The Data Transceiver Control circuit determines whether a valid read or write operation is in progress, and provides transceiver enable and data direction signals to the Data Transceivers. The Data Transceivers are enabled if both the bank address and the address lines correspond to the selected bank and a selected base address, respectively.

The General Purpose Input/Output & Timer Module (RM-65-52222)

The heart of the GPIO & Timer module is two R6522 Versatile Interface Adapter (VIA) devices. Each VIA provides two 8-bit bidirectional input/output ports, four I/O control lines, two fully programmable 16-bit timer/counters and an 8-bit shift register for serial interface. There is also control of interrupt generation from independent I/O conditions.

The two 8-bit input/output peripheral ports are fully bidirectional. Data direction registers allow each peripheral pin to independently act as either an input or an output. The four control lines can also be used for I/O or can provide handshaking for the associated data ports. Each control input can be programmed to interrupt the microprocessor on detection of a rising or falling edge.

The two 16-bit counter-timers are capable of many complex timing and counting functions. One timer provides four modes of operation: free running, with pulsed or toggled output, one-shot interval timer with a low-level output on a peripheral port line, or one-shot interval timer with a toggle output on a peripheral port line. The three modes of the second 16-bit timer provide a one-shot interval timer, a count of external pulses, or a clock for serial shift register. The shift register can shift in, or shift out, data at the system clock rate, the timer clock rate, or an external clock rate. Both timers and the shift register can be programmed to interrupt the microprocessor upon time-out or shift completion.

The Data Transceivers invert and buffer 8-bits of parallel data between the RM-65 Bus and the two R6522 VIA devices. The Data Transceivers are enabled when a valid address is presented at the Base Address Decoders. During a read operation, data is transferred from the addressed R6522 to the RM-65 Bus. During a write operation, data is transferred from the RM-65 Bus to the addressed R6522. The Address Buffers invert the five least significant address bits used to select the R6522 devices and registers.

The Bank Control circuit detects when the GPIO & Timer Module's assigned memory bank is addressed by comparing the bank address signal from the RM-65 Bus to the Bank Select Enable and Bank Select switches. The Bank Select Enable switch allows the module to be assigned common to either both banks, or to Bank 0 (lower 65K) or Bank 1 (upper 65K) depending on the Bank Select switch.

The Control Buffers drive read/write, phase 2 clock, and reset signals from the RM-65 Bus to the GPIO & Timer Module. The interrupt request and bus active signals are driven from the GPIO & Timer Module.

The Base Address Decoders use the eight most significant address lines to assign the 32 I/O addresses to a page (256 bytes) boundary. When an address is within range of the Base Address switches and the Bank Control is enabled, a chip select is generated to one of the R6522 devices.

Twelve Control Direction Jumpers allow the three bidirectional control lines (CA1, CB1, and CB2) on each R6522 to be configured for either input or output mode.

Four I/O Direction Switches provide direction control to each of the Port I/O transceivers. Four Programmed/Manual Select switches allow the direction control to be established from the Direction Control switches in the Manual mode or from a R6522 control line in the Programmed mode.

The I/O Transceivers buffer each of four 8-bit I/O ports. The direction is determined by the Direction Control logic. There are also eight buffers provided for the control lines (2 per I/O port), six of which can be configured for input or output as determined by the Handshake Direction Buffers.

The 16K PROM/ROM Module (RM65-3216)

The PROM/ROM module has eight 24-pin sockets with can accept up to 16K of either 2K, 4K, or 8K PROMs/ROMs or equivalents:

Intel 2716 or 2732 PROMs
TI TMS 2516 or 2532 PROMs
Rockwell R2316, R2332 or R2364 ROMs

The Data Buffers invert and transfer 8-bits of parallel data from the selected PROM/ROM devices to the RM 65 Bus during read operations.

The Control Buffers invert and transfer phase 2 clock, and read/write control signals from the RM-65 Bus onto the PROM/ROM module, and drive the bus active signal onto the RM-65 Bus.

The Bank Select control circuit detects when the PROM/ROM module's assigned memory bank is addressed, by comparing the bank address signal from the RM-65 Bus to the Bank Select and Bank Select and Bank Select Enable switches. The Bank Select Enable switch allows 8K of the PROM/ROM to be common memory (addressable in both Bank 0 and Bank 1) while the remaining 8K is assigned either to Bank 0 or Bank 1, as determined by the Bank Select switch.

Four Base Address Decoders allow 4K PROM/ROM sections to be independently addressed on any 4K boundary within the selected bank. When an address falls within any section (per the Base Address switches), an enable signal is sent to the Chip Select Decoder.

The Chip Select Decoder uses outputs from the Bank Select Control circuit, the Base Address Decoders, and the PROM/ROM size jumpers as well as the address lines to generate chip selects to the PROM/ROM devices. The PROM/ROM type jumpers route the chip select lines to the correct pins on the PROM/ROM sockets.

The Data Buffer Control circuit enables the Data Buffers during a read operation when an address corresponding to a selected base address is decoded and the selected PROM/ROM memory bank is addressed.

The RM65-5102 CRT Controller Module

The CRT Controller (CRTC) Module interfaces the RM-65 to a CRT monitor or television receiver. The CRTC module outputs HSYNC, VSYNC, and raw video signals for direct connection to a CRT Monitor, and composite video for connection to a CRT monitor or to a TV receiver through an rf modulator. A socketed on-board ROM generates 5 × 7 characters with two descenders in a 7 × 10 dot matrix field to provide upper and lower case alphanumerics and special symbols. The 2K bytes of on-board display RAM are memory-mapped.

A 2K-byte program ROM provides firmware to configure the display format for 80 columns by 25 rows or 40 columns by 16 rows, scan rate of 50 or 60 Hz, and a CRT display driver for AIM-65. There are also cursor control, screen editing, and utility routines.

Features

□ 4K Byte character generator ROM with:
— Upper and lower case alphabetics
— Special characters
— Numbers including subscripts and superscripts
— Math symbols
— Semi-graphics

□ On-board ROM firmware supports:
— Scrolling
— Screen editing
— Full cursor movement control
— Full screen standard or inverse video
— Predefined formats for
80 column by 25 row (50/60 Hz)
72 column by 22 row (50/60 Hz)
40 column by 25 row (60 Hz)
40 column by 16 row (60 Hz)
— Selectable format from 1 to 80 columns by 1 to 25 rows
— NTSC (60 Hz, 525 lines per frame) and European (50 Hz, 625 lines per frame) raster format
— CRT display driver for AIM-65

□ Single 5 volt operation

The CRT Controller Module block diagram is shown in Fig. 12-5 with the control commands presented in Table 12-8 and the character set shown in Fig. 12-6.

Functional Description

The Data Transceivers invert and transfer 8-bits of parallel data between the CRTC Module and the RM-65 bus, based on control signals from the Base Address Decoder and the Control Buffers. The read/write control line determines the direction, while the bus active enables the Data Transceivers.

The Address Buffers invert and transfer the 16-bit parallel address lines from the RM-65 bus to the Base Address Decoders, the R2316 ROM, the CRT Controller (CRTC) device, and to the Refresh RAM device.

The Control Buffers invert and transfer the phase 2 clock and read/write control signals from the RM-65 bus onto the module.

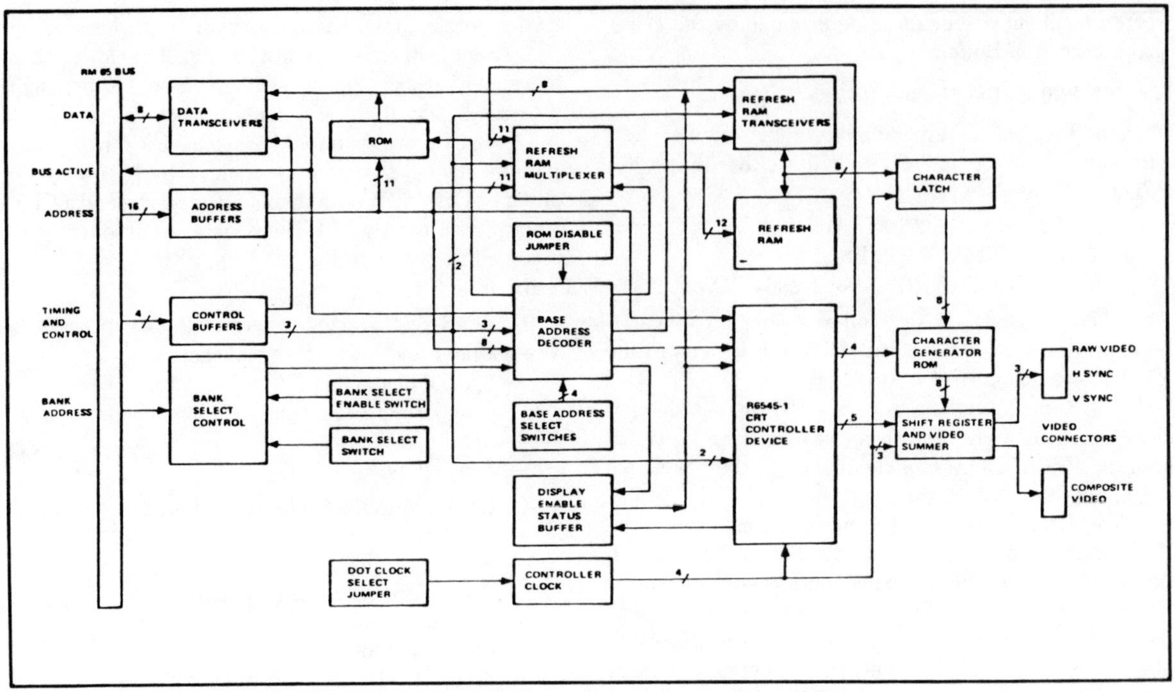

Fig. 12-5. The CRT controller module block diagram (courtesy of Rockwell International Corp.).

Table 12-8. The Control Commands for the RM 65 CRT Video Module (courtesy of Rockwell International Corp.).

RM 65 CRTC Control Commands					
Hex Code	**Character**	**Description**	**Hex Code**	**Character**	**Description**
00	CTRL @		10	CTRL P	Pass Through Next Character
01	CTRL A	Clear Line	11	CTRL Q	*
02	CTRL B	Clear to End of Line	12	CTRL R	*
03	CTRL C	Clear Screen	13	CTRL S	Toggle Insert Character mode
04	CTRL D	Clear to End of Screen	14	CTRL T	Delete One Character
05	CTRL E	Clear Screen	15	CTRL U	Insert One Line
06	CTRL F	Clear to End of Screen	16	CTRL V	Delete One Line
07	CTRL G	*	17	CTRL W	Display Cursor
08	CTRL H	Backspace (←)	18	CTRL X	Blank Cursor
09	CTRL I	Horizontal Tab (→)	19	CTRL Y	Relink AIM 65 Display
0A	CTRL J	Line Feed (↓)	1A	CTRL Z	*
0B	CTRL K	Vertical Tab (↑)	1B	CTRL [	Escape Character (ESC) (1)
0C	CTRL L	Form Feed (Clear Screen)	1C	CTRL \	Blinking Cursor
0D	CTRL M	Carriage Return (Home or Line)	1D	CTRL]	Enter Normal Characters
0E	CTRL N	Home on Screen	1E	CTRL ∧	Perform Self Test
0F	CTRL O	Home on Screen	1F	CTRL —	Reverse Video

*These characters have no effect.

(1) There are two escape sequences as follows:

Hex Code	Character Sequence	Function
1B 3D YY XX	ESC = y x	Move the cursor to the row y and column x position, with row y between top ($00) and bottom ($19), and column x between leftmost ($00) and rightmost ($4F).
1B 47	ESC G	Enter Graphics Character Mode

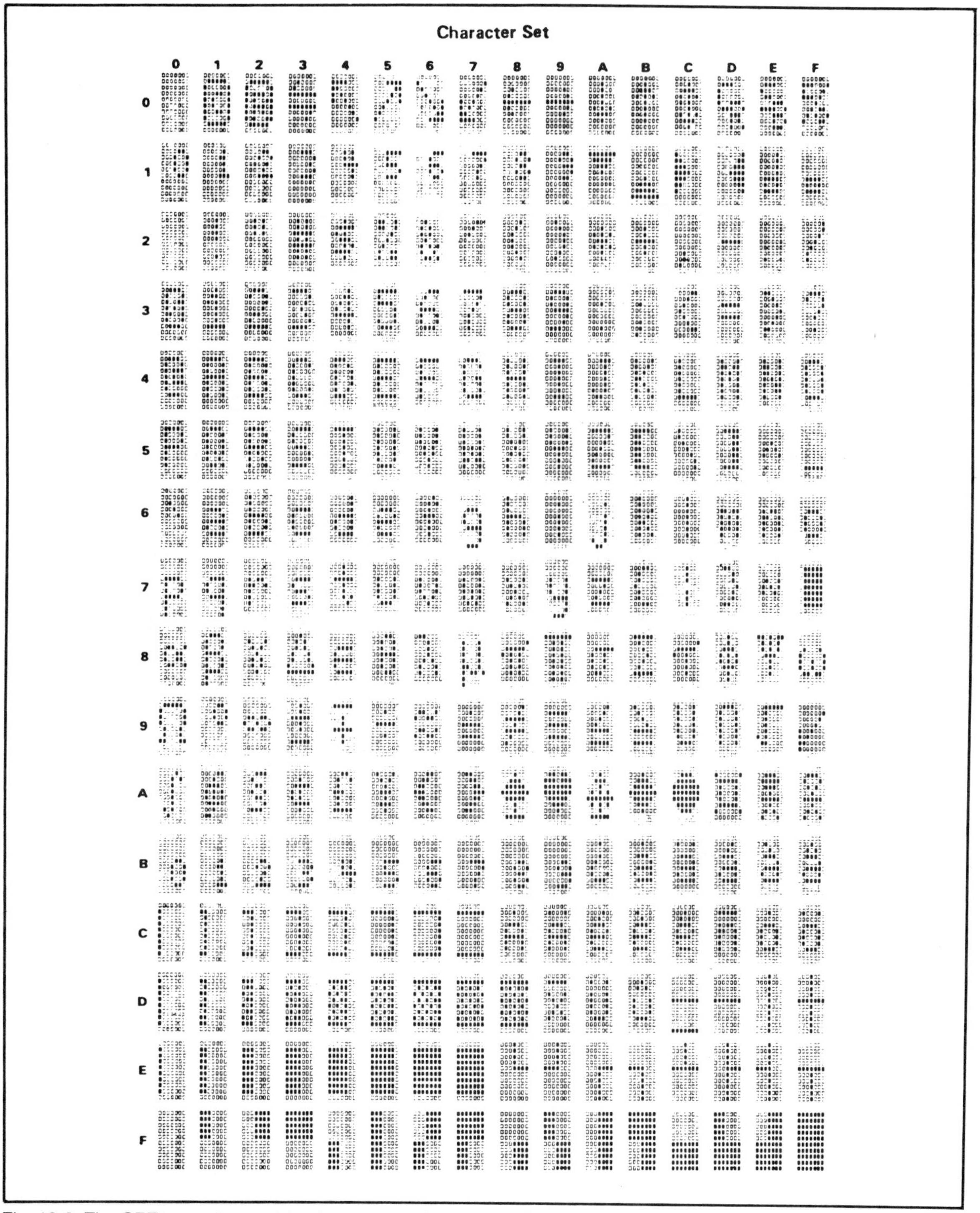

Fig. 12-6. The CRT controller module character set (courtesy of Rockwell International Corp.).

The Bank Select Control circuit detects when the module's assigned memory bank is addressed, by comparing the bank address signal from the RM-65 bus to the Bank Select and Bank Select Enable switches. The Bank Select Enable switch allows the board to reside in common memory (both Bank 0 and Bank 1) or only in the Bank set by the Bank Select switch (either Bank 0 or Bank 1).

The Base Address Decoder, with the Base Address Select switches, the Bank Select Control circuit, the ROM Disable Switch and the read/write and phase 2 clock signals, generates device selects for the on-board ROM, RAM, and I/O (CRTC device and Display Enable Status Buffer). The Base Address Select switches allow the module to be selected to any 4K block. Within the selected 4K block, the RAM is assigned to the lower 8 pages (2K bytes), and the I/O to the first 256 byte page of the upper 2K bytes. When the ROM is disabled, only the RAM and I/O can be selected and the module is assigned 9 pages (2304 bytes) in memory. When the ROM is enabled, the module is assigned the full 4K bytes, with 7 pages for ROM, in addition to the RAM and I/O.

The Controller Clock uses a crystal-controlled oscillator to derive a 6 MHz or 12 MHz reference for the shift register dot clock depending on the Dot Clock Select jumper position. With the 6-MHz clock, up to 40 characters per line can be displayed on any monitor or standard television using an rf modulator. Up to 80 characters per line can be achieved with the 12-MHz clock and a high bandwidth monitor. The dot clock is divided by seven to provide a Character Clock for the CRTC device and a load character signal for the shift register.

The Refresh RAM provides 2K bytes of display memory, for screen densities of up to 25 lines with as many as 80 characters each. The RAM is directly mapped into the RM-65 memory map, so the display can be updated by a block memory move or under DMA control. The Refresh RAM Multiplexer and RAM Transceiver allow the RM-65 bus and the CRTC device to both access the Refresh RAM, with the RM-65 bus having priority when any conflict occurs.

The Display Enable Status Buffer allows the RM-65 bus to monitor the active display times, so that display memory transfers can be made with no visible distortion.

The Character Generator ROM holds the fonts for the character set. These fonts are stored as 256 characters, each with 10 seven-bit rows. The four CRTC device row address lines and the eight Character Latch bits, which hold the character being refreshed, create an address for the character generator ROM. The output data of the ROM, which is seven parallel bits, represents the display pattern. The Shift Register takes this data and forms the serial video data. The Video Summer combines and buffers the serial video data with CRTC device timing signals to form a composite video output and a separate video, horizontal sync, and vertical sync.

The Program ROM contains the firmware for an intelligent CRT driver, in addition to utilities to aid in custom CRT display application software. There are six predefined screen formats, including 25 lines of 80 characters (50 or 60 Hz), 22 lines of 72 characters (50 or 60 Hz), 25 lines of 40 characters (50 Hz), and 16 lines of 40 characters (60 Hz). For other formats, any dimensions from 1 to 25 lines of from 1 to 80 characters can be defined (50 or 60 Hz). Full screen inverse video and 256 display characters allow flexible display capabilities.

The intelligent display driver controls all screen updating and cursor movement for the selected screen format. The cursor can be on, off, or blinking with movements including, up, down, left, right, home, and carriage return, as well as to any row and column position. There are many commands to facilitate screen editing, such as:

- Insert character or line
- Delete character or line
- Clear to end of line
- Clear to end of screen
- Clear line or screen
- Set or Clear special character mode

The firmware utilities are useful for special applications. There is also a display driver which replaces the AIM-65 on-board display with a CRT monitor and an AIM-65 Assembler listing reformatter which takes advantage of the longer display lines.

The IEEE-488 Bus Interface Module (RM65-7102)

The RM-65 IEEE-488 Bus Interface Module connects an AIM-65 or RM-65 SBC based system to the IEEE-488 General Purpose Interface Bus (GPIB). Complete controller, talker and listener functions, as defined in the IEEE-488, 1978 Standard, are implemented. The module also supports extended addressing and multiple bus controllers. On-board ROM firmware implements all 12 functions specified by the interface standard. Features not defined in the standard, but also supported, include manual talk or listen disable, dual primary addressing, and an external trigger line. Switches select the Device Talk/Listen Address, Enable Duel Primary Addressing Mode, Disable Talk, Disable Listen, and System Controller mode. The bus interface transceivers meet the electrical specifications of the IEEE 488 interface standard. An 8-inch ribbon cable mates the IEEE-488 bus with a standard 24-pin connector.

Features

- ☐ Buffered address, data and control lines
- ☐ Listen, talk, and controller functions
- ☐ IEEE-488, 1978 standard fully implemented
- ☐ Uses TI 9914 GPIB Adapter device
- ☐ On-board ROM contains bus protocol and utility firmware
- ☐ Switches for
  - — Device Talk/Listen Address
  - — Disable Talk
  - — Disable Listen
  - — Enable Dual Primary Addressing mode
  - — System Controller
  - — Base Address to page boundary for I/O
  - — Bank Selection to one or both 65K banks
- ☐ Jumper for ROM enable/disable
- ☐ LEDs show current address register contents
- ☐ Supports DMA data transfers
- ☐ +5V operation

The IEEE-488 Bus Interface Module block diagram is presented in Fig. 12-7 and the connector pin assignments are shown in Table 12-9.

The Data Transceivers invert and transfer 8-bits of parallel data between the IEEE-488 Bus Interface Module and the RM-65 bus, based on data direction signals from the Base Address Decoder.

The Address Buffers invert and transfer the 16-bit parallel address lines from the RM-65 bus to the Base Address Decoders, to the R2332 ROM and to the GPIB Adapter.

The Control Buffers invert and transfer phase 2 clock, reset, and read/write control signals from the RM-65 bus onto the module. The interrupt request is buffered and driven onto the RM-65 bus.

The Bank Select Control circuit detects when the module's assigned memory bank is addressed by comparing the bank address signal from the RM 65 bus to the Bank Select and Bank Select Enable switches. The Bank Select Enable switch allows the board to reside in common memory (both Bank 0 and Bank 1) or only in the Bank set by the Bank Select switch (either Bank 0 or Bank 1).

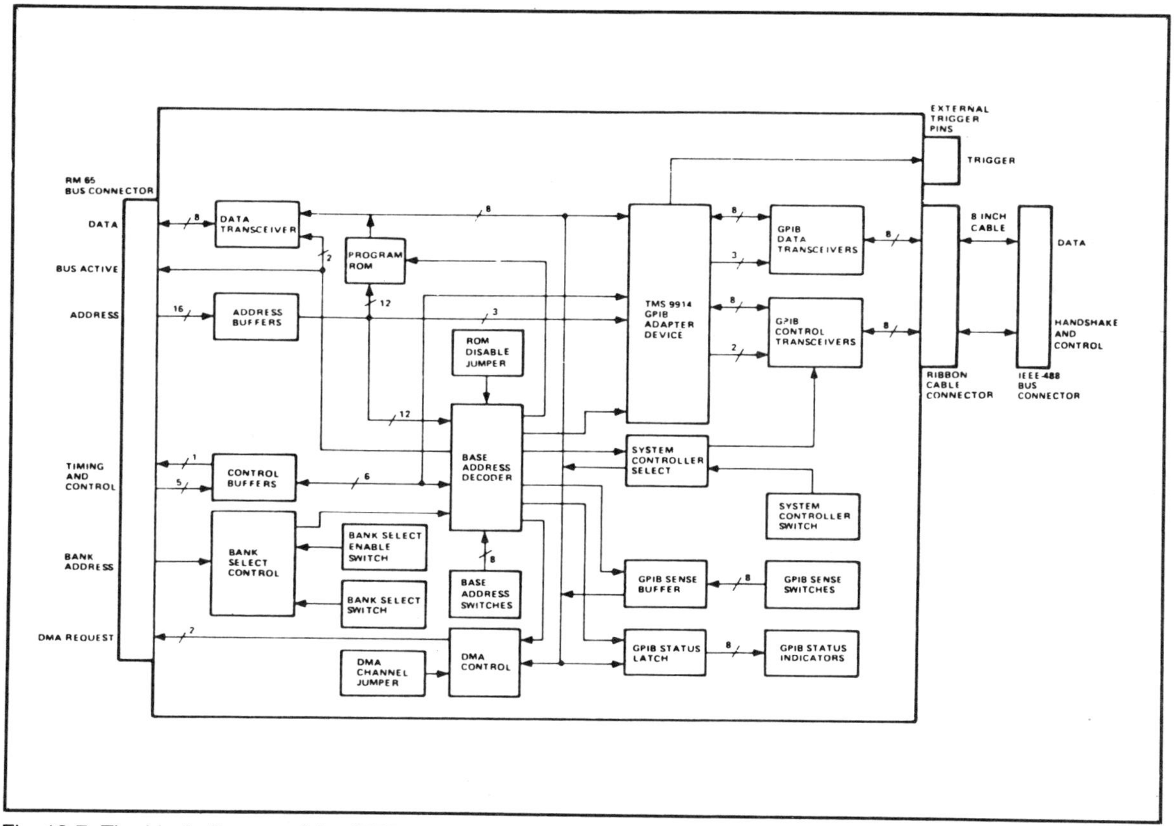

Fig. 12-7 The block diagram of the IEEE-488 interface module (courtesy of Rockwell International Corp.).

Table 12-9. The IEEE Module Connector Data (courtesy of Rockwell International Corp.).

External Trigger Pin Assignments

Pin	Signal Mnemonic	Signal Name	Input/Output
1	TRIG	Trigger Out	0
2	GND	Ground	

IEE-488 Bus Interface Connector Pin Assignments

Pin	Signal Mnemonic	Signal Name	Input/ Output	Pin	Signal Mnemonic	Signal Name	Input/ Output
1	DI01	Data Input/Output 1	I/O	13	DI05	Data Input/Output 5	I/O
2	DI02	Data Input/Output 2	I/O	14	DI06	Data Input/Output 6	I/O
3	DI03	Data Input/Output 3	I/O	15	DI07	Data Input/Output 7	I/O
4	DI04	Data Input/Output 4	I/O	16	DI08	Data Input/Output 8	I/O
5	EOI	End or Identify	I/O	17	REN	Remote Enable	I/O
6	DAV	Data Available	I/O	18	GND	Ground	N/A
7	NRFD	Not Ready for Data	I/O	19	GND	Ground	N/A
8	NDAC	Not Data Accepted	I/O	20	GND	Ground	N/A
9	IFC	Interface Clear	I/O	21	GND	Ground	N/A
10	SRQ	Service Request	I/O	22	GND	Ground	N/A
11	ATN	Attention	I/O	23	GND	Ground	N/A
12	SHIELD	Ground	N/A	24	GND	Logic Ground	N/A

The DMA Control circuit allows DMA requests from the TI 9914 GPIB Adapter device to be driven on the RM-65 bus or disabled under program control. This line is jumper selectable for either of two DMA request lines on the RM-65 bus.

The Base Address Decoder compares the eight most significant address lines to the eight Base Address switches. The ROM Disable jumper allows the module to be active in a 4K block when enabled or active in a page (256 locations) when disabled. When an address for the selected bank matches the four most significant switches and the ROM is enabled, the Data Transceivers are enabled and the bus active signal is generated. When this address also matches the four least significant switches the GPIB Adapter and I/O are selected. When there is no match on the four least significant switches, the ROM is selected. When the GPIB Adapter and I/O are selected, the four least significant address lines, phase 2 clocks, and read/write control lines are used to derive register selects for the GPIB Adapter, device selects for the GPIB Status Latch, GPIB Sense Buffers, System Controller Select, and DMA Control Circuits. The read/write control lines also determine the direction for the Data Transceivers.

The TMS 9914 GPIB Adapter device provides hardware control of the IEEE-488 bus interface, using firmware subroutines provided in ROM. All bus interface lines are buffered by the GPIB Data and Control Transceivers, to conform to the electrical specifications of the IEEE-488 Standard. These lines are brought out through a cable to a standard IEEE-488 connector. An additional connector provides an external trigger output not defined by the IEEE-488 Standard.

The System Controller Select circuit allows manual selection of System Controller capabilities in multiple controller configurations.

The GPIB Sense abuffer allows the GPIB Sense Switches to be read for Device Talk/Listen Address, Talk or Listen Disable, and Dual Primary Address Mode selection. The GPIB Status Latch latches the positions of the GPIB Sense Switches and displays them on the GPIB Status Indicators. This allows a visual verification of the Device Talk/Listen Address and Operating modes.

On-Board Program ROM Firmware

The Program ROM firmware completely supports all 12 Bus functions described in the IEEE-488, 1978 Standard, as well as features of the TMS 9914 GPIB Adapter device not defined in the Standard. These utility functions make both the Bus protocol and the GPIB Adapter device transparent to the programmer. The firmware, organized as subroutines, is linked to the user program through a jump table. Many of these routines are interrupt-driven, to minimize the processor time in servicing the module. User-alterable vectors and parameters are located in RAM, to allow custom applications. Output data or commands for the Bus are handled as tables, easing the set-up and transfer of information. Extensive error checking by the utility subroutines allow resident or user-provided error handling routines to ensure proper operation of the module, the IEEE-488 Bus and status of data transfer. Two self-test routines verify proper module operation.

The RM 65 Single-Card Adapter, Eight-Slot Card Cage and the Adapter/Buffer for the Aim-65

These three components are used to interface the RM-65 bus to the AIM-65 bus. If you add any of the RM-65 products to a SYM-1, AIM-65, or AIM-65/40 you will need to use the required card adapter.

The Single Card Adapter (RM65-7101)

The RM-65 Single-Card Adapter allows one RM-65 Bus compatible module to be connected to the AIM-65 Master Module, through the AIM-65 Expansion connector. The Adapter routes the AIM-65 address, data and control lines from the AIM-65 Expansion connector pin assignments to the RM-65 Bus pin assignments. Drive circuitry is included on the address and data lines.

The 8-Slot Card Cage and Mother Board (RM65-7008)

The 8-slot card cage consists of an 8-slot RM-65 Bus compatible motherboard in a card cage. Memory, I/O or special functions may be added to the AIM-65 Microcomputer by use of the 8-slot card cage. When connected to the AIM-65 Master Module through the Buffer/Adapter Module, the card cage may be mounted over, under, or behind the AIM-65 Master Module in a variety of orientations to meet unique application requirements. The form factor of the 8-slot card cage allows low profile placement in a tabletop or terminal style enclosure.

The 8-Slot Motherboard (RM65-7008N and RM65-7008NE) is a printed circuit board (PCB) less eight connectors, three filter capacitors, two mini-terminal strips and eight mounting blocks used to fasten the PCB to the card cage. Connectors, mini-terminal strips, filter capacitors and custom mounting blocks as needed can easily be added to meet unique installation requirements.

The Adapter/Buffer (RM65-7104)

The Adapter/Buffer extends the RM-65 Bus from the AIM-65 Expansion Connector to a compatible motherboard that is situated up to 16 inches away. Included circuitry permits the Adapter/Buffer to drive up to 15 RM-65 Bus-compatible modules. (The similar Cable Driver Adapter/Buffer, Part Number RM65-7116, provides the same drive capability for applications in which the mother board is up to six feet from the Expansion Connector.)

The Adapter/Buffer consists of an adapter module, a buffer module and two 16-inch interconnect cables. Both cables are flexible, so the motherboard may be installed in a wide variety of locations and orientations relative to the AIM-65.

AIM-65 FORTH LANGUAGE

If you are going to keep advancing the levels of your test system, sooner or later you will need a faster programming language to run the test system. Rockwell has a FORTH programming language for both the AIM-65 and the AIM-65/40 which is ideal for test system and process control. FORTH will work a lot faster than BASIC and it will pay you many times over when you take the time to learn how to use the FORTH language.

FORTH Versus Other Languages

FORTH actually provides the best of two worlds. It has the looping and branching constructs of high-level languages (DO . . . LOOP, BEGIN . . . END, IF . . . THEN and IF . . . ELSE . . . THEN) and the code efficiency of machine and assembly languages. And programmers will be pleased to know that FORTH allows you to specify addresses, operands and data in hexadecimal, octal, binary or any other number base from two to 40—a distinct advantage over languages like BASIC, where all information must be in decimal.

In most time-critical applications, at least part of the program must be written in assembly language. AIM 65 FORTH has a built-in 6502 macro assembler, and lets you drop into assembly language at almost any point in your program must be written in assembly language. AIM-65 awkward machine level linkage. FORTH programs typically run up to ten times faster than other interpretive languages, and can even approach the speed of machine language programs for some applications.

Developing FORTH Programs

FORTH is built on subroutine-like functions, called "words." These words are linked together to form a "dictionary," which is the central core of the language. Writing a program in FORTH consists of using several predefined words to define each new word. Once the new word has been added to the system dictionary, it becomes as much a part of the language as any other word that has been previously defined. In this way new features and extensions can be added by simply defining one or more new words. Adding new features to conventional languages like BASIC or PASCAL requires the language system to be completely reassembled or recompiled.

FORTH is a stack-oriented language, and is programmed in Reverse Polish Notation (RPN), the notation that is used in Hewlett-Packard scientific calculators. Using a data stack is an extremely efficient way of passing variables back and forth between operations. A data stack eliminates the need to tie up memory locations with variable tables, and allows you to use only as much memory as you need.

FORTH programs are developed using "top-down/bottom-up" techniques. That is, the programmer begins by defining the program in very general terms, then systematically breaks these definitions down into more and more detailed sub-modules. When the lowest level of sub-modules have been defined, he starts coding, in FORTH, at those levels, working back up toward the top of the program, in pyramid fashion. Each sub-module is a stand-alone component of the program, and can be completely debugged without having the complete program in the system. This type of software development is difficult, if not impossible, to do with most other high-level languages.

A FORTH Example Program

As an example of a FORTH application, suppose we have a chemical processing plant that includes two holding tanks that pump into a mixing tank. When the mixing tank is full, both pumps must shut off and allow the liquid to mix for ten minutes. Figure 12-8 shows this part of the system.

The functional steps needed to perform the operation are:

1. Start Pump #1
2. Start Pump #2
3. Wait until the Mixing Tank is full
4. Stop Pump #1
5. Stop Pump #2
6. Mix for 10 minutes

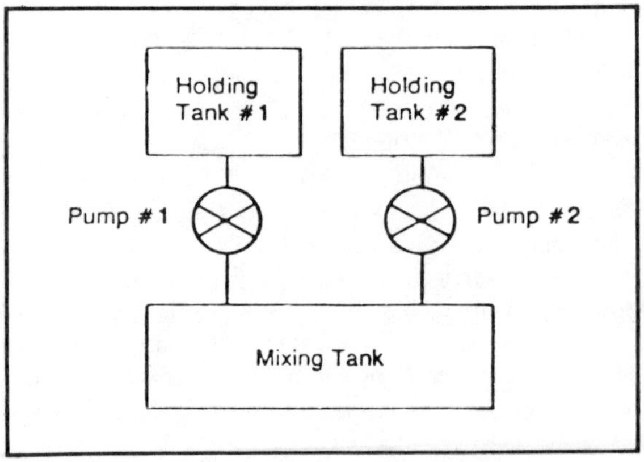

Fig. 12-8. The FORTH Language application diagram.

With the major operations now defined, we can begin writing our FORTH program. Let's call the program MIX-BATCH. It would look like this:

```
: MIX-BATCH

        START-PUMP1
        START-PUMP2
        WAIT-TIL-TANK-FULL
        STOP-PUMP1
        STOP-PUMP2
        FOR-10-MINUTES
        MIX;
```

Notice how similar this program is to our functional breakdown. It's also very readable. The colon (:) tells FORTH that we are defining a new word; MIX-BATCH, in this case. The semicolon (;) on the last line, after MIX, indicates the end of the definition. The words between MIX-BATCH and the semicolon represent the operations that will be performed when the word MIX-BATCH is executed. All of these words—START-PUMP1, START-PUMP2, WAIT-TIL-TANK-FULL and so on—must have been previously defined using AIM-65 FORTH words or other, user-defined words.

For instance, START-PUMP1 may be constructed from two general input/output control words for the AIM 65's user-dedicated R6522 VIA, as follows:

```
: START-PUMP1 PORTB1=OUTPUT SET-
        B1=HIGH ;
```

In this definition, PORTB1=OUTPUT establishes Bit 1 of the VIA as an output and SET-B1=HIGH sets the output to a +5V level, which turns on the pump motor. Either of these words (or any other FORTH words) could be defined in either FORTH or assembly language. Existing assembly language programs and subroutines may be directly used by FORTH. AIM-65 FORTH words are presented in Table 12-10.

CONCLUSION

In this chapter I have tried to present some basic information about what is in store for you when the time comes for something bigger than a single-board computer. The best suggestion I can give you is to stay with one computer system and its components. It is very hard

Table 12-10. The AIM-65 FORTH Word Dictionary (courtesy of Rockwell International Corp.).

ni = 16-bit signed number on the stack (n1 is the deepest value).
di = 32-bit signed number on the stack (d1 is the deepest value).
ui = 16-bit unsigned number on the stack (u1 is the deepest value).

STACK MANIPULATION

DUP	Duplicate top of stack.
2DUP	Duplicate top two stack items.
DROP	Delete top of stack.
2DROP	Delete top two stack items.
SWAP	Exchange top two stack items.
OVER	Copy second item to top.
ROT	Rotate third item to top.
-DUP	Duplicate only if non-zero.
>R	Move top item to return stack.
R>	Retrieve item from return stack.
R	Copy top of return stack onto stack.
PICK	Copy the nth item to top.
SP@	Return address of stack position.
RP@	Return address of return stack pointer.
SO	Return address of pointer to bottom of stack.
BOUNDS	Convert "address count" to "end-address start-address."
.S	Print contents of stack.

NUMERIC REPRESENTATION

DECIMAL	Set decimal base.
HEX	Set hexadecimal base.
BASE	Set number base.
DIGIT	Convert ASCII to binary.
0	The number zero.
1	The number one.
2	The number two.
3	The number three.

COMPARISON OPERATORS

<	True if n1 less than n2.
>	True if n1 greater than n2.
=	True if top two numbers are equal.
0<	True if top number negative.
0=	True if top number zero.
U<	True if u1 less than u2.
NOT	Same as 0=.

ARITHMETIC AND LOGICAL

+	Add.
D+	Add double-precision numbers.
−	Subtract (n1 − n2).
*	Multiply.
/	Divide (n1/n2).
MOD	Modulo (i.e. remainder from division).
/MOD	Divide, giving remainder and quotient.
*/MOD	Multiply, then divide (n1*n2/n3), with double intermediate.
*/	Like */MOD, but give quotient only.
U*	Unsigned multiply leaving double product.
U/	Unsigned divide.
M	Signed multiplication leaving double product.
M/	Signed remainder and quotient from double dividend.
M/MOD	Unsigned divide leaving double quotient and remainder from double dividend and single divisor.
MAX	Maximum.
MIN	Minii.
+−	Set sign.
D+−	Set sign of double-precision number.
ABS	Absolute value.
DABS	Absolute value of double-precision number.
NEGATE	Change sign.
DNEGATE	Change sign of double-precision number.
S −> D	Sign extend to double-precision number.
1+	Increment value on top of stack by 1.
2+	Increment value on top of stack by 2.
1−	Decrement value on top of stack by 1.
2−	Decrement value on top of stack by 2.
AND	Logical AND (bitwise).
OR	Logical OR (bitwise).
XOR	Logical exclusive OR (bitwise).

CONTROL STRUCTURES

DO . . . LOOP	Set up loop, given index range.
DO . . . +LOOP	Like DO . . . LOOP, but adds stack value to index.
I	Place current index value on stack.
LEAVE	Terminate loop at next LOOP or +LOOP.
BEGIN . . . UNTIL	Loop back to BEGIN until true at UNTIL.
BEGIN . . . WHILE . . . REPEAT	Loop while true at WHILE; REPEAT loops unconditionally to BEGIN.
BEGIN . . . AGAIN	Unconditional loop.
IF . . . THEN	If top of stack true, execute following clause THEN continue; otherwise continue at THEN.
IF . . . ELSE . . . THEN	If top of stack true, execute ELSE clause THEN continue; otherwise execute following clause. THEN continue.

OUTPUT FORMATTING

NUMBER	Convert string at address to double-precision number.
<#	Start output string
#	Convert next digit of double-precision number and add character to output string.
#S	Convert all significant digits of double-precision number to output string.
SIGN	Insert sign of n into output string.
#>	Terminate output string (ready for TYPE).
HOLD	Insert ASCII character into output string.
HLD	Hold pointer, user variable.
-TRAILING	Suppress trailing blanks.
.LINE	Display line of text from mass storage.
COUNT	Change length of byte string to type form.
	Print number on top of stack.
.R	Print number n1 right justified n2 places.
D.	Print double-precision number n2 n1.

Table 12-10. The AIM-65 FORTH Word Dictionary (courtesy of Rockwell International Corp.) (Continued from page 189.)

INPUT-OUTPUT	
CR	Carriage return.
SPACE	Type one space.
SPACES	Type n spaces.
." . . . . "	Print text string (terminated by ").
DUMP	Dump n2 words starting at address.
TYPE	Type string of n1 characters starting at address n2.
?TERMINAL	True if terminal break request present.
KEY	Read key, put ASCII value on stack.
EMIT	Output ASCII value from stack.
EXPECT	Read n1 characters from input to address n2.
WORD	Read one word from input stream, until delimiter.
IN	User variable contained within TIB.
HOLD	Waits for KEY.
BAUD	Set BAUD rate.
BL	Output a SPACE character.
C/L	Number of characters/line.
TIB	Pointer to terminal input buffer start address.
B/SCR	Number of blocks/editing screen.
QUERY	Input text from terminal.
ID.	Print <name> from name # field address (nfa).

MEMORY	
@	Fetch value addressed by top of stack.
!	Store n1 at address n2.
C@	Fetch one byte only.
C!	Store one byte only.
?	Print contents of address.
+!	Add second number on stack to contents of address on top.
CMOVE	Move n3 bytes starting at address n1 to area starting at address n2.
FILL	Put byte n3 into n2 bytes starting at address n1.
ERASE	Fill n2 bytes in memory with zeroes, beginning at address n1.
BLANKS	Fill n2 bytes in memory with blanks, beginning at address n1.
TOGGLE	Mask memory with bit pattern.

D.R	Print double-precision number n2 n1 right justified n3 places.
DPL	Number of digits to the right of decimal point.

MONITOR & CASSETTE I/O	
COLD	AIM 65 FORTH cold start.
MON	Exit to AIM 65 Monitor.
?TTY	Switch: true = TTY; false = KB.
CHAIN	Chain tape file.
CLOSE	Close tape file.
?IN	Set to active input device (AID).
?OUT	Set to active output device (AOD).
GET	Input a character from the AID.
PUT	Output a character to the AOD.
READ	Input n2 characters from AID to address n1.
WRITE	Output n2 characters to AOD at address n1.
SOURCE	Compile from the AID.
FINIS	Terminate compile from SOURCE.
−CR	Output CR to printer only.

VIRTUAL STORAGE	
LOAD	Load mass storage screen (compile or execute).
BLOCK	Read mass storage block to memory address
B/BUF	System constant giving mass storage block size in bytes.
BLK	System variable containing current block number.
SCR	System variable containing current screen number.
UPDATE	Mark last buffer accessed as updated.
FLUSH	Write all updated buffers to mass storage.
EMPTY-BUFFERS	Erase all buffers.
+BUF	Increment buffer address.
BUFFER	Fetch next memory buffer.
R/W	User read/write linkage.
USE	Variable containing address of next buffer.
FIRST	Leaves address of first block buffer.
OFFSET	User variable block offset to mass storage.
PREV	Variable containing address of latest buffer.

MISCELLANEOUS AND SYSTEM	
(<comment>)	Begin comment (terminate by right parentheses on same line)
IN	System variable containing offset into input buffer.
LIMIT	Top of memory.
QUIT	Clear return stack and return to terminal.

COMPILER-TEXT INTERPRETER	
—>	Interpret next screen.
;S	Stop interpretation.
COMPILE	Compile following <name> into dictionary.
LITERAL	Compile a number into a literal.
DLITERAL	Compile a double-precision number into a literal.
EXECUTE	Execute the definition on top of stack.

DICTIONARY CONTROL	
FORGET	FORGET all definitions from <name> on.
HERE	Returns address of next unused byte in the dictionary.

VOCABULARIES	
CONTEXT	Returns address of pointer to CONTEXT vocabulary.
CURRENT	Returns address of pointer to CURRENT vocabulary.
FORTH	Main FORTH vocabulary.
ASSEMBLER	Assembler vocabulary.
VOCABULARY <name>	Create new vocabulary.
VLIST	Print names of all words in CONTEXT vocabulary.
VOC-LINK	Most recently defined vocabulary.

SECURITY	
ABORT	Error; operation terminates.
ERROR	Execute error notification and restart system.
MESSAGE	Displays message.
WARNING	Pointer to message routine.
FENCE	Prevents forgetting below this point.
WIDTH	Controls significant characters of <name>.

PRIMITIVES

Table 12-10. The AIM-65 FORTH Word Dictionary (courtesy of Rockwell International Corp.) (Continued from page 190.)

ALLOT	Leave a gap of n bytes in the dictionary.
TASK	A dictionary marker.
'	Find the address of <name> in the dictionary.
- FIND	Search dictionary for <name>.
DP	User variable containing the dictionary pointer.
C,	Store byte into dictionary.
,	Compile a number into the dictionary.
PAD	Pointer to temporary buffer.
OBRANCH	Run-time conditional branch.
BRANCH	Run-time unconditional branch.
PUT	Stores registers and jumps to next.
ENCLOSE	Text scanning primitive used by WORD.
RO	Location of return Stack.
RP!	Initializes return Stack.
SO	Initial value of stack pointer.
SP!	Initialize stack pointer.
NEXT	The FORTH virtual machine.
DEFINING WORDS	
: <name>	Begin colon definition of <name>.
;	End colon definition.
VARIABLE <name>	Create a variable named <name> when initial value n; returns address when executed.
CONSTANT <name>	Create a constant named <name> with value n; returns value when executed.
CODE <name>	Begin definition of assembly-language primitive operation named <name>.
;CODE	Used to create a new defining word, with execution-time "code routine" for this data type in assembly.
<BUILDS . . . DOES>	Used to create a new defining word, with execution-time routine for this data type in higher-level FORTH.
CREATE	Create a dictionary header.
USER	Create a user variable.

to mix and match computers, printers, CTR boards. and system software that is required to put them all together. I have presented the RM-65 Computer System in this chapter which already has everything mixed and matched and the only problem you have is to learn how to use it. You will have plenty to learn in order to use a complete system that is ready to go when you get it. Don't put oddball items from different companies together (no matter how much cheaper it is) and expect the system to work easily.

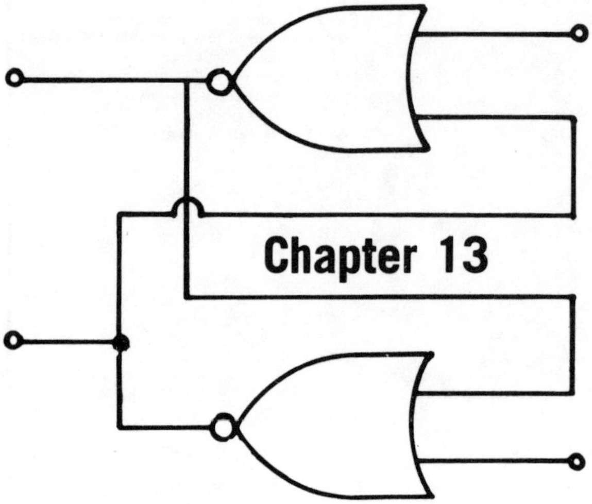

Chapter 13

The 6502 Instruction Set–an Alphabetical Presentation

This chapter presents a complete description of the 6502 instruction set from the *R6500 Microcomputer Systems Programming Manual*[1] by Rockwell International. The difference between this chaper and the programming manual is that, in this chaper, all of the instruction-set data and descriptions are presented in alphabetical order. This type of presentation will help the part-time programmer to use 6502 machine language. Table 13-1 presents the notations which are used in this chapter.

Table 13-1. These Notations are used in the 6502 Op-Code Presentations in this Chapter.

The following notation applies to this chapter:

A	Accumulator
X, Y	Index Registers
M	Memory
P	Processor Status Register
S	Stack Pointer
✓	Change
—	No Change
+	Add
∧	Logical AND
-	Subtract
⊻	Logical Exclusive Or
↑	Transfer from Stack
↓	Transfer to Stack
→	Transfer to
←	Transfer to
V	Logical OR
PC	Program Counter
PCH	Program Counter High
PCL	Program Counter Low
OPER	Operand
#	Immediate Addressing Mode

1. R. 6500 Microcomputing Systems Programming Manual, Rockwell International, 1979, Data from this publication is reproduced by permission of Rockwell International.

Table 13-2. ADC.

ADC *Add memory to accumulator with carry* **ADC**

Operation: A + M + C → A, C

(Ref: 2.2.1)

N Z C I D V
✓ ✓ ✓ — — ✓

Addressing Mode	Assembly Language Form	OP CODE	No. Bytes	No. Cycles
Immediate	ADC # Oper	69	2	2
Zero Page	ADC Oper	65	2	3
Zero Page, X	ADC Oper, X	75	2	4
Absolute	ADC Oper	6D	3	4
Absolute, X	ADC Oper, X	7D	3	4*
Absolute, Y	ADC Oper, Y	79	3	4*
(Indirect, X)	ADC (Oper, X)	61	2	6
(Indirect), Y	ADC (Oper), Y	71	2	5*

* Add 1 if page boundary is crossed.

This instruction adds the value of memory and carry from the previous operation to the value of the accumulator and stores the result in the accumulator (see Table 13-2).

This instruction affects the accumulator; sets the carry flag when the sum of a binary add exceeds 255 or when the sum of a decimal add exceeds 99, otherwise carry is reset. The overflow flag is set when the sign or bit 7 is changed due to the result exceeding +127 or −128, otherwise overflow is reset. The negative flag is set if the accumulator result contains bit 7 on, otherwise the negative flag is reset. The zero flag is set if the accumulator result is 0, otherwise the zero flag is reset.

It is a "Group One" instruction and has the following addressing modes: Immediate; Absolute; Zero Page; Absolute,X; Absolute,Y; Zero Page,X; Indexed Indirect; and Indirect Indexed.

Table 13-3. AND.

AND *"AND" memory with accumulator* **AND**

Logical AND to the accumulator

Operation: A ∧ M → A

(Ref: 2.2.4.1)

N Z C I D V
✓ ✓ — — — —

Addressing Mode	Assembly Language Form	OP CODE	No. Bytes	No. Cycles
Immediate	AND # Oper	29	2	2
Zero Page	AND Oper	25	2	3
Zero Page, X	AND Oper, X	35	2	4
Absolute	AND Oper	2D	3	4
Absolute, X	AND Oper, X	3D	3	4*
Absolute, Y	AND Oper, Y	39	3	4*
(Indirect, X)	AND (Oper, X)	21	2	6
(Indirect), Y	AND (Oper), Y	31	2	5*

* Add 1 if page boundary is crossed.

The AND instructions transfer the accumulator and memory to the adder which performs a bit-by-bit AND operation and stores the result back in the accumulator (see Table 13-3).

This instruction affects the accumulator; sets the zero flag if the result in the accumulator is 0, otherwise resets the zero flag; sets the negative flag if the result in the accumulator has bit 7 on, otherwise resets the negative flag.

AND is a "Group One" instruction having addressing modes of Immediate; Absolute; Zero Page; Absolute,X; Absolute, Y; Zero Page, X; Indexed Indirect; and Indirect Indexed.

Table 13-4. ASL.

ASL — **ASL** *Shift Left One Bit (Memory or Accumulator)* — **ASL**

Operation: C ← | 7 | 6 | 5 | 4 | 3 | 2 | 1 | Ø | ← Ø

N Ƶ C I D V
✓ ✓ ✓ — — —

(Ref: 10.2)

Addressing Mode	Assembly Language Form	OP CODE	No. Bytes	No. Cycles
Accumulator	ASL A	ØA	1	2
Zero Page	ASL Oper	Ø6	2	5
Zero Page, X	ASL Oper, X	16	2	6
Absolute	ASL Oper	ØE	3	6
Absolute, X	ASL Oper, X	1E	3	7

The shift left instruction shifts either the accumulator or the address memory location 1 bit to the left, with the bit 0 always being set to 0 and the bit 7 output always being contained in the carry flag. ASL either shifts the accumulator left 1 bit or is a read/modify/write instruction that affects only memory (see Table 13-4).

The instruction does not affect the overflow bit, sets N equal to the result bit 7 (bit 6 in the input), sets Z flag if the result is equal to 0, otherwise resets Z and stores the input bit 7 in the carry flag.

ASL is a read/modify/write instruction and has the following addressing modes: Accumulator; Zero Page; Zero Page, X; Absolute; Absolute, X.

Table 13-5. BCC.

BCC — **BCC** *Branch on Carry Clear* — **BCC**

Operation: Branch on C = Ø

N Ƶ C I D V
— — — — — —

(Ref: 4.1.2.3)

Addressing Mode	Assembly Language Form	OP CODE	No. Bytes	No. Cycles
Relative	BCC Oper	9Ø	2	2*

* Add 1 if branch occurs to same page.

* Add 2 if branch occurs to different page.

This instruction tests the state of the carry bit and takes a conditional branch if the carry bit is reset (see Table 3-5).

It affects no flags or registers other than the program unter and then only if the C flag is not on.

The addressing mode is Relative.

Table 13-6. BCS.

BCS — BCS *Branch on carry set* — **BCS**

Operation: Branch on C = 1

N Z C I D V

\- - - - - -

(Ref: 4.1.2.4)

Addressing Mode	Assembly Language Form	OP CODE	No. Bytes	No. Cycles
Relative	BCS Oper	BØ	2	2*

* Add 1 if branch occurs to same page.

* Add 2 if branch occurs to next page.

This instruction takes the conditional branch if the carry flag is on (see Table 13-6).

BCS does not affect any of the flags or registers except for the program counter and only then if the carry flag is on.

The addressing mode is Relative.

Table 13-7. BEQ.

BEQ — BEQ *Branch on result zero* — **BEQ**

Operation: Branch on Z = 1

N Z C I D V

(Ref: 4.1.2.5)

\- - - - - -

Addressing Mode	Assembly Language Form	OP CODE	No. Bytes	No. Cycles
Relative	BEQ Oper	FØ	2	2*

* Add 1 if branch occurs to same page.

* Add 2 if branch occurs to next page.

This instruction could also be called "Branch on Equal." It takes a conditional branch whenever the Z flag is on or the previous result is equal to 0 (see Table 13-7).

BEQ does not affect any of the flags or registers other than the program counter and only then when the Z flag is set.

The addressing mode is Relative.

Table 13-8. BIT.

BIT — **BIT** *Test bits in memory with accumulator* — **BIT**

Operation: $A \wedge M$, $M_7 \rightarrow N$, $M_6 \rightarrow V$

Bit 6 and 7 are transferred to the status register. If the result of $A \wedge M$ is zero then Z = 1, otherwise Z = Ø

N	Z	C	I	D	V
M_7	✓	—	—	—	M_6

(Ref: 4.2.2.1)

Addressing Mode	Assembly Language Form	OP CODE	No. Bytes	No. Cycles
Zero Page	BIT Oper	24	2	3
Absolute	BIT Oper	2C	3	4

This instruction performs an AND between a memory location and the accumulator but does not store the result of the AND into the accumulator (see Table 13-8).

The symbolic notation is M^A.

The bit instruction affects the N flag with N being set to the value of bit 7 of the memory being tested, the V flag with V being set equal to bit 6 of the memory being tested and Z being set by the result of the AND operation between the accumulator and the memory if the result is Zero, Z is reset otherwise. It does not affect the accumulator.

The addressing modes are Zero Page and Absolute.

The BIT instruction actually combines two instructions from the PDP-11 and MC6800, that of TST (Test Memory) and (BIT Test). This, like the compare test, allows the examination of an individual bit without disturbing the value in the accumulator.

Table 13-9. BMI.

BMI — **BMI** *Branch on result minus* — **BMI**

Operation: Branch on N = 1

N	Z	C	I	D	V
—	—	—	—	—	—

(Ref: 4.1.2.1)

Addressing Mode	Assembly Language Form	OP CODE	No. Bytes	No. Cycles
Relative	BMI Oper	3Ø	2	2*

* Add 1 if branch occurs to same page.

* Add 2 if branch occurs to different page.

This instruction takes the conditional branch if the N bit is set (see Table 13-9).

BMI does not affect any of the flags or any other part of the machine other than the program counter and then only if the N bit is on.

The mode of addressing for BMI is Relative.

Table 13-10. BNE.

BNE BNE *Branch on result not zero* **BNE**

Operation: Branch on Z = 0 N Z C I D V

\- - - - - -

(Ref: 4.1.2.6)

Addressing Mode	Assembly Language Form	OP CODE	No. Bytes	No. Cycles
Relative	BNE Oper	DØ	2	2*

* Add 1 if branch occurs to same page.

* Add 2 if branch occurs to different page.

This instruction could also be called "Branch on Not Equal." It tests the Z flag and takes the conditional branch if the Z flag is not on, indicating that the previous result was not zero (see Table 13-10).

BNE does not affect any of the flags or registers other than the program counter and only then if the Z flag is reset.

The addressing mode is Relative.

Table 13-11. BPL.

BPL BPL *Branch on result plus* **BPL**

Operation: Branch on N = Ø N Z C I D V

\- - - - - -

(Ref: 4.1.2.2)

Addressing Mode	Assembly Language Form	OP CODE	No. Bytes	No. Cycles
Relative	BPL Oper	1Ø	2	2*

* Add 1 if branch occurs to same page.

* Add 2 if branch occurs to different page.

This instruction is the complementary branch to branch on result minus (see Table 13-11). It is a conditional branch which takes the branch when the N bit is reset (0). BPL is used to test if the previous result bit 7 was off (0) and branch on result minus is used to determine if the previous result was minus or bit 7 was on (1).

The instruction affects no flags or other registers other than the P counter and only affects the P counter when the N bit is reset.

The addressing mode is Relative.

Table 13-12. BRK.

BRK **BRK** *Force Break* **BRK**

Operation: Forced Interrupt PC + 2 ↓ P ↓

N Z C I D V
— — — 1 — —

(Ref: 9.11)

Addressing Mode	Assembly Language Form	OP CODE	No. Bytes	No. Cycles
Implied	BRK	ØØ	1	7

1. A BRK command cannot be masked by setting I.

The break command causes the microprocessor to go through an interrupt sequence under program control (see Table 13-12). This means that the program counter of the second byte after the BRK is automatically stored on the stack along with the processor status at the beginning of the break instruction. The microprocessor then transfers control to the interrupt vector.

Other than changing theprogram counter, the break instruction changes no values in either the registers or the flags.

The BRK is a single-byte instruction and its addressing mode is Implied.

Table 13-13. BVC.

BVC **BVC** *Branch on overflow clear* **BVC**

Operation: Branch on V = 0

N Z C I D V
— — — — — —

(Ref: 4.1.2.8)

Addressing Mode	Assembly Language Form	OP CODE	No. Bytes	No. Cycles
Relative	BVC Oper	5Ø	2	2*

* Add 1 if branch occurs to same page.

* Add 2 if branch occurs to different page.

This instruction tests the status of the V flag and takes the conditional branch if the flag is not set (see Table 13-13).

BVC does not affect any of the flags and registers other than the program counter and only when the overflow flag is reset.

The addressing mode is Relative.

Table 13-14. BVS.

BVS BVS *Branch on overflow set* **BVS**

Operation: Branch on V = 1

N Ƶ C I D V
— — — — — —

(Ref: 4.1.2.7)

Addressing Mode	Assembly Language Form	OP CODE	No. Bytes	No. Cycles
Relative	BVS Oper	7Ø	2	2*

* Add 1 if branch occurs to same page.

* Add 2 if branch occurs to different page.

This instruction tests the V flag and takes the conditional branch if V is on (see Table 13-14).

BVS does not affect any flags or registers other than the program counter and only when the overflow flag is set.

The addressing mode is Relative.

Table 13-15. CLC.

CLC CLC *Clear carry flag* **CLC**

Operation: Ø → C

N Ƶ C I D V
— — Ø — — —

(Ref: 3.0.2)

Addressing Mode	Assembly Language Form	OP CODE	No. Bytes	No. Cycles
Implied	CLC	18	1	2

This instruction initializes the carry flag to a 0. This operation should normally precede an ADC loop (see Table 13-15). It is also useful when used with a ROL instruction to clear a bit in memory.

This instruction affects no registers in the microprocessor and no flags other than the carry flag which is reset.

CLC is a single-byte instruction and its addressing mode is Implied.

Table 13-16. CLD.

CLD **CLI** *Clear interrupt disable bit* **CLD**

Operation: Ø → D

N Z C I D V

– – – – Ø –

(Ref: 3.3.2)

Addressing Mode	Assembly Language Form	OP CODE	No. Bytes	No. Cycles
Implied	CLD	D8	1	2

This instruction sets the decimal mode flag to a 0. This causes all subsequent ADC and SBC instructions to operate as simple binary operations (see Table 13-16).

CLD affects no registers in the microprocessor and no flags other than the decimal mode flag which is set to a 0.

Table 13-17. CLI.

CLI **CLI** *Clear interrupt disable bit* **CLI**

Operation: Ø → I

N Z C I D V

– – – Ø – –

(Ref: 3.2.2)

Addressing Mode	Assembly Language Form	OP CODE	No. Bytes	No. Cycles
Implied	CLI	58	1	2

This instruction initializes the interrupt disable to a 0. This allows the microprocessor to receive interrupts (see Table 13-17).

It affects no registers in the microprocessor and no flags other than the interrupt disable which is cleared.

CLI is a single-byte instruction and its addressing mode is Implied.

Table 13-18. CLV.

CLV CLV *Clear overflow flag* **CLV**

Operation: Ø → V

N Z C I D V
— — — — — Ø

(Ref: 3.6.1)

Addressing Mode	Assembly Language Form	OP CODE	No. Bytes	No. Cycles
Implied	CLV	B8	1	2

This instruction clears the overflow flag to a 0 (see Table 13-18). This command is used in conjunction wth the set overflow pin which can cange the state of the overflow flag with an external signal.

CLV affects no registers in the microprocessor and no flags other than the overflow flag which is set to a 0.

Table 13-19. CMP.

CMP CMP *Compare memory and accumulator* **CMP**

Operation: A − M

N Z C I D V
✓ ✓ ✓ — — —

(Ref: 4.2.1)

Addressing Mode	Assembly Language Form	OP CODE	No. Bytes	No. Cycles
Immediate	CMP #Oper	C9	2	2
Zero Page	CMP Oper	C5	2	3
Zero Page, X	CMP Oper, X	D5	2	4
Absolute	CMP Oper	CD	3	4
Absolute, X	CMP Oper, X	DD	3	4*
Absolute, Y	CMP Oper, Y	D9	3	4*
(Indirect, X)	CMP (Oper, X)	C1	2	6
(Indirect), Y	CMP (Oper), Y	D1	2	5*

* Add 1 if page boundary is crossed.

This instruction subtracts the contents of memory from the contents of the accumulator (see Table 13-19).

The use of the CMP affects the following flags: Z flag is set on an equal comparison, reset otherwise; the N flag is set or reset by the result bit 7, the carry flag is set when the value in memory is less than or equal to the accumulator, reset when it is greater than the accumulator. The accumulator is not affected

It is a "Group One" instruction and therefore has as its addressing modes: Immediate; Zero Page; Zero Page, X; Absolute; Absolute, X; Absolute, Y; (Indirect, X); (Indirect), Y.

Table 13-20. CPX.

CPX CPX *Compare Memory and Index X* **CPX**

Operation: X - M

N Z C I D V
✓ ✓ ✓ — — —

(Ref: 7.8)

Addressing Mode	Assembly Language Form	OP CODE	No. Bytes	No. Cycles
Immediate	CPX #Oper	E0	2	2
Zero Page	CPX Oper	E4	2	3
Absolute	CPX Oper	EC	3	4

This instruction subtracts the value of the addressed memory location from the content of index register X using the adder but does not store the result; therefore, its only use is to set the N, Z and C flags to allow for comparison between the index register X and the value in memory (see Table 13-20).

The CPX instruction does not affect any register in the machine; it also does not affect the overflow flag. It causes the carry to be set on if the absolute value of the index register X is equal to or greater than the data from memory. If the value of the memory is greater than the content of the index register X, carry is reset. If the results of the subtraction contain a bit 7, then the N flag is set, if not, it is reset. If the value in memory is equal to the value in index register X, the Z flag is set, otherwise it is reset.

The addressing modes for CPX are Immediate, Absolute and Zero Page.

Table 13-21. CPY.

CPY CPY *Compare memory and index Y* **CPY**

Operation: Y - M

N Z C I D V
✓ ✓ ✓ — — —

(Ref: 7.9)

Addressing Mode	Assembly Language Form	OP CODE	No. Bytes	No. Cycles
Immediate	CPY #Oper	C0	2	2
Zero Page	CPY Oper	C4	2	3
Absolute	CPY Oper	CC	3	4

This instruction performs a two's complement subtraction between the index register Y and the specified memory location (see Table 13-21). The results of the substraction are not stored anywhere. The instruction is strictly used to set the flags.

CPY affects no registers in the microprocessor and also does not affect the overflow flag. If the value in the index register is Y equal to or greater than the value in the memory, the carry flag will be set, otherwise it will be cleared. If the results of the subtraction contain bit 7 on the N bit will be set, otherwise it will be cleared. If the value in the index register Y and the value in the memory are equal, the zero flag will be set, otherwise it will be cleared.

The addressing modes for CPY are Immediate, Absolute and Zero Page.

Table 13-22. DEC.

DEC DEC *Decrement memory by one* **DEC**

Operation: M - 1 → M

N Z C I D V
✓ ✓ - - - -

(Ref: 10.8)

Addressing Mode	Assembly Language Form	OP CODE	No. Bytes	No. Cycles
Zero Page	DEC Oper	C6	2	5
Zero Page, X	DEC Oper, X	D6	2	6
Absolute	DEC Oper	CE	3	6
Absolute, X	DEC Oper, X	DE	3	7

This instruction subtracts 1, in two's complement, from the contents of the addressed memory location (see Table 13-22).

The decrement instruction does not affect any internal register in the microprocessor. It does not affect the carry or overflow flags. If bit 7 is on as a result of the decrement, then the N flag is set, otherwise it is reset. If the result of the decrement is 0, the Z flag is set, otherwise it is reset.

Table 13-23. DEX.

DEX DEX *Decrement index X by one* **DEX**

Operation: X - 1 → X

N Z C I D V
✓ ✓ - - - -

(Ref: 7.6)

Addressing Mode	Assembly Language Form	OP CODE	No. Bytes	No. Cycles
Implied	DEX	CA	1	2

This instruction subtracts one from the current value of the index register X and stores the result in the index register X (see Table 13-23).

DEX does not affect the carry or overflow flag, it sets the N flag if it has bit 7 on as a result of the decrement, otherwise it resets the N flag; sets the Z flag if X is a 0 as a result of the decrement, otherwise it resets the Z flag.

DEX is a single-byte instruction, the addressing mode is Implied.

NOTE: Decrement of the index registers is the most convenient method of using the index registers as a counter, in that the decrement involves setting the value N on as a result of having passed through 0 and sets Z on when the results of the decrement are 0.

Table 13-24. DEY.

DEY — DEY *Decrement index Y by one* — **DEY**

Operation: Y - 1 → Y

N Z C I D V
✓ ✓ – – – –

(Ref: 7.7)

Addressing Mode	Assembly Language Form	OP CODE	No. Bytes	No. Cycles
Implied	DEY	88	1	2

This instruction subtracts one from the current value in the index register Y and stores the result into the index register Y (see Table 13-24). The result does not affect or consider carry so that the value in the index register Y is decremented to 0 and then through 0 to FF.

Decrément Y does not affect the carry or overflow flags; if the Y register contains bit 7 on as a result of the decrement the N flag is set, otherwise the N flag is reset. If the Y register is 0 as a result of the decrement, the Z flag is set otherwise the Z flag is reset. This instruction only affects the index register Y.

DEY is a single-byte instruction and the addressing mode is Implied.

Table 13-25. EOR.

EOR — EOR *"Exclusive–Or" memory with accumulator* — **EOR**

Operation: A ⊻ M → A

N Z C I D V
✓ ✓ – – – –

(Ref: 2.2.4.3)

Addressing Mode	Assembly Language Form	OP CODE	No. Bytes	No. Cycles
Immediate	EOR #Oper	49	2	2
Zero Page	EOR Oper	45	2	3
Zero Page, X	EOR Oper, X	55	2	4
Absolute	EOR Oper	4D	3	4
Absolute, X	EOR Oper, X	5D	3	4*
Absolute, Y	EOR Oper, Y	59	3	4*
(Indirect, X)	EOR (Oper, X)	41	2	6
(Indirect),Y	EOR (Oper), Y	51	2	5*

* Add 1 if page boundary is crossed.

The EOR instruction transfers the memory and the accumulator to the adder which performs a binary "EXCLUSIVE OR" on a bit-by-bit basis and stores the result in the accumulator (see Table 13-25).

This instruction affects the accumulator; sets the zero flag if the result in the accumulator is 0, otherwise resets the zero flag; sets the negative flag if the result in the accumulator has bit 7 on, otherwise resets the negative flag.

EOR is a "Group One" instruction having addressing modes of Immediate; Absolute; Zero Page; Absolute,X; Absolute,Y; Zero Page,X; Indexed Indirect; and Indirect Indexed.

Table 13-26. INC.

INC INC *Increment memory by one* **INC**

Operation: M + 1 → M

N Z C I D V
✓ ✓ — — — —

(Ref: 10.7)

Addressing Mode	Assembly Language Form	OP CODE	No. Bytes	No. Cycles
Zero Page	INC Oper	E6	2	5
Zero Page, X	INC Oper, X	F6	2	6
Absolute	INC Oper	EE	3	6
Absolute, X	INC Oper, X	FE	3	7

This instruction adds 1 to the contnets of the addressed memory location (see Table 13-26).

The increment memory instruction does not affect any internal registers and does not affect the carry or overflow flags. If bit 7 is on as the result of the increment, N is set, otherwise it is reset; if the increment causes the result to become 0, the Z flag is set on, otherwise it is reset.

The addressing modes for increment are: Zero Page; Zero Page,X; Absolute; Absolute,X.

Table 13-27. INX.

INX INX *Increment Index X by one* **INX**

Operation: X + 1 → X

N Z C I D V
✓ ✓ — — — —

(Ref: 7.4)

Addressing Mode	Assembly Language Form	OP CODE	No. Bytes	No. Cycles
Implied	INX	E8	1	2

Increment X adds 1 to the current value of the X register (see Table 13-27). This is an 8-bit increment which does not affect the carry operation, therefore, if the value of X before the increment was FF, the resulting value is 00. NX does not affect the carry or overflowing flags; it sets the N flag if the flag if the result of the increment has a one in bit 7, otherwise resets N; sets the Z flag if the result of the increment is 0, otherwise it resets the Z flag. INX does not affect any other register other than the X register. INX is a single byte instruction and the only addressing mode is Implied.

Table 13-28. INY.

INY — INY *Increment Index Y by one* — **INY**

Operation: Y + 1 → Y

(Ref: 7.5)

N Z C I D V
✓ ✓ - - - -

Addressing Mode	Assembly Language Form	OP CODE	No. Bytes	No. Cycles
Implied	INY	C8	1	2

INX is a single-byte instruction and the only addressing mode is Implied.

Increment Y increments or adds one to the current value in the Y register, storing the result in the Y register (see Table 13-28). As in the case of INX the primary application is to step through a set of values using the Y register. The INY does not affect the carry or overflow flags, sets the N flag if the result of the increment has a one in bit 7, otherwise resets N, sets Z if as a result of the increment the Y regiser is zero otherwise resets the Z flag. Increment Y is a single byte instruction and the only addressing mode is Implied.

Table 13-29. JMP.

JMP — JMP *Jump to new location* — **JMP**

Operation: (PC + 1) → PCL
(PC + 2) → PCH

(Ref: 4.0.2)
(Ref: 9.8.1)

N Z C I D V
- - - - - -

Addressing Mode	Assembly Language Form	OP CODE	No. Bytes	No. Cycles
Absolute	JMP Oper	4C	3	3
Indirect	JMP (Oper)	6C	3	5

In this instruction, the data from the memory location located in the program sequence after the OP CODE is loaded into the low order byte of the program counter (PCL) and the data from the next memory location after that is loaded into the high order byte of the program counter (PCH) (see Table 13-29).

As stated earlier, the "( )" means "contents of" a memory location. PC indicates the contents of the program counter at the time the OP CODE is fetched. Therefore (PC + 2)→PCH reads, "the contents of the program counter two locations beyond the OP CODE fetch location are transferred to the new PC high order byte."

The addressing modes are Absolute and Absolute Indirect.

The JMP instruction affects no flags and only PCL and PCH.

JMP Indirect—for indirect jump.

This instruction establishes a new value for the program counter.

It affects only the program counter in the microprocessor and affects no flags in the status register.

JMP Indirect is a three-byte instruction.

In the JMP Indirect instruction, the second and third bytes of the instruction represent the indirect low and high bytes respectively of the memory location containing ADL. Once ADL is fetched, the program counter is incremented with the next memory location containing ADH.

Table 13-30. JSR.

JSR — JSR *Jump to new location saving return address* — **JSR**

Operation: PC + 2 ↓, (PC + 1) → PCL
(PC + 2) → PCH

N Z C I D V
— — — — — —

(Ref: 8.1)

Addressing Mode	Assembly Language Form	OP CODE	No. Bytes	No. Cycles
Absolute	JSR Oper	20	3	6

This instruction transfers control of the program counter to a subroutine location but leaves a return pointer on the stack to allow the user to return to perform the next instruction in the main program after the subroutine is complete (see Table 13-30). To accomplish this, JSR instruction stores the program counter address which points to the last byte of the jump instruction onto the stack using the stack pointer. The stack byte contains the program count high first, followed by program count low. The JSR then transfers the addresses following the jump instruction to the program counter low and the program counter high, thereby directing the program to begin at that new address.

The JSR instruction affects no flags, causes the stack pointer to be decremented by 2 and substitutes new values into the program counter low and the program counter high. The addressing mode for the JSR is always Absolute.

Table 13-31. LDA.

LDA — LDA *Load accumulator with memory* — **LDA**

Operation: M → A

N Z C I D V
✓ ✓ — — — —

(Ref: 2.1.1)

Addressing Mode	Assembly Language Form	OP CODE	No. Bytes	No. Cycles
Immediate	LDA #Oper	A9	2	2
Zero Page	LDA Oper	A5	2	3
Zero Page, X	LDA Oper, X	B5	2	4
Absolute	LDA Oper	AD	3	4
Absolute, X	LDA Oper, X	BD	3	4*
Absolute, Y	LDA Oper, Y	B9	3	4*
(Indirect, X)	LDA (Oper, X)	A1	2	6
(Indirect), Y	LDA (Oper), Y	B1	2	5*

* Add 1 if page boundary is crossed.

When instruction LDA is executed by the microprocessor, data is transferred from memory to the accumulator and stored in the accumulator (see Table 13-31).

Rather than continuing to give a word picture of the operation, introduced will be the symbolic representation M→A, where the arrow means "transfer to." Therefore the LDA instruction symbolic representation is read, "memory transferred to the accumulator."

LDA affects the contents of the accumulator, does not affect the carry or overflow flags; sets the zero flag if the accumulator is zero as a result of the LDA, otherwise resets the zero flag; sets the negative flag if bit 7 of the accumulator is a 1, otherwise resets the negative flag.

The addressing modes include Immediate; Absolute; Zero Page; Absolute, X; Absolute, Y; Zero Page, X; Indexed Indirect; and Indirect Indexed.

Table 13-32. LDX.

LDX — LDX *Load index X with memory* — **LDX**

Operation: M → X

N Z C I D V
✓ ✓ — — — —

(Ref: 7.0)

Addressing Mode	Assembly Language Form	OP CODE	No. Bytes	No. Cycles
Immediate	LDX # Oper	A2	2	2
Zero Page	LDX Oper	A6	2	3
Zero Page, Y	LDX Oper, Y	B6	2	4
Absolute	LDX Oper	AE	3	4
Absolute, Y	LDX Oper, Y	BE	3	4*

* Add 1 when page boundary is crossed.

Load the index register X from memory (see Table 13-32).

LDX does not affect the C or V flags; sets Z if the value loaded was zero, otherwise resets it; sets N if the value loaded in bit 7 is a 1; otherwise N is reset, and affects only the X register. The addressing modes for LDX are Immediate; Absolute; Zero Page; Absolute Indexed by Y; and Zero Page Indexed by Y.

Table 13-33. LDY.

LDY — LDY *Load index Y with memory* — **LDY**

Operation: M → Y

N Z C I D V
✓ ✓ — — — —

(Ref: 7.1)

Addressing Mode	Assembly Language Form	OP CODE	No. Bytes	No. Cycles
Immediate	LDY #Oper	AØ	2	2
Zero Page	LDY Oper	A4	2	3
Zero Page, X	LDY Oper, X	B4	2	4
Absolute	LDY Oper	AC	3	4
Absolute, X	LDY Oper, X	BC	3	4*

* Add 1 when page boundary is crossed.

Load the index register Y from memory (see Table 13-33).

LDY does not affect the Cor V flags, sets the N flag if the value loaded in bit 7 is a 1, otherwise resets N, sets Z flag if the loaded value is zero otherwise resets Z and only affects the Y regsiter. The addressing modes for load Y are Immediate; Absolute; Zero page; Zero Indexed by X, Absolute Indexed by X.

Table 13-34. LSR.

LSR — **LSR** *Shift right one bit (memory or accumulator)* — **LSR**

Operation: 0 → [7|6|5|4|3|2|1|0] → C

N Z C I D V
0 ✓ ✓ — — —

(Ref: 10.1)

Addressing Mode	Assembly Language Form	OP CODE	No. Bytes	No. Cycles
Accumulator	LSR A	4A	1	2
Zero Page	LSR Oper	46	2	5
Zero Page, X	LSR Oper, X	56	2	6
Absolute	LSR Oper	4E	3	6
Absolute, X	LSR Oper, X	5E	3	7

This instruction shifts either the accumulator or a specified memory location 1 bit to the right, with the higher bit of the result always being set to 0, and the low bit which is shifted out of the field being stored in the carry flag (see Table 13-34).

The shift right instruction either affects the accumulator by shifting it right 1 or is a read/modify/write instruction which changes a specified memory location but does not affect any internal registers. The shift right does not affect the overflow flag. The N flag is always reset. The Z flag is set if the result of the shift is 0 and reset otherwise. The carry is set equal to bit 0 of the input.

LSR is a read/write/modify instruction and has the following addressing modes: Accumulator; Zero Page; Zero Page,X; Absolute; Absolute,X.

Table 13-35. NOP.

NOP — **NOP** *No operation* — **NOP**

Operation: No Operation (2 cycles)

N Z C I D V
— — — — — —

Addressing Mode	Assembly Language Form	OP CODE	No. Bytes	No. Cycles
Implied	NOP	EA	1	2

Table 13-36. ORA.

ORA

ORA *"OR" memory with accumulator*

Operation: A V M → A

N	Z	C	I	D	V
✓	✓	–	–	–	–

(Ref: 2.2.4.2)

Addressing Mode	Assembly Language Form	OP CODE	No. Bytes	No. Cycles
Immediate	ORA #Oper	Ø9	2	2
Zero Page	ORA Oper	Ø5	2	3
Zero Page, X	ORA Oper, X	15	2	4
Absolute	ORA Oper	ØD	3	4
Absolute, X	ORA Oper, X	1D	3	4*
Absolute, Y	ORA Oper, Y	19	3	4*
(Indirect, X)	ORA (Oper, X)	Ø1	2	6
(Indirect), Y	ORA (Oper), Y	11	2	5*

* Add 1 on page crossing

The ORA instruction transfers the memory and the accumulator to the adder which performs a binary "OR" on a bit-by-bit basis and stores the result in the accumulator (see Table 13-36).

This instruction affects the accumulator; sets the zero flag if the result in the accumulator is 0, otherwise resets the zero flag; sets the negative flag if the result in the accumulator has bit 7 on, otherwise resets the negative flag. ORA is a "Group One" instruction. It has the addressing modes Immediate; Absolute; Zero Page; Absolute,X; Absolute,Y; Zero Page,X; Indexed Indirect; and Indirect Indexed.

Table 13-37. PHA.

PHA

PHA *Push accumulator on stack*

Operation: A ↓

N	Z	C	I	D	V
–	–	–	–	–	–

(Ref: 8.5)

Addressing Mode	Assembly Language Form	OP CODE	No. Bytes	No. Cycles
Implied	PHA	48	1	3

This instruction transfers the current value of the accumulator to the next location on the stack, automatically decrementing the stack to point to the next empty location (see Table 13-37).

Noted should be that the notation ↓ means push to the stack, ↑ means pull from the stack.

The Push A instruction only affects the stack pointer register which is decremented by 1 as a result of the operation. It affects no flags.

PHA is a single-byte instruction and its addressing mode is Implied.

Table 13-38. PHP.

PHP — **PHP** *Push processor status on stack* — **PHP**

Operation: P↓

(Ref: 8.11)

N Z C I D V
- - - - - -

Addressing Mode	Assembly Language Form	OP CODE	No. Bytes	No. Cycles
Implied	PHP	Ø8	1	3

The following example shows the operations which occur during Push A instruction.

This instruction transfers the contents of the processor status register stack, as governed by the stack pointer (see Table 13-38).

The PHP instruction affects no registers or flags in the microprocessor.

PHP is a single-byte instruction and the addressing mode is Implied.

Table 13-39. PLA.

PLA — **PLA** *Pull accumulator from stack* — **PLA**

Operation: A ↑

(Ref: 8.6)

N Z C I D V
✓ ✓ - - - -

Addressing Mode	Assembly Language Form	OP CODE	No. Bytes	No. Cycles
Implied	PLA	68	1	4

This instruction adds 1 to the current value of the stack pointer and uses it to address the stack and loads the contents of the stack into the A register (see Table 13-39).

The PLA instruction does not affect the carry or overflow flags. It sets N if the bit 7 is on in accumulator A as a result of instructions, otherwise it is reset. If accumulator A is zero as a result of the PLA, then the Z flag is set, otherwise it is reset. The PLA instruction changes content of the accumulator A to the contents of the memory location at stack register plus 1 and also increments the stack register.

The PLA instruction is a single-byte instruction and the addressing mode is Implied.

Table 13-40. PLP.

PLP — **PLP** *Pull processor status from stack* — **PLP**

Operation: P ↑

N Ƶ C I D V
From Stack

(Ref: 8.12)

Addressing Mode	Assembly Language Form	OP CODE	No. Bytes	No. Cycles
Implied	PLP	28	1	4

This instruction transfers the next value on the stack to the Processor Status register, thereby changing all of the flags and setting the mode switches to the values from the stack (see Table 13-40).

The PLP instruction affects no registers in the processor other than the status register. This instruction could affect all flags in the status register.

PLP is a single byte instruction and the addressing mode is Implied.

Table 13-41. ROL.

ROL — **ROL** *Rotate one bit left (memory or accumulator)* — **ROL**

Operation:

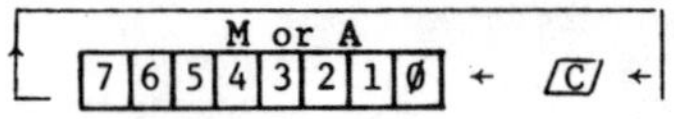

N Ƶ C I D V
✓ ✓ ✓ — — —

(Ref: 10.3)

Addressing Mode	Assembly Language Form	OP CODE	No. Bytes	No. Cycles
Accumulator	ROL A	2A	1	2
Zero Page	ROL Oper	26	2	5
Zero Page, X	ROL Oper, X	36	2	6
Absolute	ROL Oper	2E	3	6
Absolute, X	ROL Oper, X	3E	3	7

The rotate left instruction shifts either the accumulator or addressed memory left 1 bit, with the input carry being stored in bit 0 and with the input bit 7 being stored in the carry flags (see Table 13-41).

The ROL instruction either shifts the accumulator left 1 bit and stores the carry in accumulator bit 0 or does not affect the internal registers at all. The ROL instruction sets carry equal to the input bit 7, sets N equal to the input bit 6, sets the Z flag if the result of the rotate is 0, otherwise it resets Z and does not affect the overflow flag at all.

ROL is a read/modify/write instruction and it has the following addressing modes: Accumulator; Zero Page; Zero Page,X; Absolute; Absolute,X.

Table 13-42. ROR.

ROR — ROR *Rotate one bit right (memory or accumulator)* — **ROR**

Operation: → /C/ → [7 | 6 | 5 | 4 | 3 | 2 | 1 | 0] (M or A)

(Ref: 10.4)

N Z C I D V
✓ ✓ ✓ - - -

Addressing Mode	Assembly Language Form	OP CODE	No. Bytes	No. Cycles
Accumulator	ROR A	6A	1	2
Zero Page	ROR Oper	66	2	5
Zero Page,X	ROR Oper,X	76	2	6
Absolute	ROR Oper	6E	3	6
Absolute,X	ROR Oper,X	7E	3	7

The rotate right instruction shifts either the accumulator or addressed memory right 1 bit with bit 0 shifted into the carry and carry shifted into bit 7 (see Table 13-42).

The ROR instruction either shifts the accumulator right 1 bit and stores the carry in accumulator bit 7 or does not affect the internal registers at all. The ROR instruction sets carry equal to input bit 0, sets N equal to the input carry and sets the Z flag if the result of the rotate is 0; otherwise it resets Z and does not affect the overflow flag at all.

ROR is a read/modify/write instruction and it has the following addressing modes: Accumulator; Zero Page; Absolute; Zero Page,X; Absolute,X.

Table 13-43. RTI.

RTI — RTI *Return from interrupt* — **RTI**

Operation: P↑ PC↑

(Ref: 9.6)

N Z C I D V
From Stack

Addressing Mode	Assembly Language Form	OP CODE	No. Bytes	No. Cycles
Implied	RTI	40	1	6

This instruction transfers from the stack into the microprocessor the processor status and the program counter location for the instruction which was interrupted (see Table 13-43). By virtue of the interrupt having stored this data before executing the instruction and the fact that the RTI reinitializes the microprocessor to the same state as when it was interrupted, the combination of interrupt plus RTI allows truly reentrant coding.

The RTI instruction reinitializes all flags to the position to the point they were at the time the interrupt was taken and sets the program in the microprocessor.

RTI is a single-byte instruction and its addressing mode is Implied.

Table 13-44. RTS.

RTS — **RTS** *Return from subroutine* — **RTS**

Operation: PC↑, PC + 1 → PC

N Ƶ C I D V
— — — — — —

(Ref: 8.2)

Addressing Mode	Assembly Language Form	OP CODE	No. Bytes	No. Cycles
Implied	RTS	6Ø	1	6

This instruction loads the program count low and program count high from the stack into the program counter and increments the program counter so that it points to the instruction following the JSR (see Table 13-44). The stack pointer is adjusted by incrementing it twice.

The RTS instruction does not affect any flags and affects only PCL and PCH. RTS is a single-byte instruction and its addressing mode is Implied.

Table 13-45. SBC.

SBC — **SBC** *Subtract memory from accumulator with borrow* — **SBC**

Operation: $A - M - \overline{C} \rightarrow A$

Note: $\overline{C}$ = Borrow (Ref: 2.2.2)

N Ƶ C I D V
✓ ✓ ✓ — — ✓

Addressing Mode	Assembly Language Form	OP CODE	No. Bytes	No. Cycles
Immediate	SBC #Oper	E9	2	2
Zero Page	SBC Oper	E5	2	3
Zero Page, X	SBC Oper, X	F5	2	4
Absolute	SBC Oper	ED	3	4
Absolute, X	SBC Oper, X	FD	3	4*
Absolute, Y	SBC Oper, Y	F9	3	4*
(Indirect, X)	SBC (Oper, X)	E1	2	6
(Indirect), Y	SBC (Oper), Y	F1	2	5*

* Add 1 when page boundary is crossed.

This instruction subtracts the value of memory and borrow from the value of the accumulator, using two's complement arithmetic, and stores the result in the accumulator (see Table 13-45). Borrow is defined as the carry flag complemented; therefore, a resultant carry flag indicates that a borrow has not occurred.

This instruction affects the accumulator. The carry flag is set if the result is greater than or equal to 0. The carry flag is reset when the result is less than 0, indicating a borrow. The overflow flag is set when the result exceeds +127 or −127, otherwise it is reset. The negative flag is set if the result in the accumulator has bit 7 on, otherwise it is reset. The Z flag is set if the result in the accumulator is 0, otherwise it is reset.

It is a "Group One" instruction. It has addressing modes Immediate; Absolute; Zero Page; Absolute,X; Absolute,Y; Zero Page,X; Indexed Indirect; and Indirect Indexed.

Table 13-46. SEC.

SEC SEC *Set carry flag* **SEC**

Operation: 1 → C

N Z C I D V

(Ref: 3.0.1) — — 1 — — —

Addressing Mode	Assembly Language Form	OP CODE	No. Bytes	No. Cycles
Implied	SEC	38	1	2

This instruction initializes the carry flag to a 1 (see Table 13-46). This operation should normally procede a SBC loop. It is also useful when used with ROL instruction to initialized a bit in memory to a 1.

This instruction affects no registers in the microprocessor and no flags other than the carry flag which is set.

SEC is a single-byte instruction and its addressing mode is Implied.

Table 13-47. SED.

SED SED *Set decimal mode* **SED**

Operation: 1 → D

N Z C I D V

(Ref: 3.3.1) — — — — 1 —

Addressing Mode	Assembly Language Form	OP CODE	No. Bytes	No. Cycles
Implied	SED	F8	1	2

This instruction sets the decimal mode flag D to a 1 (see Table 13-47). This makes all subsequent ADC and SBC instructions operate as a decimal arithmetic operation.

SED affects no registers in the microprocessor and no flags other than the decimal mode which is set to a 1.

Table 13-48. SEI.

SEI — **SEI** *Set interrupt disable status* — **SEI**

Operation: 1 → I

(Ref: 3.2.1)

N Z C I D V
— — — 1 — —

Addressing Mode	Assembly Language Form	OP CODE	No. Bytes	No. Cycles
Implied	SEI	78	1	2

This instruction initializes the interrupt disable to a 1 (see Table 13-48). It is used to mask interrupt requests during system reset operations and during interrupt command.

It affects no registers in the microprocessor and no flags other than the interrupt disable which is set.

SEI is a single-byte instruction and its addressing mode is Implied.

Table 13-49. STA.

STA — **STA** *Store accumulator in memory* — **STA**

Operation: A → M

(Ref: 2.1.2)

N Z C I D V
— — — — — —

Addressing Mode	Assembly Language Form	OP CODE	No. Bytes	No. Cycles
Zero Page	STA Oper	85	2	3
Zero Page, X	STA Oper, X	95	2	4
Absolute	STA Oper	8D	3	4
Absolute, X	STA Oper, X	9D	3	5
Absolute, Y	STA Oper, Y	99	3	5
(Indirect, X)	STA (Oper, X)	81	2	6
(Indirect), Y	STA (Oper), Y	91	2	6

This instruction transfers the contents of the accumulator to memory (see Table 13-49)

This instruction affects none of the flags in the processor status register and does not affect the accumulator.

It is a "Group One" instruction and has the following addressing modes available to it: Absolute; Zero Page; Absolute,X; Absolute,Y; Zero Page,X; Indexed Indirect; and Indirect Indexed.

Table 13-50. STX.

STX STX *Store index X in memory* **STX**

Operation: X → M

N Z C I D V

\- - - - - -

(Ref: 7.2)

Addressing Mode	Assembly Language Form	OP CODE	No. Bytes	No. Cycles
Zero Page	STX Oper	86	2	3
Zero Page, Y	STX Oper, Y	96	2	4
Absolute	STX Oper	8E	3	4

Transfers value of X register to addressed memory location (see Table 13-50).

No flags or registers in the microprocessor are affected by the store operation. The addressing modes for STX are Absolute, Zero Page, and Zero Page Indexed by Y.

Table 13-51. STY.

STY STY Store index Y in memory **STY**

Operation: Y → M

N Z C I D V

\- - - - - -

(Ref: 7.3)

Addressing Mode	Assembly Language Form	OP CODE	No. Bytes	No. Cycles
Zero Page	STY Oper	84	2	3
Zero Page, X	STY Oper, X	94	2	4
Absolute	STY Oper	8C	3	4

Transfer the value of the Y register to the addressed memory location (see Table 13-51). STY does not affect any flags or registers in the microprocessor. The addressing modes for STY are Absolute; Zero Page; and Zero Page Indexed by X.

Table 13-52. TAX.

TAX — TAX *Transfer accumulator to index X* — **TAX**

Operation: A → X

N Z C I D V
✓ ✓ – – – –

(Ref: 7.11)

Addressing Mode	Assembly Language Form	OP CODE	No. Bytes	No. Cycles
Implied	TAX	AA	1	2

This instruction takes the value from accumulator A and transfers or loads it into the index register X without disturbing the content of the accumulator A (see Table 13-52).

TAX only affects the index register X, does not affect the carry or overflow flags. The N flag is set if the resultant value in the index register X has bit 7 on, otherwise N is reset. The Z bit is set if the content of the register X is 0 as a result of the operation, otherwise it is reset. TAX is a single-byte instruction and its addressing mode is Implied.

Table 13-53. TAY.

TAY — TAY *Transfer accumulator to index Y* — **TAY**

Operation: A → Y

N Z C I D V
✓ ✓ – – – –

(Ref: 7.13)

Addressing Mode	Assembly Language Form	OP CODE	No. Bytes	No. Cycles
Implied	TAY	A8	1	2

This instruction moves the value of the accumulator into index register Y without affecting the accumulator (see Table 13-53).

TAY instruction only affects the Y register and does not affect either the carry or overflow flags. If the index register Y has bit 7 on, then N is set, otherwise it is reset. If the content of the index register Y equals 0 as a result of the operation, Z is set on, otherwise it is reset.

TAY is a single-byte instruction and the addressing mode is Implied.

Table 13-54. TYA.

TYA TYA *Transfer index Y to accumulator* **TYA**

Operation: Y → A

N Z C I D V
✓ ✓ - - - -

(Ref: 7.14)

Addressing Mode	Assembly Language Form	OP CODE	No. Bytes	No. Cycles
Implied	TYA	98	1	2

This instruction moves the value that is in the index register Y to accumulator A without disturbing the content of the register Y (see Table 13-54).

TYA does not affect any other register other than the accumulator and does not affect the carry or overflow flag. If the result in the accumulator A has bit 7 on, the N flag is set, otherwise it is reset. If the resultant value in the accumulator A is 0, then the Z flag is set, otherwise it is reset.

The addressing mode is Implied and it is a single-byte instruction.

Table 13-55. TSX.

TSX TSX *Transfer stack pointer to index X* **TSX**

Operation: S → X

N Z C I D V
✓ ✓ - - - -

(Ref: 8.9)

Addressing Mode	Assembly Language Form	OP CODE	No. Bytes	No. Cycles
Implied	TSX	BA	1	2

TXS is a single-byte instruction and its addressing mode is Implied.

Another application for TXS is the concept of passing parameters to the subroutine by storing them immediately after the jump to subroutine instruction.

This instruction transfers the value in the index register X to the stack pointer (see Table 13-55).

TXS changes only the stack pointer, making it equal to the content of the index register X. It does not affect any of the flags.

Table 13-56. TXA.

TXA TXA *Transfer index X to accumulator* **TXA**

Operation: X → A

N Z C I D V

✓ ✓ - - - -

(Ref: 7.12)

Addressing Mode	Assembly Language Form	OP CODE	No. Bytes	No. Cycles
Implied	TXA	8A	1	2

This instruction moves the value that is in the index register X to the accumulator A without disturbing the content of the index register X (see Table 13-56).

TXA does not affect any register other than the accumulator and does not affect the carry or overflow flag. If the result in A has bit 7 on, then the N flag is set, otherwise it is reset. If the resultant value in the accumulator is 0, then the Z flag is set, otherwise it is reset.

The addressing mode is Implied, it is a single-byte instruction.

Table 13-57. TXS.

TXS TXS *Transfer index X to stack pointer* **TXS**

Operation: X → S

N Z C I D V

\- - - - - -

(Ref: 8.8)

Addressing Mode	Assembly Language Form	OP CODE	No. Bytes	No. Cycles
Implied	TXS	9A	1	2

This instruction transfers the value in the stack pointer to the index register X (see Table 13-57).

TSX does not affect the carry or overflow flags. It sets N if bit 7 is on in index X as a result of the instruction, otherwise it is reset. If index X is zero as a result of the TSX, the Z flag is set, otherwise it is reset. TSX changes the value of index X, making it equal to the content of the stack pointer.

TSX is a single-byte instruction and the addressing mode is Implied.

Power Supplies

Chapter 14

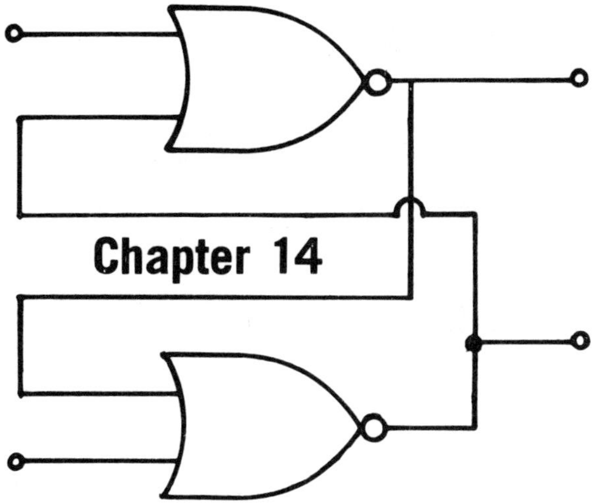

The power supply is a common electronic circuit which is used in almost all electronic instruments. Even the electronic instrument that uses a battery will usually have a voltage-regulator circuit in it to supply a constant current or a constant voltage to the electronic circuits. Most generally, the power supply is a simple circuit which can be built easily or can be purchased at a low cost. Unless you are a school student who cannot afford fifty dollars for a power supply, I would advise that you buy commercially made units. If you add up the time that it takes to construct a power supply, it will far exceed the cost of a purchased power supply even if you only make a few dollars per hour. When you consider the fact that a 5-volt 3-amp power supply can be purchased for about forty dollars, a test system engineer cannot afford to fix a power supply; just replace it and throw the bad unit away.

A lot of the good books have been published about designing power supplies, and so we will not compete with them by presenting a long and dry essay on power supply designing. It will be, however, the aim of this chapter to describe some commercial power supplies and their characteristics, plus supply you with several power supply schematics that you can build. Included in these schematics will be a programmable power supply which can be controlled by your computer. All of these power supplies can be built with electronic components that are usually available at a local electronics hobby store. Now, go out and buy a good supply of one- and three-amp fuses, and we will continue on this chapter!

COMMERCIALLY MANUFACTURED POWER SUPPLIES

The power supplies that I will be describing are manufactured by Standard Power Incorporated, I am not selling Standard power supplies, but all three of the electronic supply houses that I buy from sell Standard Power power supplies and I also just happen to have a few around, one of which is shown in Fig. 14-1. There are several other competing companies which manufacture equivalent power supply units that probably function as well and are competitively priced. I have had very little trouble with the purchased power supplies that I have used, and I can generally state that if they work the first twenty-four hours, they will work for the next two or three years unless you put it to them in some way.

The commercially manufactured power supplies are generally protected from overloads and it is really hard to burn one of them up if they are used properly. The overload protection does not mean that you can run a power supply into a short circuit because sooner or later the power supply will heat up and the higher leakage currents that are caused by the heat will wipe out one of the circuit components. If the power supply that you are using is rated at 3 amps and you are only pulling three-quarters of an amp in your circuit, put a one amp fuse in

Fig. 14-1. This is a commercially manufactured power supply (courtesy Standard Power Inc.).

the dc output line and protect everything; some day you will be glad you did. We will now go through a short discussion of what each of the power supply specifications means.

Universal Input 115/230 Vac, 47-440 Hz

The *universal input* means just that. You can connect the power supply to either a 115 Vac or a 230 Vac line voltage, using the proper input connections, and the power supply outputs will be within specification. The input line frequency can be anything from a 47 Hz sine wave to a 440 Hz sine wave which covers about all of the input line frequencies that you will ever see.

Temperature Compensated Circuitry

The temperature compensation comes from the integrated-circuit chip that is used in the voltage regulation circuit. Temperature compensation means that the output specifications will be maintained as long as the power supply is operated within its temperature range.

Adjustable Output Voltage

The output voltage may be controlled by adjusting a wire wound pot on the pc board.

Floating Output

The floating output means that neither of the dc output terminals (+ or −) are connected to ground. So, you can use this power supply as either a positive or negative supply by connecting the proper output terminal to ground.

Wire Wound Pots/Metal Film Resistors

This is a general description of the type of components that are used in the construction of the power supply to make it a dependable unit.

Input Voltage: 115/230 Vac ± 10%, 47-440 Hz

The input voltage specifications means that you can vary the power-supply line voltage ± ten percent from the specified values and the output will remain within the specified limits.

- Universal input 115/230 Vac, 47-440 Hz
- Temperature compensated circuitry
- Adjustable output voltage
- Floating output
- Wire wound pots/metal film resistors

"Blue Line" dc power supplies also feature: current limit adjustment . . . optional overvoltage protection . . . computer grade capacitors . . . compact design/low cost.

General Specifications:

Input voltage: 115/230 Vac ± 10%, 47-440 Hz
Line regulation: ±0.1%
Load regulation: ±0.1% 0 to full load
Ripple: 0.1%, typically 0.5 to 2 mv rms
Short circuit protection: fold-back type, current limiting, adjustable from 20% to 150% of load. Factory set at 110%
Response time: 50 microseconds
Temperature coefficient: 0.02%/°C
Temperature rating: 0° to 50°C (to 70°C derated)
Adjustable voltage range: ±10%

Fig. 14-2. A Blue Line power supply specification. (courtesy Standard Power Inc.).

Line Regulations: ± 0.1%

The line regulation specification means that the output voltage will remain within ± .01 % of its set value if the input line voltage is varied over the +/− 10% range.

Load Regulation: ± 0.1% 0 to Full Load

The load regulation specification means that the output voltage will remain with ±0.1% of its set value from a no-load condition to the full load condition.

Ripple: 0.1%, Typically 0.5 to 2 mV rms

The ripple specification specifies that the output voltage will not have over a 0.1% ripple content on it when the power supply is supplying the full load current.

Short Circuit Protection: Fold-back Type, Current Limiting, Adjustable from 20% to 150% of Load. Factory Set at 110%.

The over load protection specification indicates the type of protection circuitry that is used, and specifies that you can adjust the output current level from 20% to 150% of the power-supply current rating. It also indicates that the factory setsthe current limiting control to110% of the power-supply rating when the unit leaves the factory. Short circuit protection *does not mean* that you can leave a short circuit across the power supply output continuously without damaging the power supply.

Response Time: 50 Microseconds

The response time tells you how long it will take for the voltage regulation circuit to react to a changing load condition.

Temperature Coefficient: 0.01% Per Degree C

The temperature coefficient specifies that the output voltage will not change more than 0.02% from its set voltage value per degree of temperature change. (Temperature is in degrees centigrade).

Temperature Tating: 0 Degrees to 50 Degrees C (to 70 Degrees C Derated)

The temperature rating indicates that the power supply will operate over a temperature range of 0 to 50 degrees centigrade, and can function at a temperature of 70 degrees centigrade if its output is derated by a given amount.

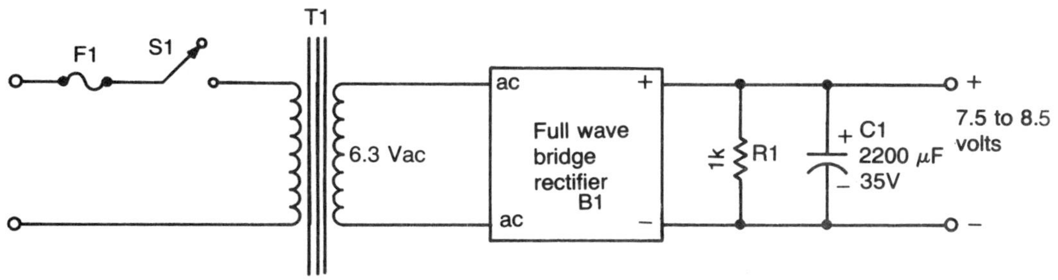

Parts List: Unregulated Positive Voltage Power Supply

F1 - Fuse 1 amp
S1 - 3 Amp 120 Vac switch
T1 - Radio Shack 273-1505
B1 - Radio Shack 276-1180
R1 - 1k ½ watt resistor
C1 - 220 μF at 35 Vdc

This power supply is unregulated and the output voltage will vary indirectly with the output current. The dc output voltage will generally be somewhere around 1.25 (± 10 percent or so) times the ac input voltage when you are using a full wave bridge rectifier and a filter capacitor. This means that a 6.3 volts ac secondary will give you about 8 volts dc or so if the power supply load is not too heavy.

Fig. 14-3. A basic unregulated power supply.

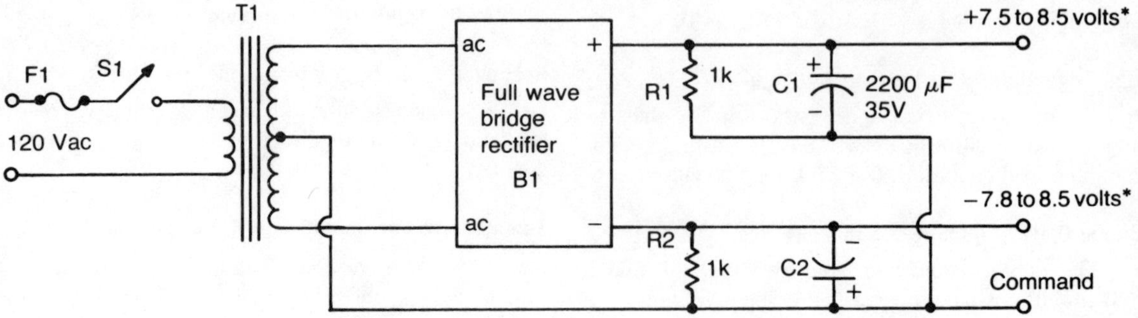

Parts List: Unregulated ± Power Supply

F1 - Fuse 1 amp
S1 - 3 Amp 120 Vac switch
T1 - Radio Shack 273-1505
B1 - Radio Shack 276-1180
R1, R2 - 1k ½ watt resistor
C1, C2 - 2200 μF at 35 Vdc

This power supply is unregulated and the output voltage will vary indirectly with the output current. The dc output voltage will generally be somewhere around 1.25 (± 10 percent or so) times the ac input voltage when you are using a full wave bridge rectifier and a filter capacitor. This means that a 6.3 volts ac secondary will give you about 8 volts dc or so if the power supply load is not too heavy.

Fig. 14-4. A basic positive and negative unregulated power supply.

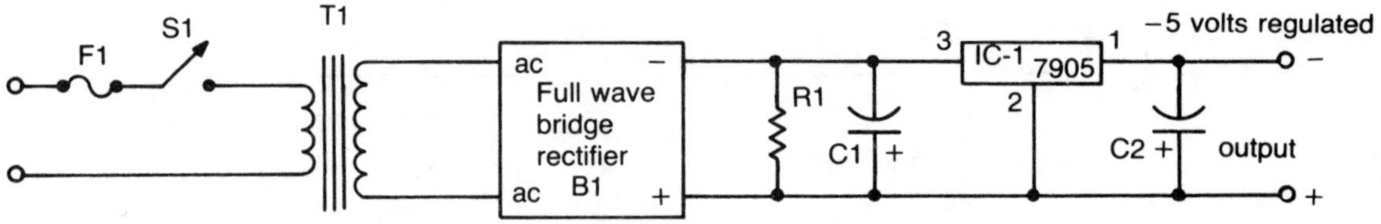

Parts List for Regulated −5 Volts Power Supply

F1 - Fuse 1 amp
S1 - 3 Amp 120 Vac switch
T1 - Radio Shack 273-1505
B1 - Radio Shack 276-1180
R1 - 1k ½ watt resistor
IC1 - 7905 - Radio Shack 276-1773
C1 - 2200 μF at 35 Vdc
C2 - 1 to 5 μF at 16 Vdc

This power supply will deliver over 1 amp of dc current at a regulated output voltage of negative 5 volts. The IC regulator contains a circuit for short circuit protection and a thermal overload protection. The unit must have a proper heat sink if it is going to regulate at maximum current levels. You can estimate the IC heat dissipation by multiplying the dc current through the IC times the voltage drop across the IC.

Fig. 14-5. A negative 5 volt power supply.

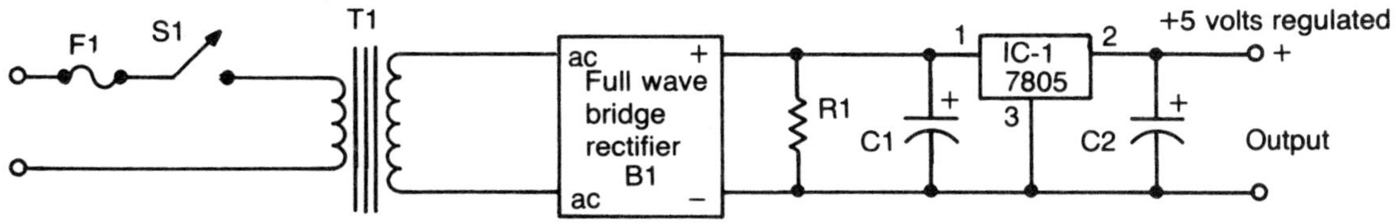

Parts List for Regulated 5 Volts Power Supply

F1 - Fuse 1 amp
S1 - 3 Amp 120 Vac switch
T1 - Radio Shack 273-1505
B1 - Radio Shack 276-1180
R1 - 1k ½ watt resistor
IC1 - 7805 Radio Shack 276-1770
C1 - 2200 μF at 35 Vdc
C2 - 1 to 5 μF at 16 Vdc

This power supply will deliver over 1 amp of dc current at a regulated output voltage of 5 volts. The IC regulator contains a circuit for short circuit protection and a thermal overload protection. The unit must have a proper heat sink if it is going to regulate at maximum current levels. You can estimate the IC heat dissipation by multiplying the dc current through the IC times the voltage drop across the IC.

Fig. 14-6. A positive 5 volt power supply.

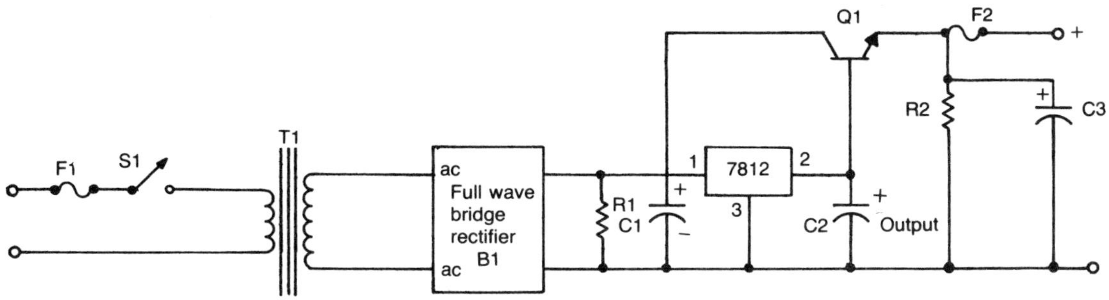

Parts List for High Current Power Supply

F1 - Fuse 3 amp
F2 - Fuse 5 amp
S1 - 3 Amp 120 Vac switch
T1 - Radio Shack 273-1513
B1 - Radio Shack 276-1185
R1,R2 - 1k ½ watt resistor
IC1 - 7805 Radio Shack 276-1770
C1 - 2200 μF at 35 Vdc
C2, C3 - 1 to 5 μF at 16 Vdc
Q1 - Radio Shack 276-2020

This power supply will deliver over 5 amps of dc current at a regulated output voltage of 5 volts. The voltage regulation of this circuit is not great, but it is good enough for hobby, ham radio projects, and other average applications. The circuit must have a proper heat sink if it is going to operate at the maximum current levels. You can estimate the heat dissipation of Q1 by multiplying the dc current through the transistor times the voltage drop across the transistor.

Fig. 14-7. A 5 amp, 5 volt power supply.

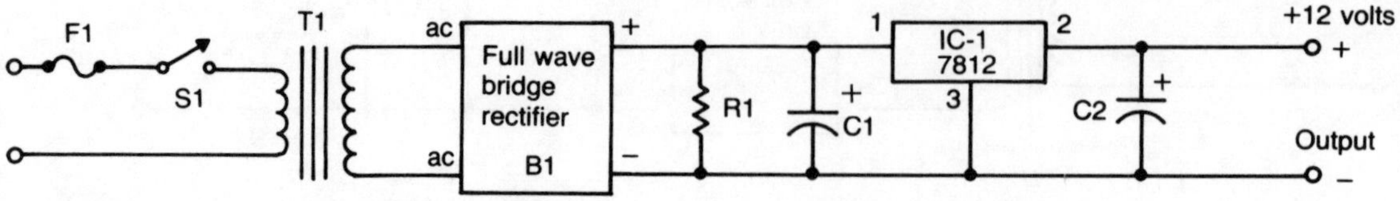

Parts List for Regulated 12 Volts Power Supply

F1 - Fuse 1 amp
S1 - 3 Amp 120 Vac switch
T1 - Radio Shack 273-1515
B1 - Radio Shack 276-1180
R1 - 1k ½ watt resistor
IC1 - 7812 Radio Shack 276-1771
C1 - 2200 μF at 35 Vdc
C2 - 1 to 5 μF at 16 Vdc

This power supply will deliver over 1 amp of dc current at a regulated output voltage of 12 volts. The IC regulator contains a circuit for short circuit protection and a thermal overload protection. The unit must have a proper heat sink if it is going to regulate at maximum current levels. You can estimate the IC heat dissipation by multiplying the dc current through the IC times the voltage drop across the IC.

Fig. 14-8. A 12.0 volt power supply.

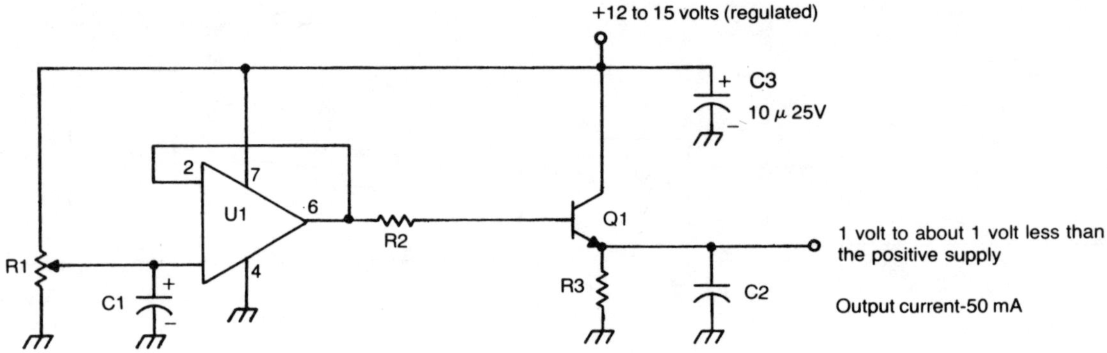

Parts List for the Series Voltage Controlling Circuit

R1 - 1k trim pot
R2 - 27 ohm resistor
R3 - 1k ohm resistor
C1 - 1 μF 16 Vdc
C2 - .1 μF 50 Vdc
C3 - 10 μF 25 Vdc
U1 - 741 Op-amp
Q1 - 2N2222 transistor

This circuit is a series voltage controlling circuit for use on a circuit board to develop variable low current voltages as required. This circuit is more accurate and stable than a voltage divider circuit, and the parts are easy to secure also. The circuit should be operated from a regulated supply voltages. (Max output current is 50 mA).

Fig. 14-9. An op-amp controlled power supply.

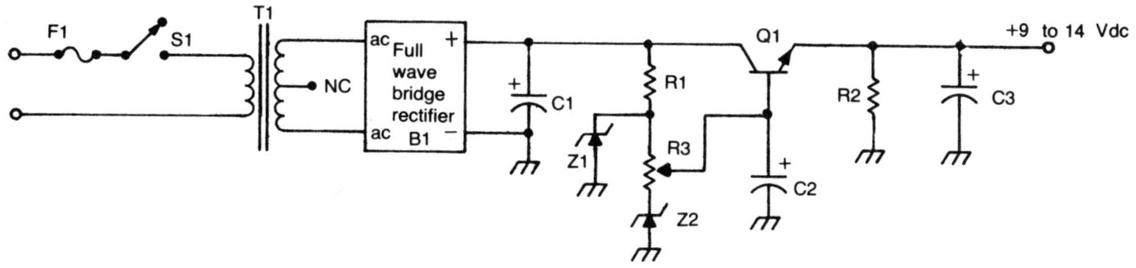

Parts List for the Junk Box Power Supply

F1 - Fuse 1 amp
S1 - 3 amp 120 Vac switch
T1 - Radio Shack 273-1515
B1 - Radio Shack 276-1180
C1 - 2200 μF at 35 volts
C2 - 1000 μF at 16 volts
C3 - 1 μF at 16 volts
R1 - 390 ohms at 1 watt
R2 - 1k at ½ watt
R3 - 500 ohm 2 watt pot
Q1 - Radio Shack 276-2020
Z1 - 14 zener
Z2 - 9V zener

This power supply is adjustable between 9 and 14 volts and can deliver up one amp of dc current. The voltage regulation of this power supply is not as good as a power supply with a commercial IC regulator unit, but this power supply can usually be built from junk box parts and little else.

Fig. 14-10. An adjustable power supply.

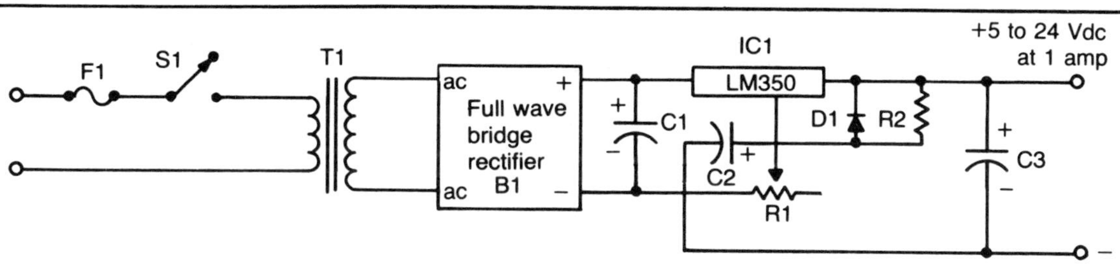

Parts List for the Adjustable Voltage Power Supply

F1 - Fuse 1 amp
S1 - 3 amp 120 Vac switch
T1 - Radio Shack 273-1512
B1 - Radio Shack 276-1180
C1 - 2200 μF at 35 volts
C2 - 4.7 μF at 16 volts
C3 - 2 μF at 16 volts
R1 - 5k Radio Shack 271-1720
R2 - 240 ohms at 1 watt
D1 - 1N4004
IC1 - LM 350

This power supply will deliver between 5 to 24 volts at a dc current of 1 amp. As with the other IC regulated power supplies, an adequate amount of heat sinking for IC1 is important if this power supply is going to be operated at full power.

Fig. 14-11. An adjustable IC regulated power supply.

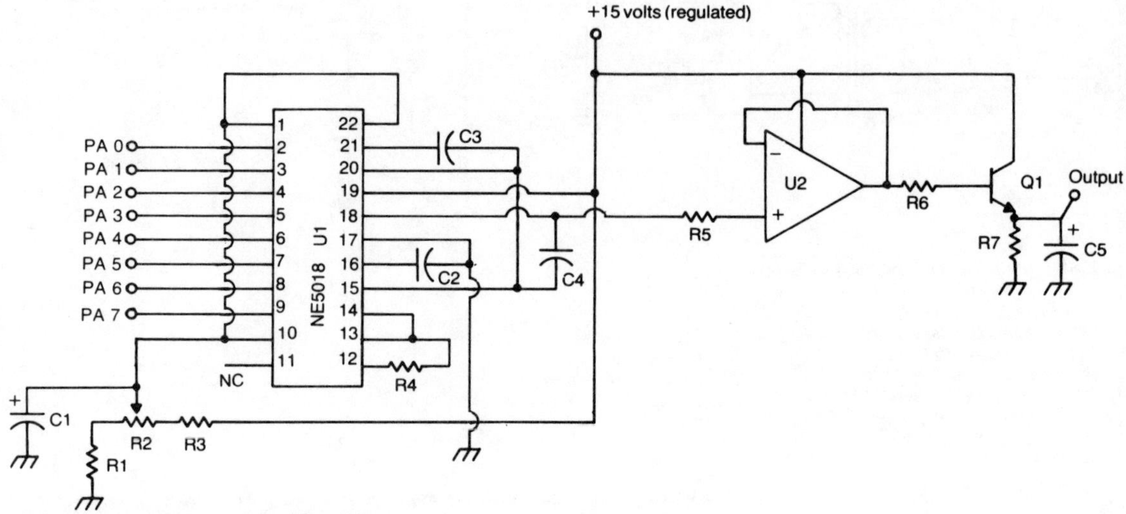

The Programmable Power Supply Parts List

U1 - D to A converter NE5018
U2 - UA 741 Op-amp
Q1 - Radio Shack 276 2017
C1 - 220 μF at 16 volts
C2 - .05 μF at 50 volts
C3 - 2000 pF
C4 - 180 pF
C5 - .47 μF at 50 volts
R1, R3 - 100 ohm at ½ watt
R2 - 500 ohm pot at 2 watt
R4 - 6.8k at 1/4 watt
R5, R7 - 1k at ¼ watt
R6 - 27 ohm at ¼ watt

This power supply that is presented in this schematic is a programmable power supply. The power supply is designed so you can program a voltage in steps of .1875 volts over an area of six volts. The six volts area can be moved by adjusting R2 so you can cover any six volts area between about 13.5 volts and 3.0 volts. The power supply does not have a regulator circuit, so it must be connected to a regulated supply voltage which will control the regulation of this circuit. The maximum output current is about one half amp dc, and the output voltage can be varied as fast as the 741 op-amp will permit. If a faster voltage response time is required, you should replace IC U2 with a faster op-amp. The one-half amp of dc current which this circuit will pass should be enough to handle any test circuitry that requires an automatic variable voltage source.

The computer programs that can be used to control the programmable power supply are presented in Tables 14-4 to 14-7.

Fig. 14-12. A single-board computer controlled power supply.

Adjustable Voltage Range: ± 10%

This specification indicates the output voltage may be varied plus or minus ten percent from the specified output voltage by turning an on-board wire-wound pot control.

The above specifications pretty well characterize the performance that you can expect from the power supply. If these specifications leave anything unmentioned, all of the power supply manufacturers have application engineers that will be happy to answer any questions you may have about one of their products.

POWER SUPPLY CONSTRUCTION PROJECTS

The power supplies that are described in the rest of this chapter can be constructed with hobby store parts. But, they are still very good power supplies and will do just as good of a job for you as a commercially manufactured unit with the same voltage and current ratings. The main thing that you will have going if you build your own power supply is the fact that you will be able to easily repair it with parts that you can buy. Sometimes it is not very easy to find the parts that are in the commercially manufactured power supplies.

All of the required parts for the power supplies that are shown in Figs. 14-3 through 14-12 can be purchased at Radio Shack or most other hobby electronics shops (also see Tables 14-1 through 14-7). I have built each one of the power supplies at one time or another and you should

Table 14-1. An AIM-65 Sawtooth Waveform Program for the Power Supply in Fig. 14-12.

```
A. This program can be used to generate sawtooth waveforms
using the programmable power  supply shown  in Fig. 14-12
with an AIM-65 Microcomputer.
B. This program uses Port A as an output port to  supply the
drive to the D to A converter in the power supply.
C. If  the  op-amp in your programmable power supply  is not
fast enough to  follow  this waveform,  place  a  time delay
routine  from  Chapter 5  before  the  JUMP  instruction  at
program location 218 to slow the program down a little.

The machine-language  program  using  the  AIM-65  'dissembly
format.
200  A9  LDA  #FF
202  8D  STA  A003
205  A9  LDA  #81
207  8D  STA  A001
20A  A9  LDA  #00
20C  8D  STA  0300
20F  AD  LDA  0300
212  8D  STA  A001
215  EE  INC  0300
218  4C  JMP  020F

NOTES: A.  When the single-board computer is turned  on, the
power supply output will be low  until you program it to  be
something else.
       B. Change location  215  to CE  (DEC)  to reverse the
waveform output.
```

Table 14-2. A KIM-1 Sawtooth Waveform Program for the Power Supply in Fig. 14-12.

```
A. This program can be used to generate sawtooth waveforms
using the programmable  power supply shown in  ig. 14-12
with a KIM-1 Microcomputer.
B. This program uses Port A as an output port to  supply the
drive to the D to A converter in the power supply.
C. If  the  op-amp in your programmable power supply  is not
fast enough to  follow  this waveform,  place  a  time delay
routine  from  Chapter 5  before  the  JUMP  instruction  at
program location 218 to slow the program down a little.

Address--Instructions--Mnemonic--Description
Location B1--B2--B3
200        A9  FF        LDA
202        8D  01  17    STA       MAKE PORT A AN OUTPUT PORT
```

Table 14-2. A KIM-1 Sawtooth Waveform Program for the Power Supply in Fig. 14-12. (Continued from page 227.)

```
205     A9  81       LDA
207     8D  00  17   STA    PLACE HEX DATA 81 IN OUTPUT
                            PORT A WHICH WILL SET THE
                            POWER SUPPLY OUTPUT TO MID
                            RANGE.
20A     A9  00       LDA
20C     8D  00  03   STA    STORE 00 IN LOCATION 0300H
20F     AD  00  03   LDA
212     8D  00  17   STA    PLACE THE DATA IN LOCATION
                            600H INTO OUTPUT PORT A
215     EE  00  03   INC    INCREMENT 0600H BY 1
218     4C  0F  02   JMP    LOOP BACK TO 20F

NOTES: A. When the single-board computer is turned on, the
power supply output will be low until you program it to be
something else.
       B. Change location 215 to CE (DEC) to reverse the
waveform output.
```

Table 14-3. A SYM-1 Sawtooth Waveform Program for the Power Supply in Fig. 14-12.

```
A. This program can be used to generate sawtooth waveforms
using the programmable power supply shown in Fig. 14-12
with an AIM-65 Microcomputer.
B. This program uses Port A as an output port to supply the
drive to the D to A converter in the power supply.
C. If the op-amp in your programmable power supply is not
fast enough to follow this waveform, place a time delay
routine from Chapter 5 before the JUMP instruction at
program location 218 to slow the program down a little.

The machine language program using the AIM-65 dissembly
format.


200  A9  LDA  #FF
202  8D  STA  A003
205  A9  LDA  #81
207  8D  STA  A001
20A  A9  LDA  #00
20C  8D  STA  0300
20F  AD  LDA  0300
```

Table 14-3. A SYM-1 Sawtooth Waveform Program for the Power Supply in Fig. 14-12. (Continued from page 228.)

```
212   8D   STA   A001
215   EE   INC   0300
218   4C   JMP   020F


NOTES: A.  When the single-board computer is turned on, the
power supply output will be low until you program it to be
something else.
       B. Change location 215 to CE (DEC) to reverse the
waveform output.
```

Table 14-4. This is a KIM-1 Program which will Control the Output Voltage of the Power Supply in Fig. 14-12.

```
A.  This program can be used to control the programmable
power supply of Fig.14-12 with a KIM-1 Microcomputer.
B. This program uses Port A as an output port to drive the
D to A converter in the power supply.

Address--Instructions--Mnemonic--Description
Location B1--B2--B3
200        A9   FF          LDA
202        8D   01   17     STA       MAKE PORT A AN OUTPUT PORT
205        A9   81          LDA
207        8D   00   17     STA       PLACE HEX DATE 81 IN OUTPUT
                                      PORT A WHICH WILL SET THE
                                      POWER SUPPLY OUTPUT TO MID
                                      RANGE.
20A        UU   UU   UU     JMP       JUMP TO NEXT PROGRAM
                                      LOCATION.

NOTES: A. An FF in program location 206 will set the power
supply output voltage to low output.
       B. An 00 in program location 206 will set the power
supply output voltage to high output.
       C. When the single-board computer is turned on, the
power supply output will be low until you program it to be
something else.
       D. UU indicates that data is furnished by the user.
```

Table 14-5. This is a SYM-1 Program which will Control the Output Voltage of the Power Supply in Fig. 14-12.

```
A.  This program can  be  used to  control  the programmable
power supply of Fig. 14-12 with a SYM-1 Microcomputer.
B. This program uses Port A as an  output  port to drive the
D to A converter in the power supply.

Address--Instructions--Mnemonic--Description
Location B1---B2---B3
200        A9   FF         LDA
202        8D   03   A0    STA       MAKE PORT A AN OUTPUT PORT
205        A9   81         LDA
207        8D   01   A0    STA       PLACE HEX DATE 81 IN OUTPUT
                                     PORT A WHICH WILL SET THE
                                     POWER SUPPLY OUTPUT TO MID
                                     RANGE.
20A        UU   UU   UU    JMP       JUMP TO NEXT PROGRAM
                                     LOCATION.

NOTES: A. An FF in program location 206  will set  the power
supply output voltage to low output.
       B. An  00  in program location 206 will set the power
supply output voltage to high output.
       C. When the single-board computer  is turned on, the
power supply output will be low  until you program it to  be
something else.
       D. UU indicates that data is furnished by the user.
```

Table 14-6. This is a Model III Program which will Control the Output Voltage of the Power Supply in Fig. 14-12.

```
A.  This is a  program  for the  Model  III  using  a  BASIC
program with  a USR  (1) instruction and  a machine-language
subroutine which  will control the programmable power supply
circuit of Fig. 14-12.
B. This program must be used with the 80-I/O-PIB.
C. The machine-language routine will start at 7F00H.
D. Limit the BASIC memory size to 32245. SEE NOTES

THE MODEL III MACHINE LANGUAGE ROUTINE
Address--Instructions--Mnemonic--Description
Location B1---B2---B3
7F00       F3              DI          DISABLE INTERRUPTS
7F01       3E   10         LD          LOAD 10H INTO REGISTER A
7F03       D3   EC         OUT         PLACE 10H IN PORT ECH
7F05       3E   81         LD          PLACE HEX 81 IN REGISTER A
```

Table 14-6. This is a Model III Program which will Control the Output Voltage of the Power Supply in Fig. 14-12. (Continued from page 230.)

```
7F07      D3  6F        OUT       PLACE HEX 81 IN PORT 6FH
7F0A      C9            RET       RETURN TO BASIC PROGRAM

THE MODEL III BASIC PROGRAM (LIMIT MEMORY SIZE TO 32245)

10 PRINT "PROGRAM OUTPUT VOLTAGE TO XXXX VOLTS"
20 POKE 16526,00:POKE 16257,127
30 X=USR (1)
40 PRINT "POWER SUPPLY VOLTAGE IS XXXX OUTPUT VOLTS"
50 END
```

NOTES: A. Load the machine-language routine in first using the DEBUG program and then reset the machine and bring up the BASIC program limiting the memory size to 32245.

B. Line 20 is the subroutine ram starting location data. See the Model III reference manual, page 191 and 192.

C. An FF in program location 7F06 will set the power supply output voltage to low output.

B. An 00 in program location 7F06 will set the power supply output voltage to high output.

C. When the Model III Computer is turned on, the power supply output will be low until you program it to be something else.

D. XXXX indicates that data is furnished by the user.

Table 14-7. This is an AIM-65 Program in BASIC which will Control the Output Voltage of the Power Supply in Fig. 14-12.

A. This program can be used to control the programmable power supply of Fig. 14-12 with a 4K AIM-65 Microcomputer with BASIC.

B. This program uses Port A as an output port to supply data that is required by the D to A converter in the power supply.

C. Limit the BASIC memory size to 3072.

The machine-language routine using the AIM-65 disassembly format.

```
0FE0    A9   LDA   #FF
0FE2    8D   STA   A003
0FE5    A9   LDA   #81
0FE7    8D   STA   A001
0FEA    60   RTS
```

Table 14-7. This is an AIM-65 Program in BASIC which will Control the Output Voltage of the Power Supply in Fig. 14-12. (Continued from page 231.)

```
THE AIM-65 BASIC PROGRAM (LIMIT THE MEMORY SIZE TO 3037)

10 PRINT "PROGRAM OUTPUT VOLTAGE TO XXXX VOLTS"
20 POKE 04,224:POKE 05,15
30 X=USR (1): PRINT X
40 PRINT "POWER SUPPLY IS SET TO XXXX OUTPUT VOLTS"
50 END

NOTES: A.  An FF in program location 0FE6 will set the power
supply output voltage to low output.
       B. An 00 in program location  0FE6 will set the power
supply output voltage to high output.
       C. When the single-board computer is  turned on,  the
power supply output will  be low until you program it to  be
something else.
       D. XXXX  indicates that  data  is  furnished  by  the
user.
```

have no problem building them. Make sure that all of the power transistors and IC regulators are connected to a heatsink that has been coated with a silicon for heatsink compound for good heat transfer between the active circuit element and the heatsink. The majority of all problems that you will encounter in a power supply will usually be heat related in some way.

Always be sure that you fuse your power supply for its protection and your protection. An unfused power supply can cause large amounts of smoke and pungent smells. Also, an unfused ac power line can burn off the tip of a small screwdriver or burn a pretty good hole in a pair of wire cutters (which then can be used to strip number 10 and larger insulated wire).

Model III BASIC Programs for the Electronic Test Engineer

Chapter 15

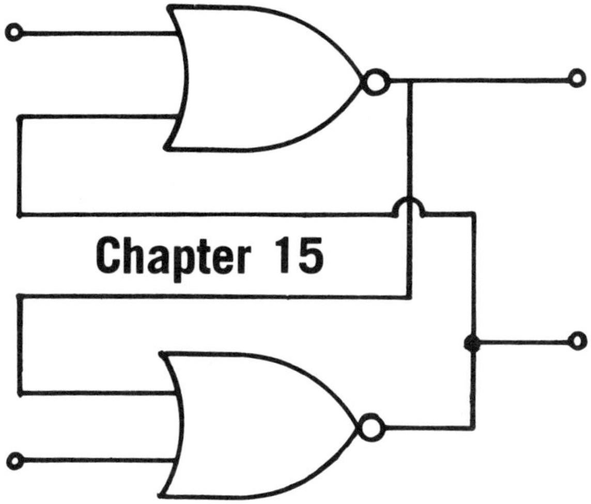

Throughout this book, we have been presenting methods that can be used to control electronic test circuits and manufacturing equipment with a single-board computer. In this chapter we will present a few BASIC programs that can be used by the test systems engineer for circuit design functions. Although the programs have been written for a Model III, they should function with very little extra effort on an AIM-65, AIM-65/40, and a Model I level II computer system.

A LUMPED ELEMENT FILTER DESIGN PROGRAM

The first program that is presented in Table 15-1 is a Lumped Element Filter Design Program[1] which will calculate all of the circuit element values that will be needed to build a PI or T filter with up to twenty sections that will function at frequencies into the microwave spectrum. After the program is loaded and running, you can select the type of filter you need and its characteristics. Figures 15-1 through 15-4 show a typical bandpass PI filter design for the circuit of Fig. 15-5. When the program requests the choice of filter, enter 5 for the bandpass PI filter program. The program will then ask for the number of sections you need and the permissible ripple content; enter 3, 1.5 (three sections and a ripple content of 1.5 dB). The program will then ask for the lower and upper bandwidth points and the filter input and output impedance (The input and output impedance must be the same); enter 7.0, 7.3, 50. (7.0 MHz, 7.3 MHz, and 50 ohms). The filter program now has all of the information that is required to design a bandpass filter which has three sections, a bandpass of 7 to 7.3 MHz with a maximum ripple of 1.5 dB. The program will take about two seconds to run and display all of the circuit element values. After the filter design is complete, the program will ask if you want to design another filter.

1. Lumped Element Filter Design Program, G. Greer, Greer Computer Consultants, 1982

A VOLTAGE, POWER, CURRENT, AND RESISTANCE PROGRAM

This is a really nice program that will work out Ohm's law and all the other basic electrical formulas (Table 15-2). When you enter and bring up the program, it will quiz you as to what parameter you are looking for as shown in Fig. 15-6. In Fig. 15-6, a "P" was entered for power. The program then asked for the variables that are needed to determine the circuit power usage which is shown in Fig. 15-7. For this run of the program, we knew the circuit voltage was 10 volts and the circuit current is 10 amps. A zero (0) was entered for resistance because that variable was not required. If you enter three variables, the program will tell you to start over. With the two variables of voltage and current entered, the program

Table 15-1. A Lumped Element Filter Design Program which will Calculate the Required Circuit Values for the PI Filter in Fig. 15-5. This Program will Design a Twenty-Section Filter if Needed (courtesy Greer Computer Consultants).

```
10 'LUMPED ELEMENT FILTER DESIGN
20 DIM A(20),G(20),B(20),LP(20),LS(20),CP(20),CS(20)
25 GOTO 90
30 XX=1/(SGN(X)*(ABS(X)>99)-1+2/(EXP(2*X*(ABS(X)<=99))+1)):RETURN
40 XX=(EXP(X)-1/EXP(X))/2:RETURN
50 XX=R/(2*PI*FC)*G(X)*1E9:RETURN
60 XX=R/(2*PI*FC)/G(X)*1E9:RETURN
70 XX=1/(R*2*PI*FC)*G(X)*1E12:RETURN
80 XX=1/(R*2*PI*FC)/G(X)*1E12:RETURN
90   CLS: PI=3.14159265
100 PRINT"HIGH PASS....PI(1)...T(2)":PRINT"LOW PASS.....PI(3)...T(4)"
110 PRINT"BAND PASS....PI(5)...T(6)"
120 INPUT"CHOICE";Q:Q=INT(Q):IF Q<1 OR Q>6THEN 120
130 INPUT"NUMBER OF SECTIONS, & RIPPLE ARE";D,L
140 IF Q>4THEN 160
150 INPUT"Fc, INPUT IMPEDANCE";FC,R
160 IF L=0THEN 230
165 X=(L/(40/LOG(10))):GOSUB 30
170 B=LOG(XX)
175 X=B/(2*D):GOSUB 40
180 Y=XX
190 IF D=INT(D/2)*2 THEN 220
200 G(D+1)=1
210 GOTO 230
215 X=B/4:GOSUB 30
220 G(D+1)=(XX)[2
230 FOR K= 1TO D
240 A(K)=SIN(PI*(2*K-1)/(2*D))
250 IF L=0THEN 270
260 B(K)=Y*Y+SIN(PI*K/D)[2
270 NEXT
280 IF L <>0THEN340
290 FOR K=1TOD
300 G(K)=2*A(K)
310 NEXT K
320 G(D+1)=1
330 GOTO380
340 G(1)=2*A(1)/Y
350 FOR K=2 TOD
360 G(K)=4*A(K)*A(K-1)/(B(K-1)*G(K-1))
370 NEXT K
380 IF Q<5 THEN 410
390 INPUT"F1, F2, IMPEDANCE";F1, F2, R
400 FC=F2-F1:FOGM=SQR(F1*F2)
410 ON Q GOTO 420,510,600,690,780,920
420 PRINT"HIGH PASS PI FILTER"
430 PRINT
440 FOR Y=1 TO D STEP2
450 X=Y:GOSUB 60:LP(Y)=XX
460 X=Y+1:GOSUB 80:CS(Y+1)=XX
470 CS(D+1)=0
480 PRINT"L parallel";Y;")=";LP(Y);"nH";TAB(30);"C series";Y+1;"=";CS(Y+1);"pF"
490 NEXT Y
500 GOTO100
510 PRINT"HIGH PASS T FILTER"
520 PRINT
530 FOR Y=1 TO D STEP 2
540 X=Y:GOSUB 80:CS(Y)=XX
550 X=Y+1:GOSUB 60:LP(Y+1)=XX
560 LP(D+1)=0
570 PRINT"C series";Y;")=";CS(Y);"pF";TAB(30);"L parallel";Y+1;"=";LP(Y+1);"nH"
```

```
580 NEXT Y
590 GOTO100
600 PRINT"LOW PASS PI FILTER"
610 PRINT
620 FOR Y=1 TO D STEP 2
630 X=Y:GOSUB 70:CP(Y)=XX
640 X=Y+1:GOSUB 50:LS(Y+1)=XX
650 LS(D+1)=0
660 PRINT"C parallel";Y;")=";CP(Y);"pF";TAB(30);"L series";Y+1;"=";LS(Y+1);"nH"
670 NEXT Y
680 GOTO100
690 PRINT"LOW PASS T FILTER"
700 PRINT
710 FOR Y=1 TO D STEP 2
720 X=Y:GOSUB 50:LS(Y)=XX
730 X=Y+1:GOSUB 70:CP(Y+1)=XX
740 CP(D+1)=0
750 PRINT"L series";Y;")=";LS(Y);"nH";TAB(30);"C parallel";Y+1;"=";CP(Y+1);"pF"
760 NEXT Y
770 GOTO 100
780 PRINT"BAND PASS PI FILTER"
790 PRINT
800 FOR Y=1 TO D STEP 2
810 X=Y:GOSUB 70:CP(Y)=XX
820 X=Y+1:GOSUB 50:LS(Y+1)=XX
830 LS(D+1)=0:CS(D+1)=0
840 LP(Y)=(1/(2*PI*FOGM))[2/(CP(Y)*1E-12)*1E9
850 IF LS(Y+1)=0 THEN 870
860 CS(Y+1)=(1/(2*PI*FOGM))[2/(LS(Y+1)*1E-9)*1E12
870 PRINT"L parallel";Y;")=";LP(Y);"nH";TAB(30);"C parallel";Y;")=";CP(Y);"pF"
880 IF CS(Y+1)=0 THEN 900
890 PRINT"L series";Y+1;")=";LS(Y+1);"nH";TAB(30);"C series";Y+1;")=";CS(Y+1);"p
F"
900 NEXT Y
910 PRINT:GOTO100
920 PRINT"BAND PASS T FILTER"
930 PRINT
940 FOR Y=1 TO D STEP 2
950 X=Y:GOSUB 50:LS(Y)=XX
960 X=Y+1:GOSUB 70:CP(Y+1)=XX
970 CP(D+1)=0
980 CS(Y)=(1/(2*PI*FOGM))[2/(LS(Y)*1E-9)*1E12
990 IF CP(Y+1)=0 THEN 1010
1000 LP(Y+1)=(1/(2*PI*FOGM))[2/(CP(Y+1)*1E-12)*1E9
1010 PRINT"L series";Y;")=";LS(Y);"nH";TAB(30);"C series";Y;")=";CS(Y);"pF"
1020 IF CP(Y+1)=0 THEN 1040
1030 PRINT"L parallel";Y+1;")=";LP(Y+1);"nH";TAB(30);"C parallel";Y+1;")=";CP(Y+
1);"pF"
1040 NEXT Y
1050 PRINT:GOTO 100
1060 END
```

knows that it is to use the formula P=IE which will give you an answer of 100 watts as shown in Fig. 15-8. At this point the program will ask you if there is another problem to run. The formulas in this program can be used with a USR(X) function and a few digital meters to do actual in circuit measurements with a single-board computer.

A SERIES AND PARALLEL RESISTANCE, INDUCTANCE, AND CAPACITANCE PROGRAM

The program that is presented in Table 15-3 will determine the total resistance, inductance, or capacitance of a series or parallel circuit. When the program is entered and run, it will ask if the circuit is a series or

```
High pass . . . . PI (1) . . . T(2)
Low pass . . . . PI (3) . . . T(4)
Band pass . . . PI (5) . . . T(6)
Choice? 5
```

Fig. 15-1. The initial program set-up for the filter-design program requesting a filter design choice which in this figure was #5 for a PI bandpass filter design.

parallel resistor, inductor, or capacitor combination. In Fig. 15-9 a "3" was entered telling the program that the circuit is a series capacitor circuit. The program then asks for the number of components in the circuit which, in Fig. 15-10, was answered with a "3" for three capacitors. The program now requests the value of capacitor "No. 1" which was answered with the data of 10 E-6 indicating a 10 μF capacitor which is also the value that is entered for capacitors two and three. After the value for capacitor three was entered, the program figured the total circuit capacitance as 3.33333E-6 farads and then set-up to receive data on the next circuit.

A RESONANT FREQUENCY PROGRAM

The resonant frequency program of Table 15-4 is a neat little program based on the formula:

$$F = \frac{1}{2\pi \sqrt{LC}}$$

This formula gives you the resonant frequency for an LC circuit. The program is set-up so it will figure out the unknown value given the two other variables. When the program is entered and run, it will ask for two known values which in Fig. 15-11 were 0.1 millihenrys and .001 μF. The program then figured the resonant frequency as 0.503292 MHz. After the program has determined the value of the unknown quantity, it sets up for the next calculation.

AN L AND C REACTANCE PROGRAM

This program, which is presented in Table 15-5, will determine the value of reactance which a capacitor or inductor will exhibit at a specified frequency. When this program is entered and ran, it will request the specified frequency and a value of capacitance or inductance. As shown in Fig. 15-12, a frequency of 1,000 Hz and an inductance of .001 henrys is entered into the program. The program then calculates the inductive reactance at 6.28319 ohms as shown in Fig. 15-13. Note that a zero (0) was entered for the capacitance. The program can only calculate the value for one characteristic at a time and the unit (capacitance or inductance) that is not used must be represented by a zero (0).

CONCLUSION

The last three programs (Tables 15-6, 15-7, and 15-8) are data modification programs that are needed every once in a while to round off a number, find a min or max number, or find an average number. Once you have studied and used the programs that have been presented in this chapter, you will have no problem applying the same programming style to other basic electronic formulas.

```
Number of selections, & ripple are?
3 , 1.5
```

Fig. 15-2. The program data request for the number of filter sections and the maximum ripple content. For this program run, the values of "3" and "1.5" have been used.

```
F1, F2, impedance? 7.0, 7.3, 50
```

Fig. 15-3. The program data request for F1 and F2 frequency cut-off points and the filter input-output impedance. The data inputs here are "7" and "7.3" for a bandpass of 7 to 7.3 MHz and "50" for an input-output impedance of 50 ohms.

```
Bandpass PI filter

L parallel 1 ) = 1.96271E+07 nHC parallel 1 )
                = 2.52559E+10 pF
L series 2 ) = 2.405593+10 nH C series 2 )
                = 2.06062+07 pF
L parallel 3 ) = 1.96271E+07 nHC parallel 3 )
                = 2.52559E + 10 pF
High pass . . . . PI(1) . . . T(2)
Low pass . . . . PI(3) . . . T(4)
Band pass . . . . PI(5) . . . T(6)
Choice?
```

Fig. 15-4. The program display of the designed circuit values for Fig. 15-5.

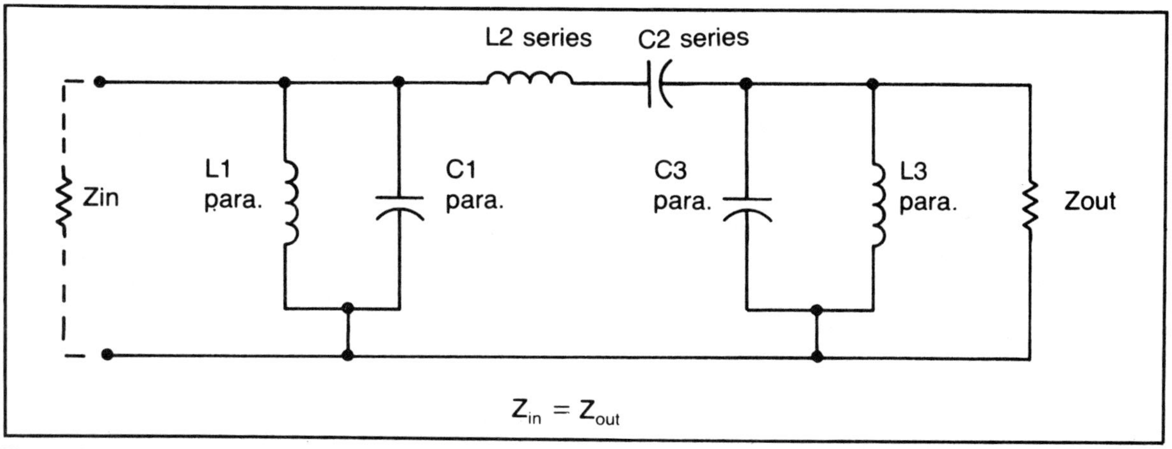

Fig. 15-5. A Butterworth PI bandpass filter.

Table 15-2. The Basic Dc Circuit Parameters can be Determined Using this Program.

```
5 CLS:A$(1)="VOLTAGE IS":A$(2)="POWER IS":A$(3)="CURRENT IS":A$(4)="RESISTANCE I
S": B$(1)="VOLTS":B$(2)="WATTS":B$(3)="AMPS":B$(4)="OHMS"
1Ø PRINT"ENTER THE UNKNOWN VARIABLE"
15 PRINT
2Ø PRINT"VOLTAGE(E), POWER(P), CURRENT(I), OR RESISTANCE(R)";:INPUTA$
3Ø PRINT"ENTER ZERO (Ø) FOR THE UNUSED VARIABLE AND THE VALUES OF THE OTHER TWO
VARIABLES"
4Ø IF A$="E" OR LEFT$(A$,1)="V" THEN Z=1 ELSE IF LEFT$(A$,1)="P" THEN Z=2 ELSE I
F A$="I" OR LEFT$(A$,1)="C" THEN Z=3 ELSE IF LEFT$(A$,1)="R"THEN Z=4 ELSE 1Ø
42 PRINT
45 C=Ø:W=Ø
5Ø FOR X=1 TO 4
6Ø IF X=Z THEN 8Ø
7Ø PRINTA$(X);:INPUTC(X)
75 IF C(X)=Ø THEN C=C+1:D=X
8Ø NEXT
9Ø IF C<>1 THEN PRINT"SORRY BUT ONE VARIABLE MUST BE ZERO(Ø), TRY AGAIN":GOTO 45
1ØØ FOR X=1 TO 4
11Ø FOR Y=1 TO 4
115 W=W+1
12Ø IF Z=X AND D=Y THEN Q=W
13Ø NEXT Y,X
14Ø ON Q GOTO 5,15Ø,16Ø,17Ø,18Ø,5,19Ø,2ØØ,21Ø,22Ø,5,23Ø,24Ø,25Ø,26Ø,5,
15Ø A=C(3)*C(4):GOTO 27Ø
16Ø A=SQR (C(2)*C(4)):GOTO27Ø
17Ø A=C(2)/C(3):GOTO 27Ø
18Ø A=C(3)*C(3)*C(4):GOTO27Ø
19Ø A*C(1)*C(1)/C(4):GOTO27Ø
2ØØ A=C(1)*C(3):GOTO27Ø
21Ø A=SQR(C(2)/C(4):GOTO 27Ø
22Ø A=C(1)/C(4):GOTO27Ø
23Ø A=C(2)/C(1):GOTO27Ø
24Ø A=C(2)/C(3)*C(3):GOTO27Ø
25Ø A=C(1)/C(3):GOTO27Ø
26Ø A=C(1)*C(1)/C(2)
27Ø PRINT:PRINT"    THE   ";A$(Z);A;B$(Z):PRINT
28Ø GOTO1Ø
29Ø END
```

```
Enter the unknown variable
Voltage (E), Power (P), Current (I), or Resistance (R)?  P
```

Fig. 15-6. The initial program set-up requesting what parameter is to be calculated.

```
Enter zero (0) for the unused variable and the values of
the other two variables
Voltage is? 10
Current is? 10
Resistance is? 0
```

Fig. 15-7. The program data request for the known circuit parameters. Here the known parameters are 10 volts and 10 amps. The resistance is not required, so a zero (0) is entered.

```
The power is 100 watts
Enter the unknown variable
Voltage (E), Power (P), Current (I), or Resistance (R)?
```

Fig. 15-8. The calculated data display showing a calculated power of 100 watts. Note that the program is now requesting data for the next calculation.

```
Type of circuit   series  parallel
Resistor ..... (ohms) ............. 1 ................ 4

Inductor ...... (henrys) ........... 2 ................ 6
Capacitor ... (farads) ........... 3 ................ 6
```

Fig. 15-9. The initial program set-up requesting data for the proper calculation. A "3" is entered telling the program that the calculation will be for a series capacitor circuit.

```
Number of components? 3
No. 1 capacitor is ? 10 E-6
No. 2 capacitor is ? 10 E-6
No. 3 capacitor is ? 10 E-6
The total capacitance is 3.33333E-06 farads
Type of circuit   series  parallel
Resistor ..... (ohms) .............. 1 ................ 4
Inductor ...... (henrys) ........... 2 ................ 6
Capacitor ... (farads) ............ 3 ................ 6
?
```

Fig. 15-10. The program data request for the number of circuit components and the component values. For this calculation, there will be "3" capacitors each with a value of 10 μF (10 E-6).

Table 15-3. This Program will Calculate the Values of Series and Parallel Resistor, Inductor, and Capacitor Circuits.

```
2 CLS
4 D$(1)=" RESISTOR IS ":D$(2)=" INDUCTOR IS ":D$(3)="CAPACITOR IS ":D$(4)=D$(1):
D$(5)=D$(2):D$(6)=D$(3):A$="ANCE":C$(1)="OHMS":C$(2)="HENRYS":C$(3)="FARADS":C$(
4)=C$(1):C$(5)=C$(2):C$(6)=C$(3)
5 PRINT"TYPE OF CIRCUIT  SERIES  PARALLEL"
10 PRINT"RESISTOR...(OHMS)........1........4"
15 PRINT
20 PRINT"INDUCTOR...(HENRYS)......2........6"
25 PRINT
30 PRINT"CAPACITOR..(FARADS)......3........6"
40 INPUT T:T=INT(T):IF T<1 OR T>6 THEN 40
50 INPUT "NUMBER OF COMPONENTS";N:T0=0
60 FOR X=1 TO N:PRINT"NO.";X;D$(T);:INPUT S:ON T GOSUB 70,70,80,80,80,70:NEXT:IF
 T=3 OR T=4 OR T=5 THEN T0=1/T0
65 PRINT"THE TOTAL "MID$(D$(T),1,7)+A$+" IS";T0;C$(T):GOTOXXX 5
70 T0=T0+S:RETURN
80 TO=T0+1/S:RETURN
```

Table 15-4. This Program will Calculate the Resonant Frequency of a LC Circuit.

```
5 CLS:P1=3.14159265
10 PRINT" THE L C CIRCUIT RESONANT FREQUENCY":PRINT
20 PRINT"ENTER ZERO(0)FOR THE UNKNOWN VARIABLE"
30 INPUT"INPUT -- Fr IN MHz, L IN MILLIHENRYS, C IN uF";F,L,C
40 IF F=0AND L<>0AND C<>0THEN 50 ELSE IF L=0 AND F<>0 AND C<>0THEN 60 ELSE IF C=
0 AND F<>0 AND L<>0 THEN 70 ELSE 30
50 F=1/(2*P1*SQR(.001*L*1E-6*C)):PRINT"THE RESONANT FREQUENCY IS";F/1E6;"MHZ":GO
TO10
60 L=(1/(2*P1*F))[2/C:PRINT"THE INDUCTANCE IS";L/1E3;"MILLIHENRYS": GOTO 10
70 C=(1/(2*P1*F))[2/L:PRINT"THE CAPACITANCE IS";C*1E-3;"uF":GOTO10
80 PRINT:PRINT:PRINT:PRINT
90 END
```

The L C circuit resonant frequency

Enter zero(0) for the unknown variable
Input — Fr in MHz, L in millihenrys, C in μF? 0, .1, .001
The resonant frequency is .503292 MHz
The L C circuit resonant frequency

Enter zero (0) for the unknown variable
Input — Fr in MHz, L in millihenrys, C in μF?

Fig. 15-11. The resonant frequency program data display showing the program functions. This program run will calculate the resonant frequency. (A zero was entered for Fr) for a LC circuit with the values of .1 millihenry (L) and .001 μF (C). The Fr is .503292 MHz.

Table 15-5. A Program that will Determine the Reactance Value for a Capacitor or Inductor at a Specified Frequency.

```
5 CLS:P1=3.14159265
6 PRINT:PRINT:PRINT
10 PRINT" L AND C REACTANCE VALUES":PRINT
20 PRINT"ENTER ZERO(0) FOR THE UNUSED  VARIABLE"
30 INPUT"INPUT -- F IN Hz, L IN HENRYS, C IN FARADS";F,L,C
40 IF  L=0 AND F<>0 AND C<>0THEN 70 ELSE IF C=0 AND F<>0 AND L<>0 THEN 60 ELSE I
F F=0 THEN 85 ELSE 30
50 F=1/(2*P1*SQR(.001*L*1E-6*C)):PRINT"THE RESONANT FREQUENCY IS";F/1E6;"MHZ":GO
TO10
60 XL=2*P1*F*L:PRINT"THE INDUCTIVE REACTANCE IS";XL;"OHMS":GOTO 80
70 XC=1/(2*P1*F*C):PRINT"THE CAPACITIVE REACTANCE IS";XC;"OHMS":GOTO 80
80 PRINT:PRINT: GOTO10
85 PRINT"FREQUENCY CAN NOT BE ZERO - TRY AGAIN":GOTO30
90 END
```

```
L and C reactance values

Enter zero (0) for the unused variable
Input — F in Hz, L in henrys, C in farads? 1000, .001,0
```

Fig. 15-12. The program data request for the frequency and either the circuit capacitor or inductor value. For this program run, a frequency of 1000 Hz and an inductance of .001 henry was used.

```
The inductive reactance is 6.28319 ohms

L and C reactance values

Enter zero (0) for the unused variable
Input — F in Hz, L in henrys, C in farads?
```

Fig. 15-13. The program calculation data display showing a calculated reactance of 6.28319 ohms reactance for the .001 henry inductor at 1000 Hz.

Table 15-6. A Number Round-Off Program.

```
10 REM ROUND OFF
20 INPUT"NUMBER OF DECIMAL PLACES";N:N=INT(10[INT(N)+.1)
30 INPUT"NUMBER TO ROUND OFF";A
40 B=INT(A*N+.5)/N
50 PRINTB
60 GOTO 20
70 END
```

Table 15-7. A Min-Max Number Program.

```
10 REM MIN MAX NUMBERS
20 DIM A(50):L0=1:H1=1
30 INPUT"HOW MANY NUMBERS DO YOU HAVE";N
40 FOR X=1 TO N
50 INPUT"ENTER NUMBER";A(X)
60 IF A(L0)>A(X) THEN L0=X ' DETERMINES LOWEST NUMBER
70 IF A(H1)<A(X) THEN H1=X ' DETERMINES HIGHEST NUMBER
80 NEXT X
90 PRINT"LOWEST NUMBER IS";A(L0)
100 PRINT"HIGEST NUMBER IS";A(H1)
110 END
```

Table 15-8. An Average Value Number Program.

```
5 A=0:B=0:CLS:PRINT"A PROGRAM FOR THE AVERAGE OF A GROUP OF NUMBERS"
8 PRINT"LIST NUMBERS"
10 INPUT"NUMBER IS";N
20 A=A+N
30 B=B+1
40 INPUT"DO YOU HAVE ANOTHER NUMBER (Y, N)";A$
50 IF A$="N" THEN 60 ELSE 10
60 PRINT "AVERAGE OF THESE NUMBERS IS";A/B
70 PRINT:PRINT:PRINT"FINISHED"
80 END
```

Using the VIC-20 Computer as a Test Controller

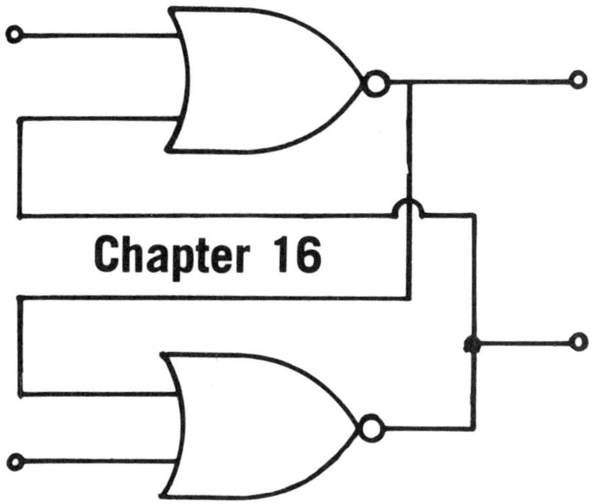

The VIC-20 computer is one of the better computers that you can use to study computing. In this chapter, we will show you how to connect the VIC-20 to the EXP-6522 and then present an example of how to measure the duty cycle of a square wave. The VIC-20 will be used as purchased from the store with no modifications. It will be suggested that you purchase the machine-language monitor program and the *Programmer's Reference Guide* for the computer. The Programmer's Reference Guide will have the technical information required to use all of the computer's functional abilities. I have used all of the popular small computers and only the VIC-20 has the complete documentation that is required for using a small computer as a test controller.

THE BASIC VIC-20

The basic VIC-20 as it is purchased from the store falls nicely within the scope of this book because it has two 6522 VIA chips in the computer and one of the chips has Port B brought out to the USER Port on the back of the computer. The computer has 5K of memory of which 3.5K is available for programming in either BASIC or machine language. It is possible to control any test circuit presented in this book with the basic VIC-20 and nothing else. You will have to move the machine-language routine addresses to the proper RAM area and we will present two examples later.

There is really no easy way to program the computer for the presented circuits unless you buy the VIC-20 Programmer's Reference Guide. This guide gives you all the technical information that is needed for controlling the test circuits with USER Port's 6522 VIA. The VIA is located in memory between addresses 9110 and 911F. The memory locations that you will be using are shown in Fig. 16-1. Check the Reference manual on page 176 for the complete memory map and the computer schematic in back of the manual for the wiring details of the VIA.

Connecting the VIC-20 to the EXP-6522 experimenter's board that was presented in Chapter 4 only requires the use of the interface cable that is presented in Fig. 16-2. If you are familiar with the computer, you know that you can control the EXP-6522 using the POKE command, but that does not give you the total control that is required to completely use the computer's total abilities. It will be necessary to secure the VICMON 6502 machine-language monitor program to easily use the EXP-6522 and other routines that will be presented later for the computer.

RUNNING THE VIC-20 WITH MACHINE LANGUAGE

The computer has 3.5K of memory which can be used for programs. The computer does not request that you set an upper limit of usable memory for the BASIC program so the computer will use it all if the BASIC

VIA #1 Memory Map Data

Hex Address	Via Function	Decimal Address
9110	I/O Data Register B	37136
9112	Data Direction Reg B	37138
9114	Timer #1 L - Low	37140
9115	Timer #1 L - High	37141
9116	Write T1 Latch Low	37142
9117	Write T1 Latch High	37143

Check page 176 of the VIC-20 Programmer's Reference Guide

Fig. 16-1. The VIA memory map data.

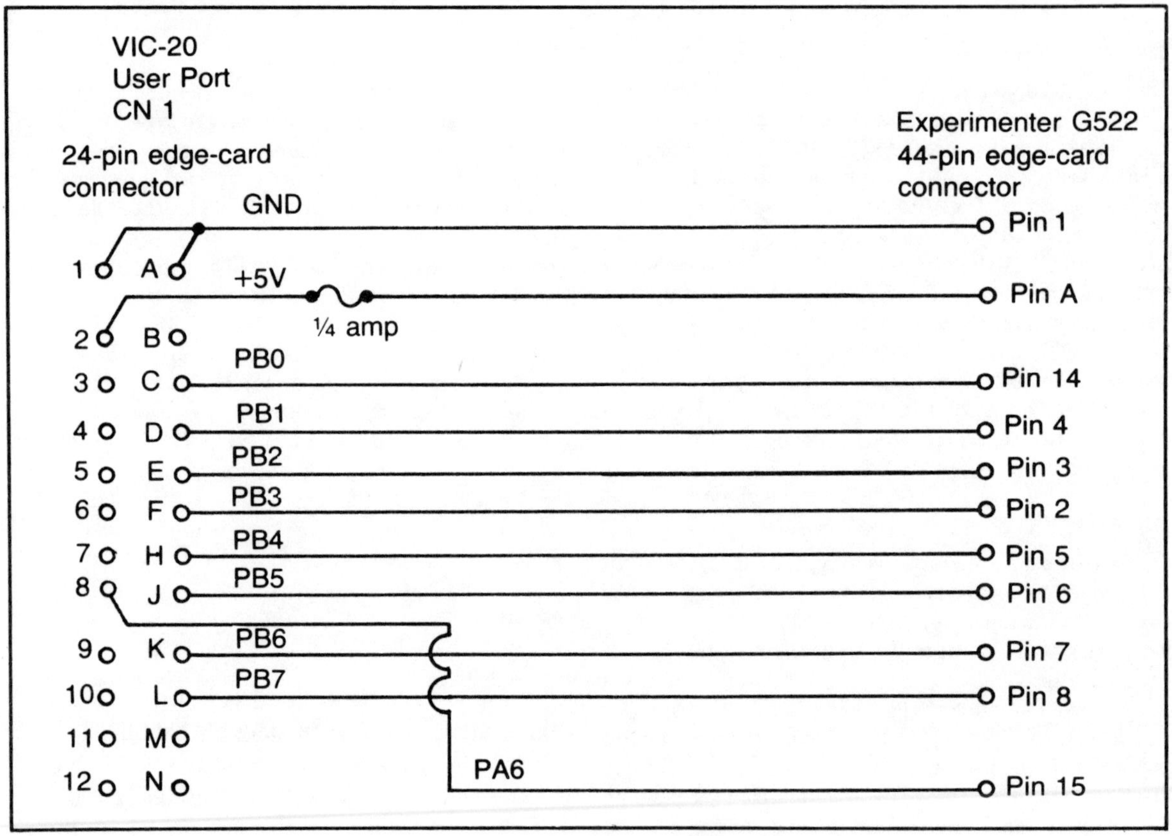

Fig. 16-2. The cable connections for connecting the VIC-20 to the Exp-6522.

Table 16-1. Converting Hexadecimal to Decimal.

HEXADECIMAL	---	DECIMAL
1C20	--	7200
1C30	--	7216
1C40	--	7232
1C50	--	7248
1C60	--	7264
1C70	--	7280
1C80	--	7296
1C90	--	7312

program is large enough. We will set-up our system so the machine-language routines will be located starting at memory location 1C20 which is decimal location 7200. This starting location will give you at least 100 memory locations for your machine-language routine, and you will soon learn that you can do a lot with 100 bytes of memory. As with the other single-board computers, the machine-language data is in hexadecimal. If you are not familiar with the hexadecimal and decimal numbers, Table 16-1 will help out in that area. All machine-language routines will be given in the VICMON assembly-language presentation.

Table 16-2 presents a push-to-test routine for the VIC-20 which was first presented in Chapter 5 for the SYM-1. This is a machine-language-only routine and must be run using VICMON. Table 16-3 presents a push-to-test routine which uses both BASIC and machine language and it was first presented in Chapter 5 for the AIM-65 computer. The other computers that we have used in this book required the application of a USR function to combine a BASIC program and a machine-language routine together. The USR function required the POKING of information which told the computer where the machine-language program started. The VIC-20 has a command called SYS which makes mixing a machine-language routine and a BASIC program a little easier. The SYS command is presented on page 33 of the reference manual and this command will be used in the presented programs of this chapter. The push to test circuits can be constructed on the EXP-6522 as described in Chapter 5 or as shown in Fig. 16-3.

MEASURING THE DUTY CYCLE OF A SQUARE WAVE

A good demonstration of the ability of the VIC-20 is to measure the duty cycle of a square waveform. The software that is presented in Tables 16-4 and 16-5 uses TIMER #1 in VIA #1 to perform such a measurement function. The computer receives the square wave from the interface circuit of Fig. 16-3 on PB7. The CMOS IC VIA will interface any waveform that is between about

Table 16-2. A Push-to-Test Routine for the VIC-20.

```
A. This routine will  perform a Push-To-Test function  using
input port bit PB6.
B.  This  routine  is  presented  in  the  VICMON  assembly
format.

A   1C20   LDA #$00
A   1C22   STA $9112
A   1C25   BIT $9110
A   1C28   BVC 1C25
A   1C2A   BRK              (OR JSR TO NEXT ROUTINE)

NOTE:    The  bit  test only takes a  few microseconds to  run
and branch  back for  another test, so care must be taken to
insure  that there is no  noise or voltage spikes allowed on
the PB6 input line from outside circuits.
```

Table 16-3. A Push-to-Test Routine for the VIC-20 Using Both Machine Language and BASIC.

```
A. This routine will  perform a Push-To-Test function  using
input port bit PB6.
B.  This  routine  is  presented  in  the  VICMON  assembly
format.
C. Use SYS7200 to enter the machine-language routine.

A   1C20  LDA #$00
A   1C22  STA $9112
A   1C25  BIT $9110
A   1C28  BVC 1C25
A   1C2A  RTS

THE BASIC PROGRAM
10 PRINT " A PUSH TO TEST ROUTINE "
20 PRINT " PUSH START BUTTON TO RUN TEST"
30 SYS7200
40 PRINT " STARTING TEST"
50 END

NOTE: A.  The bit test only takes a few microseconds  to run
and branch  back for  another test, so care must be taken to
insure  that there is no  noise or voltage spikes allowed on
the PB6 input line from outside circuits.
      B. The BASIC program test routine would start at line
50 when one is used.
```

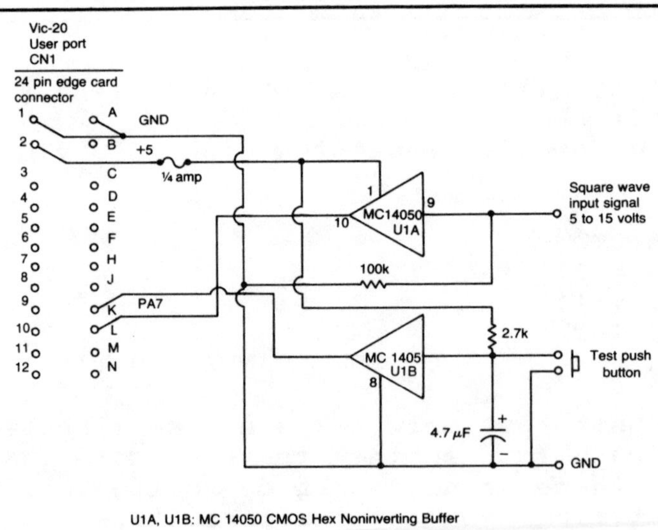

Fig. 16-3. A push-to-test circuit schematic.

Table 16-4. A Machine-Language Routine for Measuring the Duty Cycle of a Square Wave.

This is a machine-language routine for the VIC 20 which uses timer #1 of VIA #1 to measure the duty cycle waveform parameters of a square wave. This routine must be used with the BASIC program of Table 16-5

The routine is presented in the VICMON assembly format.

```
A  1C20  NOP
A  1C21  NOP
A  1C22  NOP
A  1C23  LDA  #$FF
A  1C25  STA  $9116
A  1C28  STA  $9117
A  1C2B  BIT  $9110
A  1C2E  BMI  $1C2B
A  1C30  BIT  $9110
A  1C33  BPL  $1C30
A  1C35  LDA  #$FF
A  1C37  STA  $9115
A  1C3A  BIT  $9110
A  1C3D  BMI  $1C3A
A  1C3F  LDA  $9114
A  1C42  STA  $1A00
A  1C45  LDA  $9115
A  1C48  STA  $1A01
A  1C4B  BIT  $9110
A  1C4E  BPL  $1C4B
A  1C50  LDA  $9114
A  1C53  STA  $1A02
A  1C56  LDA  $9115
A  1C59  STA  $1A03
A  1C5C  RTS
A  1C5D  BRK
A  1C5E  BRK
```

NOTES: A. This routine will require the use of the VICMON Machine Language Monitor Program.

B. This routine stores the TIMER #1 data in locations 1A00, 1A01, 1A02, and 1A03.

Table 16-5. A BASIC Routine for Measuring the Duty Cycle of a Square Wave.

This is a BASIC program for the VIC 20 which will measure the duty cycle of a square wave signal that is applied to PB7 of the User Port. This program must be used with the machine-language routine of Table 16-4.

```
1 QA=1
3 Q=65535
5 W=265
6 Y=100
7 REM  USE SYS7261 TO RE-ENTER VICMON
10 PRINT "DUTY CYCLE TEST NO. ";
15 PRINT QA
20 PRINT " "
25 PRINT " "
30 SYS7200
40 GOSUB 1500
50 DC=INT(HC/FC*Y*Y)/Y
60 PRINT "DUTY CYCLE IS ";
70 PRINT DC;
75 PRINT " %"
80 FOR I=1 TO 1000: NEXT
85 PRINT " "
86 PRINT " "
87 PRINT " "
90 QA=QA + 1
95 GOTO 3
1500 B=PEEK (6656)
1505 A=PEEK (6657)
1510 D=PEEK (6658)
1520 C=PEEK (6659)
1530 HC=Q-(A*W+B)
1540 FC=Q-(C*W+D)
1550 RETURN
```

NOTES: A. Line 30 jumps to the machine-language routine that is located at 1C20.

B. The data at decimal locations 6656, 6657, 6658, and 6659 is the measured waveform time parameters of the square wave signal. The total period of the waveform must not exceed 65 milliseconds.

four to fifteen volts peak-to-peak to the computer safely.

The program is simply a machine-language routine which uses TIMER #1 and a few bit-test functions to secure the on and off times of the waveform. The measured waveform data is then stored in memory for later use by the BASIC program using a few PEEK functions. The duty-cycle data is measured and displayed on the TV screen by the BASIC program which will continue to loop back to make another measurement until you stop the program.

This program is a very good example of how you can convert the hexadecimal data from the VIA timers into presentable decimal data for test-measurement video presentation and print-out.

Some people consider the VIC-20 and other computers in its class as a toy computer. But, if you only need one I/O port, you can do just about anything with a VIC-20 that you can do with any other instrument-level single-board computer.

Index